From Witches to Crack Moms

Women, Drug Law, and Policy

Susan C. Boyd

CAROLINA ACADEMIC PRESS
Durham, North Carolina

Library of Congress Cataloging-in-Publication Data

Boyd, Susan C., 1953–
From witches to crack moms : women, drug law, and policy / by Susan C. Boyd.
p. cm.
Includes bibliographical references.
ISBN 0-89089-127-3
1. Women—Drug use—United States—History. 2. Women—Drug use—Canada—History. 3. Women—Drug use—Great Britain—History. 4. Drug abuse—Government policy—United States. 5. Drug abuse—Government policy—Canada. 6. Drug abuse—Government Policy—Great Britain. 7. Drugs of abuse—Law and legislation—United States—Criminal provisions. 8. Drugs of abuse—Law and legislation—Canada—Criminal provisions. 9. Drugs of abuse—Law and legislation—Great Britain—Criminal provisions. I. Title.

HV5824.W6B686 2003
362.29'082—dc22 2003065407

Carolina Academic Press
700 Kent Street
Durham, NC 27701
Telephone (919) 489-7486
Fax (919) 493-5668
www.cap-press.com

Revised Second Printing

Printed in the United States of America

From Witches to Crack Moms

For my parents

Catherine and Andrew Boyd

Contents

Foreword

The Gender and Justice series responds to two of the most profound changes in criminal justice over the last quarter-century, one well-known, the other almost unrecognized.

The well-known change is the introduction of gender into the study of crime and its consequences. In the early 1970s, scholars and practitioners began to realize that gender, the social effects of being men and women, has an enormous impact on both the kinds of crimes men and women commit and the ways in which social systems respond to those offenses. Studying the effects of gender is necessarily an ongoing project, partly because gender roles themselves are in a constant state of flux and partly because scholars are constantly uncovering new facets of gendered existence—new historical meanings of gender and previously overlooked variations in gender by age, ethnicity and nationality, sexuality, and social class. Consequently, one of the primary goals of this series is to explore the ramifications of gender in the arena of crime and justice.

The second change, which is barely recognized but equally profound, involves the conceptualization of *justice*. Citizens of democracies like to think that the concept of justice is unchangeable, that justice has always meant equal treatment under the law. Unfortunately, this is not the case. Ideas of justice, like ideas of gender, change over time. In the 1970s, many criminal justice officials assumed that black and Hispanic prisoners should be segregated and provided fewer resources than white prisoners; similarly, nearly everyone assumed that women prisoners should be treated differently than their male counterparts. While differential treatment by race has been rejected, many people continue to advocate differential treatment by gender, at least during some stages of the criminal justice process. If we aim to treat men and women the same, it is essential that we acknowledge our reliance on a masculine model of prisoner policy. The dominance of this model, which draws on assumptions developed in reaction to men, is logically rooted in the fact that men have always outnumbered women as offenders and convicts. The debate over whether treatment should be dependent on gender is ever-changing and continuous. Therefore, the second objective of this series is to explore the evolving meanings of justice as it relates to gender—to investigate ways in which people try to achieve gender equity in an unfair world.

Susan C. Boyd's *From Witches to Crack Moms* addresses these issues in the context of drug use, an arena in which ideas of what constitutes crime and justice have changed radically in recent years. For much of the twentieth century, the use and abuse of addictive substances was defined—at least in part—as a treatment issue. The close of the twentieth century, however, brought an increasingly punitive approach to bear on the use of certain drugs. Harsh mandatory sentencing laws that left little room for judicial discretion or treatment alternatives filled the prison system with, not "kingpin" distributors, but small-time users and even non-users who had the misfortune to live with sellers and users. These laws reversed earlier beliefs about what constitutes "justice" in drug cases.

This dramatic reversal affected men and women differently. As Boyd skillfully documents, seemingly even-handed laws can have different consequences for males and females. Boyd traces gender differences in definitions and results of substance use back to the persecution of witches in the Middle Ages, taking a longer historical view of her subject than most scholars. In addition, Boyd pays close attention to ways in which the consequences of what is defined as substance abuse vary by race, class, and ethnicity, as well as gender, to produce a whole spectrum of drug problems, from the alcoholic suburbanite to the titular "crack mom"

At the most fundamental level, Boyd's analysis is concerned with the regulation of women—our health, reproduction, and daily activities. She casts a broad net geographically, covering the drug laws of three countries (Britain, Canada, and the United States) in depth, and devotes an entire chapter to the impact of U.S. drug policies on women in Colombia. She covers the full procedure of the criminal justice system, from the impulses that generate drug laws in the beginning, all the way through imprisonment. Her analysis is decidedly feminist, but everything she says has implications for men as well as women. Boyd draws on years of experience as a community activist to question the arbitrary nature of current drug policies and to recommend more effective means of achieving social justice. *From Witches to Crack Moms* provides forceful, closely reasoned, and in-depth coverage of one of the foremost issues in gender and justice today.

Nicole Hahn Rafter
Northeastern University

Preface

This book grew out of my own need to understand the efforts to persecute women suspected of illegal drug use. I wanted to provide a comprehensive study of how drug law and policy affect women in the United States, and illuminate similarities and differences in Britain and Canada. The impact of the war on drugs on women and indigenous peoples in Columbia is also discussed in order to reveal the connections between the regulation of drug use in Western liberal states and non-Western states.

For twenty-five years I have worked with women and youth in my community. My positions have ranged from counselor to front-line and outreach worker. Every day I have been reminded how all women, but especially poor women (both white women and women of color) and women who use illegal drugs, are regulated. My community work and earlier research on mothers who use illegal drugs have brought me face to face with women's daily struggles. However, my interest in the regulation of illegal drug users also derives from my earlier history. In the late 1960s and 1970s, I along with millions of other youth in Britain, Canada, and the United States, experimented with a wide range of drugs that were criminalized by the state. The state and a host of "authorities" responded. It was not immediately evident how quickly the prison industrial-complex and the drug treatment industry would expand in the United States and elsewhere. The conservative policy of Margaret Thatcher in Britain, Ronald Reagan and George Bush Sr. in the United States, and Brian Mulroney in Canada paved the way for a narrower view of family values and a new depiction of those threatening it. Illegal drug users, especially if they were single-parent mothers, were increasingly depicted as deviant and immoral and the cause of social, economic, and family breakdown. However, this view is in sharp contrast to my own view of myself, or of other women I knew who then used, or currently use, illegal drugs.

In 1990, I spent ten weeks in the hospital in Canada while I was pregnant. Early labor contractions signaled concern and I was confined to bed rest. During my stay at the hospital I was offered an array of legal drugs including narcotics, sleeping pills, muscle relaxers, and over-the-counter drugs to counter nausea. I have to admit that I was shocked by the array of legal drugs offered to me to "save" my unborn child and to make me more comfortable. During my first pregnancy in the mid-1970s, I had little contact with the medical profession and maternity wards because I received care from a lay midwife and delivered my daughter at home. I mistakenly believed that the midwifery and natural-birth movement had influenced the practices of medical professionals in relation to pregnancy and birth, and to a certain extent they have. However, women's quest to take back control of their reproduction takes place against the medical profession's persistent reliance on a variety of legal drugs and technology to manage pregnancy in order to "protect and save" the fetus.

I had just begun my graduate studies a few months before landing up in the hospital. My thesis topic was about the regulation of mothers who used illegal drugs. I could not help but compare my situation in the hospital with women in the United States who were being demonized and later prosecuted for maternal drug use and child abuse. How was their drug use different from mine? The pharmacology of the drugs were often the same. Not knowing the specific circumstances or the reasons for women's illegal drug use during pregnancy led me to question my own situation. Women are prescribed legal drugs to alleviate physical and emotional pain and distress, to lessen anxiety and depression, and to cure illness and disease. Women are also prescribed a host of legal drugs to manage their reproduction and pregnancies. Women who use illegal drugs and legal drugs in ways not recommended by their doctors are also managing anxiety, depression, and pain. Sometimes, they too, are trying to feel better, whether their drug of choice is marijuana, heroin, or cocaine. However, when women self-medicate they are constructed as irresponsible, immoral, capable of damaging the fetus, and incapable of parenting. When women take prescribed drugs they are constructed as compliant for following medical advice and their drug use is viewed as therapeutic. Women who follow medical advice while they are pregnant are viewed as maternal and responsible, those who do not are seen as irresponsible and unfit.

Growing up in a working-class family in the United States, I experienced and witnessed the coercive power of the state. Nor was I protected from the regulation of the "helping" professions. These experiences have contributed to my lack of faith in the criminal justice system and in various "expert" opinions about regulating the poor and those who are labeled as deviant. Although drugs like marijuana, cocaine, and heroin and the people associated with them have been constructed as dangerous, it is difficult for me to understand what all the fuss is about. Nothing I have witnessed or read leads me to believe that these drugs in themselves, or the people who use them, are inherently evil. Nevertheless, in Britain, Canada, and the United States, women who use these drugs are constructed as being even more deviant than their male counterparts. Theoretically we can point to conventional beliefs about the sanctity of the home, mothering, sobriety, and morality culminating into negative views about women who are suspected of using illegal drugs. In this book I explore how these beliefs and race, class and gender inequalities inform drug law and policy and how they affect women's daily lives. I was at a public forum a few years ago where a woman in the audience asked the speakers how they could separate illegal drug use from race. I wonder about this question, too. I believe it is important to recognize that illegal drug use is racialized, just as it is gendered and class-based. However, racial categories are also essentialist and social constructions. By examining the history of the regulation of altered states of consciousness, we can see how women's drug use has become racialized, sexualized, pathologized, and criminalized. We can also see how women conform or resist.

Why This Book?

Since the late 1950s and 1960s, critical writers have been writing about drug law and policy. Sociohistorical studies by researchers in the U.S., such as Howard Becker's *Outsiders: Studies in the Sociology of Deviance*; Alfred Lindesmith's *The Addict and the Law*; Brecher and associates' *Licit & Illicit Drugs*; and David Musto's edition of *The American Disease*, provided a framework for many critical drug researchers. Since these groundbreaking studies emerged, a number of critical books and articles have followed that criticize drug law and policy in Britain, Canada, and the U.S. Many of these studies highlight the experiences of illegal drug users while others analyze both law and policy. However, until the 1980s, few studies examined the lives of women who use illegal drugs.

In 1981, Marsha Rosenbaum's ethnographic study of women in California who used heroin, *Women and Heroin*, broke the impasse, and a number of feminist ethnographies and qualitative studies written by sociologists and criminologists have followed her lead. These works include, but are not limited to Avril Taylor's study on injection drug users in Glasgow, *Women Drug Users*; Lisa Maher's study of marginalized users in, *Sexed Work: Gender, Race and Resistance in a Brooklyn Drug Market*; Claire Sterk's study *Fast Lives: Women Who Use Crack Cocaine*; and Sheigla Murphy and Marsha Rosenbaum's study which provides insight into the experience of pregnant women, *Pregnant Women on Drugs*. My own book, *Mothers and Illicit drugs: Transcending the Myths* provides in-depth interviews with mothers who used drugs in Western Canada and analyzes the social construction of neonatal abstinence syndrome (NAS); and British researchers Hilary Klee, Marcia Jackson, and Suzan Lewis also examine the lives of mothers who use illegal drugs in their book *Drug Misuses and Motherhood*. All of these works highlight the experiences of the women interviewed. In addition, Nancy Campbell's *Using Women: Gender, Drug Policy, and Social Justice* explores the historical regulation of drugs and women in the U.S. and the ideological underpinnings of policy.

Other feminist books on women and drugs focus on drug treatment and recovery models and the female drug user, drug use and pregnancy, and the pharmaceutical industry and its impact on women.[1] There are many critical studies about illegal drug use that offer insight into the lives of illegal drug users. This book would not be possible without their collective wisdom, and I draw on them throughout this study. However, there are no theoretical critical feminist books that compare how women are regulated by drug law and criminal justice, social service, and medical policy in Britain, Canada, and the U.S. Consequently, I decided to fill this gap by writing *From Witches to Crack Moms: Women, Drug Law, and Policy*. This book offers a critique of drug law and policy and its impact on women in all three nations and provides insight into how the war on drugs and the regulation of reproduction intersect. It also provides a brief sociohistorical account of the regulation of altered states of consciousness and women's role in those events. I also explore how punitive drug laws inform and shape social service and medical policy, and highlight how the mainstream media, politicians, and nonstate organizations construct drug issues that inform national and international policy.

1. See Bepko 1991; Ettorree 1992; Kandall 1999; Kasl 1992; Rapping 1996; Siney 1999; and McDonnell 1986.

Acknowledgments

I would like to thank Nicole Rafter for envisioning the Gender and Justice Series and inviting me to submit a proposal. Her thoughtful comments and direction contributed to this work. Special thanks to Ron Weinhardt for editing my original proposal, and to both him and Marilyn Green for visiting and providing such great company back east. I am also deeply grateful to Karlene Faith and Dorothy Chunn for reading my unwieldily preliminary draft and whose critiques shaped the final manuscript. Both have provided steady support over the years. I would also like to thank Faye McCrory and Mary Hepburn for taking the time to read through parts of the manuscript and providing comments, and Kim Fate for discussing her observations about Canadian prisons with me. In addition, I would like to thank Lynn Paltrow for her comments and expertise on maternal-state conflicts in the U.S. I also appreciate the theoretical discussions with Karlene Faith and John McMullin. However, any mistakes in the book are my own.

I am grateful to Dennis Sullivan for taking an interest in my thoughts on altered states of consciousness and inviting me to submit an article to *Contemporary Justice Review*, and for permission to reproduce these copyright material. Sections in chapter 1 appeared in *Contemporary Justice Review*, 4, no.1, (2000): 75–100. I would also like to thank Sue Johnson, Catherine O'Connor, Reuben Ayres, and Carolina Academic Press for their interest and encouragement in the publication of this book. I am indebted to Starla Anderson for her support and thoughtful editorial comments and to Beth McAuley and Arlene Wells for their copy-editing skills.

Finally, I would like to thank all of my family and friends. I am indebted to Morgan LeBlond for her encouragement and for making the fleece pants I wore almost every day while working on the manuscript. This manuscript would never have been written without the accompaniment of music, especially my daughter Jade Boyd's compilations. I would also like to thank Nuszia Mordasiewicz and Jeannie Kamins for their support, inspiration, and the artistic beauty that they bring into my life. Thank you to Cheryl Anderson, Carolyn Crichton, and Gloria Watkins, whose friendships continue to sustain me. A special acknowledgement to my mother, Catherine Boyd, to all of my brothers and sisters—Diana, Jean, Robert, Tommy, Eddie, and Howard,—and to my sister-in-laws Nancy, Tamara, and Suzanne. My last thank you is reserved for my two children, Jade Lanore and Iain Ruby. Both enrich my life in more ways than I can count.

From Witches to Crack Moms

Introduction

On May 15, 1999, Regina McKnight, a young twenty-two-year-old black woman, delivered a stillborn girl at Conway Hospital in South Carolina. Although she was distraught and grieving, Regina was approached by medical staff minutes after her delivery and asked to provide a urine sample. She was not informed that the findings from the urine sample might have legal consequences. Nor did she give consent for the urine sample to be tested for that purpose. Later that evening, Regina McKnight was again approached by a nurse and asked to sign a form entitled "Informed Consent for Drug Testing." The form explained that she had tested positive for drugs in the earlier urine sample and now she was being asked to give consent for another urine sample to "confirm or deny" the earlier findings. The form also made clear that the findings of the urine sample could be used for legal purposes; however, there was no explanation of how the consequences of a positive urine sample might affect her life.

One of the nurses at the hospital later claimed that she "probably" read the consent form to Regina McKnight. Little attention was given to the facts that Regina McKnight had an IQ of 72 and that she was still suffering from the trauma of the stillbirth and the loss of her daughter. Nor is there any evidence that Regina McKnight understood what the nurse "probably" read out to her. Armed with the results of the urine sample, police arrested Regina McKnight on October 7, 1999, and charged her with the crimes of homicide by child abuse and distribution of crack cocaine to her unborn child. The state argued that Regina's cocaine use, which was delivered to the fetus, caused its death. They claimed that the stillborn fetus was seven to eight months in term, thus "viable" and would have been able to live outside "the body without aid or assistance" had it not been for the effects of the ingested cocaine.[1]

Regina McKnight's first trial resulted in a mistrial because the jury was unable to reach a verdict. However, even though she had no prior criminal record, Regina's retrial resulted in a conviction of homicide, and she was sentenced in 2001 to twenty years in prison, with eight years suspended sentence. Her conviction rested solely on the state's evidence that she had used cocaine during her pregnancy. Although witnesses at her second trial could not identify the exact cause of fetal death, the state argued that because there was no clear cause that could be determined, "the drugs that she consumed killed her child." The state relied on a diagnosis by exclusion even though they did not perform all the necessary tests that would have ruled out other possible causes of death. In fact, the leading pathologist who examined the baby after birth, and other medical witnesses, stated that there were other diseases that might have contributed to the stillbirth, confirming that the baby did *not* test positive for fatal levels of cocaine. In fact, it was questionable whether the infant tested positive at all. The trauma of Regina's personal loss of her baby was thus compounded by the states effort to blame and punish her. Furthermore, there was no evidence that Regina McKnight had any criminal *intent* of causing harm to her fetus, nor was it established that she was aware of the issues surrounding fetal viability, "live children," and culpability.[2] These factors are important because they are the necessary elements in the charges laid. The South Carolina child abuse statue was never intended to punish women who suffer stillbirths, or to include the behavior of pregnant women. Nor does the word "child" in the Homicide by Child Abuse Statute cover "fetuses."

Shortly after Regina McKnight's conviction hit the media in the United States another case emerged that exposed the contradiction at the centre of U.S. drug policy. Noelle Bush, a young twenty-four-year-old woman, the niece of President Bush Jr. and the daughter of Jeb Bush, the governor of Florida, rose to national prominence after she was arrested in January 2002 for buying Xanax, an anti-anxiety

1. *State of South Carolina v. Regina D. McKnight* 2001: 153.
2. Ibid.

drug, with a fraudulent prescription at a pharmacy in Tallahassee, Florida. She had forged a prescription for the drug. Rather than facing a criminal trial, Noelle sought treatment through the drug courts, which offer drug rehabilitation, and was sent to the Center for Drug-Free Living. While still in residence at the Center, Noelle was found possessing a prescription drug and subsequently, in July 2002, the drug court judge ordered her to spend two days in jail for her offense. In September 2002, the police were called to the drug treatment center after another patient reported that Noelle was again in possession of an illegal drug, this time crack cocaine. A small amount of crack cocaine was found in Noelle's shoe; however, four drug treatment workers refused to cooperate with the police and when the State Attorney's Office subpoenaed them to court, the judge ruled that the four workers did not have to testify because federal regulations protected the privacy of people in drug treatment.

While it is true that Florida courts make an exception for records involved in drug treatment, these same rules do not apply to drug courts. Since the first drug court emerged in Miami, Florida, in 1989, their courtrooms have been open. In fact, judges and drug court workers have claimed that the open courtroom is an essential component of rehabilitation for drug court participants. Nevertheless, in October 2002, Noelle Bush's attorney asked the drug court judge to close the court proceedings (related to the possession of crack cocaine) to the public in her case and in all future drug court hearings. Her lawyer argued that Noelle and other clients in drug court programs would be less likely to be honest if their infractions of drug court policy were aired in open-court proceedings, and this would undermine their treatment. He stated that drug court clients should be assured privacy in court. Governor Jeb Bush is now claiming that he too believes the drug courts should be "protected from public scrutiny."[3] In sharp contrast, critics state that Noelle Bush should not be granted preferential treatment. They argue that the drug courts are criminal courts and that the public is interested in the outcome of Noelle's case because it strikes at the heart of the

3. The Associated Press 2002: 2.

hypocrisy of the war on drugs—drug treatment for the rich and prison for the poor.

Following Noelle's arrest, Florida Governor Jeb Bush, Noelle's father, told reporters, "This is a private issue as it relates to my daughter and myself and my wife.... The road to recovery is a rocky one for a lot of people who have this kind of problem."[4] These words sound quite compassionate, as does his current argument that drug courts should remain closed so that clients are granted privacy. However, Jeb Bush is contradicting his earlier 1998 campaign message in which he claimed that drug use is not a private matter. At that time, he adamantly argued that drug use is a criminal rather than a medical matter, and drug users should not be granted leniency or a second chance. He claimed that tougher laws and larger budgets were needed to punish drug users. Since he was elected as governor of Florida, Jeb Bush has been instrumental in cutting back resources for drug treatment and supporting "tough-on-crime" legislation that sends drug offenders to prison. In the meantime, his brother in the White House, George W. Bush Jr., has attempted to further demonize illegal drug users by linking drug use to terrorist groups and the attacks on the World Trade Center on September 11, 2001.[5] The hypocrisy of the Bush men is evident when we consider that Noelle's drug use is viewed as a private matter to be dealt with by the family and drug treatment experts, while the poor and less privileged are publically reprimanded and sent to prison. The attempt by Noelle's attorneys to close the drug court to the public was a thinly veiled effort to shelter her from scrutiny, especially if she received preferential treatment. However, her lawyer was unsuccessful and the drug court remained open to the public. Noelle was sent back to jail for ten days for her infraction.

Although I am opposed to punishing any women suspected of using illegal drugs, the cases of Regina McKnight and Noelle Bush bring up important issues related to the war on drugs in the United States. The Regina McKnight case exemplifies not only how women

4. Saunders 2002: F2.
5. Ibid.

who are suspected of using illegal drugs are being punished but also how punishment for illegal drug use is class-based, gendered, and racialized. The Noelle Bush case speaks to class privilege, the failure of the war on drugs, and points to corrupt politicians who subvert the political and judicial system to meet their own needs. Noelle's case also highlights the conflicts between the medical and the criminal model of regulating illegal drug users. In addition, it calls into question the role of drug courts. Prosecution of women like Noelle Bush is rare in the United States. Prosecution of poor women and women of color like Regina McKnight is common.

Regina McKnight's case also exemplifies both the challenges to women's reproductive autonomy and the increased regulation of mothering that have occurred in the United States, Britain, and Canada. Since the 1980s, the war on drugs and the war on abortion and women's reproductive rights have converged. Women in the U.S. have been most vulnerable to these shifts. It is here that drug war ideologies and the subordination of women's bodies intersect, culminating in a volatile mix. Myths and ideologies about morality, sexuality, reproduction, and mothering shape policy. The mother-fetus relationship is viewed as adversarial, and the mother is seen as a danger to the fetus, especially in relation to illegal maternal drug use. Increased surveillance of mothers suspected of using drugs has led to families being ripped apart.

Myths and Ideologies

Drug laws are supported by myths and ideologies that intensify the regulation of women. Ideology is significant in relation to understanding the thinking that is involved in the moral regulation and disciplining of women who use illegal drugs. Ideology is a set of beliefs that often succeeds in maintaining and upholding the world as fair, acceptable, and natural, when it is basically unfair and corrupt.[6] The myths and ideologies that we hold shape our world and may limit our

6. Cohen 1985.

imagination, making "other ways of interpreting the world unthinkable."[7] The myths support the views that some drugs are so "dangerous" that they must be criminalized, that there are good and bad drugs, and that only drugs prescribed by one's doctor are good. Illegal drugs are thought to be so dangerous that it is "noble" to restrict their use. Drug laws are linked to the moral regulation of women and the loss of control over their own sexuality and reproduction. They are also linked to the rise of the modern-day prison-industrial complex, a system of class and racial apartheid and economic interests that profit from punitive penal governance. Drug laws are also associated with colonization, and the loss of Indigenous peoples' control over their healing and spiritual practices.

Myths about "dangerousness" also fuel the war on drugs. We are told daily that the government, police, and drug agencies need more special powers, budgets, and repressive laws so that we can be "protected" and the "drug trafficker" caught and brought to justice. However, in contrast to the myth, the drug "user," not the drug trafficker, is at most risk of being arrested in the U.S., Britain, and Canada. Eighty percent of all U.S. and 85 percent of all British drug convictions are for possession.[8] Thus, women in the U.S. who are arrested for small amounts of illegal drugs, as little as $10.00 worth, receive criminal records and are sentenced to prison. As well, most drug convictions are for marijuana, not for cocaine or heroin, as is often proclaimed by criminal justice officials and the media. However, as illustrated by the Regina McKnight and Noelle Bush cases, not all women are treated equally in the war on drugs—it is poor women and women of color who are most vulnerable to arrest in Britain,[9] Canada, and the United States.

At the end of 2001, almost seven million people were under criminal justice control on any given day in the U.S. Two million of these

7. Pfohl 1994: 416.

8. DrugScope 2001; USDJ 2000b: 4.

9. Throughout the book, Britain refers to England and Wales unless specified.

people were in prison and the others were under probation and parole supervision.[10] The U.S. imprisons a significantly higher proportion of people than any other nation in the world. Much of this increase in imprisonment and criminal justice regulation of the last twenty years stems directly from the war on drugs. In Britain, Canada, and the U.S., a similar pattern has emerged over the last thirty years—even though there are more men in prison for drug offenses than women, the percentage of women in prison convicted of drug offenses is significantly higher than their male counterparts, despite the fact that drug-use surveys and research demonstrate that men use one half to two times more illegal drugs than women and they are more likely to be involved in selling illegal drugs than women. In all three nations, the female prison population has increased two- and-threefold since 1970, and drug convictions account for much of the increase in Britain and the U.S. Furthermore, in Britain, Canada, and the U.S., poor women and women of color are overrepresented in relation to arrest, conviction, and imprisonment for drug offenses.

Women of color make up two-thirds of the population of women in American prisons.[11] In 2002, 89 percent of the women imprisoned for nonviolent drug offenses in New York State were women of color.[12] In 2000, of the 39 percent of the female prison population in Britain who were serving time for a drug offense, 70 percent were foreign national women, and over half of these women were black.[13] In Canada, First Nations and black women are disproportionately overrepresented in prison, and the Commission on Systemic Racism in the Ontario Criminal Justice System in 1995 noted that since 1992 black women were more affected by tough drug policy than were white women in their province.[14] In Britain, Canada, and the U.S., drug offenses are both racialized and gendered, and poor women (both white women and women of color) are most vulnerable to drug arrests and conviction.

10. BJS 2002b: 1.
11. CANY/WPP 2000.
12. CANY/WPP 2002b.
13. Ibid.:1–4; Wedderburn 2000: 12–13.
14. Commission on Systemic Racism in the Ontario Criminal Justice System 1995.

Historically, poor women and women of color have experienced more intrusive regulation and state violence in Britain, Canada, and the U.S. Thus, this book is informed by the work of feminist writers whose work is antiracist and anticolonial. Globally, women of color have been at the forefront of moving the feminist movement boundaries by challenging white supremacy.[15] Their adoption of an antiracist agenda provides a lens that helps us to understand the historical impact of colonization on women. It also provides us with a framework for understanding today's drug laws and policies.

This book challenges current conventional ideas about illegal drugs and women and highlights some individual and collective resistance to the war on drugs and to the continued regulation of women's reproduction. Because the U.S. is the only superpower in the world today, and one of the most ardent supporters of the war on drugs within and outside its borders, special attention is given to U.S. policy, including the "Americanization" of international and criminal law globally. Thus, *From Witches to Crack Moms* examines how punitive drug laws lend legitimacy to other repressive practices and policies against women, including arrest and imprisonment, maternal-state conflicts, child apprehension by the state, and drug treatment centers and courts. Criminal justice, welfare, medical treatment, and international policy have been restructured due to the war on drugs. In addition, the war on drugs is linked to larger economic and political shifts, and to neoliberalism. For example, myths about the "dangerousness" of drugs and the immorality of women who use illegal drugs have justified welfare cutbacks and the putting into place of more stringent eligibility criteria for federal housing in the U.S. In all three nations, surveillance of women suspected of using illegal drugs has increased. In Third World nations like Colombia, U.S. aid is accompanied by free trade, privatization, deregulation, and repressive drug policy. In Third World nations and Britain, Canada, and the U.S., poor women are disadvantaged while the rich benefit, as do corporations, criminal justice, and the military. The links between eco-

15. See Collins 1991; hooks 1984, 1993, 1995; Monture-Angus 1999, 2000; and Razack 1998.

nomic and drug policy in Western and Third World nations is explored.

The historical roots of drug prohibition and the role women played in such events as the witch hunts, the gin craze of the early to mid-1700s, colonization, and the temperance movement exemplify how, in many ways, the war on drugs is not new and point out that Western imperialist and colonial practices continue to shape it. History demonstrates that the social construction of good and bad drugs, and the regulation of illegal drug use is linked to the loss of control over women's own sexuality and reproduction. In this book, I advance the idea that the war on drugs is linked to the social control of *all* women and is being waged on many fronts, and that it is legitimized by both national and international law which is fueled by and contributes to colonization, global capitalism, and oppression. I also address how the latest "war on terrorism," sparked by the terrorist attacks on the World Trade Center and the Pentagon on September 11, 2001, is linked to the "war on drugs." Both "wars" have been instrumental in intensifying racial profiling and eroding civil rights.

Although the focus of this book is on women's experience of the war on drugs, it in no way intends to ignore the plight of men who move through the criminal justice system and who are caged in numerous prisons throughout the world. Rather, it intends to examine how law and policy affect women in similar and different ways, and how the social control of male drug users affects women, families, and communities.

Like their alcohol-prohibitionist sisters in the last century, women today tend to see illegal drugs as a threat to the family and to home life and often promote prohibition and abstinence as the solution. Although feminist activists and writers have challenged the medicalization of women's lives through overprescribing and the dispensing of harmful legal drugs, there has been little challenge to the war on drugs until recently. Nor has there been much interest in discussing how the line dividing illegal and legal drugs is a social construction, one that has nothing to do with dangerousness. Our legal drugs—tobacco and alcohol—are our most toxic drugs and more dangerous than marijuana, our most benign drug, and cocaine and heroin. Only recently have feminist organizations begun to scrutinize the war on drugs, acknowledging that it is causing more harm than the drugs themselves. Today, women active in the anti-drug, peace, abolitionist, and reproductive autonomy movements, are speaking out against the war on drugs.

A Feminist Sociological Perspective

The arguments in this book are informed by two schools of thought: feminist and critical sociological, which encompass critical social control and social construction theory. A critical sociological perspective highlights how a person's drug use is shaped by the social and cultural environment, as well as by drug laws and by social service, medical, and nongovernment policy. As C. Wright Mills notes, "The sociological imagination enables us to grasp history and biography and the relation between the two within society" and to distinguish "between 'the personal troubles of milieu' and 'the public issues of social structure.'"[16] Critical sociological theory is concerned with the interplay between the individual and society and how the social structure both limits and constrains individuals. Central to this theory is the claim that "historical and structural conditions also have everything to do with social power."[17] Critical perspectives in sociology draw from a range of theories, including anarchist, Marxist, feminist, criminological, transformative justice, anticolonial, and antiracist theory. In addition, critical perspectives challenge us to link our everyday/every night lives to "historical organizations of power."[18] If we fail to examine larger structural factors, such as the political economy of crime and law, we lose sight of the erosion of democracy taking place in the world today and how this is affecting women, communities, cultures, and nation states. Our current individualistic focus on illegal drugs as the cause of social pathology and deviant behavior obscures how the New World

16. Mills 1975: 6, 8.
17. Pfohl 1994: 402.
18. Ibid: 469.

Order of capitalism contributes to violence and to the destruction of the self and communities.[19] Thus, this book calls attention to the social-structural factors that shape the lives of women.

Drawing on a feminist sociological perspective allows us to move away from male-centered and individualistic psychological theorizing about drug use. The war on drugs and women's (and men's) experience of illegal drug use is mediated by race, class, and gender, in conjunction with history, culture, politics, and the legal and socioeconomic environment. A sociological perspective informed by feminist theory allows us to understand how all women, but especially women suspected of using illegal drugs, are socially controlled in ways that differ from men. The social control of women is gender specific. The regulation of women centers on reproduction, mothering, double standards of morality, social and legal subordination, and an ideology that places women in the role of mother, wife, and daughter—each of whom is relegated to the private sphere of the home.[20]

Since the 1980s, a wide array of feminist research about women who use illegal drugs has emerged which demonstrates that men are not subject to the same gendered forms of legal, medical, social service, and nonstate regulation. These controls are directed at all women, but have a greater impact on women in relation to sexuality, pregnancy, birth, and mothering. Paloma Sales and Sheigla Murphy's study of pregnant drug users in the U.S. notes that "being a woman was a strike against them, being a pregnant women was a second strike, and being a drug using pregnant women was the third and final blow in their social standing."[21] However, illegal drug users are not all viewed equally, and being poor is another strike against a woman, as is being a woman of color. Women who are suspected of using illegal drugs are vulnerable to interlocking, and often competing, spheres of informal and formal regulation. Women are regulated by formal drug laws and the criminal justice system, family law, social service policy, medical policy, and nonstate agencies such as Nar-

---

19. Chomsky 1994.
20. Smart and Smart 1978: 3.
21. Sales and Murphy 2000: 695.

cotics Anonymous (NA) and Children Requiring a Caring Kommunity (CRACK). The social control of women rests heavily on moral rhetoric that argues for increased regulation due to moral degeneracy, loss of control, and danger to the fetus.

For many women, social justice rather than criminal justice is the goal that they are working toward in order to restore women's control over their own sexuality, reproduction, and the drugs that they consume. Social justice encompasses the belief that the world we live in can be transformed. That we can go beyond rejecting capitalism, imperialism, colonization, violence and war. Many social justice activists strive toward eliminating power hierarchies and race, class, and gender inequality, as well as transforming how we mediate conflict and our relationships in the public and private spheres. By changing the social-structural conditions that limit and restrain people, we can transform our home life and our workplace, as well as our ideas about peace.[22] Ending the war on drugs is one strategy on the road to achieving social justice.

Social Control

A number of critical researchers have developed the term social control to explain relationships between the powerless and the powerful.[23] Stanley Cohen writes that social control has been used as a conceptual tool to give unity to a wide range of attempts and practices to identify, contain, manage, and punish groups and individuals. Cohen states that social control is "the organized way in which society responds to behavior and people it regards as deviant, problematic, worrying, threatening, troublesome or undesirable in some way or another."[24] He states that the organized response to perceived deviance may include punishment, treatment and rehabilitation, and

22. See Faith 2000; Pepinsky and Quinney 1997; and Sullivan and Tifft 2001.

23. Edwards 1988. See McLaren, Menzies, and Chunn's discussion of social control, governmentality, and moral regulation in their book, *Regulating lives: Historical essays on the state, society, the individual and the law.*

24. Cohen 1985: 1.

that the behavior in question is "classified" as immoral, criminal, or sick. The professions—social work, criminology, psychology, and the judiciary—view these people from different vantage points. Since the criminalization of such drugs as heroin, cocaine, and marijuana, users have been viewed sometimes as criminals, sometimes as victims, or sometimes as a combination of the two. Prior to and following the criminalization of these drugs, users have been also viewed as immoral, sick, and pathological.

Critical social control theory has been criticized because it ignores agency and conceptualizes power as coercion from above. It also views the state as monolithic and static when, in fact, it is not. However, social control can be perceived as both formal and informal, and both direct and indirect. Social control is not limited to state repression, rather it can apply to "more autonomous methods of applying pressure to groups and individuals."[25] I believe critical social control theory is useful when speaking about the regulation of illegal drugs and the people who are suspected of using them. Anyone who has experienced the power of the state through imprisonment, or who has had their child apprehended, understands social control and the punitive power of the state. Granted, not all power emanates from above, nor is all power coercive. However, in relation to the war against drugs, state agencies and criminal law are significant in the regulation of both women and men.

Some theorists have drawn from Michel Foucault's work on moral regulation to expand their analysis and to highlight how individuals and groups are regulated by the state and state agencies, as well as by various nonstate agencies and professions which have developed a wide range of knowledges and techniques to categorize and manage people. Foucault emphasized how moral regulation occurs at diverse sites.[26] Moral regulation is central to defining illegal drug use as a social problem. Drawing on Foucault, feminist writer Karlene Faith provides insight into how discourses and the institutions that certify them affect women:

---

25. McLaren, Menzies, and Chunn 2002: 10.
26. Foucault 1979.

> Gendered power relations are specifically organized according to interplay among the traditional discourses that have controlled women's bodies. Consider religious, economic, and familial ideologies through which women have been physically and sexually subservient; legal, medical, and welfare discourses that pathologize the female body, and exercise state sanctioned (expert, professional, primarily male) authority over its reproductive functions; psychiatry and other "psy" professions, that similarly issue policy and treatment that sexualize the female, who is viewed as an unfortunate product or victim of her biology in the ways it affects her psyche; the law, for its part, has criminalized female sexuality and sexualized female criminality. The strategic relations between and among these discourses, and the institutions that pronounce and certify them, determine how, by whom, and for what purpose the female body can be classified, confined and turned into capital.[27]

Women who use illegal drugs have long been constructed as the "Other," who is outside the norms of proper moral and gendered female behavior. Traditional discourse about the female illegal drug user is embedded with gendered power relations.

Foucault referred to a much broader understanding of institutions and the state, including "systems of welfare, social services, medicine, and urban planning, that encourage individuals to behave in ways commensurate with the interests of a liberal, well-tempered, regulated society."[28] Foucault also developed the term "governmentality" to explore the increased surveillance of individuals and groups and how they are disciplined and managed, and sought to show how government "infuses the social and penetrates the self. It radiates in all directions."[29]

For the purposes of this book, the term social control encompasses a wider analytical understanding of both state and nonstate regula-

---

27. Faith 1944: 58.
28. Hyatt 2001: 205.
29. Mclaren, Menzies, and Chunn 2002: 14.

tion, including knowledges developed to manage and discipline, and practices and technologies of categorization, normalization, and punishment. Social control will also be linked to self-governance, shifts in the moral regulation of drug use, and how these regulatory practices converge. Criminology, medicine, psychiatry, statistics, social work, and sociology all developed new knowledges and techniques for the identification, management, surveillance, and discipline of populations. These professions compete and overlap in their moral regulation of all women, especially those suspected of using illegal drugs. Drawing from British feminist theorist Carol Smart, I too assert that legal discourse "sets itself above other knowledges."[30] This is especially evident when the war on drugs and the regulation of reproduction intersect.

Social Construction and Feminist Research

The writings of Howard Becker and other theorists contributed to the emergence of the labeling perspective in the 1960s. Becker claimed that "deviance is not a quality of the act the person commits, but rather a consequence of the application of rules and sanctions to an 'offender.' The deviant is one to whom the label has successfully been applied; deviant behavior is behavior that people so label."[31] Becker and other labeling theorists also wrote about moral entrepreneurs. Becker explored the origins of the Marijuana Tax Act of 1937 and the role of moral entrepreneur Commissioner Harry J. Anslinger, who ran the U.S. Federal Bureau of Narcotics. Anslinger spread misinformation about marijuana and linked it to immorality, insanity, and murder. Becker points out that the Federal Bureau of Narcotics and Anslinger's claims were aired on radio shows, depicted in films like *Reefer Madness* (1937), and published in magazine articles. However, marijuana smokers had no forum to publicize their experiences and claims. Subsequent legislation to criminalize marijuana passed unopposed, and marijuana smokers became a new class of deviant out-

30. Smart 1989: 10.
31. Becker 1963: 9.

siders. Sociologist Craig Reinarman expands on Becker's theory by adding another dimension. He refers to "politico-moral entrepreneurs" who have either financial or political interests of their own which are unrelated to drugs (for example, being "tough on drugs" wins elections).[32]

Similar to sociological research on "moral entrepreneurs," social constructionist theorists wish to draw our attention to how social problems are constructed. Social construction theorists identify "claimsmakers" who bring our attention to a social issue and mold our thoughts about the "problem" at stake. Vocal claimsmakers "typify" social problems by defining the nature of the problem.[33] Illegal drug use and addiction has been constructed predominantly by criminal justice (e.g., police and judges), the medical profession (e.g., physicians, psychiatrists, and psychologists), and the media. However, social workers, teachers, and academics also claim expertise in defining the "problem." Alongside these "authorities" are self-help and recovery groups which have emerged to stake their claim.[34] These groups compete for ownership of the "drug problem" and produce "knowledge" that they use to inform the public about drug issues.[35]

Sociologist Joel Best claims that social constructionist theory should be understood as a perspective that can help us understand the world we live in. On a daily basis, newspapers, radio, and television highlight the voices of claimsmakers while those impacted by the policy that emerges out of claimsmaking and the construction of social problems are less likely to be heard. As researchers Neil Websdale and Jeff Ferrell point out, "crime, deviance, and control exist as socially and culturally constructed phenomena, rather than as random events in the 'natural' world."[36]

---

32. Reinarman 2000.

33. Best 1995.

34. See Joel Best's discussion of claimsmakers and the victim industry in his1999 book, *Random violence: How we talk about new crimes and new victims.*

35. Reinarman 2000.

36. Websdale and Ferrell 1999: 355.

Feminist writers have drawn our attention to how women in conflict with the law are depicted in the mainstream media. These writers have contributed to our understanding of race, class, and gender representation in film and print media.[37] Critical and feminist writers have also written solely about print media and representations of illegal drugs, users, and sellers. Criminologist Drew Humphries explores how the network news in the U.S. fueled a moral panic and drug scare about crack and pregnancy in the 1980s and 1990s. Even though cocaine use had been declining since the late 1970s, and women were less likely to use crack than men, the media constructed the *crack baby* and their mothers as poor women of color who were criminals and powerless to resist crack.[38] In addition, legal researcher Laura Gomez reviewed articles about drugs, pregnancy, and child abuse in two California newspapers between 1985 and 1992. She argues that the news media played a crucial role in constructing the "crack crises" and "crack baby" as well as bringing it to the attention of the public. She also demonstrates how the news media informed California legislative debates, policy making, and prosecutors' actions, and their subsequent role in the "institutionalization of a social problem."[39] In Canada, researcher Lorraine Greaves and her colleagues analyzed thirty articles concerning mothers and substance use in three Canadian newspapers in 1999 and 2000. Of these thirty articles, 87 constructed the fetus as being at risk due to maternal drug use and mothers were consistently constructed as being a risk to their children.[40]

Sociologist Craig Reinarman, who examines drug scares in the U.S., states that drug scares have been a popular media creation throughout the twentieth century. He points out that dramatic and sensationalized stories about illegal drugs and drug users spread misinformation. Today's "war on drugs" is characterized by the "routinization of caricature," which promotes worst case scenarios as the

37. See Birch 1994; Chesney-Lind 1999; Clover 1999; Faith 1993; McCaughey and King 2001.

38. Humphries 1999.

39. Gomez 1997: 123.

40. Greaves et al. 2002: 28.

norm and sensationalizes and distorts drug issues in the media.[41] Drug scares also link illegal drugs with racial and ethnic minorities, with youth, and with concerns about mothering and the breakdown of the family. While the media offer narrow misrepresentations of drugs, drug use, and selling, they also attempt to shape public opinion about illegal drug use and women.[42]

Sexuality, the Family, and Mothering

Ever since the witch hunts of the Middle Ages, women who use illegal drugs have been portrayed as amoral and sexually promiscuous by Christian religious authorities and, in the centuries following, by the mainstream media and white middle-class reformers. Studies of female drug use also demonstrate an interest in women's sexual lifestyle that is rarely extended to male drug users. This interest is reinforced by research that claims "one effect of all forms of cocaine, including crack, is the release of normal inhibitions on behavior, including sexual behavior."[43] James Inciardi and his co-writers also maintain and perpetuate misguided myths about the "crack whore," and state that many women addicted to crack will have "any manner of sexual activity, under *any* circumstances, in private or in public, and with multiple partners of either sex."[44] However, a wide array of research refutes the construction of female illegal drug users as promiscuous and immoral.[45]

The discussion of sexuality and women drug users is often linked to concerns about pregnancy and mothering, for if women are having sex, they may also be having children. Pregnancy and single-parent status of women suspected of illegal drug use is of special concern to moral reformers and to legal, medical, and social service professionals. U.S. prosecutors claim that women who use illegal

41. Reinarman and Duskin 1999: 49.
42. Reinarman and Levine 2000.
43. Inciardi et al. 1993: 96.
44. Ibid. 1993: 96.
45. See Bourgois 1995; Macdonald, Waldorf, Reinarman, and Murphy 1988; and Rosenbaum et al. 1990.

drugs have multiple partners and violate family norms.[46] Studies that evaluate birth control methods to prevent pregnancy carry the underlying message that sexual promiscuity is rampant among women who use illegal drugs. In addition, women who smoke crack are viewed as losing their maternal instincts.[47] The threat to the reproductive autonomy of women who use illegal drugs has negative implications for all women. Women who use illegal drugs are seen not only as tearing apart the family due to their immorality and compulsion to use illegal drugs but also as unfit to parent. This is not a new theme, though it has taken on a particular viciousness since the mid-1980s in North America.

Following the more liberal 1960s and 1970s, political shifts ushered in a new temperance and conservative ideology that centered on personal responsibility and narrow family values. With these political and cultural shifts, women's inroads into the public sphere and gains in reproductive autonomy have been challenged, and maternal-state conflicts came into sharper focus. Nancy Campbell states that mothers who use drugs have been viewed as refusing to act as "women," which signals "social decay" and "deviance."[48] Women are supposed to keep the family intact and when they are perceived as failing in their gender-specific role, they are seen as contributing to society's breakdown. White women have been, and continue to be viewed as the moral barometers of Western society, which has constructed them as inherently more moral and virtuous than men; however, women of color are not embraced by this ideology. Rather, they have been viewed at various historical moments as savage, unfit, immoral, criminal, and incapable of nurturing their own children.[49] Because illegal drug use is racialized, when white women use illegal drugs, it is seen as "the end of respectability as a form of social control and the failure of modernity's civilizing mission."[50] White women's illegal drug use is continually linked to racial domination,

---

46. Gomez 1994.
47. Bourgois 1995.
48. Campbell 2000 221, 224.
49. Gupta 1995; hooks 1992
50. Campbell 2000 57.

corruption, immorality, and promiscuity, which many consider as contributing to the breakdown of the home.

The nuclear family, consisting of a white middle-class heterosexual couple with biological children, is the legal norm in Western nations. Families that do not conform are often viewed as deviant in the eyes of criminal and social service agencies. Although more positive attitudes towards single-parent mothers have developed over the last few decades, they are mostly reserved for rich women who can earn their own way. Women on social assistance, who have children in care or whose relatives are raising their children, are often constructed as deviant, regardless of the circumstances that lead to these arrangements and to their extended family values and practices. The courts see these mothers as fallen women, and their sentencing is harsher than those who maintain custody of their children.[51] Conventional beliefs about the gender-specific role of women shape criminal court proceedings, family court decisions, and social service and medical policy. Police, judges, social workers, and a host of nongovernment workers internalize assumptions about the proper role of women and the family. These ideologies have little to do with the social reality of most women's lived experience of the family, for the nuclear family represents a small portion of the population. As well, the state has historically been quite intent in systematically preventing the formation of families for people of color. Slavery, residential schools, internment camps, economic policy, drug and immigration laws, and racial profiling have torn families apart.

The family and motherhood are central to the debates surrounding women and drugs. Canadian writer Lorna Turnbull states that we know little about the real life experiences of mothers, although there are many stereotypes and myths that misinform us.[52] The ideology of mothering in Western nations portrays women as selfless, giving and pure.[53] However, not all women are embraced by this ideology; some women, especially poor women and women of color, are deemed

51. Carlen 1983; Chunn and Gavigan 1991; Eaton 1983; Gavigan 1988.
52. Turnbull 2001: 39.
53. Glenn 1994.

unfit, and incapable of caring for their children. Single-parent mothers in Britain, Canada, and the U.S. have been singled out as contributing to the breakdown of family values and the overburdening of social programs.[54] Single mothers, especially those suspected of illegal drug use, are also viewed as suspect and as contributing to an underclass of children who may become criminals. Women of color and the poor are depicted as immoral and incapable of socializing their children.[55]

The morality of women of color and poor women and their role as mothers have historically been questioned in the nations of the colonizer and the colonized. Women of color and poor women have struggled to gain control over their own bodies and their reproduction, and over having children and keeping the ones they do have. Slavery, residential schools, immigration policy, the eugenics movement (in all its manifestations), forced sterilization, child apprehension, and the medical diagnoses neonatal abstinence syndrome (NAS) which justifies the removal of children from a mother's care, have prevented women from having and keeping their children. The ideology of mothering masks the difficulties women face in their struggles to keep their families intact, to find a safe haven from racism, class inequality, and sexism, and to counter all interventions by the state. Since the 1980s, women suspected of using illegal drugs have faced increased surveillance, civil and criminal charges and intervention into their families. Central to the debates are whether they are fit to parent and whether they are a risk to the unborn fetus.

* * *

In chapter 1 of *From Witches to Crack Moms*, I take a closer look at women and their relationship to illegal and legal drugs. Chapter 1 also offers a brief account of the historical underpinnings that have shaped present drug policy, and examines the history of the regulation of altered states of consciousness and its links to the oppression of women and Aboriginal peoples. In addition, women's legal drug

---

54. Bashevkin 2002.
55. Collins 1991; Gupta 1995.

use and the drug-use rates for British, Canadian, and U.S. women are discussed. Chapter 2 focuses on medical, social service, and legal regulation of women suspected of using illegal drugs. It examines fetal rights, maternal drug use, maternal-state conflicts, and criminal and civil cases against women who use illegal drugs in the U.S. and highlights alternative programs in England and Scotland. Chapter 3 explores the restructuring of social services in Britain, Canada, and the U.S. and discusses how women suspected of using illegal drugs are identified and regulated in these countries. Chapter 4 presents a sociological view of drug use and examines drug treatment and alternative options for women who use drugs. It concludes with a discussion about drug treatment courts in the U.S. and Canada and their significance for women. Chapter 5 explores routes to imprisonment for women who are suspected of possessing, selling, or transporting illegal drugs; sentencing and prison time; and the restructuring of the prison in all three nations to accommodate the war on drugs. Chapter 6 links the domestic war on drugs in the U.S. to international policy, and explores how U.S. drug policy in Colombia has fueled and contributes to violence against women and Indigenous peoples.[56] This chapter also highlights women's peace groups active in Colombia. The final chapter, chapter 7, highlights alternatives to the war on drugs.

---

56. As noted earlier, even though racial categories are essentialist social constructions, illegal drug use is racialized. Throughout this book the terms Indigenous, Aboriginal, Native Indian, and First Nations are used to describe those peoples and their descendants who inhabited what is now referred to as North and South America. There is no firm agreement about these descriptive terms amongst Aboriginal peoples themselves. Similarly, the terms Hispanic and Latino are used to describe those peoples and their descendants who are from diverse regions in South America, Mexico, Puerto Rico, etc. The descriptive terms white, black, and women of color are also used to refer to diverse groups of people.

Chapter 1

Women and Illegal and Legal Drugs

We may assume that we know quite a bit about specific drugs, but often our information comes from mainstream media, pharmaceutical, and government sources. Critical sociologists, historians, ethnobiologists, and drug users themselves often present a different story about specific drugs. The justification of the criminalization of specific drugs is based on their perceived "dangerousness," thus, it is worthwhile examining whether these assumptions are valid and why and how women use drugs. Protecting women against drugs has been used by law-and-order pundits to justify punitive drug laws. The point here is not to replace one set of ideologies about dangerousness with another; but to explore how the line dividing illegal and legal drugs is a social construction, and to better understand that the taking of drugs is central to most people's lives.

Everyday, people in Western nations consume the drug caffeine in coffee, tea, and soda-pop. Others smoke cigarettes which contain nicotine, our most toxic drug. Still others frequently use over-the-counter and prescribed drugs. The majority of adults in Britain, Canada, and the U.S. drink alcohol. Rarely do we consider these legal drugs we use each day. However, illegal drugs are no more dangerous than the legal ones we readily consume. Rather than fearing illegal drugs, we can begin to shift our assumptions by becoming more informed about the social factors that shape drug use. Perhaps we can move toward understanding drug use as "normal" and as socially and culturally based, rather than as sexualized, racialized, medicalized, and criminalized. In this chapter, I explore what a drug is and look at some of the historical factors that shape the regulation of drugs and, in turn, the regulation of women.

Drugs: What Are They?

Determining what a drug is can be complex. Traditionally, drugs have been defined as "any substance that in small amounts produces significant changes in the body, mind, or both." However, Andrew Weil and Winifred Rosen point out in their celebrated book, *From Chocolate to Morphine*, that this definition may apply to food and poisons as well. In addition, psychoactive drugs—those substances that alter "mood, perception, and thought"—are difficult to categorize.[1] For example, should alcohol be considered a food, drug, or poison? Drugs can also be classified as natural, refined, semisynthetic, or synthetic. Natural or organic drugs which come from plants, consist of complex mixtures that contribute to the effect of the drug. For example, the coca leaf contains fourteen drugs, cocaine being only one of them. The other drugs in the coca leaf appear to modify the stimulating effect of cocaine.

A number of researchers have pointed out that organic drugs seem to be less toxic than synthetic drugs and have less potential for abuse.[2] Isolating active principles from drug plants and creating synthetic drugs has led to the emergence of our modern-day pharmaceutical industry, which promotes the production of more potent and purer drugs; however, these drugs may have more potential for abuse. It appears that synthetic drugs made in laboratories (e.g., Valium, Prozac) may be the most problematic. The coca leaf rarely contains more than 0.5 percent cocaine; in contrast, refined cocaine can be 100 percent pure (although cocaine sold on the illegal market is usually around 60 percent pure).[3] Thus, chewing coca leaves differs from smoking, sniffing, and injecting cocaine.

Since the nineteenth century, the use of organic plants, rather than refined and legally prescribed synthetic drugs, has been perceived as

1. Weil and Rosen 1998: 9.
2. Morgan and Zimmer 1997; Weil and Rosen, 1998.
3. Weil and Rosen, 1998: 45, 46.

"unscientific." Organic drugs such as marijuana, opium, and coca are often described in Western society as "bad drugs," originating from Third World countries.[4] British writers John Davies and David Shewan note that the present categorization of legal and illegal drugs stems from the "historical dominance of Western societies," climate, and geography.[5] Grains and hops grow well in England and Scotland, providing malt whiskies and beer, whereas the coca plant is central to areas in South America. Marijuana was originally a native plant of Asia, and of the 120 hallucinogenic plants found today, fewer than twenty are found outside the Americas. Indigenous peoples throughout the world have shown evidence of "pharmacological genius" in their experimentation with drugs; ethnobiologists have no understanding of how Indigenous peoples first made their discoveries.[6] Drug researchers Ross Coomber and Nigel South explore how some forms of drug use are normalized and how drug use differs in different settings and cultures. They examine how forms of drug use do not fit the "Western" notion of drug use as "*essentially* damaging." Rather, they highlight how some forms of drug use are positive, enhancing cohesiveness as well as the social-health of groups of people.[7]

Imperialism, colonization, the search for new markets and territory, global travel, and the emergence of synthetic drugs and the modern-day pharmaceutical industry have expanded the array of drugs available to people throughout the world today. Western societies continue to demonize drugs that they "perceive" as originating outside their borders, even when logically this is not true. For example, today a significant portion of marijuana in Canada and the U.S. is grown domestically (from one-third to one-half), and not imported from other countries, and it is the largest cash crop in some areas of these countries.[8] Although many "experts" and political leaders claim that drugs are dangerous, there is no consensus about *which* drugs are dangerous. In Canada, Britain, and the U.S.,

4. Boyd 1991.
5. Davies and Shewan 2000: 233.
6. Davis 1998: 163.
7. Coomber and South 2004: 16.
8. Schlosser 2003.

alcohol and tobacco are legal and tolerated. In Muslim societies, alcohol is banned.

A Brief History of Drug Regulation and Women

The criminalization of drugs cannot be separated from the regulation of altered states of consciousness, imperialism, colonization, and the subordination of women in Western history. Drug reformers have constructed certain drugs as agents that lead white moral women into addiction, immorality, and sexual slavery at the hands of devious men of color. Immoral women and women of color are viewed as more deviant than their moral counterparts. The moral regulation of drugs in its many guises attempts to erase any memory of ritual, spiritual, and medicinal use of plants that alter consciousness and to engender political dissent. It also attempts to render invisible our considerable legal drug use which is constructed as therapeutic.

The current war on drugs is similar to other wars of persecution. Drug users are treated similarly to witches and heretics during the Inquisition, the dispossessed poor in England in the eighteenth century, and political dissidents in Third World countries that experience social unrest. Drug researcher Bruce Alexander notes that in each instance, the deviant is blamed for society's ills, and society allays its "fears symbolically by organized persecution."[9] Yet moral regulations do "not arise out of the primal unconscious of the populace. They are constituted through the coming together of historically specific cultural, political, and legal tools."[10] This is evidenced by the persecution of women during the witch hunts of earlier times and the drug war of today. Canadian writer Sherene Razack states that "without history and social context, each encounter between unequal groups becomes a fresh one, where the participants start from zero, as one human being to another,

9. Alexander 1990: 50, 51.
10. Moore and Valverde 2003: 306.

each innocent of the subordination of others."[11] The roots of our present drug war and the subordination of women begin with the witch hunts.

Witch Hunts

I am not so concerned with the history of the witch hunts, which is diverse, but rather with its relation to the regulation and subordination of women and its link to the regulation of altered states of consciousness, which undermined women's control of their own sexuality and reproduction, and their independence. Although Christianity emerged much earlier, it was not until the twelfth century that the Roman Catholic Church became the first male-dominated centralized authority with the political, military, and religious power to define and persecute pagans and subordinate women.[12] Pagan believers honored the "earth as the 'Great Mother'" and honored the spiritual importance of women.[13] Their belief and practice of diversity and reconciliation was replaced by Christian patriarchal conceptions of retribution, and in the thirteenth century, the Inquisition was established by the Roman Catholic Church as a tool to identify and punish witches and heretics.[14]

In the name of God, torture, mass burnings, trials and executions occurred throughout Europe up until the eighteenth century, and as many as one to nine million people were sentenced to death.[15] People were charged with the crime of "heresy" and "witchcraft," and the majority of those charged and convicted were poor women in rural areas, the midwives and healers of the community, unruly women, and political dissenters. Until recently little attention was given to the gendered nature of the witch hunts. However, it is estimated that 80–85 percent of condemned witches were women.[16]

11. Razack 1998: 8.
12. Bianchi 1994; Cayley 1998; Faith 1993.
13. Pfohl 1994.
14. Cayley 1997.
15. Ehrenreich and English 1973; Faith 1993; Pfohl 1994.
16. Ehrenreich and English 1973: 8.

Most witches were identified by secret informers, and torture and death was the ultimate outcome of their trials. Furthermore, family members and neighbors who informed on women suspected of witchcraft benefited by acquiring their property and material goods after their death.

Witches were believed to have supernatural powers; thus, the Church's suppression of paganism and its denouncement of the ritual use of plants for spiritual practice and healing. "During ancient times," plants were used as "medicines, poisons, and sacraments."[17] It was believed that witches used hallucinogenic plants such as "belladonna, mandrake, henbane, and datura,"[18] and those suspected of altering consciousness were condemned. Religious authorities thought that plants that had hallucinogenic properties were rubbed on the skin or ingested by women they identified as witches. It was also believed that witches enticed innocent young virgin girls to join them, interfered with reproduction and male virility, killed newborn babies, and raised hailstorms.[19] It was thought that the eating of herbs assisted their evil power. The Church saw all women as sexually immoral, but especially those women suspected of being witches. Christian authorities claimed that witches deserved the heaviest punishment of all criminals.

Canadian theorist Sheila Noonan notes that many of these women quite possibly possessed "extraordinary abilities."[20] The construction of women healers as witches denied their considerable healing powers and their knowledge about various plants/drugs to relieve pain and suffering.[21] During the witch hunts, midwives and healers threatened the Catholic church because healing was considered to be in the domain of God, not of laypeople. Thus, women who possessed healing knowledge, especially related to reproduction, and who knew how to use plants/drugs were constructed as witches who were unscientific, dangerous, and non-Christian. *The*

17. Kunitz 2001: 91, 92.
18. Davis 1998: 164.
19. Kramer and Sprenger 1971.
20. Noonan 2002.
21. See Palmer and Horowitz 2000 and their discussion about women and drugs.

Malleus Maleficarum (The Witches' Hammer) written in 1484 by two Dominican monks, served as a tool for religious and secular authorities to identify and punish women suspected of witchcraft. The monks were suspicious of the various herbal remedies midwives and healers used and noted that many people believed that magic was central to witches' healing powers. However, it is evident that woman healers and midwives of this period relied on many medicines still used today.[22] Key elements that fueled the witch hunts were the control of female reproduction and sexuality and control of women's independence.

Eventually, the writings of Enlightenment thinkers, the Protestant Reformation of the sixteenth century, and the break from the Roman Catholic Church contributed to conflicting Christian religious and political beliefs in Europe. In practice, this meant there was no longer a consensus about who was the deviant (i.e., witches). Middle- and upper-class people began to protest public executions once it became apparent that they too could be arrested.[23] By the early 1700s, the regulation of women and the drugs they consumed began to shift.

The Gin Craze

In Britain, as in the rest of Europe, women identified as witches were blamed for social and private problems. Poverty shaped the lives of the masses of people in Britain during the fifteenth and sixteenth centuries, and child mortality rates may have been as high as 40–45 percent.[24] Beer was the beverage of choice for adults and children because unpolluted drinking water was scarce and beer itself was a food source. One hundred years later conditions had not improved for the ordinary citizen in Britain, as feudalism and peasant labor was replaced by industrial capitalism and the modern nation state.[25] The ordinary citizen was poor, uneducated, and illiterate, and women had few rights.

22. Ehrenreich and English: 1973.
23. Pfohl 1994.
24. Thomas 1973: 6.
25. Culhane 1998: 43 44.

Drunken, unruly behavior was common, and beer was the affordable drug for the masses of poor women, men, and children in London.[26]

Although distilled alcohol has been available since the late sixteenth century, only the rich could afford to drink it regularly. The poor in Britain used it medicinally and for special celebrations. However, use of distilled alcohol shifted in the early 1700s when gin and other distilled alcohols were produced cheaply and became more available to the poor. Historian Jessica Warner claims that gin became the "first modern drug" and its new popularity became known as the "gin craze" beginning in 1720 and ending in 1751.[27] The poor's consumption of gin threatened the social and economic arrangements of the status quo. The poor were afforded few rights and their living and work conditions were appalling. However, wealthy moral reformers perceived gin to be the cause of numerous social ills, including poverty, social decay, immorality, and the loss of maternal instinct. Gin was constructed as a health hazard for women, especially mothers and those women who looked after young children, and poor women were constructed as less moral and less maternally fit than their wealthier counterparts. Moral reformers condemned women's presence and behavior in the public sphere. Beer consumption, however, was not targeted and its use remained high during the gin craze.

In 1736, witchcraft was dropped as a statutory offense in Britain. This is the same year that "one of the most infamous gin acts was passed."[28] It took a tremendous effort by wealthy moral reformers to convince poor women that they had no place in the public sphere and to force them to retreat to the private sphere, the home.

Colonization and the Regulation of Altered States of Consciousness

From the 1500s to the 1800s, while the majority of people in Britain and Europe struggled to survive, the colonization of "back-

26. Thomas 1973.
27. Warner 2002.
28. Ibid.: 81.

wards heathens" and "uncivilized" peoples was legitimized. During this period, Britain and other European nations explored the world searching for resources and markets. The slave trade forced "20 million Africans to the New World" between the 1500s and the mid-1800s. Roughly two-thirds died in the slave forts that were built to hold them and during transit to other parts of the world. African men, women, and children were stolen from their homes to provide the labor for plantations and farms in the New World. Slavery was also legal in some regions of Canada.

Slave codes in the U.S. and elsewhere prohibited slaves from gathering in groups of more than four or five people "without whites present," and this was enforced to prevent not only rebellion but also religious practices. Thus, spiritual beliefs and traditional healing practices were driven underground as slave masters strove to "transform primitive black savages into civilized, God-fearing agricultural workers."[29] African men, women, and children who were transported against their will to the New World and the generations of black people who were later born into the institution of slavery in the U.S. and elsewhere were exploited and treated as nonhuman. Christian religious and racial theories supporting white supremacy justified such practices. Black women suffered at the hands of their slave masters who regarded them as not only sources of labor but also as breeders. Slave women were vulnerable to sexual exploitation and their children were the property of the slave master.[30] Britain, Canada, and the U.S. share an interconnected history of the colonization and subjugation of African and Aboriginal peoples. However, it is debatable whether representatives of Western culture were in any way more "developed" or "civilized" than the Aboriginal and African peoples they encountered.[31]

Hungry for resources and new markets, English law was already in place to legitimize colonization. England never colonized a land that was uninhabited, and many Aboriginal societies were not conquered,

29. Websdale 2001.: 14, 19, 16.
30. Collins, 1991; hooks 1981.
31. Culhane 1998; hooks 1995; Paul 2000.

nor were treaties signed. Nevertheless, as sociologist Dara Culhane writes, "Already inhabited nations were simply legally *deemed to be uninhabited* if the people were not Christian, not agricultural, not commercial, not 'sufficiently evolved' or simply in the way" (italics in the original).[32] Historically, Britain, Canada and the U.S. failed to honor Aboriginal collective and treaty rights.

Arriving in the New World, the colonizers brought not only their laws but also their drug of choice, alcohol, and their religion, Christianity. All three were to have a devastating impact on Aboriginal peoples and their communities. Prior to colonization, North America was essentially alcohol free, the exception being a small group of southwestern Aboriginal societies that made alcoholic beverages. For example, the Pima and the Papago participated in ritual use of alcohol and the Apache used alcohol on secular occasions. From all accounts, Aboriginal drinking was infrequent and of a peaceful nature.[33] There are no accounts of negative drug use in North America prior to colonization. Initially, in their first contact with Europeans, Aboriginal peoples in Canada and the U.S. steadfastly declined to drink or drank modestly. The writings of early Jesuit missionaries, traders, and explorers repeat the same story, "The Indians... entertain a strong aversion to ardent spirits, which they regard as poison."[34] Early recorded accounts of heavier drinking patterns reveal no violent or abusive behavior, and drunken disorder did not prevail.[35]

Although Aboriginal societies in North America rarely used alcohol, they have historically recognized the benefits of plants to alter consciousness during spiritual worship and to heal the sick. The ritual use of tobacco was common, and some societies used hallucinogens during spiritual practice. As well, following the criminalization of the Sun Dance in the U.S. in 1890, the Kiowa were denied "their essential act of faith" and the ritual use of peyote emerged as an "affirmation of their fundamental religious ideas."[36] Non-Christian vi-

32. Culhane 1998: 48.
33. MacAndrew and Edgerton 1969.
34. Howay, as cited in MacAndrew and Edgerton 1969: 114.
35. MacAndrew and Edgerton 1969.
36. Davis 1996: 81, 82.

sionary experience, shamanic traditions, and ritual use of plants which altered consciousness were demonized by colonizing nation states, the church (both Protestant and Catholic), and zealous missionaries. Catholics were believed to be more tolerant toward the transgressions of the sinner than Protestants;[37] however, this tolerance was reserved for the rich and the powerful, rather than the colonized.

Canadian writer Sherene Razack uses a "language of color to describe the politics of domination and subordination," and white "is the color of domination."[38] In the 1800s, legislation was enacted in Canada and the U.S. to regulate all areas of Aboriginal peoples' lives. Genocide and assimilation were the goals of restricting cultural, political, and spiritual practices. One consequence was that Aboriginal religions were "driven underground."[39] As Aboriginal peoples in North America lost their "stewardship" of the land—as well as loss of their language, spiritual practices, medicines, and political and social control of their own destinies—they were introduced to alcohol by "scheming fur-traders," white settlers, and "hard-drinking soldiers" who displayed negative behavior when they drank.[40] The fact that Aboriginal societies were introduced to a model of drinking that was negative is "beyond dispute."[41] They witnessed white people drinking to excess, accompanied by dramatically negative changes in their behavior, including violence. In Canada, trading posts run by the Hudson Bay Company would arrange drinking parties when the hunting season was over. Barrels of whiskey would be supplied for Aboriginals and Europeans alike.[42]

In the United States, federal legislation was enacted in 1832 to prohibit Aboriginal peoples from drinking alcohol, and although some state and local laws remained, the federal legislation was repealed in 1953.[43] In Canada, one of the provisions of the Indian Act of 1868

37. Wagner 1997; Weber 1976.
38. Razack 1998: 11.
39. Zion 1998: 139.
40. Maracle 1993: 9, 45.
41. MacAndrew and Edgerton 1969: 145.
42. Maracle 1993.
43. MacAndrew and Edgerton 1969: 106.

was to prohibit Aboriginal peoples from buying or possessing alcohol. This legislation was not completely repealed until 1985. Brian Maracle discusses the impact of alcohol prohibition in Canada:

> Thousands of people were arrested and jailed as a result of the law, many of them dozens of times. The law against Indian drinking was not added to the books just to appease churches or temperance groups. It was a convenient social control measure that could be arbitrarily used by the Indian agents and the police against whomever they wanted to target.[44]

However, prohibition did not stop Aboriginal peoples from drinking; it just changed the way they drank. The law forced them to drink their alcohol covertly and as quickly as possible in order to avoid arrest.[45] In order to drink legally (and to vote), Aboriginal peoples in Canada had to sign away their legal status. Constructing Aboriginal peoples as *outsiders* to Anglo-Saxon life was essential to colonial practices. Aboriginal women who drank alcohol were especially stigmatized because drinking was viewed as the domain of men. Their drinking not only provided evidence of their criminality and transgression of their proper gender role, it also confirmed their immorality. By the mid-1800s, Christian religious authorities generated fear about the mixing of the races by focusing on Aboriginal women leaving reservations in the U.S., and reserves in Canada, to live with non-Native men. The mixing of the races was perceived as a serious problem which contributed to Anglo-Saxon race suicide—it was criminalized in the U.S. and discouraged in Canada. The children of Aboriginal women and non-Native men were labeled "half-breeds" and they were constructed in British Columbia as central players in supplying alcohol to "status Indians" who were prohibited by law from drinking.[46]

Throughout five hundred years of colonization, Aboriginal women were increasingly viewed as evil by missionaries and as second-class "Indians" by government. Researcher Nancy Shoemaker notes that

44. Maracle 1993: 44.
45. Ibid.
46. Mawani 2002; Nelson 2002

George Washington, the first president of the U.S., articulated his plan for Aboriginal women to be transformed into "chaste, orderly housewives."[47] In order to accomplish this goal, the role and status of Aboriginal women in the family and community and in spiritual, political, and social life had to be dismantled. In addition, all ritual uses of plants and all spiritual practices were criminalized, and the medicinal use of plants for healing, which was in opposition to European and later Canadian and U.S. medicine, was also discouraged and criminalized. For example, Aboriginal healers were arrested and charged with witchcraft and fraud in the early 1900s in British Columbia.[48]

The Regulation of Coca

Similar to the British, the Spanish colonizers in South America were also intolerant of Indigenous knowledge, including spiritual, social, and political knowledge that might challenge early capitalist and Christian hegemony. Spain also forged campaigns of genocide against Aboriginal peoples in South America in the late sixteenth century. Fueled by their hunger for gold, the Spaniards proclaimed both legal and religious authority and systematically destroyed communities and murdered and tortured Aboriginal peoples of South America for their non-Christian spiritual beliefs.[49] Religious terrorism forged new markets and opened up access to land and resources. But shamanic traditions were "deeply embedded in the culture."[50] The use of coca preceded the Inca empire by hundreds of years, and many Indigenous people viewed the plant as sacred and magical, beliefs which were expressed in myths. Drug "abuse" did not exist prior to colonization. Then, as now, the coca leaf contained more vitamins and minerals than fifty other foods that were regularly consumed in South America; the amount of calcium in the plant was higher than any other ed-

---

47. Purdue, as cited in Anderson 2001: 62.
48. Kelm 2001: 158.
49. Burkholder and Johnson 1990; Davis 1996.
50. Davis 1996: 141.

ible plant.[51] The coca leaf was not a drug per se, rather a food and a mild stimulant and an essential part of Indigenous people's diet in South America.

Originally, the Roman Catholic Church attempted to outlaw coca due to its association with pagan beliefs, but Spanish colonists resisted because they benefited economically by growing and selling coca, and found that Indigenous miners refused to work without coca. A compromise emerged in the mid-1500s. The Church sanctioned the growing and selling of coca, but the religious use of the leaf was criminalized and "punishable by death."[52] The cultivation of coca became an important part of the colonizer's economy and the Church's revenues.

Spiritual belief, shamanic traditions, and the ritual use of plants to alter consciousness varied throughout the Americas. What did not vary was the response to Indigenous knowledge and spiritual belief by Christian nations in their quest to spread the word of God and to expand their markets. Yet violence and punitive colonization practices have not been successful in suppressing Aboriginal knowledge and resistance.

Western Drug Use: Women's Use of Opiate Remedies

While the healing practices of and plants used by Aboriginal peoples were criminalized, the elixirs and patent medicines used by the colonizer were not initially scrutinized by Christian authorities and moral reformers. During the nineteenth century, North American, British, and European medicine cabinets contained many elixirs, patent medicines, and cough suppressants that contained narcotics, cocaine, and marijuana. These drugs were viewed very differently than the plants they were derived from (such as coca and poppy). Many of the elixirs were specifically for "women's problems" and for soothing sick infants. Opiates were used for a wide range of ailments, including pain management, intestinal problems, respiratory conditions, mental disorders, and infections. Historians Virginia Berridge

51. Ibid.: 425.
52. Ibid.: 425.

and Griffith Edwards note that in Britain, as elsewhere, opium use was acceptable in society during the 1700s and early 1800s.[53] It was a commodity that people used freely and it was not restricted to medicinal use. There was no distinction between medical and nonmedical use of opium at this time.

Opiates have a long history of use for women's ailments. Most women could not afford the services of a doctor and self-medicated for treatment of painful menstruation, childbirth (during and after birth), and puerperal fever. They also treated their children, spouses, and the elderly in their care. For most women in rural areas, doctors were not only too expensive but also few and far between. A wide array of patent medicines, many containing opium, were listed in Eaton's and Sears, Roebuck and Co.'s mail-order catalogues and advertised widely elsewhere.[54] Right up until the 1930s, women's magazines in Canada stated, "It is of paramount importance that every woman, especially mothers, should know what remedies to use in the treatment of slight ailments—little matters for which a physician would not be consulted but which, if neglected, may lead to grave disorders."[55] A doctor was not called for by mothers until all other patent medicines and home remedies had been exhausted.

In the medical system, opiates were prescribed for nervous disorders that were thought to be gender specific. Interestingly, opium was used during the eighteenth and nineteenth century for the treatment of insanity; however, by the early twentieth century, it was heralded as the cause of insanity.[56] Morphine was used to treat "hysterical women" in the nineteenth century, and later self-administered by women using the newly invented hypodermic needle.[57] With its discovery came cases of "chronic morphine use." In fact, the first person to die of a morphine overdose was the wife of Alexander Wood of Edinburgh, who is generally credited with the discovery in 1843 of the hypodermic method of "injecting drugs under the skin in liquid

53. Berridge and Edwards 1981.
54. Kandall 1996.
55. Mitchinson 2002: 31.
56. Musto 1987: 64.
57. Berridge and Edwards 1981: 68.

form."[58] She was also the first person on record to become addicted to the drug.[59]

In Britain, Canada, and the U.S., it was quite common for physicians to prescribe opiates for menstrual and menopausal discomforts. Upper-class women, as opposed to poor women who could not afford to see doctors, were prescribed Laudanum (an opiate derivative) for many of their ills, and the majority of those women did not become addicted.[60] Upper-class women also visited opium dens and smoked opium for recreational purposes. Opium eating was often perceived as an "aristocratic vice" because wealthy and educated women (and men) participated in it.[61] Many people became familiar with opiate use and addiction through the works of literary figures like Thomas De Quincey and Samuel Taylor Coleridge. However, critics note that these atypical users should not be generalized to the rest of society at that time. More typical opium users were Elizabeth Barrett Browning, "a well-balanced addict" who took opium and morphine regularly, and Florence Nightingale, who used opium for medical reasons after she returned from the Crimea and to "counteract the effect of the ending of her work there."[62]

Marijuana and Cocaine Use

Following criticism about opium's positive qualities by anti-opium causes, doctors began to look to cocaine and marijuana to treat illness. Marijuana is one of our oldest drugs, and a product of the hemp plant, *cannabis sativa*. There are more than 460 known compounds in the marijuana plant, one of them being THC. The hemp plant is diverse, providing oil, fibre, rope, paper, and seeds; it is also used as a medicine. The first recorded report of using marijuana for medicinal purposes was found in a Chinese herbal book, which suggested using it for female disorders, malaria, constipation, rheumatic pains,

58. Terry and Pellens 1970: 65, 67.
59. Weil and Rosen 1998.
60. Berridge and Edwards 1981.
61. Brecher et al. 1972: 18.
62. Berridge and Edwards 1981: 59.

and absentmindedness.[63] It was also used in Africa, India, and in medieval Europe. Although its healing qualities were recognized for thousands of years, marijuana as a medicine became popular in the West in the mid-nineteenth century. Many patent medicines contained marijuana. At that time, Western doctors praised marijuana and wrote about its healing qualities. They prescribed it for a wide range of ills, including migraines, asthma, gastric ulcer, depression, and painful menstruation.

Similarly, coca's medicinal properties were not recognized by Western healers until the 1800s, and then it was not the leaf with its various nutrients and vitamins that caught their attention but cocaine, which was isolated and extracted from the coca leaf as hydrochloride. By the late 1800s, the use of cocaine in tonics and wines became popular in Europe and North America.[64] Vin-Mariani wine contained cocaine, as did Coca-Cola and many patent medicines, home remedies, and tonics. Several types of coca wine were consumed by women and children, especially the sweet wine called Malaga.[65] Cocaine was also used as a local anaesthetic and a cure for people addicted to opiates. Doctors also prescribed cocaine for many medical problems, especially "women's problems." In the Victorian era, middle- and upper-class women were perceived as weak, passive, and ruled by their biology, more specifically, their reproductive system. They were treated with cocaine for a wide range of illnesses, including reproductive problems and "neurasthenia," which were defined as nervous conditions.[66]

Once cocaine was isolated from the coca plant and marketed in Europe and North America, it wasn't long before its potential as a recreational drug was discovered.[67] Although it was not necessarily constructed for nonmedical use at the time, cocaine began to be used for recreational purposes in the late 1800s, mostly by middle- and upper-class women (and men). However, this use was generally confined to ingesting the various tonics, patent medicines, and tablets available.

---

63. Grinspoon and Bakalar 1997.
64. Morgan and Zimmer 1997; Weil and Rosen 1998.
65. Berridge and Edwards 1981: 221.
66. Kaplan 1996.
67. Grinspoon and Bakalar 1976.

Women's Drug Use: A Personal Matter

Prior to the mid-1800s, if a woman's use of liquid opiates (or, for that matter, her use of marijuana or cocaine in patent medicines) was discussed at all, it would have been discussed as a personal matter, or a bad habit not subject to legal sanctions.Women who used opiates were not cut off from the rest of society, nor were they stigmatized. In fact, the words "addict" and "addiction" were only introduced to describe "negative" drug/alcohol use in the mid-1800s. Before then, addiction was associated with pursuits such as reading, and it wasn't assumed that the regular use of accepted Anglo-Saxon drugs/alcohol was a negative or destructive activity.[68] The prevailing view of the opiate user in the U.S. before the nineteenth century was of a middle- or upper-class woman (or man) who was a law-abiding citizen. Prior to criminalization of opiates in the U.S., 80 percent of people addicted to narcotics had "jobs, home, families, and reputations."[69] It has been noted that it was more acceptable for upper- and middle-class American women to use narcotics than alcohol. In fact, historian Stephen Kandall suggests that the women's temperance movement of the mid-1800s to1920s may have fueled women's narcotic use, as alcohol was not considered an alternative option.[70] It was commonly known that "husbands drank alcohol in the saloon; wives took opium at home."[71] The emergence of both temperance ideology and the new professions, however, would redefine drug use.

Temperance Ideology

By the nineteenth century, poor women's gin consumption and immorality were forgotten when the women's temperance movement, spurred on by religious conviction of self-control, morality, and abstinence,[72] emerged to champion women as the sober and moral defenders of home, family, and abstinence. Rather than focus on gin,

68. Alexander 1990; Brecher et al. 1972.
69. Gray 1999: 12.
70. Kandall 1996.
71. Brecher et al. 1972: 17.
72. Gusfield 1972: 5.

the temperance movement condemned all alcohol use; sobriety and self-control became the template of middle-class respectability in North America and other Western nations. Temperance researcher Joseph Gusfield explores how Western Protestants adopted religious dedication and temperance as symbols of social status that separated them from lower-class citizens and Catholics. In general, Protestant religious beliefs fostered individualism, self-control, labor, and material wealth as visible signs of God's favor. The capitalist system, as Max Weber pointed out, "so needs this devotion to the calling of making money."[73] It is not surprising that those countries that had large temperance movements in the nineteenth and twentieth centuries tended to be predominantly Protestant (Canada, Finland, United States).[74] As the impact of industrialization, social unrest, and non-Protestant immigration threatened Protestant hegemony in North America, the temperance movement gained ground and alcohol was blamed for a host of social ills.

Women have been at the center and have often been the leaders of prohibition movements in North America and Britain. In Canada and the U.S., the Women's Christian Temperance Union (WCTU) emerged in the late 1800s and gained a larger following by the early 1900s. White middle-class reformers regarded sobriety and morality as innate to the female sex, and therefore by extension, it was women's responsibility to protect it. Women reformers, who saw themselves as moral defenders of the home and community, were concerned with what they perceived as the disintegration of family values and identified alcohol as the main culprit of society's ills such as poverty, violence, wife beating, and criminality. Contrary to early Christian views that women were inherently evil, the new temperance movement depicted women as naturally moral. However, some women were constructed as more moral than others. Poor women and women of color, immigrants, and "fallen women" were viewed as immoral and deviant. Reformers sought to transform these "immoral" individuals, and fought for prohibition against alcohol.[75]

73. Weber 1976: 72.

74. Levine 1992.

75. Hannah-Moffat 2001.

Prohibition came into law in the U.S. in 1919 when the United States Constitution's Eighteenth Amendment was ratified. However, prohibition generated social unrest, overburdened the court system, and contributed to police violence. Poor and working-class people felt the brunt of the law during the prohibition era. After several years, however, support for prohibition lessened, and in 1933, the Twenty-First Amendment to repeal prohibition became part of the U.S. Constitution. National prohibition in Canada only lasted for one year, although several provinces continued to criminalize the sale of alcohol. Interestingly, both prohibitionist and anti-prohibitionist women drew upon the concept of protecting the home from evil to advance their movements.[76] Historically, the United States has been more attached to temperance ideology than Britain and Canada.

Ideological Overlap Between the Anti-opiate and Prohibition Movement

Many writers note that there was considerable overlap between the earlier international and national anti-opium movements of the late 1800s and the temperance movement. "Anti-opiumists" believed that moderate use of opium was impossible, as did temperance reformers with reference to alcohol. Both movements argued that moderate users did not exist, and some doctors were willing to support this thesis. In Britain, many doctors "moved easily between temperance, anti-opium and medical organizations studying inebriety."[77] As well, the anti-opiumist and the temperance movement expressed interest in both the physical and the moral decline of users; thus, they influenced the emergence of "hybrid" medical and moral theory.[78] Their focus often centered on those perceived to be *outsiders* to white middle-class Christian morality. Thus, the smoking of opium by Chinese laborers in Britain, U.S., and Canada came under attack, with little attention being paid to the copious amounts of

---

76. Rose 1996.
77. Berridge and Edwards 1981: 154–155.
78. Ibid.155, 193.

opium white Westerners consumed in elixirs and patent medicines. Opium smokers were constructed as *foreigners*, and a threat to women, the family, and the nation. The opium den was depicted as a place of evil where a "cunning Chinaman wreathed in opium fumes"[79] corrupted moral white women.

In the 1920s, moral entrepreneurs such as Canadian Emily Murphy, a Canadian police magistrate and juvenile court judge, and Sara Graham-Mulhall, a former U.S. First Deputy Commissioner in the Department of Narcotic Drug Control in New York state, were significant in producing new discourses about women, drug users, and traffickers.[80] Moral reformers argued that opium smoking was an epidemic that needed to be contained before it spread any further into the white population. Fears related to preserving racial purity, women's morality and victimization, the breakdown of the family and the Anglo-Saxon way of life fueled drug prohibition in Britain, Canada, and the U.S. British writer Marek Kohn notes that if the "ultimate menace of drugs had to be summarized in a single proposition, it would be that they facilitated the seduction of young white women by men of other races."[81]

Contemporary Drug Regulation

Current laws can be linked to Christian morality, colonial practices, and the anti-opiate and temperance movements. U.S. opiate laws were fueled by anti-Asiatic and economic tensions as well as by fears that white supremacy and white women's morality was threatened by foreign outsiders. As early as 1835, San Francisco adopted an ordinance to prohibit opium smoking in "dens." Other cities followed suit, and tariffs were raised on opium to discourage use.[82] In 1914, The Harrison Act (federal drug law) was passed. Because it did not appear to be as controversial as alcohol prohibition, the legislation

79. Ibid. 197.
80. See Graham-Mulhall 1981; and Murphy 1973.
81. Kohn 1992: 2.
82. Brecher et al. 1972.

went unnoticed and the public did not oppose the broadening of police powers.[83] Journalists, congressmen, physicians, and pharmacists had already informed the public that there was widespread drug use and that cocaine could lead black men to violence and Chinese men to devious deeds. In fact, there was no evidence to support these wild claims, and most documented cases of problematic cocaine use had to do with white professional men, many of whom were doctors.[84] The public in the United States assumed the early legislation would be confined to controlling specific foreign *outsiders* and "problem" sections of the population (and not themselves), restricting drug use from reaching middle-class consumers.[85] Moral entrepreneur Harry J. Anslinger, who ran the U.S. Federal Bureau of Narcotics, spread misinformation about marijuana and other drugs and linked them to immorality, crime, and insanity. Drug users had no forum to publicize their experiences. Thus, the legislation was unopposed and *illegal* drug users became a new class of criminals.

Canada's first federal drug legislation, part of the Indian Act of 1868, was enacted one year after Confederation. It lasted for 117 years, serving as an oppressive colonial tool.[86] Canada's federal opiate legislation, The Opium and Narcotic Act, was enacted in 1908 in response to moral entrepreneur Mackenzie King's recommendations following the anti-Asiatic riots in Vancouver in 1907. The riots were set off by white workers who were motivated by economic and racial fears. It is well documented that the Chinese in Western Canada and the United States were perceived as an economic threat to white laborers after the completion of the railway. King came to Vancouver to settle damage claims from the riots after being approached by two opium merchants seeking restitution. King was surprised by the unregulated Chinese opium industry in the city. However, it was not until several affluent Chinese Canadians complained about the opium industry that he saw a way of getting "some good out of this

83. Musto 1987.
84. Grinspoon and Bakalar 1976: 39.
85. Musto 1987; Solomon and Green 1988.
86. Maracle 1993: 44.

riot."[87] He recommended that the importation, sale, and manufacturing of opium be regulated. King had no evidence that opiates caused physiological harm, nevertheless he was able to convince the federal government that white women were being corrupted by Chinese opium merchants and that fairly large profits were being made. The public assumed that the Opium Act would not be used on "ordinary" white middle-class citizens, rather it was believed that it was enacted to control a small minority of users—the Chinese in Western Canada.

Similar to Canada and the U.S., the framework for Britain's current drug policy is linked to their past history. Much has been written about the Opium War of 1840–42 in which the Chinese were forced to open their ports to large-scale opium exports by the British. Opium sales brought huge profits to the East India Company. However, by the late 1800s, the U.S. was pressuring Britain to restrict the opium trade, and in 1909, British representatives agreed to attend the Shanghai Commission, which set the groundwork for international drug control. Their concern centered on opium smoking, considered to be the practice of "inferior peoples,"[88] rather than on patent medicines containing opiates, which most Westerners used. In 1911, the International Conference on Opium (introduced by the U.S.) formalized drug control by introducing a treaty to regulate opium production and distribution, opium smoking, and the manufacture, sale, and use of cocaine and morphine outside of medical use. Britain ratified the treaty in 1914.

The first domestic drug legislation enacted in Britain was the Pharmacy Act of 1868, which regulated the sale of poison.[89] In 1908, Britain passed The Poisons and Pharmacy Act, to regulate patent medicines (which often included opiates and cocaine). The Act was a response to the medical professions' growing power and class tensions, which culminated in their concern over recreational opium use and "infant doping" (administering opium to children) by the poor.[90]

---

87. Boyd 1984: 115.
88. Mott and Bean 1998.
89. Ibid.
90. Berridge and Edwards 1981.

The Defence of the Realm Act Regulation 40 B of 1916 was passed to restrict cocaine possession. Interestingly, this legislation was enacted to deal with "suspected" cocaine use by Canadian soldiers. The Home Office and the police were granted the responsibility of controlling drug use; researchers in the field have interpreted this decision as a step towards criminal justice control.[91] In Britain, a new debate about drugs emerged in 1916 and peaked in the mid-1920s. Women, including chorus girls, flappers, actresses, and lower-class girls, were at the heart of the debate. Their perceived independence was linked to drug use and seduction by men of color. The high profile overdose death of actress Billie Carleton in 1918 sparked the nation's interest in the "sexualized menace" of the drug subculture. Chinese and black men continued to be constructed as culprits who corrupted white women by the media.[92] By the early 1920s, panic about white women's sexual immorality and the "mixing of the races" were behind the push for drug regulation.[93]

As we know today, drug legislation and the social control of drug users and dealers has not been confined to people of color. However, in many Western nations, racial profiling remains prevalent, and the criminal justice system has not deterred from its original intent in criminalizing minorities and the poor. In fact, more drugs were added to the federal list of prohibited drugs—marijuana in 1924 in Canada, 1928 in Britain, and 1937 in the U.S.—even though there was no "evidence" demonstrating that they were more harmful than a host of legal drugs.

Drug Regulation since the 1950s

In the U.S., a distinct shift in drug use and perceptions about drug use occurred after World War II. The beat writers of the 1950s, who included Jack Kerouac, Bonnie Frazer, Joyce Johnson, Allen Ginsberg, Hettie Jones, William Burroughs, and Gregory Corso, challenged the social and political beliefs and literary styles of American culture, and

91. Mott and Bean 1998.
92. Kohn 1992: 7.
93. Kohn 1992.

supported the "use of drugs in the name of art."[94] The beat writers were intent on exploring and bringing to light state-sanctioned death and destruction—including the bombing of Hiroshima and Nagasake—the Cold War, and McCarthysim. They argued that the "sane" state and the social arrangements it supported were dangerous, and they opened to challenge all preconceptions about conventional lives.[95] They believed drugs could lead to mystical experiences, self-transcendence, and cultural revolution.

The period between the late 1950s and the early 1970s, known as the 1960s counterculture movement, has often been characterized by the media and the state as a time of massive illegal drug use, permissive behavior, and liberalism. "Drugs, sex and rock 'n' roll" was the conventional mantra. However, active participants in the social and political movements of the 1960s saw it very differently than the state and the media. Drugs, sex, and rock 'n' roll were certainly present, but for many people and not just the youth, "the '60s" represented an era of political and social activism, "the disruption of late-capitalist ideological and political hegemony,"[96] and the opportunity to alter one's consciousness through many activities, including drug use. However, in many groups, drug use was discouraged and the pursuit of pleasure was considered apolitical.[97]

Although there is some disagreement about which groups led the overall political movement of the '60s,[98] it is generally recognized in North America that the Civil Rights movement, the beat movement, the anti-war movement, the Black Panther movement, the American Indian Movement, and the challenge to the "work ethic, the family ethic, monogamy, prudery, even rational consciousness"[99] were integral to it.[100] Also, during this period the feminist movement emerged

94. Schumacher 1992: 284.
95. Schumacher 1992.
96. Sayres, Stephanson, Aronowitz, and Jameson 1984: 2.
97. Aronowitz 1984; Wagner 1997.
98. See Aronowitz 1984; Breines 1982; Ehrenreich 1989; Wagner 1997.
99. Wagner 1997: 14.
100. The writing about the '60s era is mostly written by political and cultural leaders, and little attention has been paid to the thousands of people in

and the primacy of heterosexuality was challenged as gays and lesbians became more vocal. Women formed "consciousness-raising" groups and explored the artificial "boundaries between private/personal life and public/political life" and coined the expression "the personal is political."[101] This was a time when the personal and the political merged and the movement to create a different social reality was shared by many different groups even if the visions and means to obtain it differed between them. The 1960s movement was multilayered as people experimented with drugs, communalism, and new family formations. A new politics was adopted, one that was anti-authoritarian, anti-hierarchical, nonviolent, and egalitarian.[102] For women, this meant challenging many of the gender constraints placed on them by conventional society.

The discovery of LSD (lysergic acid diethylamide) in the 1940s, and its use as a legal therapeutic tool in the 1950s and early 1960s exposed many members of the beat and '60s movement to the drug. Similar to the beat writers, the youth of the 1960s associated drugs with altered states of consciousness and political dissent. Marijuana, LSD, and other psychedelics were viewed as positive mind-enhancing drugs, and millions of middle-class youths experimented with them in Britain, Canada, and the U.S. Firsthand accounts of illegal drug use was positive and created a challenge to official state propaganda that these drugs had no positive value. In fact, the state, represented by the Central Intelligence Agency (CIA), regarded LSD as an hallucinogenic drug that mimicked psychosis and, therefore, one that could be used

---

Britain, Canada, the U.S., and Europe who tried to live the revolution in their families, homes, and workplace. In many ways, the '60s movement had a life force of its own regardless of its "leaders." Many self-appointed and media-constructed leaders had little connection with the masses of people challenging the status quo. As well, there are many important differences in relation to the British, Canadian, and U.S. experience. In Britain and Canada, many of the cultural and political issues differed from the U.S., as did the responses.

101. Michals: 2002: 48.

102. Breines 1982: 56.

as a weapon of war by breaking people down.[103] The rise of the modern-day pharmaceutical industry also shaped legal and illegal drug use. However, the '60s was a time of experimentation with more than just drugs; it was a challenge—both inside and outside North America—to authority, militarism, and the capitalist state.

Following the more liberal 1960s and 1970s, the conservative governments of Ronald Reagan and George Bush Sr., in the U.S., Margaret Thatcher in Britain, and Brian Mulroney in Canada, ushered in a political culture that sought to dismantle the modern welfare state. "Personal responsibility" was their mantra as they slashed social programs and attempted to regulate personal behavior, including drug use. Reproductive, social, and economic gains made by women in the 1960s and 1970s were challenged. Women's drug use was constructed as evidence of their transgression from conventional family values and proper gender roles. In addition, their drug use was perceived as *dangerous* and seen as evidence of their immorality and irresponsibility. In this political and cultural climate, women's personal behaviors became subject to increased surveillance, and maternal-state conflicts arose.

The period between the late 1950s and the early 1970s can be viewed as a break from former temperance ideology. However, David Wagner considers this period to be an exception to the rule. He writes about the "new temperance movement" in the U.S. which emerged as a challenge to this more liberal period. Wagner sensitizes us to the shift in regulation that has emerged since the early 1970s. The current temperance movement is conservative, with a focus on social control, and the "de-contextualization" of personal behavior (drugs, sex, food) from race, class, gender, and social circumstances, and the punishment of those who fail to conform. Thus, personal behaviors are scrutinized and women and men are blamed for a rapidly ex-

---

103. By the early 1950s, CIA investigators began to experiment with LSD, ingesting it themselves and covertly giving it to civilians, while CIA doctors began to administer massive doses to prisoners and psychiatric patients without their consent (See Lee and Shlain 1992).

panding host of societal problems, rather than the social and political structures that shape their lives.[104]

Since President Nixon's presidency, the U.S. has stepped up its fight against illegal drugs. The Bush Sr. and Clinton administrations, for example, were responsible for unprecedented federal spending and imprisoning of U.S. citizens, most of them victims of the war on drugs. In the 1970s and 1980s, Congress and many state legislatures enacted mandatory minimum sentencing "the 2–3 strikes out" legislation in the U.S. Although, white middle-class youth were the focus of drug regulation during the 1960s, by the 1970s and 1980s it became apparent that the poor and people of color were most vulnerable to police profiling.

As the list of prohibited drugs grew, the police were granted greater powers and allowed to use controversial procedures (no other crime outside of treason, terrorism, and murder warrants similar powers) in order to investigate and arrest suspected drug offenders. Some of the changes in drug legislation and procedures that have expanded police powers include powers of forfeiture, search and seizure, conspiracy laws, electronic surveillance, and the use of informants and undercover agents. Today, "we seem largely incapable of imagining a world that doesn't vigorously police our consciousness, despite the fact that... such a world existed for thousands of years."[105] Drug researchers note that temperance ideology, prohibition, the war on drugs, and the expanding prison-industrial complex are particularly predominant in the United States. It is true that many other Western nations, including Britain and Canada, have criminalized specific drugs and imprisoned illegal drug users and sellers, and that prohibition and temperance movements have emerged in Britain, Canada, England, and Scandinavia. Nevertheless, historically, the United States has been the country most attached to temperance ideology, which has culminated in alcohol prohibition and several drug scares, the war on drugs being the most recent.

Still, since the earliest drug legislation was enacted up until the present, illegal drug use has not been contained in the U.S., Britain, and

---

104. Wagner 1997: 69.
105. Kunitz 2001: 91.

Canada. In this sense drug legislation has been a failure. In defiance of current drug policy, new generations of youth are creating their own rituals in order to experience sensual pleasure and altered states of consciousness. In direct challenge to state programs, like DARE and zero drug-tolerance policies in schools, and levels of surveillance unimaginable to most 1960s participants, the youth of today continue to look for altered states of consciousness that are not state sanctioned. The popularity of raves, and women's participation in them, where music and dance are the focus and MDMA (ecstasy) is the drug of choice, is a strong example of how extensively drug regulation and normative ideas about rational consciousness are being challenged.[106] On April 10, 2003, The AMBER Alert bill (a child abduction bill) was passed by the U.S. House and Senate and later signed by President Bush Jr. At the last moment, the Illicit Drug Anti-Proliferation Act, more commonly known as the RAVE Act which was rejected by both the House and Senate over the last year, was added to it. This Act expands the powers and discretion of prosecutors and is not limited to raves, in fact, diverse public gatherings could be targeted.

In essence, the current "drug war" is seen as the conservative response to the liberal antiauthoritarianism of the 1960s, and the subsequent loss of state and corporate control; the "war on drugs" is "about getting it back."[107] It is a war on any form of consciousness that competes with the ideology of hierarchal power, whether manifested in the church, through continued colonization, in the patriarchal state, or in capitalist economic institutions. Today, George Bush Jr.'s administration, which holds Republican majorities in every branch of government, supports more conservative and Christian Fundamentalist values of family norms, women's reproductive rights, drug use, and civil liberties than previous administrations. The war on drugs is linked to the war on terrorism, and illegal drug users are constructed as subverting the "war effort." Increased corporate power, police, prison and military expansion, and racial profiling have accompanied these changes, and women's reproductive autonomy has also come under attack.

106. Hinchliff 2001; McCall 2001.
107. Willis 1992: 251.

Legal Drugs: Tobacco, Alcohol, and Prescribed Drugs

Although this book is about illegal drugs, the social control of female illegal drug users and sellers cannot be understood unless we challenge the social construction of drug categories. Contrary to official propaganda, we are all drug users, as evidenced by the amazing amounts of legal drugs that we consume. Tobacco and alcohol are billion-dollar industries that can legally advertise and promote their drugs.

Tobacco

Tobacco is a stimulant that affects the central nervous system. Nicotine, the most active chemical found in tobacco, is our most toxic drug. Tobacco has an interesting history because it was, and still is, considered to be a consciousness-altering drug and is cultivated in many parts of the world for ritual and spiritual use (including Canada and the U.S.).[108] In the past, tobacco was quite toxic and could only be used sparingly. It was not until the colonization of North and South America in the 1500s that Europeans discovered tobacco, and they have experimented with its use since then. Originally, Western governments categorized tobacco as a potent drug and sought to prohibit its use. Yet prohibition of tobacco was futile as more and more Europeans began to smoke it and as governments began to use it as a tax revenue. As milder tobacco was cultivated and slow-burning cigarettes developed, regular use of tobacco became possible, giving rise to our modern-day tobacco industry. Until recently, rather than condemning tobacco use, Western governments claimed that tobacco helped people to relax and to concentrate,[109] and cigarette rations were given to U.S. soldiers right up until the 1950s.

In the early 1900s, wishing to capture the market of women smokers, American tobacco companies paid women to march and to

---

108. Davis 1996; Weil and Rosen 1998.
109. Weil and Rosen 1998.

smoke cigarettes at women's suffrage protests. These events were framed as a sign of women's liberation—they too could smoke cigarettes just like men. Today, ad campaigns like those of *Virginia Slims* that claim women "have come a long way" also play on women's liberation and their right to smoke just like men. Feminist activists argue that tobacco advertising is gendered, for tobacco use is associated not only with liberation but also with thinness, beauty, and a happy life.[110] We never see any of the young slender women in tobacco ads gasping for breath.

In the U.S., over 25 percent of females aged twelve and older reported current use of tobacco in 2000.[111] In Canada, 26 percent of women reported that they smoked in 1996–97; by 1994 it was noted that teenage girls were slightly more likely to smoke cigarettes than teenage boys (15.6 percent and 14.9 percent, respectively).[112] In 1998, 26 percent of adult women smoked in Britain compared with 33 percent of men (the gap being smaller if you rule out pipe and cigar use).[113] In all of these countries there has been a recent increase in teenage smoking, especially among teenage girls. Feminist activists have pointed out that several tobacco companies have targeted teenagers in their ad campaigns. For example, the producers of Camel cigarettes use ads that associate smoking with weight and appetite control to appeal to young girls. Although tobacco advertising is restricted in Canada and Britain, it is not restricted in the U.S., so that Canadian, British (because they have access to U.S. media) and U.S. residents are subjected to a wide range of tobacco advertising in U.S. magazines. Tobacco companies also pay producers large sums to have their products displayed on TV and in movies. Although smoking has long been associated with women of lower socioeconomic backgrounds, its use continues to be associated with the glamorous and ultrathin life-style presented in shows like *Sex in the City*.[114] Women in Third World countries and Japan are also targeted by a tobacco in-

110. Norsigian 2001.
111. National Household Survey on Drug Abuse 2000.
112. Single, Van Truong, Adlaf, and Ialomiteanu 1999: 82, 85.
113. DrugScope 2001: 67.
114. Norsigian 2001.

dustry competing to find new markets as public disapproval of smoking in Western nations increases.

Tobacco use is associated with "the number one preventable cause of death and disease" in many Western societies. In Canada, the percentage of tobacco-related deaths for women is rising faster than those for men, and although tobacco-related death is still higher for men, it is feared that women will soon match and eventually exceed male rates.[115] In addition, with the advent of milder tobaccos and quick-burning cigarettes, it is difficult for smokers to maintain an occasional or recreational relationship with tobacco. Many people become addicted to it, and ceasing use is problematic, even more so than ceasing use of alcohol or even heroin.[116] One of the main reasons for this is the fact that when tobacco is inhaled deeply into the lungs, it reaches the bloodstream and then the brain and the central nervous system within seconds, faster than when a drug is injected, eaten, or sniffed. Similar to smoking crack, the effect of smoking tobacco is not only intense but quick, and many smokers light up many times a day to repeat the experience.

The number one tobacco-related disease is lung cancer. Women who smoke are also vulnerable to other forms of cancer, heart disease, and stroke. Although, not every woman who smokes cigarettes suffers from tobacco-related diseases or death, there is a substantial amount of evidence to suggest that not every smoker can escape the ill effects of tobacco. The U.S. Surgeon General's Report 2001 states that since 1980, approximately three million women in the U.S. have died "prematurely of smoking-related diseases."[117] Yet, while government and health officials often condemn and publicize the health problems associated with tobacco use, governments continue to heavily subsidize tobacco cultivation and ignore corporate pollution of the environment associated with forms of cancer and other diseases. It is interesting that social condemnation of individual behavior is more acceptable than criticism of state and corporate practices.

---

115. Greaves and Barr 2000: 2.

116. Weil and Rosen 1998.

117. CDC 2001: 1

Despite the possibility of developing health problems associated with using tobacco, many women enjoy smoking and consider it a positive experience. Although tobacco is a stimulant, women (and men) note that it has a calming influence on them and contributes to their stability. Anyone who has ever shared a cigarette with another person can also attest to its social function.

Alcohol

Alcohol is one of our oldest drugs and was probably first discovered when fruit fermented in the heat. It comes in many forms—spirits, liquors, beers, wines—and has historically been used for medicinal and social purposes. Alcohol is a depressant and depresses the central nervous system. Andrew Weil and Winifred Rosen point out that alcohol is difficult to categorize because it is a food, a drug, and a poison.[118] Beer easily falls into these three categories. Beer was the most common drug used by people in Britain and by white settlers during the 1700s in the new colonies (in what is now the U.S. and Canada). It was cheap and consumed regularly by men, women, and children. In the late 1800s women were encouraged to drink beer, such as Guinness or stout, because of its food value.[119] In the 1950s, doctors recommended beer to pregnant women for its sedative qualities and its nutritional value. Today, Western doctors condemn its use during pregnancy.

Distilled alcohol, which is much more potent than beer because the alcohol content is higher, is a fairly new product. Most women have experimented with alcohol and have maintained a casual relationship with it. In general, women, outside of those who abstain for religious, health, and ideological reasons, see alcohol as a part of social life and associate its use with pleasure, celebration, relaxation, and recreation. Although women's patterns of alcohol consumption are varied, most personal accounts are positive and recreational drinking is the norm. Similar to the use of illegal drugs, young

118. Weil and Rosen 1998: 60, 61.
119. Ritson and Thorley 2000.

women drink the heaviest; however, this is situational and patterns of use shift as women grow older. Most women who "drift" into negative drinking patterns are able to limit their alcohol consumption without any therapeutic intervention.[120]

There are many health problems associated with recurrent drinking, some of which are irreversible. Acute gastritis and acute pancreatitis may accompany heavy drinking over a long period of time. Car accidents, cirrhosis of the liver, and suicide account for the largest alcohol-related deaths in Canada.[121] Of these, alcohol-related traffic accidents lead the list. Of the total deaths related to car accidents in 1996, 35 percent of drivers were over the legal alcohol limit in Canada; in the U.S., 40 percent were over the legal alcohol limit in 2000. In 2000, a U.K. source noted that one in seven road deaths there were alcohol-related.[122] Accidental falls and nonfatal car accidents that occur while under the influence of alcohol result in hospitalization. Alcohol overdose, or "poisoning," can lead to coma and death. Withdrawal from heavy drinking can be quite serious (more so than with narcotics), and some people experience what is known as delirium tremens (D.T.'s), which can cause death. Furthermore, alcohol use is often a factor in violence against women in Western nations. Although alcohol in itself does not make people violent, it has been noted that Westerners associate alcohol with violence and may excuse people's negative behavior if they are intoxicated. Furthermore, more offenders are under the influence of alcohol than illegal drugs during crimes of violence in Britain, Canada, and the U.S. Drunken unruliness has been a common occurrence in Western nations for centuries. Nevertheless, it has also been noted that "some of the greatest literature, music, poetry and scientific and philosophical concepts have been created or developed out of a setting of not a little intoxication."[123]

Although men drink more alcohol than women, women are more stigmatized than men when they become addicted to it and when it

120. Plant and Cameron 2000.
121. Single et al. 1999.
122. Ibid.: 18; NHTSA 2000a; Ritson and Thorley 2000: 20.
123. Ritson and Thorley 2000: 34.

is believed that they drink to excess. However, because alcohol is legal in Britain, Canada, and the U.S., women who drink are not subject to the same marginalization and criminalization that shape the lives of the many women who use illegal drugs in these countries.

Prescribed Drugs

In addition to tobacco and alcohol, women regularly consume over-the-counter and medically prescribed drugs. The pharmaceutical industry targets women, and doctors prescribe more mood altering drugs to women than men. Not all of these drugs, however, have been beneficial and some have been dangerous. Initial drug legislation in Western nations required that patent medicines list their ingredients and restricted the use of specific ingredients such as cocaine, which paved the way for the development of the pharmaceutical industry. In 1803, isolating morphine from opium marked the beginning of the pharmaceutical industry's quest for refined drugs with greater potency. The most significant shift occurred in the mid-1800s when pharmaceutical companies synthesized "entirely new compounds—not otherwise found in nature."[124] The manipulation of organic molecules offered a range of new compounds that were not previously available, including drugs, soaps, pesticides, and cosmetics. The shift from natural drugs such as opium to refined and synthetic drugs was promoted by the emerging pharmaceutical industry, which was (and continues to be) interested in patents, profits, and new markets.[125] Organic drugs such as opium cannot be patented, thus their potential for profit is limited. Although refined and synthetic drugs have a much higher potential for toxicity, the pharmaceutical industry continues to promote their curative powers.

Pharmaceutical companies became responsible for the "creation" and advertisement of new drugs in the early 1900s. In Britain, Canada, and the United States, the state regulated the trade but granted the medical profession the right to prescribe specific drugs.

---

124. Healy 1997: 18.
125. Lexchin 1984.

Consequently, intense lobbying and advertising by pharmaceutical companies have been directed at doctors and, in some nations, consumers, in order to expand legal drug use. In 1952, Thorazine was discovered and it was followed by the discovery of antidepressants.[126] The development of such drugs as Librium and Valium also ushered in a new era of prescribing tranquilizers to deal with the stress of everyday life.[127] During the late 1950s and early 1960s, the pharmaceutical industry was transformed through the creation of these drugs. In the 1960s, books like Jacqueline Susann's *The Valley of the Dolls* depicted women's widespread use of these new drugs.

Since the psychopharmaceutical revolution of the 1950s, there has been a wide array of drugs to choose from. In 2002, there were 9,500 prescription drugs on the market compared with 300 in 1965.[128] This unprecedented manifestation has changed the face of drug use for both legal and illegal users. There is no question that many of the drugs created since the 1950s have improved health and many people would be unable to live or enjoy life without the aid of these modern drugs. Nevertheless, a growing body of evidence demonstrates that not all legal drugs are safe or effective. Pharmaceutical companies favor synthetic drugs over natural drugs, because as previously noted natural drugs cannot be patented as easily as synthetic drugs; also, a limitless array of new compounds await discovery and marketing. At the same time, pharmaceutical companies are aware of the potential market that genes from certain plants may offer them in the future and have been rushing to claim patents on and to colonize indigenous plants in Asia and the Amazon through the Genome Project.[129]

Feminist Research

Feminists have been writing about the medicalization of women's lives since the 1970s. Feminist research and activism centers on

126. Healy 1997: 43.
127. Hughes and Brewin 1979.
128. NIHCM 2002; NCPA 2002.
129. Robinson 2001.

women's role as the guardian of health in the family, the overprescribing of legal drugs to women (especially minor tranquilizers and selective serotonin reuptake inhibitors known as (SSRIs), and the dumping of unsafe drugs in Third World countries.[130] Pharmaceutical companies target women because they visit doctors more than men due to their reproductive needs, and because they are the caretakers of their families' health. Because women are prescribed more drugs than men, they are more vulnerable to harm.[131] Women are also the sole users of most birth-control products, which has created a huge market for pharmaceutical corporations. All areas of women's health, including menstruation and menopause, are seen as sites of illnesses that need to be treated with drugs. Women are also prescribed more mood-altering drugs than men to help them cope with problems that stem from their subordinate status in society, for doctors are quick to tranquilize women who do not comply with traditional gender roles.[132] However, women need more than chemical solutions to poverty, racism, sexism, lack of housing, poor nutrition, environmental pollution, and violence.

Feminist research has also documented how legal drugs such as thalidomide, DES (diethylstilbestrol), the Dalkon Shield, and the Copper 7 IUD (to name a few) have harmed many women and their children. Thalidomide was a drug prescribed in Canada and Europe to pregnant women in the 1960s for nausea during pregnancy (it was not prescribed in the U.S.). Babies were born without limbs or with malformed limbs. DES, the first synthetic hormone to be developed, was widely prescribed to pregnant women from 1941 to 1971 to prevent miscarriages. Pharmaceutical ads to physicians heralded its effectiveness for *all* pregnancies, stating that its use would lead to "bigger and stronger babies." It was prescribed to millions of women worldwide under two hundred different brand names, even though it was found to be ineffective after the first twenty years and despite

130. See Cooperstock and Hill 1982; Ettorre 1992; Lexchin 1984; McDonnell 1986; and Penfold and Walker 1983.

131. Single et al. 1999; Ettorre 1992; Lexchin 1984; McDonnell 1986; Mintzes 2000; Penfold and Walker 1983.

132. Lexchin 1984.

the fact that animal studies demonstrated that it might cause cancer.[133] About 4.8 million women in the U.S. and between two hundred to four hundred thousand women in Canada were prescribed DES.[134] Quite different from thalidomide babies, DES-exposed infants did not exhibit any health problems at birth. It was not until thirty years after it was created that DES was known to cause breast cancer in mothers and daughters. Many daughters born to mothers who took DES have malformed reproductive organs, fertility problems, endometriosis, immune-system disorders, and cancer.[135] As well, a higher rate of menstrual problems has been noted and a small number of daughters have developed clear cell adenocarcinoma of the vagina (1 out of 1,000).[136] Sons also have a wide range of health problems, including reproductive abnormalities and fertility problems.

When the medical profession realized that the fetus was vulnerable to toxic drugs, they began to perceive mothers as a danger to and separate from the fetus, rather than perceiving the fetus as part of the mother' body and as vulnerable as any of her internal organs. Feminist sociologist Barbara Rothman notes that it wasn't the pharmaceutical industry and doctors who were seen as a danger to the fetus and the mother—for creating, marketing, and prescribing these drugs—it was the mother who was a danger to the developing fetus. As a consequence, women's activities have become suspect when they are pregnant, and the level of instruction to and surveillance of them by the medical professions have increased.[137]

Prescribing drugs that may endanger women's health is not confined to the recent past. Today, drugs such as Diane-35 are prohibited in Europe because of their toxicity. Diane-35 is being marketed to North American women as a cure for acne and as a contraceptive; however, because of its association with liver toxicity and high risk of fatal blood clots, Diane-35 has been approved in Canada as a treatment for severe acne that is to be used only after all other treatments

---

133. Mintzes and Baraldi 2001.
134. Ibid.
135. Reynolds 2001.
136. DES Action Canada 2000.
137. Rothman 1989.

have failed.[138] Ads for Diane-35 have been displayed on university and college campuses across Canada and the U.S., even though direct advertising of prescribed drugs to consumers is illegal in Canada.

Norplant is another contraceptive that is very controversial. It is a fairly new hormonal contraceptive that lasts for five years; however, it requires surgical implantation and removal from under a woman's skin. It is controversial for several reasons. First, there is risk related to the surgical implantation, and although some health benefits and clinics cover the cost of inserting Norplant, they do not always cover the cost of removing it. Secondly, there are risks of adverse side effects for women who have diabetes, heart disease, and high blood pressure. Many women who use this drug may not be aware of these risks, and the risks are ignored by legislators and moral reformers who have argued that women convicted of child abuse, maternal drug use, and those on welfare should be forced to have Norplant implanted. These practices affect black women in the U.S. disproportionately, as they have higher incidences of health problems that interact with Norplant and are targeted by medical and welfare agencies as likely recipients for the drug.[139]

SSRI Prescribing and the Disciplinary Society

Feminist research brought our attention to the overprescribing of minor tranquilizers for women. The creation of minor tranquilizers and SSRIs (selective serotonin reuptake inhibitor), including Prozac and Paxil, has transformed drug-use patterns for women in Western societies. It was not initially apparent that some users of major tranquilizers such as Thorazine would experience permanent effects such as *tardive dyskinesia* after several years of use and that some users of minor tranquilizers (eg. Valium), and later SSRIs (eg. Seroxat and Paxil), would experience dependence and withdrawal symptoms. The discovery and wide use of these drugs are discussed by psychi-

---

138. Mintzes and Baraldi 2000.
139. Bond, 2001; Roberts 1997.

atrist David Healy who notes that dependency on drugs has not been confined to illegal drugs and that "psychopharmacology was faced with a political problem. The problem was how to distinguish drugs which restored social order from drugs which subverted the social order." Thus, "political" rather than "scientific" decisions were made about drugs and drug categories. In relation to SSRI use, he states that the "depression that we have lived through in the 1990s in the West has arguably been a politically and economically constructed era that bears little relationship to any clinical facts." A new corporate psychiatry emerged in the 1990s which works "out what they have to sell and then prepare[s] the market so that we will want those products."[140]

Even though Prozac was approved by the U.S. Federal Drug Administration (FDA) for chronic depression, it has been advertised and prescribed to women for a wide range of social and psychological ills, including obsessive-compulsive disorder, bulimia, and premenstrual syndrome (PMS). Women are treated more often than men for depression and mood disorders.[141] Critics note that the popularity of Prozac is linked to conceptions of the "self" when medicine "appears to modify, change, even 'improve' the personality of its users."[142] In North America, Prozac has widely been prescribed to women and young children (as young as one year old, although it has never been approved or tested on children in relation to its safety) and to dogs. Since it was brought on the market in 1988, it is estimated that over 40 million people have used Prozac worldwide and that sales have exceeded U.S.$2.5 billion.[143]

Medicine, whether under the rubric of psychiatrists and physicians (who most often prescribe SSRIs in North America), functions to normalize and discipline society through the use of some drugs. Human diversity and the rich tapestry of life are lost today as we rigidly quantify all human behavior so that many fall outside the "new norms" that have been set up. This has been especially devastating for

140. Healy 2001: 5, 6, 7.
141. Penfold and Walker 1983; Ussher 1991.
142. Fracassa 1999: 23.
143. Robinson 2001: 9.

"overactive" children who are constructed as falling outside the "norm" and are prescribed Prozac and Ritalin, and for women who have historically been targeted by the pharmaceutical industry. Surprisingly, clinical trials of "legal drugs" rarely demonstrate that they work. Healy claims that if drugs such as Prozac worked, we would not have three times as many people detained in hospitals and fifteen times more admissions and longer stays "for mood and other disorders" as we have today.[144]

The Legal/Illegal Divide

Unfortunately, new drugs can be harmful and many have a long list of "effects," which are misleadingly termed as "side effects." Many of these drugs may not be better than older, safer drugs. In a recent study that looked at hospital deaths in the U.S. over the last thirty years, it was discovered that between 75,000 to 100,000 people die each year from "normal" medicine use—not from overdoses or mistakes, but from the normal use of legally prescribed drugs.[145] Our focus on the dangerousness of illegal drugs masks the risks we take everyday by consuming legal ones.

Of course, we cannot solely blame the pharmaceutical companies and doctors for overprescribing; women themselves need to challenge their reliance on and faith in science, medicine, and chemicals. Rather than looking toward science and medicine, we might look at social factors that lead to poor health and oppressive living conditions. In addition, not all aspects of life need to be medicated; perhaps at times we need to feel life, rather than anaesthetize ourselves from it. It is important to note, however, that minor tranquilizers and SSRIs are not always legally prescribed to reduce pain, sometimes they are prescribed to temper diversity and reduce those "modern anxieties" created in part by corporate psychiatry and the pharmacy industry. Although drugs are often used to escape painful reality, we should keep in mind

144. Healy 2001: 9.
145. DES Action Canada 2000.

(as discussed earlier) that, historically, drugs have been used for ritual, spiritual, and healing purposes as well as for recreational use.

Nor do legal drugs stay neatly tucked behind the line socially constructed for their "official use." They are used in a variety of inventive ways, that are not recommended by one's doctor. Drug users have also developed a wealth of knowledge about "legal" drugs and their various uses. Books like *Pills-a-go-go* chronicle America's love for pills. The author, Jim Hogshire, states that "the pill is the quintessential icon of Western Civilization."[146] The pills we love to consume are also under legal control and women who consume these drugs on the illegal market are subject to arrest. The state assumes that self-prescribing users are more dangerous than the pharmaceutical companies and doctors who offer these same drugs.

The state and the pharmaceutical industry have created fictional boundaries to define what constitutes a legitimate pharmaceutical to be dispensed by the industry and prescribed by doctors. Illegal drugs are separated from these drugs when their use is criminalized. However, the status of specific drugs can change over time, and "illegal drugs can be transformed into legal drugs if they are prescribed for relief from pain or the treatment of illness. And legal drugs can be transformed into illegal drugs if they are used without a physician's approval"[147] or sold on the illegal market. Various legal drugs are quite popular on the illegal market, including Valium, Ativan, and an array of pain killers, sleeping pills, and stimulants such as Ritalin. We also tend to overlook how legal drugs are similar to illegal drugs. Some drug users refer to Ritalin as the "poor person's cocaine," and Ritalin and Talwin (another legal drug) as the "poor man's heroin." The fact that Ritalin is prescribed to hyperactive children to calm them speaks to the paradox of drug categories and to the official and unofficial uses of drugs.

Since the early 1900s, drug categories have not remained static. Criminologist Neil Boyd notes that it is the line separating "pleasure and pain" that distinguishes forms of illegal and legal drugs, point-

146. Hogshire 1999: 1.
147. Boyd 1991: 108.

ing out that the "taking of medicine is socially acceptable; the taking of drugs is not."[148] Politicians have an interest in making sure that the fictional lines that separate legal and illegal drugs remain in place. Former President Bush Sr. was on the board of Eli Lilly before he began his presidential campaign and owned U.S.$145,000 of its stock. Dan Quayle was also a large share holder of Eli Lilly stock.[149] Contributions of U.S.$60 million from American pharmaceutical corporations helped to secure the Republican victory at mid-term elections in 2002.[150] Certainly, the quest by pharmaceutical companies to extend patent rights on U.S. products in order to benefit from their profits has been aided by these influential politicians when negotiating free trade agreements.

Critics of the pharmaceutical industry like Canadian writer Joel Lexchin also question who the real drug "pushers" are. He claims that globalization is an "overarching international system: which has gone hand-in-hand with trade liberalization and right in the middle has been the pharmaceutical industry."[151] The aggressive advertising used by pharmaceutical companies to target women, the elderly, and, more recently children, and Third World countries expose the profit motive inherent in marketing, as opposed to the promotion of health. This reality is often submerged in the drug-war rhetoric, as is the contradictory reality of the billion-dollar tobacco and alcohol industry that legally "pushes" their drugs.

Advertising and Profit

The pharmaceutical industry spent U.S.$13.9 billion worldwide advertising their products in 1999, more than was spent on research and development.[152] Most research on "legal" drugs is conducted and funded by pharmaceutical corporations, which may contribute to bias

148. Boyd 1990: 44.
149. Robinson 2001: 36, 37.
150. Monbiot 2003.
151. Lexchin 2001: 1.
152. No Free Lunch 2003; Robinson 2001.

and omissions. Similar to the tobacco industry, pharmaceutical corporations know that it is not in their interest to fund research that may discover adverse effects or hazards to health because this would increase legal liability. Over the last thirty years, the pharmaceutical industry has been rated as one of the most profitable sectors by *Fortune* magazine. Recent mergers have not contributed to women's health but to profit, for managing disease is "big business."[153] The pursuit of profit over health is exemplified by the fact that pharmaceutical researchers are more interested in developing drugs to meet the needs of wealthy nations that can afford to purchase their products.

Eighty percent of the world's legal drug market live in North America, Europe, and Japan. Africa makes up 1 percent of the drug market, even though several serious infectious diseases such as AIDS, malaria, and tuberculosis have reached epidemic proportions. But most people in Africa cannot afford the high price of patented drugs (some times marketed at a thousand times more than their cost), and the pharmaceutical industry has consistently refused to allow cheaper generic drugs to be offered to consumers in Africa and other Third World nations.[154] For example, about 80–85 percent of the world HIV-positive population lives in Africa, and over 55 percent of those infected are women. Activists speak to the gendered nature of HIV transmission, for women have little power over their "own bodies [and] sexual lives" and are socially and economically subjugated.[155] However, until recently, pharmaceutical companies refused to lower their prices.

Even with lower prices, drugs are still out of reach for most poor women. In addition, pharmaceutical industry contributions to Third World Nations have been piecemeal and leave patent protections in place. Drug dumping is also common in Third World nations, where international pharmaceutical companies sell drugs that are restricted

153. Robinson 2001.
154. Ibid.: 14, 38.
155. Albertyn 2000: 1.

in Western nations because of the dangers associated with their use, or donate drugs (which are written off as tax deductible) that are no longer being used for specific diseases or are near their expiration date. However, when it suits their own political purposes, governments in Western societies have been quick to ignore patent laws, as in the case of the anthrax scandal in Canada in 2001—former Minister of Health, Allan Rock ignored patent laws in order to purchase and stockpile drugs to combat anthrax poisoning.

Resistance

A number of organizations have been active in challenging the legal/illegal construction of drugs and the influence of the pharmaceutical industry. No Free Lunch is a group in the U.S. that educates the public about the power of the pharmaceutical companies and their bias in research findings.[155] They also question the practices of medical professionals receiving free samples and being invited to conferences and gatherings hosted by the pharmaceutical companies. Feminist activist groups have been at the forefront of the women's health movement since the late 1960s, challenging pharmaceutical companies and the medical profession. The Boston Women's Health Collective, which published the groundbreaking book *Our Bodies, Ourselves*, speaks to women's reproductive health and the impact of the medical and pharmaceutical industries on women. The National Women's Health Network and the Women's Group on Women and Health Protection in the U.S., and Working Group on Women and Health Protection in Canada are made up of activists and researchers who write and educate the public about women's health, the pharmaceutical industries and its effects on women's health, and advertising and funding. Groups like D.E.S. Action Canada represent the interests of women and men who have been exposed to that drug, actively educating the public about the effects and health consequences of D.E.S.

156. No Free Lunch 2003.

Contemporary Drug Use Rates

Finding accurate information about legal drug use, excluding tobacco and alcohol use, can be a frustrating endeavor. Government agencies cite numerous studies that highlight illegal drug use and tobacco and alcohol use. However, data on prescribed and over-the-counter drug use are not included. Thus, the conventional construction of drug use remains firmly in the domain of illegal drug use and tobacco and alcohol use. A 1996–97 National Population Health Survey claimed that over 11 percent of Canadians used a prescription medication in the previous month. In the province of British Columbia 15 percent of those surveyed stated they had used a prescription drug in the previous month. Narcotics were used by 4.7 percent of Canadians aged 15 or older surveyed about their drug usages in the previous month, antidepressants by 3.6 percent, sleeping pills by 3.5 percent, and tranquilizers by 2.7 percent of Canadians aged 15 and older in the previous month of the study.[157] There is no current Canadian data available on national prescription use. However, research on prescription-drug expenditures can provide some insight into legal drug use in Canada and the U.S. In the U.S., spending on prescription drugs has increased sharply since 1997 (U.S.$78.9 billion). From 2000–01, outpatient prescription spending rose 17.1 percent (from U.S.$131.9 billion to $154.5 billion). Antidepressants were the top-selling drugs, culminating in U.S.$12.5 billion in retail sales. Narcotic painkillers ranked fifth and account for U.S.$5.4 billion in retail sales. OxyContin, a narcotic on the market, ranked 15 in the top 50 drugs for retail sales in 2001. In 1999, doctors prescribed "146 drugs for every 100 office visits, up from 109 drugs per 100 office visits in 1985." A total of 3.3 billion prescriptions were filled in the U.S. in 2001.[158] In Britain and Canada, prescription drug use and costs are rising too. In Canada, prescribed-drug spending has risen from Can$8.4 billion in 1997 to $12.3 billon in 2002.[159] Although part of this increase is due to the higher cost of drugs, prescribing practices

157. Single et al. 1999: 113.
158. NIHCM 2002: 2, 6, 11, 13, 3, 7.
159. Gagnon 2002.

may have shifted as well. As noted earlier, the pharmaceutical industry devotes enormous sums to promote the use of legal drugs. Furthermore, legal drug use cannot be confined to purely medical use. The line that separates social and medical use is illusory. Nor are legal drugs prescribed for purely medical reasons.

Drug-use surveys should be approached with caution, but they do provide some limited information about drug use. What is most evident in the drug surveys for Britain, Canada, and the U.S. is that alcohol is the drug of choice for youths and adults by a very wide margin. In 1999, over 73 percent of U.S. high-school students claimed that they used alcohol over the last year, even though most are under age, and 37 percent stated they used marijuana over the last year. In the same year, U.S. college and university students reported that in the prior year, 34 percent used marijuana.[160] In an earlier report, 88 percent claimed they used alcohol, a slightly higher rate than their peers outside of college.[161] In the U.S., according to the 2000 Substance Abuse and Mental Health Administration National Household Survey on Drug Abuse, 87 million residents over the age of twelve claimed they had used an illicit drug at least once in their lifetime. That is 39 percent of the U.S. population.[162] Given these rates of illegal drug use, one has to ask if the war on drugs has been effective in the U.S. and if it is reasonable to believe that the behavior of 39 percent of the population can be criminalized?

When one looks at trends in illegal drug-use surveys, it becomes obvious that drug use of men is about twice that of women. As well, the age group who uses the most legal and illegal drugs and who are most at risk for arrest are those between the ages of eighteen and twenty-five. However, most youth tend to abandon illegal drug use as they grow older. Although the media and some U.S. presidents have tried to persuade us that crack is the drug of choice in America, statistics do not support these claims. Sociologists Craig Reinarman and Harry Levine note "that at the peak of crack use, 96% of Amer-

160. Bureau of Justice Statistics 2000.
161. Marlatt and Baer 1997: 245.
162. Bureau of Justice Statistics 2002a.

ica's high school seniors had never tried crack, much less gone on to more regular use, abuse, or addiction"; as well, high-school crack use has declined from 1986 on. In fact, a couple of years prior to the crack scare in the mid-1980s and the rush to enact Draconian drug legislation, crack use was declining.[163]

In the U.S., the National Institute on Drug Abuse Survey in 1999 claimed that 4.9 percent of women had used an illegal drug at least once in the prior month.[164] As noted earlier, over 25 percent of females aged twelve and over were current cigarette smokers in 2000. Drug use in the United States has not been increasing as many politicians and media pundits claim. In fact, outside of a small increase in heroin use, there has been a downward trend in illegal drug use over the last twenty years. Women's illegal drug use declines as they grow older, as does their cigarette and alcohol use.[165] The media construction of women who use illegal drugs is of poor women of color. However, in 1998, U.S. drug surveys demonstrated that Native, black, and Hispanic women were less inclined to use alcohol than white women. And when it came to illegal drugs, black and Hispanic women used less illegal drugs, including marijuana, cocaine, inhalants, hallucinogens, psychotherapeutics, and stimulants, than white women.[166] The survey also showed that black women used more crack than white women (2.7 versus 1.2) in their lifetime, but crack use in the year prior to 1998 differed little (0.3 versus 0.8 respectively), and white women's lifetime rate for powder cocaine was higher than black and Hispanic women.[167]

Contrary to media depictions of rampant crack and heroin use by women, marijuana remains the most popular illegal drug for all women. Lifetime rates for all women in 1998 were 27.9 percent, and use over the prior year was 6.5 percent.[168] Use of cocaine, heroin, and

---

163. Reinarman and Levine 1997: 32.

164. NIDA 2000.

165. NIDA 2001; Misra 2001.

166. Misra 2001: 125, 127.

167. See Misra 2001: 127. The rates for having used cocaine during one's lifetime were white non-Hispanic women, 9.2 percent; black women, 5.6 percent; and Hispanic women, 5.8 percent.

168. Misra 2001:127.

prescribed drugs used illegally pales in comparison to marijuana use. As well, it is estimated that over 9 million people used prescription drugs for nonmedical reasons in the U.S. in 1999 (mostly narcotics, benzodiazepines such as Valium, Librium, and Xanax, and stimulants such as Ritalin), and women were more likely than men to be prescribed these drugs.[169]

Canadian Drug Trends

According to the Canadian Addiction Survey in 2004, about 45 percent of Canada's adult population stated that they had used an illegal drug in their lifetime, and marijuana was identified as the most commonly used illegal drug.[170] Only 13.2 percent claimed they tried LSD, speed, or heroin in their lifetime, and only 1.3 percent claimed that they had used these drugs in the last year; 10.6 percent claimed that they had used cocaine in their lifetime, and 1.9 percent claimed using it in the last year. In contrast, 79.3 percent of Canadians reported drinking alcohol in the past year.[171] Women's lifetime and yearly illegal drug use in Canada is about half of the national average, or half of men's use. Similar to the U.S. and Britain, marijuana is the most widely used illegal drug by Canadian women and men. Women's lifetime rate of marijuana is 39.2 percent compared with men's rate of 50.1 percent.

British Drug Trends

The British Crime Survey (BCS) only includes Britain and Wales, and those sixteen to sixty years of age. Because the survey is carried out by the Home Office, the findings may be quite conservative,[172] but

169. NIDA 2001: 1.
170. Adlaf et al. 2004: 3.
171. Ibid.: 10.
172. DrugScope 2001: 12.

it can be used as a general guide, similar to surveys in Canada and the U.S. Men are about 1.4 times more likely than women to have used an illegal drug in their lifetime. In 2000, the BCS reported that cannabis was also the most widely used illegal drug, and though men were more likely to report using it (27 percent had used it in their lifetime), use was highest for young people at about 40 percent. As well, white people use more drugs than black and Asian people. Cocaine was used by those with the highest income levels. Black people in the sixteen to nineteen age group had a 1 percent higher use of crack (2 percent for whites versus 3 percent for blacks, 2 percent for Indian, 0 percent for other ethnic groups) in their lifetime; 10 percent of white people in this age group reported cocaine use versus 6 percent for black people, 7 percent Indian, 1 percent other ethnic groups. Cocaine use by women reported in the past year was 3 percent, although heroin and crack use was so low it did not represent even 1 percent. Of course women between the ages of sixteen to twenty-four reported higher use of drugs; 26 percent of young women had used cannabis; 3 percent had used cocaine; and 4 percent had used ecstasy in the last year; however, the yearly reported use of crack and heroin remained the same as lifelong use.[173] In addition, over 90 percent of adults in Britain drink alcohol, although amounts vary widely. Alcohol consumption and public houses, or pubs, are a much more integral part of the cultural setting than in North America.

The Diversity of Drug Use

We can see that drug-use patterns for women in Britain, Canada, and the United States are quite similar. Men use more illegal drugs than women, and both men and women use more legal and illegal drugs in their youth. Alcohol use is by far the most popular legal drug, and marijuana is our most popular illegal drug. Women are prescribed and use more mood-altering drugs than men. Thus, drug-use patterns vary by age and gender, at different moments in history,

173. Ramsay et al. 2001: vi, 14, 52, 23, 86, 87, 76, 77, 80, 81.

and from region to region. For example, port cities may have a larger heroin using population than cities located in the interior where synthetic narcotics like Percodan bought on the illegal market are more accessible. In the early 1900s, white middle-to-upper-class women made up the majority of people addicted to opiates. As we can see from the drug rate survey findings above, more men than women use illegal narcotics. Women's illegal drug use is more distressing to the public especially when it is visible; and when it is visible, it is subject to racial, gender, and class profiling by the police and by social service and medical professionals. But illegal drug use that is hidden from view does not claim our attention in the same way and thus can privilege white upper-class use of drugs.

Today, women who use illegal drugs in Britain, Canada, and the U.S. come from diverse class and racial/ethnic backgrounds. However, the consequences of drug use are not the same, because the consequences are mediated by race, class, gender, and law. Poor women and women of color are most vulnerable to police profiling and arrest, social service intervention, and harsh treatment by the medical profession. As well, the drug of choice, the route of administration, the duration of the drug's effect, and the cost all mediate drug use, as does occasional, regular, and addicted use. For example, the effects of heroin last about four to six hours, whereas the effects of cocaine last from twenty to forty-five minutes. Thus, a small percentage of intravenous users might inject cocaine ten or more times in one day, which increases their risk of infection and of taking an overdose. LSD can last for up to eight or more hours and most women find it too exhausting to use it on a regular basis; its potential for abuse is very low when self administered.[174]

Drugs can be taken in many different ways. They can be taken orally, absorbed through inhalation (smoking), administered through the mucous membranes of the mouth or nose (sniffing or snorting), or administered by injection, either intravenous or subcutaneous.[175] The route one chooses shapes a woman's relationship with her drug

174. Weil and Rosen 1998.
175. Ibid.

of choice. For example, drinking coca or opium tea is quite a different experience than injecting cocaine or heroin. However, choice is restrained due to the fact that organic drugs such as coca tea are unavailable in Western nations.

For many women who use illegal drugs, secrecy, social stigma, and lifestyles can be difficult. Social attitudes about women's illegal drug use are quite negative, especially in relation to women who are mothers. Yet women who use illegal drugs have commented on their positive value. Drug use can be fun, even though most research, especially about women and drugs, tends to dwell on only the negative consequences of use. This has been problematic for several reasons. First, people's experiences, especially their initial experiences with specific drugs, are often positive, thus there is a tendency to throw out all government-sanctioned information, especially as a lot of the government information is incredibly propagandist and ignores critical research and cross-cultural studies. Denying that drug use can be positive is barely credible since we credit legal drugs with positive value, and illegal drugs share the same pharmacological properties as many of these drugs. Furthermore, this propaganda ignores the many firsthand reports of the positive value of specific drugs reported by women.[176] Most women who use illegal drugs experiment with marijuana, and to a lesser extent with drugs like ecstasy, rather than heroin, and their use is predominately unproblematic. I don't think that recognizing the positive value of drug experiences in any way detracts from reports of negative addiction and episodes of problematic use. As I discuss later on, set and setting may be more important or just as important as the pharmacology of a drug. Thus, it is not the drug per se, but whether we have a negative or a positive relationship with that drug that matters. Of course this relationship is shaped by the legal and social constraints surrounding illegal use.

Unfortunately, the illegal status of drugs like heroin and cocaine dramatically alters and shapes one's relationship with the drug. Buying heroin on the illegal market increases one's risk of overdose, in-

176. See Boyd 1999; Faith 2001; Henderson 1993; Rosenbaum 1981; Taylor 1993.

fection, inflated prices, arrest, rip-offs, and associated illegal market violence. Poor women who are addicted to illegal drugs usually cannot afford to buy substantial amounts of their drug at one time and are subject to finding and buying it more often in small amounts, which is more expensive in the long run and increases their risk of rip-offs, violence, and arrest (and other problems associated with the illegal market) due to increased visibility. Potency and quality are unknowns which can fluctuate dramatically, depending on availability of the drug. All drugs, legal and illegal, have risks, but prohibition ensures that women who use criminalized drugs are subject to a host of dangers that would not exist otherwise. It also ensures that women who use illegal drugs are viewed as deviant by medical, social service, and legal agents. Since the 1980s, women's bodies have become the new terrain for the war on drugs and mothers, in particular, are major targets. Maternal-state conflicts, which emerged in the 1960s and 1970s, have culminated in the enactment of child welfare legislation and criminal charges against mothers who are drug users in the U.S.

Chapter 2

The Medical, Legal, and Moral Regulation Of Women

The regulation of altered states of consciousness and drug control was realized early on and it became more volatile as it was linked to the regulation of women's sexuality and reproduction. Women's bodies have long been the site of medical and legal intervention; since the mid-1980s women who use illegal drugs in North America have been subject to increased medical, social service, and legal control. It is assumed that women who use illegal drugs are unfit parents and a danger to the developing fetus.

The Regulation of Reproduction

In Britain, Canada, and the U.S., the state has intervened in the families of those labeled deviant, and in the families that are marginalized due to race, class, and gender inequality (which are often one and the same). However, regulation and intervention vary at different historical moments. Surveillance of families is also related to the state's interest in controlling women's bodies and reproduction. Although one Canadian politician proclaimed that "the state has no place in the bedrooms of the nation,"[1] women's access to birth control and abortion are regulated by the state. For many women, pregnancy is the first time that they encounter the power of the state and

1. Former Prime Minister P.E. Trudeau.

the ideology of mothering, for pregnancy is both a biological and a social event. In Western societies, women have very little privacy in relation to their pregnancies. The state, parenting groups, medical and social service agencies, concerned friends, and complete strangers believe that they have a right to comment on, and curtail, women's behavior during their pregnancies. The state and the law have been "concerned" with the "ownership" of women's bodies and what they produce. Feminist writer Carol Smart concludes that women's bodies are also used as "a point of entry for social values and norms."[2] When women are suspected of using illegal drugs both surveillance and intervention increases.

When we look at the medicalization of women's bodies and the history of drug use in Western societies, it becomes apparent that the two histories converge, widening the net of moral regulation. The anti-abortion movement and the war on drugs both draw from early ideological assumptions about women's role in society. With the rise of the nuclear family in the nineteenth century, motherhood became the central role for women and it was expected that their behavior would be virtuous. Thus, suspected gender-role deviation was constructed as aberrant, justifying social control. Researcher Elizabeth Armstrong notes that maternal-state conflicts arose in the 1960s and early 1970s as women challenged gender roles and sought equality in the home, in the workplace, and in politics. In the 1960s as women were gaining more control over their reproduction with the introduction of oral contraceptives and the legalization of abortion, medical discourse about the fetus as separate from the pregnant woman emerged. In addition, moral entrepreneurs in the field of medicine "discovered" new syndromes with little proof.

Although there was some earlier interest by physicians in relation to infants exposed to narcotics, medical regulation of women who used narcotics emerged in the 1960s. Armstrong notes how ironic it is that fetal alcohol syndrome (FAS) was first diagnosed in 1973.[3] In 1979, neonatal abstinence syndrome (NAS) was reported and diag-

---

2. Smart 1989: 113.
3. Armstrong 1998: 2037.

nosed and guidelines for care were established. The regulation of maternal cocaine use emerged in the 1980s.[4] Armstrong argues that sometime a new syndrome is the result of serendipity, but most often it is the "result of determined investigation and scientific entrepreneurship. In the case of FAS moral fervor powered the discovery as much as medical curiosity."[5] The same analysis can be applied to the diagnosis of NAS. Although medical entrepreneurship led the way, social workers, criminal justice officials, and a host of other professionals also saw maternal drug use as a new and expanding field of research and practice.

In the U.S., recent maternal-state conflicts have led to the enactment of child welfare legislation and criminal child abuse laws related to prenatal exposure to drugs. The state considers pregnant women to be a potential danger to their fetuses and prosecutors have criminally charged women in the U.S. for behavior that they see as being harmful to the developing fetuses. In Canada, attempts have been made by social services to detain pregnant women suspected of using drugs and to extend "legal personhood" to the fetus. Reproductive discourse about the adversarial relationship between pregnant women and their fetuses emerges out of the medical model of birth. Legal, social service, and medical regulations overlap, and medicine lends legitimacy to law that seeks to regulate women's bodies.

Since the mid-1980s the war on drugs has centered on maternal drug use and the persecution of women suspected of using illegal drugs. Little attention is given to the fact that in the U.S. drug treatment—like health and prenatal care—is unavailable for most women, especially pregnant women. Even Britain and Canada have few treatment centers specifically for women. Unlike Britain, which has universal health care, and Canada, which has provincial and federal programs, women in the U.S. have limited access to any health insurance. Since 1965, Medicaid has become the health insurance program for some poor women in the U.S.; however, each state has different eligibility criteria and coverage. Prior to the 1996 Personal Responsibility

4. Boyd 1999: 27–29.
5. Armstrong 1998: 2025.

and Work Opportunities Act, all those families deemed eligible for welfare assistance were signed up for Medicaid. Today, families in the U.S. must meet stricter criteria; time limits on aid and work requirements have also been initiated, leaving many women uninsured. Further, women are not eligible for care until they are three months pregnant. Many women are left uninsured, including poor working-class families, the homeless, and poor single women.

Medicalization

Women's bodies have long been under the gaze of medical and public scrutiny, and women's individual responsibility for the outcome of their pregnancies places a burden on them that is unrivaled in any other area outside of parental responsibility. Women's concern for their pregnancies is fed on by medical professionals who construct new reproductive technologies (RTs) as positive and necessary and as providing a "choice" for women. However, the new reproductive technologies have not necessarily created more choice; choice and access to some RTs is severely restricted for those not rich and white enough. At the same time that health care, education, housing, and social services have been cut, funding for reproductive technologies has increased, even though there is little scientific evidence to suggest RTs improve maternal outcomes.

As social factors that shape pregnancy, such as nutrition and poverty, are ignored, some women are offered expensive, intrusive, and selective technology to improve their chances of becoming pregnant. However, our love affair with technology is misguided. At the same time that the medical profession and much of the public praise reproductive technologies—such as in vitro fertilization, which often results in multiple births due to fertility drugs—they are also making efforts to limit the reproduction of women of color, the poor, and those suspected of using illegal drugs. Racial and eugenic ideologies and practices shape reproductive technologies, risk assessment, "care," and maternal drug policy.

Lynn Paltrow, of the National Advocates for Pregnant Women, notes that we place women who use fertility drugs and have multiple births (up to six children) on a pedestal and those suspected of using illegal drugs like cocaine during pregnancy in prison.[6] As medical professionals seek to help "some" women conceive with fertility drugs and new reproductive technologies, women who use illegal drugs are offered sterilization. White women, and their multi-birthed in vitro infants, have graced the cover of popular magazines such as *People.* They are proclaimed as heroes, and individual, religious, and corporate sponsors have rewarded them, giving them free homes, diaper service, groceries, and money. Most of these women also took fertility drugs to stimulate multiple ovulation, which contributes to multiple births. Unlike the national attention given to mothers using illegal drugs, little attention has been given to the severe health problems many of these multi-birth in vitro infants are born with and the health problems many of them will experience as they mature. Because a woman's uterus cannot physically hold five full-term infants, multi-birth infants are born prematurely, leaving them vulnerable to health problems such as visual disabilities and respiratory distress syndrome.[7] There are also risks to the mother, including negative side effects from the fertility drugs and rupturing of the uterus. For those mothers who take fertility drugs in conjunction with in vitro fertilization, further risks associated with the surgical procedure are involved.

Moral reformers are not rallying to criminalize women who take fertility drugs to induce ovulation, even though the negative impact on their fetuses and the negative birth outcomes are undisputed. For these mothers are constructed as upholding conventional gender-role norms, and are seen as self-sacrificing and maternal. Outside the obvious ramifications of trying to care for three to five infants at the same time, disabilities are five times more common and immediate and long-term health problems more prevalent in multi-birth children than single-born children.[8] While moral reformers claim that infants born to mothers who use illegal drugs will be a drain on medical, social, and legal resources, they fail to note that premature

6. Paltrow 2001.
7. Koren 1997; Strong 2000.
8. Launslager 1994: 122.

infants whose mothers used fertility drugs are also a drain on these resources. Nor do they comment on the cost of care in intensive care units, which can run up to U.S. $210,000 for an infant under 2.2 lbs.[9] In addition, the fact that fertility drugs and in vitro fertilization are experimental is rarely explored. Critics note that in vitro fertilization failure rates are as high as 85–90 percent, very expensive, and are neither accessible nor a "choice" for all women.[10]

Our collective love affair with medical technology, which is constructed as an aid to those who can afford it, especially in the United States, deflects our attention from questions about the quality of life and who gets selected to reproduce and to parent. It also diverts us from asking why illegal drug use during pregnancy is seen as harmful (given the evidence of such harm is sketchy at best), when some legal drugs and reproductive technologies can contribute to poor birth outcomes and permanent disability.

A Social Model of Health

In contrast to the medical model of health, which perceives pregnancy and birth as a medical problem where intervention is necessary, most midwives and nonallopathic healers adopt a social model of health which views pregnancy and birth as a normal process and which, like all aspects of health, is shaped by social factors such as nutrition, social and economic support, and housing. Midwives in Scotland and England have been leaders in the care of women who use illegal drugs during pregnancy. Midwives are not antitechnology; rather, they acknowledge that social factors, rather than technology, have improved both maternal and child health. Low birth weight is considered to be the largest contributor to infant mortality. However, there is no modern medical technological intervention that can effectively eliminate low birth weight; only social supports can achieve that.[11] Income distribution, nutrition, and housing have a major im-

9. Strong 2002: 12.
10. See Basen, Eichler, and Lippman 1993.
11. Oakley 1992.

pact on birthing outcomes. As feminist writer Ann Oakley so effectively expresses it, "[T]he fact that 'science' cannot prove that medicine produces health is a major weakness of the quantitative paradigm."[12]

In the Netherlands and Britain, midwifery-attended births are the norm. In Canada and the U.S., midwifery is only legal in some provinces and states and is not covered by all medical plans. Therefore, women's access to midwifery services is still very limited. In relation to other areas of reproductive care, women in Britain and Canada have access and health coverage for abortion, in contrast to the U.S. where Medicaid will not cover abortions, although it covers sterilization. In 1996, 86 percent of U.S. counties lacked abortion providers for women.[13] Abortion in the U.S. and Canada, and to a lesser degree in Britain, is a politically contested issue. Canada is one of the only Western societies that has no abortion law, although it is unconstitutional to deny women access to abortion. Abortion in the U.S. is highly regulated and restricted, and eligibility and access differ from state to state. Recent proposals and new legislation in the U.S. are attempting to restrict women's access to abortion and to grant legal "personhood" to the fetus.

Due to systemic racism, sexism, and economic marginalization in the U.S., the burden of poverty falls disproportionately on black, Hispanic, and Native American women and children, and negatively affects their health.[14] Although the U.S. is the most powerful nation in the world, it ranks twenty-fifth in infant mortality and twenty-first in maternal mortality. One Canadian newspaper claimed that if infant death rate in the U.S. dropped even to the Canadian level, 4,000 infants a year would be saved.[15] Instead of examining the association between infant mortality, poverty, and lack of health care, moral reformers blame women who use illegal drugs during pregnancy for poor maternal outcomes and accuses them of draining already-limited health and social resources.

12. Oakley 1992: 11.
13. Misra 2001: 181.
14. Ibid.
15. *The Globe and Mail*, July 7, 2001b: A12.

Fetal Rights

A number of excellent studies have examined the emergence of the fetal rights movement. Feminist writer Rosalind Petchesky describes how the fetus has become the central focus of the anti-abortion movement.[16] Petchesky and others highlight how mothers are constructed as separate from and adversarial to the developing fetus. It is believed by anti-abortion advocates that their movement to criminalize abortion will benefit from the fetus being redefined as a legal person under the law, for it may grant the fetus the same rights as a born child. In 2002, the Bush Jr. administration announced that the definition of a "child" had been broadened so that low-income women could receive prenatal care. Rather than extend health care to women who were pregnant, the new definition of a "child" was extended to conception. Thus, the developing fetus would be eligible for health care under the State Children's Health Insurance Program. This new interpretation of the word "child" is just one of many proposals and actions that is attempting to grant legal status to the fetus and to limit the rights of women.

The impact of fetal rights is also highlighted in a review of court-ordered obstetrical interventions in the U.S. Overwhelmingly black, Asian, and Hispanic women made up the majority of court-ordered interventions (81 percent), and all were at public hospitals.[17] Court-ordered interventions, including Caesareans, inform women that they have little legal status. New medical technology and prenatal interventions have advanced fetal rights and encouraged societal attitudes that see women as nothing more than vessels.[18] The state has made clear its interest in the fetus, and that interest is shaped by medical technology and what is labeled "fetal viability." As modern technology extends fetal viability, the laws related to women's reproductive autonomy are challenged.

In the U.S., the Supreme Court noted in *Roe v. Wade* 1973 that once a fetus is viable and can live outside of its mother's body, the state's

16. Petchesky 1990.
17. Kolder, Gallagher and Parsons 1987: 1192.
18. Gallagher 1989.

interest becomes compelling. In Canada, the Supreme Court justices in *Morgentaler v. The Queen* 1988 voiced the state's interest in the fetus. In Britain, as in the U.S. and Canada, medical abortion is legal (although more highly restricted in the U.S.), but the state also seeks to protect fetal life. British writer Carol Smart highlights how the state and law respond differently to emerging fields regarding "in vitro fertilization, surrogacy, contraceptive," and the rights of the fetus.[19] The state's "interest" can be interpreted in many ways. She explains how the ideology of creating healthy babies is "transported" into oppressive law and policy, which are initially viewed as benevolent and integral to public health. Conservative ideology supports the view that once women conceive, they have a moral obligation to the fetus and to avoid harm that could come to it. Thus, forced medical (including surgery) and drug treatment, civil commitment, and imprisonment to protect the fetus is deemed appropriate, and in some cases noble. So, too, is the criminalization of abortion. The fetal rights movement has little to do with health, eliminating poverty, and maternal drug use; rather, it is a tool to further regulate women's activities and their bodies.[20] As well, "personhood" is a "decision," not a legal or medical discovery.[21] In the U.S., attempts to grant legal personhood to the fetus have been more successful than in Canada and Britain, and many of these challenges have centered on maternal drug use.

Pregnancy and Drugs

As noted earlier, it is in the area of maternal drug use that maternal-state conflicts have become most volatile, especially in the U.S. Since the 1980s, over two hundred women have been arrested for suspicious behavior during their pregnancies and most of these arrests are based on suspicions of illegal drug use.[22] Women have been arrested for trafficking to the fetus, manslaughter, assault with a deadly

19. Smart 1989: 97.
20. Ibid.: 102.
21. Callahan and Knight 1992.
22. Center for Reproductive Law and Policy 1996.

weapon, and homicide.[23] These charges refer to taking drugs during pregnancy and raise the question of a fetus's legal personhood. It is assumed that drug use during pregnancy is harmful to the fetus and is the sole cause of risk. Furthermore, thousands of women and their children are negatively affected by state laws that equate illegal drug use with child abuse. The majority of these women are poor and women of color. However, drugs are only one of the factors that shape pregnancy, maternal outcomes, and mothering. Historical, social, cultural, and economic factors also shape pregnancy and may be even more important in shaping maternal outcomes and parenting than illegal drug use.

Maternal Drug Use and Infant Doping: A Historical Perspective

Some of our current assumptions about maternal drug use and mothering emerged in the 1700s and 1800s. Condemnation of "parents" who drank emerged during this time. As early as 1725, the "gin craze," as it was referred to, was condemned by British religious and medical moral reformers of the time. They wrote about pregnant women, mothers, and caretakers drinking to excess in their campaign to prohibit the consumption of gin. They believed that mothers and caretakers who drank gin failed to care for the children in their charge, and were critical of pregnant women and mothers who nursed their infants while consuming gin.[24] In 1730, Stephan Hales, an Anglican priest, wrote that "unhappy mothers habituate themselves to these distilled liquors, whose children, when first born, are often either of a diminutive, pigmy size, or look withered and old, as if they had numbered many years, when they have not, as yet, alas! Attained to the evening of the first day."[25] Rather than recognize that poverty, lack of housing, disease, and poor sanitation contributed to the ill health of poor women and their children, moral reformers

23. Paltrow 2001.
24. Musto 2002: 16–26; Warner 2002: 68, 69.
25. Musto 2002: 21.

blamed gin consumption as the cause of poor health, social decay, and immorality.

Historians Virginia Berridge and Griffith Edwards examine the moral panic in Britain in the mid-1800s related to mothers and drugs, which centered on infant doping and the practice of giving infants soothing syrups such as Godfrey's Cordial, Mrs. Winslow's Soothing Syrup, and Daffy's Elixir—which contained opiates to settle upset stomachs. By the mid-1800s, British medical attention and parliamentary inquiries focused on working-class women, especially on factory workers who were employed outside the home, and on unqualified nurses who were suspected of drugging infants to keep them sleeping while their mothers worked. The public health movement made the general public aware of the dangers of adults and infants using opiates, and the "Ladies Sanitary Association acted as a propagandist body" at the national level. Working-class childrearing practices were scrutinized and the root of the problem was assumed to be the mother's employment and her absence from the home. Moral reformers took little note of the fact that most working-class mothers were not employed in factories, did not hire nurses to care for their children, and many did not work when their children were young. Domestic employment was still more common and children often accompanied their mothers. Berridge and Edwards also note that although infant doping and poisoning occurred, there was no evidence to suggest that a mother's employment outside of the home was the root of the problem. Similar to current constructions of drug use, "both the culture of poverty and the economic realities of working-class life were ignored."[26] The author's state:

> For opium was at least a palliative for the gastro-intestinal complaints which, in conditions of poor housing and sanitation, in fact caused most infant deaths. Its ability to quieten infants made fretful by these and other digestive complaints aggravated by feeding habits based on "scraps" should not be underestimated. Despite the undoubted dangers in-

26. Berridge and Edwards 1981: 98, 100, 102.

> volved in overdosing, opium did have a role to play in a very imperfect system of infant management.[27]

Furthermore, what most moral reformers ignored was the fact that mothers, and the general public, believed in the positive and "beneficial properties of opium for a baby." As well, infant doping by those outside the working class was ignored. Physicians and nurses in wealthy homes used opium to soothe children, although these practices never came under attack.Thus, a distinction between professional use and lay use was constructed. Middle- and upper-class children in the care of nurses, a common practice in Britain, did not cause concern. In contrast, the use of opium by working-class mothers and the unqualified nurses they hired caused panic. As today, this focus diverted attention from the wider context of poor women's living conditions and environment.[28]

Worries about infant doping were not restricted to Britain. In 1832, a New York doctor named W.G. Smith claimed that "the youthful, inconsiderate mother and the idle nurse, too frequently resort to opium to hush the infant's cries." He added, "[T]he gay and youthful mother, rather than forego the pleasures of a crowded assembly, or the gaudy charms of a dramatic scene, a single evening, not unfrequently commits the unfortunate infant to its cradle under the influence of opium."[29] He also worried about the indiscriminate use by fellow doctors and women of "higher circles" who consumed opiates.

By the late 1800s, other Western doctors recorded the impact of opium use on women during pregnancy and its effect on the fetus and the newborn infant. Charles Terry and Mildred Pellens' classic book, *The Opium Problem*, first published in 1928 by the Bureau of Social Hygiene in the U.S., reviewed the medical research on narcotic addiction to date. The authors also examined the medical literature on maternal drug use from the late 1800s to the early 1900s. Similar

27. Ibid.:102.
28. Ibid.:102, 104.
29. Terry and Pellens 1970: 61.

to the medical literature of today, doctors' reports on the impact of maternal drug use on the fetus and newborn infant were anecdotal and contradictory throughout this time period. Many doctors noted that children born to mothers who used opiates were "normal." Some doctors wrote about their concerns about opiate withdrawal during pregnancy, others described infant withdrawal occurring in some instances, but not all. They noted that some infants of mothers who used opiates were restless and cried, and that small doses of laudanum comforted them. Nursing by the mother after the third day was also recommended to soothe the infant, as small amounts of the drug would be present in her milk. One doctor stated that "narcotic habits in the ancestors produced descendants in whom the normal checks on excessive nervous action were removed, so that paranoiacs, periodical lunatics, epileptics, hysterics, congenital criminals, congenital paupers or otherwise degenerable beings result." The *American Textbook of Applied Therapeutics* of 1886 claimed that "the moral and mental strength of these children is so far below par as to make them liable to much subsequent suffering."[30] As we can see, the fear of producing an underclass of children is not new. The eugenics movement was also influential during this time period and many doctors were leaders in the movement. Their interest in maintaining white supremacy and race purity may have informed their analysis of maternal drug use.

On of the first possible cases of maternal drug testing occurred in 1882, when a physician named T.J. Happel collected the blood from the cord immediately after a women's delivery and tested it for morphine. It was positive. Although it is not surprising that morphine passes through the cord to the placenta, Happel noted that there was no previous record of this fact being demonstrated.[31] Nothing happened to the mother in this case. The difference being that today, mothers who test positive for narcotics are persecuted in the U.S. and come under medical, social service, and legal control.

30. Ibid.: 411, 414.
31. Ibid.: 414.

Identifying Pregnant Women Who Use Drugs and Drug Testing

After the criminalization of specific drugs, including heroin, cocaine, and marijuana, doctors began to view maternal drug use quite differently. Earlier on, when doctors reported withdrawal symptoms in infants, they did not consider the mothers as suspects. Nor did they contact legal and social service agencies. But changing societal attitudes about mothering and reproduction shaped the increasing regulation of women. The criminalization of drugs lent credibility to punitive practices by social service, medical professionals, and non-state agencies that sought to regulate women suspected of using drugs, especially during pregnancy. Since the 1950s, Canadian and U.S. doctors have written about their mistrust of women whom they suspected of using illegal drugs when pregnant. They discuss their denial and manipulation and suggest techniques of surveillance such as subjecting "these girls" to repeated pelvic examinations during their hospital stays because they hide drugs in their vaginas.[32] Other doctors claim that pregnant women suspected of using illegal drugs are "unreliable historians" and lie about the length of their labor, delaying their arrival at the hospital so that they can "satisfy their need for a last 'fix' before submitting to authority."[33] These attitudes still exist, as one British obstetrician recently stated, "I'm sorry but I don't believe a word any of them say."[34] Although women suspected of using illegal drugs are depicted as liars, unpredictable, and incapable historians of their own birth process, all women are suspect to a certain degree.[35]

Because it is assumed that pregnant women who use illegal drugs lie, observation, intake history, and urine screening are used to identify them when they arrive at the hospital for delivery in the U.S. and Canada. In many cases, urine screening has been administered without the mother's consent. Some doctors advocate the use of meco-

32. Hofmeister 1971: 723.
33. Stone et al. 1971: 718.
34. Jackson and Klee 2002: 113.
35. Oakley 1984.

nium testing and hair analysis to detect prenatal exposure to illegal drugs. These new tools of surveillance are described as "promising techniques,"[36] which are used to socially control women with little thought given to ethics and consent. However, drug testing is highly unreliable and tells us very little about a woman's drug use. For example, alcohol is difficult to detect due to its quick metabolization and excretion in the urine, whereas marijuana can be tested for up to thirty days. Over-the-counter drugs and foods like poppy seed cake consumed by the mother can produce false positives. Criminologist Drew Humphries notes that there is race and class bias in drug testing in the U.S. and that drug testing cannot distinguish between the first-time user, the occasional user, or the dependent user.[37] Black women were tested ten times as frequently as white women in one Florida study.[38] In addition, drug testing cannot provide any information about whether maternal drug use has a negative impact on the developing fetus or on one's parenting abilities. Still, in the U.S., drug testing is regularly used by hospital staff.

Since the 1980s, the rationale behind the surveillance and drug testing of women who are suspected of maternal drug use has been that they need to be identified by medical staff and then diverted to social service and legal authorities. A number of medical, social service, and legal professionals consider persecuting mothers as "saving" the fetus and the newborn from the risk of both the mother and the drugs they have consumed. However, societal concern about illegal drugs and pregnancy is misguided. In the 1990s, a California study[39] tested 29,494 women who delivered in 202 public and private hospitals for drug use, of whom 20.17 percent tested positive (using urine analysis and self report). On closer examination, it becomes clear that 6.72 percent tested positive for alcohol use and 8.82 percent tested positive for tobacco use. Prescription drugs (benzodiazepines, barbiturates, and amphetamines) accounted for 1.71 percent of the positives. *Illegal drugs accounted for 3.49 percent of the total positives, and*

36. Albersheim 1994; Robins and Mills 1993.
37. Humphries et al. 1992.
38. Chasnoff et al. 1990.
39. Vega et al. 1993.

positive THC/marijuana tests accounted for 1.88 percent of this total. Consequently, illegal methamphetamines, cocaine, methadone, and opiates accounted for only 1.61 percent of the total 20.17 percent positives. This study was unique in that it included women from private and public hospitals.

Most research associated with maternal illegal drug use in the U.S. includes only poor women at public hospitals. The California study showed, however, that although there were differences related to race/ethnicity and although black women had the highest maternal drug rates, "nonblack women constituted four fifths of all women in California who tested positive for any licit or illicit drug other than alcohol," and three-fifths of the total tobacco smokers were white women.[40] It seems evident that a majority of women are likely to be using legal drugs during their pregnancies; however, I am not suggesting that their use be subject to control.What I am pointing out is that our focus on illegal drugs is political. Most often moral reformers fail to point out low prevalence rates of illegal drug use and highlight the total results for all maternal drug use (legal and illegal) to support increased regulation and monitoring of pregnant women. Consequently, the negative ideologies associated with illegal drugs remain intact.

Up until the 1990s, feminist writers had little to say about maternal illegal drug use. The social construction of NAS was not explored and it was assumed that illegal drugs caused both risk and harm to the developing fetus. Thus, feminist writers focused on the need for voluntary drug treatment and prenatal care, rather than on criminal sanctions, for women who use illegal drugs. Since then, a wealth of research has emerged that challenges conventional views about maternal drug use. Early predictions by some medical professionals, prosecutors, and moral reformers about the new underclass of crack babies have been unfounded. In fact, there was never substantial medical evidence to support earlier claims that maternal illegal drug use would cause permanent disability. The arguments about harm to the fetus are often not based on fact, but are largely shaped by politics and the quest to further regulate women.

40. Ibid.: 854.

Neonatal Abstinence Syndrome

Neonatal abstinence syndrome (NAS) refers to long- and short-term symptoms associated with neonatal exposure to maternal narcotic use. A recent Canadian government report states that infants born to mothers who use heroin and cocaine have serious problems, and they need special care and support. The report claims that "many of these babies face a lifetime of social, physical, and psychological disability...and as adults they may live with unemployment and poor social skills."[41] It points out that "everyone is concerned when babies are born impaired by exposure to drugs."[42] Some doctors have also warned that a NAS infant will experience long-term problems, such as aggressiveness, poor self-confidence, defective communication skills, and impaired growth.[43] However, there is no evidence to substantiate these claims. It is true, in the present political climate, that many people and groups are interested in maternal drug use. However, the research on neonatal abstinence syndrome is very controversial. Government reports have been misleading and rarely point out that poverty, rather than illegal drugs, have the most negative impact on fetal health and birth outcomes. As well, state research and policy documents tend to conflate both illegal and legal drug rates and drug effects as if their use and impact are similar.

Dr. Mary Hepburn, the founder of the Women's Reproductive Health Service in Glasgow, notes that women worry about the impact of their drug use on the developing fetus in relation to withdrawal and developmental anomalies. She argues that there "is no good evidence of teratogenesis by any of the drugs that are commonly used illicitly."[44] Poor women who use illegal drugs have a higher rate of perinatal death, preterm deliveries, low birth weight, and sudden infant death syndrome (SIDs). However, these are non-specific effects and the same incidence is found for women who smoke cigarettes and

41. British Columbia Provincial Health Officer 1998: 122.
42. Ibid.
43. Sunny Hill Hospital for Children 1992.
44. Hepburn 2002: 252.

for those who are poor and nondrug users. Although illegal drug use is a risk in pregnancy it cannot be viewed as a cause of harm, for we cannot say the drugs cause poor pregnancy outcomes. When illegal drugs are eliminated, the birth outcome may remain the same.[45]

Cocaine and Pregnancy

The crack scare of the 1980s generated writing that warned if infants were prenatally exposed to cocaine they would suffer long-term problems; however, these warnings have been found to be untrue. Barbara Myers, Heather Olson, and Karol Kaltenbach were some of the first researchers to note that to date all of the prenatal studies related to cocaine were conducted on poor women and their infants.[46] Thus, the effects of poverty are mistaken for the effects of cocaine exposure. They also argue that the majority of infants exposed to cocaine are not premature and do not have a low birth weight, and they note that this is especially true when women have been provided good prenatal and nutritional support.

Subsequent research on prenatal exposure to cocaine also challenged earlier claims related to short- and long-term problems.[47] Deborah Frank and her colleagues reviewed studies on prenatal exposure to cocaine from 1984–2000.[48] They conclude that most infants exposed to prenatal exposure are "indistinguishable" from nonexposed infants. They also state that there is no evidence that prenatal exposure to cocaine is related to negative effects that are more severe than a host of other risk factors such as tobacco use and poverty. Withdrawal related to prenatal exposure to cocaine does not exist. Rather, problems are a "consequence of antenatal complications rather than from true withdrawal."[49]

---

45. Hepburn 1999.
46. Myers et al. 1992.
47. Chasnoff et al. 1992; Frank et al. 2001; Frank and Zuckerman 1993; Greider 1995; Hawley and Disney 1992; Hepburn 2002; Mayes et al. 1992; Morgan and Zimmer 1997; Robins and Mills 1993.
48. Frank et al. 2001.
49. Hepburn 2002: 253.

Narcotics and Pregnancy

Narcotic withdrawal is specific to prenatal exposure to narcotics, not cocaine. As well, withdrawal is the only specific effect of maternal narcotic drug use. However, not all infants exposed to narcotics (whether legal or illegal) may experience withdrawal symptoms. Narcotic withdrawal is both transitory and unpredictable. Not all infants exposed to maternal drug use experience withdrawal and it is not dose related. Research on narcotic withdrawal in infants varies widely from nation to nation. In the U.S. and Canada, researchers state that anywhere from 60–95 percent of infants exposed to maternal narcotic use will experience withdrawal. In contrast, at the Women's Reproductive Health Service in Glasgow, of 200 infants born to women who used drugs during pregnancy, only 7 percent required treatment for withdrawal symptoms, and fewer still were admitted to a special-care nursery.[50] Dr. Mary Hepburn, who established the service, notes that poor pregnancy outcome "may be due not so much to the drugs as to the underlying socioeconomic deprivation or the effects of drug use on lifestyle."[51] It is clear that social deprivation is linked to poor maternal outcomes, thus Canadian and U.S. researchers are mistaking the effects of poverty with the effects of drugs.[52] Differences in withdrawal and maternal outcomes between the U.S. and countries like Scotland and Britain highlight their divergent health, economic, and social service support systems. In the U.S., women have no access to universal health care and have fewer economic and social supports than their counterparts in Britain and Scotland. These social and economic facts shape maternal health and research findings.

Tobacco and Pregnancy

Tobacco use during pregnancy is linked to low birth weight, and many maternity services attempt to educate women about this in

50. Hepburn 1993.
51. Ibid.: 54.
52. Myers et al. 1992; Siney 1995.

order to reduce their smoking.[53] Tobacco use during pregnancy is also linked to prematurity and sudden infant death syndrome (SIDs),[54] and to vasoconstruction (which is also associated with cocaine exposure). Deborah Frank and her fellow researchers, note that there is little public discourse about "tobacco babies," in contrast to "crack babies," even though when "prenatal cocaine and tobacco exposure are compared dispassionately, it becomes clear how sociopolitical forces shape discrepant interpretations of similar scientific data."[55] Our assumptions about low-birth-weight babies are laden with moral judgments that ignore the political and social factors that shape women's experience of their pregnancies and their maternal outcomes.

Feminist researcher Ann Oakley describes how antenatal educational material and tactics at clinics are directed at women who smoke during pregnancy. Women are instructed not to smoke "for the sake of the baby."[56] Most often poor women are targeted to "change" their behavior. Oakley discusses how the weighing of babies at birth is one of the techniques employed in the commodification of human life. All babies in Western societies are weighed at birth and categories of "normal" and "low" birth weights have been created. Moral significance is placed on those babies that fall into the low-birth-weight category. She states, "The labels attached to the different birth weight categories imply a judgement about the weights that infants should be. This ignores some important considerations, including birth weight distribution of different populations, and a consideration of the standpoint of mothers as the people who 'produce' babies with differently quantified bodies."[57]

Alcohol Use and Pregnancy

Historical references to alcohol use did not center on damage to the fetus. Rather, women and men were warned not to drink because

53. Koren 1997; Oakley 1992; Siney 1999.
54. Koren 1997.
55. Frank et al. 2001: 1620.
56. Oakley 1992: 61.
57. Ibid.: 258.

it might affect conception. Later, in the mid-1700s, religious and medical moral entrepreneurs focused on the poor and the consumption of distilled alcohol that led to immorality and unfit parenting. Religious and medical reformers also wrote about the reproduction of feeble children. Claims made by religious and medical reformers during the gin craze are antidotal, and although they provide evidence of the moral fever of reformers and their disdain for poor women who transgressed "proper" feminine behavior, they provide little evidence related to fetal alcohol syndrome (FAS). Alcohol researcher Elizabeth Armstrong states that "quasi-historical allusions" about FAS are "misconstrued." She notes that contemporary FAS researchers have unearthed historical references because they "were faced with the task of explaining why, when women have been drinking and giving birth for thousands of years... an association between drinking and birth defects had never been, in their collective memory, commonly acknowledged."[58]

One of the earliest documents about the dangers of distilled alcohol was written by the College of Physicians in London in 1725. The physicians noted that infants born to parents who drank distilled alcohol were 'weak, feeble, and distemper'd children, who must be, instead of an advantage and strength, a charge to their country."[59] However, their concern was not related to fetal harm. Rather, it centered on parental unfitness. During the gin craze, maternal drinking was linked to the survival of the nation because it was believed it reduced the "numbers of fitness of the next generation of soldiers, sailors, and laborers."[60]

Today, in contrast to tobacco, alcohol use during pregnancy is fraught with many of the same ideological problems as maternal illegal drug use. Fetal alcohol syndrome was introduced as a diagnosis in 1973 by medical researchers at the University of Washington School of Medicine in Seattle. The researchers associated maternal alcohol use with a specific pattern of birth defects. The

58. Armstrong 1998: 2033, 2034.
59. Musto 2002: 25.
60. Warner 2002: 71.

"main features of this pattern are pre and/or postnatal growth retardation, characteristic facial abnormalities, and central nervous system dysfunction, including mental retardation."[61] Since then, new symptoms have been added and diagnosis expansion has occurred. In addition, medical researchers, practitioners, teachers, and lay people have racialized and gendered fetal alcohol syndrome in North America. Native Indian women are associated with giving birth to FAS infants. However, race profiling and subjectivity regarding FAS diagnoses comes into play. Early and contemporary research demonstrates that only chronic heavy drinking is associated to FAS and fetal anomalies.[62] The medical research on FAS is very inconsistent, and it is still not known how much alcohol consumed, or when, during pregnancy, causes harm to the fetus. Thus, the actual teratogen effect of alcohol is uncertain in pregnancy, and highly subjective.

The first research to use the term FAS was conducted on eight poor mothers on welfare assistance in the U.S. who were chronic drinkers during their pregnancy. Thus, the social and economic deprivation that these mothers experienced was high. The second study conducted by the same members of the Seattle medical team was even smaller, consisting of three cases. All three were Native Indian infants. The early research also made clear that the mother was to clearly have an "identifiable"drinking problem. Alcohol researcher Moira Plant claims that this factor has been repeatedly ignored in later research and practice. She also states that fetal alcohol effects (FAE) emerged later as a new diagnosis. However, "initially this was the diagnosis, '*possible* fetal alcohol effects', babies found to have individual features of FAS."[63] She quotes FAS researcher Ernest Abel: "The 'possible' was subsequently dropped and, like fetal alcohol syndrome, the term *fetal alcohol effects* (FAE) took on a life of its own."[64] Plant notes that FAE is used as a diagnosis for any abnormality that cannot be explained. Teachers, social workers, doctors, and counselors who have no train-

61. Stratton et al., as cited in Armstrong and Abel 2000: 276.
62. Koren 1997.
63. Plant 2000: 35.
64. Abel, as cited in Plant 2000: 35.

ing in the diagnosis of FAS label children FAE. Foster care and adoptive parents are often participants in the labeling process because they are led to believe that they will be able to access resources from social services if their children are labeled as "special needs." In addition, the diagnosis can be perceived as the cause of their children's behavioral and developmental problems.[65]

Drawing from the results of a large study, which aimed to establish "whether or not birth abnormalities are associated with self-reported rates of drinking by pregnant women," Plant interviewed and followed 1,008 women through one of Edinburgh's antenatal departments in the early 1980s. Blood tests and clinic case notes were also obtained. The women were divided into three groups, high, medium, and low drinkers, according to their self-reported levels of alcohol use in their twelfth week of pregnancy. Their infants were assessed at birth and when they were three months old. In contrast to the many studies that include only poor women and heavy drinkers, the women in Plant's study reflected the general population of Edinburgh and most of them were not heavy drinkers. Plant concludes that the results of the study show that "birth abnormalities were slightly *associated* with but not caused by maternal alcohol consumption" (italics in original). She notes that, although heavy drinkers were more likely to produce infants with abnormalities, it was evident that "something other than their alcohol consumption" caused the damage. Plant states that tobacco, other drug use, maternal age, stress, birth weight of the mother, and economic deprivation shape pregnancy outcomes. She also concludes that alcohol-related birth damage did not constitute a "syndrome" in her study.[66]

Later research confirms Plant's findings; however, the biomedical research community has been constructing FAS as a national health problem in Canada and in the U.S. FAS researchers Elizabeth Armstrong and Ernest Abel state that the "greater the national panic, the higher the research budgets."[67] Women are viewed as giving birth to

65. Schellenberg 2002: 8.
66. Plant 1985: 99–100.
67. Armstrong and Abel 2000: 279.

social problems, including FAS, NAS, and criminal children. However, the actual incidence of FAS is very low and there is no epidemic. FAS is associated with poverty and binge drinking and cannot be generalized to social or moderate drinkers.[68]

The focus on FAS and mothers masks other realities associated with alcohol that have a much greater impact on people's lives. Alcohol is associated with impaired driving leading to injury and death, injuries in the home, hospitalization, and a myriad of health problems, including cirrhosis of the liver. In 2000, 40 percent (16,653 of 37, 409) of all fatal car crashes in the U.S. were alcohol-related.[69] Every day six children are killed and 797 people are injured in motor vehicle crashes in the U.S.[70] Even though there are groups like Mothers Against Drunk Drivers (MADD) that rally for stricter laws, there is little challenge to our love affair with cars and this form of transportation, even though there are significant environmental concerns and children and adults are at risk of injury and death. My point is that moral reformers are very selective when it comes to creating social problems and demanding retribution, most often they ignore the activities of the status quo, and those that they participate in, even when those behaviors are associated with greater harm than those they condemn. Rather, they tend to favor "a rhetoric of *individual* responsibility, and private moral choice of drinkers" instead of corporate interests—including the alcohol industry—and the social and economic factors that shape alcohol problems.[71]

The research on FAS is inconclusive, even though teachers, counselors, doctors, and foster care and adoptive mothers themselves continue to inaccurately label children FAS and FAE. The labels FAS and FAE, which can stigmatize children, do little to alleviate the host of social and economic factors that harm children and families. In addition, women are constructed as individually failing in their maternal role and producing unfit children.

68. Ibid.
69. NHTSA 2000a; NHTSA 2002.
70. NHTSA 2000b.
71. Reinarman 1988: 105.

Marijuana and Cultural Factors

Marijuana has few health-related problems. Contrary to propaganda about its ill effects, there is no known incident of death caused by the drug. In fact, over 65 million people in the U.S. have tried marijuana.[72] Its one risk factor is irritation of the respiratory track, which is caused by inhalation of smoke. However, compared with tobacco smokers who can inhale the smoke of up to sixty cigarettes a day, marijuana smokers inhale much lower amounts. The British research institute DrugScope states that "there is still no conclusive evidence that long-term cannabis use causes lasting damage to physical or mental health."[73] However, this has not distracted supporters of harsh penalties for marijuana possession and sale from claiming otherwise. Law and order advocates claim that THC (tetrahydrocannabinol, an active chemical in cannabis) is dangerous and has a negative psychological and health impact on marijuana users. They claim that marijuana today has higher THC levels than it did thirty years ago. However, THC is a fairly benign drug, much less toxic than alcohol, tobacco, and a host of other legal drugs prescribed every day by doctors, and there is no research that demonstrates that higher levels of THC in marijuana causes negative health problems. Higher levels of THC might actually decrease respiratory health problems because marijuana users can smoke less of the drug to achieve the effect they want.[74]

Marijuana is the drug of choice for most people who use illegal drugs, and this is apparent in maternal drug testing as well. Although some researchers claim that marijuana use during pregnancy is harmful to the fetus and that infants may experience "irritability and tremulousness" at birth,[75] others dispute these claims. Cross-cultural researcher Kevin Nugent[76] examines how concepts of *risk* and *normality* are cultural constructions, which may not be valid outside the

72. Annas 1997.
73. DrugScope 2001: 48.
74. Boyd 1998.
75. Chasnoff 1988: 276.
76. Nugent 1994.

culture in which they were constructed. Cross-cultural studies have emphasized this discrepancy and the negative effects of placing one's own cultural values on other communities which may not share the same values or practices. Melanie Dreher, Kevin Nugent, and Rebekah Hudgins have demonstrated in their examination of maternal drug use in Jamaica that medical models of risk are cultural constructions. The researchers note that U.S. medical data suggest that infants are negatively affected by maternal marijuana use; therefore, they expected their research on maternal marijuana use in Jamaica to have similar results. However, this was not the case. Their study demonstrated that Jamaican women who used marijuana heavily during pregnancy had healthier babies than women who were light users or nonusers of marijuana. The authors stated:

> The heavily exposed neonates were more socially responsive and were more autonomically stable at 30 days than their matched counterparts. The quality of their alertness was higher; their motor and autonomic systems were more robust; they were less irritable; they were less likely to demonstrate any imbalance of tone; they needed less examiner facilitation to become organized; they had better self-regulation; and were judged to be more rewarding for caregivers than the neonates of nonusing mothers at 1 month of age.[77]

The Jamaican women who were defined as heavy users of marijuana were better educated, more financially independent, had fewer children and childcare responsibilities, and shared their home with more adults than the other women in the study. Their marijuana use did not indicate their lack of concern; rather, they believed that marijuana had healing properties and could be useful in relation to pregnancy and birth. For example, many of the heavy marijuana users in the sample said that marijuana increased their appetite and relieved nausea during pregnancy. Others noted it relieved fatigue and provided some rest during pregnancy.

77. Dreher, Nugent and Hudgins 1994: 258.

Many women in Jamaica are Rastafarian and they smoke marijuana regularly. They view marijuana as a sacred herb and recognize its healing properties for all types of health problems and for maintaining overall health, including during pregnancy and birth. The authors note that in Jamaica, the heavy users of marijuana in their study had minimal or no tobacco, alcohol, and illegal drug use outside marijuana use during pregnancy. This is in sharp contrast to the research samples in the U.S. where marijuana use is largely recreational. U.S. researchers have not controlled for social and environmental factors such as poverty, nutrition, support, and polydrug use in relation to maternal marijuana use. The researchers of the Jamaican study conclude that environmental influences, such as cultural, social, and economic characteristics of the mother, may override drug effects, and that marijuana is just one variable affecting maternal outcome. They stress the importance of "understanding the cultural context of drug use to explain outcomes."[78] In understanding maternal drug use and its consequences, we would do well to heed their advice, for repeatedly, researchers, the media, moral reformers, and the state fail to include social and economic factors into their research designs. Thus, in North America, the effects of poverty on pregnancy and maternal outcomes are often mistaken for the effects of illegal drugs.

Risk Categories

Risk categories, appearing neutral and scientific, deflect attention away from how they are used as gendered, class-based, and racialized measurements. Poor women and women of color are subjected the most frequently to risk assessment in relation to maternal drug use. Risk categories, and risk labels, are central to the medical model of health and draw attention to groups of women who have poor pregnancy outcomes in order to provide them with specialized care. Maternal drug use is viewed as a risk, although the extent of the "risk" is controversial. A number of researchers have pointed out that risk assessments of mothers and their infants for maternal drug use are sub-

78. Ibid.: 259.

jective and sometimes discriminatory.[79] As well, the assessments ignore the punitive outcomes of being labeled high risk. Risk categories related to maternal drug use ignore the constraints of one's environment on achieving optimum maternal health and ignore the mothers' perspective about themselves and their infants' health. Maternal health continues to be referred to as the mother's individual choice, rather than as an outcome of the social environment. Rather than examine the social contexts of women's lives, moral reformers question whether mothers exhibit responsibility to their developing fetuses and whether they are following medical advice. This advice often ignores the reality of women's everyday and everynight experiences. In the U.S., where most poor women have little access to health care, drug treatment, and social and economic support, risk categories can be a tool of repression.

Worldwide, researchers acknowledge that social deprivation (poverty) is linked to poor maternal outcomes. Yet this fact is ignored and women are increasingly held solely responsible for the outcomes of their pregnancies. Risk labels also reinforce power inequalities between women and medical professionals. When women fail, or refuse, to curtail at-risk behavior, such as using illegal drugs during pregnancy, they have been subjected to civil and criminal sanctions. Infants who are labeled at risk for NAS are also affected. Often they are isolated from their mothers in the hospital after they are born, and are later apprehended by the state. Mothers in North America who use illegal drugs are often perceived as incapable of caring for NAS-labeled infants. Many of these infants are labeled as NAS even though they do not exhibit any symptoms. Their mothers' suspected maternal illegal drug use is viewed as evidence of NAS harm and parental unfitness.

The Criminalization of Pregnancy: Maternal-State Conflicts

Political and cultural shifts in the 1980s ushered in a new conservative ideology that focused on personal responsibility and narrow

---

79. Morrison and Siney 1996.

family values and gender roles. Since the 1980s, zealous prosecutors in the U.S. have targeted pregnant women who use illegal drugs, and legislators have introduced numerous bills ranging from forced sterilization, Norplant implantation, and involuntary detention. Of those women charged with criminal offenses (most related to illegal drug use) between 1985 and 1992, 70 percent were women of color.[80] Biased reporting by media and initial, unconfirmed medical claims about harm to the fetus and unfitness of mothers who use illegal drugs are used by court prosecutors as "facts" rather than as social constructions.[81] Many people are still unaware of the new challenges to women's reproductive autonomy. This section describes a few cases.

Moral entrepreneur Paul Logli is a prosecutor from Illinois who has been active in charging women who use illegal drugs during pregnancy with a criminal offense. Along with Jeff Deen, another prosecutor from Florida, Logi educated millions of TV viewers about how women's prenatal cocaine exposure could harm the fetus and how these women were culpable.[82] Logli made it clear on national news and in his writing that the "plight" of cocaine babies inspired his actions to prosecute women who use illegal drugs during pregnancy. He stated that prosecutors in the U.S. have been successful in expanding the war on drugs to a "controversial new battlefield—the mother's womb,"[83] and he argued that prosecutors have a duty to protect the fetus from the destructive behavior of mothers who use illegal drugs.

In 2000, activists Lynn Paltrow, David Cohen, and Corinne Carey[84] reviewed state responses to women who use alcohol and illegal drugs in the U.S. They assessed the use of criminal statutes, civil child abuse statutes, third party liability, and civil (involuntary) commitment of pregnant women. Civil child welfare statutes vary from state to state. Some states can bring a family court or child welfare

80. Paltrow 1992.
81. Gomez 1997.
82. Humphries 1999: 34–35.
83. Logli 1990: 23.
84. Paltrow, Cohen, and Carey 2000a, 2000b, 2000c.

charge against a mother and apprehend her child if she tests positive for an illegal drug or for alcohol. Other states require other evidence in addition to a positive drug test, such as the infant exhibiting symptoms of NAS. Some states have amended their laws to allow for civil detention of women who test positive for illegal drugs, which essentially means that the woman is imprisoned or sent to drug treatment during her pregnancy. The justification for civil commitment rests with the assumption that the pregnant woman is a danger to the developing fetus.

The first criminal case against a woman in the U.S. occurred in 1977 when Margaret Velasquez Reyes was charged by the state of California with two counts of felony child endangerment.[85] Margaret's twin infants exhibited symptoms of NAS after their birth, as a result of their mother's heroin use. On appeal, the case was dismissed because the state's law did not apply to the fetus, only to live children. The next case was much more public and occurred in the middle of the crack scare in the U.S. In 1987, Pamela Rae Stewart, a young white woman, was charged in California with failing to follow medical advice after her infant son died five weeks after his birth. The prosecutor in this case claimed that Pamela had not followed advice to abstain from methamphetamine use and sexual intercourse during her pregnancy (the man was not charged). She had severe bleeding at her delivery due to placenta previa. Her son suffered from brain damage and tested positive for methamphetamine after he was born. Even though the doctor who delivered her son testified that the slight traces of methamphetamine found were not the cause of brain damage or death, Pamela was charged. The charges were eventually dismissed; however, this did not deter other zealous prosecutors from targeting pregnant women by extending criminal statutes intended for other purposes to the fetus and to pregnant women. Nor did it stop medical and social workers from contacting legal authorities when they suspected a woman of maternal drug use. Legal scholar Laura Gomez notes that this case was significant because of the media attention it received and its construction of a new social problem,

85. Roth 2000: 145.

namely, maternal drug use. In addition, feminist organizations and civil rights groups viewed the charges against Pamela Rae Stewart as being more than about maternal drug use; they saw it as a threat to women's reproductive rights.[86]

Prosecutor Paul Logli claims that society has a right to impose criminal sanctions against women who engage in maternal drug use, as he did when he charged Melanie Green in 1989 with manslaughter after her newborn died. This was the first time a woman had been charged with manslaughter in relation to prenatal drug use. Logli argued that her infant's death was due to her cocaine use during pregnancy and claimed that "to ignore that is unconscionable. It borders on barbarism."[87] Thus, Melanie was depicted as less moral than other mothers. The grand jury did not agree and the charges were dropped.

Jennifer Johnson's arrest is also a landmark, because it represents the first time that a prosecutor attempted to charge a woman for trafficking a controlled substance to her newborn infant and her older child (who had earlier tested positive for drugs). Jennifer, a young black women, was convicted in 1989 of delivering a controlled substance to a minor. This case is very important to women for several reasons. Because Florida drug laws do not apply to fetuses, the prosecutor argued that Jennifer had delivered cocaine to her children after their births through the attached umbilical cord in the seconds before it was cut. Therefore, the drugs were not delivered to the fetuses but rather to the live children seconds after their births. However, it was never determined if the infants tested positive for cocaine at birth because of fetal exposure, or from delivery after birth via the umbilical cord. Regardless of this fact, the judge sentenced her to a year at a residential drug treatment program and to fourteen years of probation. If she was not successful in treatment, or could not comply with her probation order, a prison term awaited her. Jennifer also had to undergo random drug testing and the court attempted to regulate any future pregnancies by mandating that she report to the court if she became pregnant. Lynn Paltrow headed the American Civil Lib-

86. Gomez 1997: 43.
87. Stein, as cited in Humphries 1999: 72.

erties Union (ACLU) team of lawyers that appealed Jennifer Johnson's conviction. Although the court of appeals upheld the conviction, the Florida Supreme Court disagreed. They held that the drug trafficking statute was misapplied (*Johnson v. State* 1992). However, Jennifer was imprisoned and separated from her children because of the earlier court decision.

In *Whitner v. State* 1997, the South Carolina Supreme Court determined that pregnant women who harm the "viable" fetus can be prosecuted. Pregnant women suspected of using illegal drugs can be charged under the state's criminal child endangerment statute and imprisoned for up to ten years. The state's mandatory child abuse reporting law assures that medical and social service providers report women suspected of using illegal drugs during pregnancy. South Carolina's Drug Dealer Liability Act also assures that "any individual who was exposed to an illegal controlled substance in utero" can "bring an action for damages caused by an individual's use of an illegal controlled substance."[88] In South Dakota, pregnant women suspected of using alcohol or illegal drugs can be involuntarily committed to a drug treatment center. A woman's husband, doctor, relative, administrator of a drug treatment program, or any "responsible" person can petition to have a woman committed involuntarily. The petitioner only needs to "allege" that the woman abuses alcohol or illegal drugs, "lacks self-control," or is pregnant. In New Jersey, a person's prison term will be doubled if she or he is convicted of selling drugs to a woman who is pregnant, even if the seller is unaware of the woman's pregnancy. Similarly, it is a Class D felony to sell drugs to a pregnant woman in North Carolina.

Civil Child Welfare Law

In 2002, over eighteen states in the U.S. had some type of civil child welfare law that regulates women's drug use during pregnancy.[89] In Oklahoma, a "deprived child" is one that tests positive for illegal

88. Ibid.: 57.
89. Paltrow, Cohen, and Carey 2000b.

drugs at birth. Recently, they considered House Bill No. 1185, which would amend their civil child abuse statue to the unborn viable fetus. This legislation is directly related to the controversial Julie Starks case (*Starks v. State* 2001). Julie Starks was arrested on August 23, 1999, and the trial court later determined that her fetus was a "deprived child" because she was approximately seven months pregnant and on the site of an alleged methamphetamine lab. Julie was arrested with Jimmy Cook (the father of her unborn child), and initially charged with manufacturing and possession of methamphetamine. It is interesting to note that his bail was set at U.S.$25,000, whereas Julie's was raised to U.S.$200,000. The trial court took temporary emergency custody of Julie's "viable fetus," so that after bail was obtained she was ordered into foster care until her child was born. The court also ordered Julie to complete an alcohol and drug assessment after she was released from jail and to make her living arrangements known and open to inspection to the Department of Human Services. She also had to submit to random urine analyses and attend pre-natal visits once a week.[90] Prison conditions could easily be perceived as a clear danger to Julie and her fetus. Julie remained in jail for thirty-six days where she was fed an inadequate diet, developed a sinus infection, lost fourteen pounds, and became dehydrated. She subsequently went into premature labor and was rushed to the hospital. There she was given medication to stop her labor and she had to continue taking the medication until a few days prior to her delivery. Julie states that she never used drugs during her pregnancy; in fact, she never tested positive for drugs.[91]

The state's case rested solely on the perceived danger to the fetus due to Julie's presence at the methamphetamine lab. The day after Julie's baby was born, the Department of Human Services took emergency custody of him. A little over a week later, the district attorney filed a petition claiming the baby was a "deprived child" due to Julie's arrest. On appeal, Julie and her lawyer, Barbara Teichner, argued that the trial court lacked jurisdiction to assume custody of her fetus and

90. Starks v. State 2001.
91. Barbara A. Teichner (Personal communication, April 2, 2002).

that they violated her right to privacy and autonomy, due process, and equal protection based on gender and the right to travel. As a result of the efforts of Julie and her lawyer, Julie and her son are now together.

Another disturbing case relates to the search and arrest of pregnant women who came to a state hospital to deliver in South Carolina (*Ferguson v. The City of Charleston, South Carolina* 2001). This case brought up many important issues related to personal privacy and to the ethics of health care providers and the trust placed in them by patients. The Supreme Court reviewed the policy of a state hospital program in Charleston implemented in 1989. The program was created by the local police department, the prosecutor, and the medical staff. The medical staff worked with the police for five years, searching pregnant women and those who had just given birth for evidence of drug use. This was done without the women's consent and without warrants. Medical personnel (nurses and doctors) decided which women would be searched and given urine tests; the results provided evidence for criminal proceedings. This program affected poor women, particularly black women. Lynn Paltrow notes that all but one woman was African American. If evidence demonstrated that a woman had used drugs (i.e., tested positive for drugs, especially cocaine), she was arrested on the spot. Some women were shackled immediately after birth and escorted to prison in their hospital gown while still bleeding, in pain, and recovering from childbirth. Others were shackled to their beds prior to and after childbirth. Complaints led to the creation of a treatment component in 1990, since none was available for pregnant women, or mothers, in the entire state. However, all of the women were sent to the same treatment program that was run by people who had no experience with pregnant women. The hospital staff argued that given the danger to the developing fetus from maternal cocaine use, their policy was justified. They also assumed that the threat of legal sanctions would deter pregnant women from using drugs.

Ten women challenged the policy and sued the state for violating their civil rights; however, in 2000, the U.S. Court of Appeals for the Fourth Circuit ruled that the hospital's policy did not violate the women's constitutional rights, for the need to deter women from drug use was deemed an exception to promote health. The case was brought to the Supreme Court. There it was argued by the plaintiffs that there was no evidence that legal sanctions deter pregnant women from using drugs. In fact, they stated that it is known that "threat-based approaches" do not work. The plaintiffs also argued that the "assumption of cocaine's unique danger when ingested during pregnancy" is not supported by empirical evidence. In 2001, the Supreme Court agreed, and recognized that "government physicians and nurses should not act as agents of law enforcement, nor should they use 'routine' medical examinations to covertly gather evidence for use against patients in criminal proceedings."[92] The Supreme Court recognized that the Fourth Amendment to the U.S. Constitution protects "Americans," including women who are pregnant, from unreasonable searches.

This case is significant because the Supreme Court's decision recognized the infringement of women's rights related to the search and arrest of pregnant women and the breach of trust and pain the women experienced at the hospital and afterwards in jail and in treatment. Little attention was given to the fact that they were separated from their infants at birth, which also contributed to their suffering. In addition, without the challenge initiated by the ten women who opposed the punitive policy of arresting and imprisoning obstetrical patients, the civil-rights law suit would not have been able to proceed. This is the first civil-rights law suit in the U.S. to challenge a policy of arrest in federal court. Linda Paltrow, Executive Director of the National Advocates for Pregnant Women, initiated the suit. She, and over seventy physicians, researchers, and civil rights, medical, and public health organizations, filed an amicus curiae (friend of the court) brief to oppose the policy implemented at the hospital. Their concerted effort made this success possible.

Another case, which I outlined in my introductory chapter, has not had a successful outcome yet. In 2001, Regina McKnight was convicted of homicide by child abuse (*County of Horry, State of South Carolina v. Regina D. McKnight* 2001). Regina is a young black

92. Goldberg, Abrahamson, and Waldman 1999: 27, 3.

woman who gave birth to a stillborn infant in 1999 and was subsequently charged with crimes of homicide by child abuse. Her first trial was declared a mistrial because the jury was unable to reach a verdict. At her retrial in 2001, Regina McKnight was convicted of homicide and sentenced to twenty years, with eight years suspended.

The court transcripts in this case are quite telling. It is obvious that the state attempted to keep African Americans off the jury by using four of six strikes to eliminate them during the jury-selection process. In addition, potential jurors were not chosen if they, or a family member, had a history of drug use. In relation to the evidence presented at the trial, the first pathologist to examine the infant, and who actually conducted the autopsy, stated that three factors may have contributed to the death of the infant. The first two factors were the diseases choriamnionitis and funisitis; the third factor was the presence of benzoylecgonine, a breakdown product in the metabolism of cocaine, which the infant tested positive for. The first two diseases on their own could have caused the infant's death.

The first pathologist and three other doctors gave evidence that women who do not use drugs can also develop chorioamnionitis and funisitis, which can result in stillbirths. Only one other doctor claimed that these diseases did not cause the stillbirth. The defense also noted that a baby can be born with cocaine in its system as opposed to benzoylecgonine. It was never determined, without a doubt, how the benzoylecgonine ended up in the stillborn baby and whether it was a breakdown product from cocaine. It was never established that the level of benzoylecgonine found in the stillborn baby's system could have caused death. Nevertheless, the state argued that since the cause of death by disease was "undetermined," it must have been the cocaine which was introduced through the placenta.

The state claimed that while other pregnant women care for the developing fetus, "Regina McKnight was sucking on a crack pipe. While most mothers would jump in front of a school bus to protect a young child; the crack pipe is still there."[93] In less than fifteen minutes the jury found Regina guilty of homicide by child abuse. The state con-

---

93. *State of South Carolina v. Regina D. McKnight* 2001: 438.

structed Regina as a women whose compulsion to use crack overrode her maternal instincts. Thus, she was depicted as "unnatural" and the opposite of the selfless mother so esteemed in Western ideology.

Lynn Paltrow and a coalition of groups worked on Regina McKnight's appeal. In January 2003, the Supreme Court of South Carolina upheld her conviction in a 3–2 decision and later that year the U.S. Supreme Court refused to review her case. Regina's conviction has implications for any woman who suffers a miscarriage or a stillbirth, for any behavior that is deemed dangerous to the fetus could result in criminal charges. It also contributes to legal discourse that views women as only vessels—vessels that are antagonistic and dangerous to the developing fetus. In addition, it extends the legal rights of a born child to the fetus. Some have questioned whether Regina was "fit" to stand trial, and note that she may be mentally handicapped as her IQ is indicated to be only 72. She was also homeless. Rather than receiving much needed support, Regina, and other pregnant women who suffer stillbirth and who are suspected of drug use are charged with a criminal offense.

Another recent case in Arizona which is still pending, also demonstrates how prosecutors attempt to frame maternal drug use and its harm to the born child. On November 9, 2001, Demitres Robertson's infant daughter died only ten days after her birth. Initially, it was alleged that the baby died from prenatal exposure to secondhand crack cocaine smoke. However, in Arizona, prenatal substance use is not a crime. After a nine-month investigation, Demitres was charged by prosecutors with first-degree murder and child abuse, and her mother was charged with two counts of child abuse. The prosecutors claim that the child died from exposure to secondhand crack cocaine smoke after she was born, rather than during the pregnancy, and that the exposure caused a lethal bowel condition called necrotizing enterocolitis. A panel of doctors examined the case and commented that there is no medical evidence to support the prosecutors' allegations. Necrotizing enterocolitis is associated with premature babies.[94]

94. Baker 2002; Bland 2002.

Nongovernment Initiatives

Initiatives to limit women's reproductive autonomy also derive from nongovernment groups like Children Requiring a Caring Kommunity (CRACK), which has twenty-one affiliates across the U.S. and which targets poor women who have used illegal drugs. The organization, founded by Barbara Harris, offers U.S.$200 to drug users (almost all have been women) who will submit to permanent sterilization or long-term birth control like Norplant. Barbara Harris assumes that maternal drug use permanently impairs children and that it equals child abuse. Although she claims that she is not targeting poor black women, her website for CRACK does precisely that. CRACK is a modern eugenics program that perpetuates myths about women who use illegal drugs and exaggerates the risks to them and their infants. As poor women in the U.S. are denied medical care, social and economic support, they are increasingly the targets of coercive interventions, including sterilization. In addition, social services often target women who use drugs, and intervention in the family is common in Canada and the U.S. However, in the U.S., fundamentalist Christian beliefs (including those in the White House) also shape reproductive issues.

Alternative Maternity Services

In contrast to programs like CRACK, which seek to limit women's reproduction, maternal services in Britain and Scotland seek to insure that women who use illegal drugs have access to maternal care so that their birth experiences are similar to nondrug using women. Consequently, the most interesting information about maternal drug use has emerged out of these countries. These successful maternal services recognize that midwifery is both safe and inexpensive and can promote healthy pregnancies and births. These services offer pregnant women nonjudgmental prenatal and infant care without the threat of child apprehension. Despite high-risk categories, maternal outcomes have improved without legal and unwarranted medical intervention. Random drug testing is not practiced and treatment is not coerced. Rather, voluntary maternal services for women have been set up which offer social, prenatal, and economic care to all women. As a result, birth outcomes for women who use illegal drugs are similar to nondrug using women who use these services. Dr. Mary Hepburn's Women's Reproductive Health Service in Glasgow became a model for many other midwifery programs throughout the U.K., including the programs set up by Catherine Siney in Liverpool and by Faye Macrory in Manchester.

Glasgow

Dr. Mary Hepburn's service emerged when she opened a clinic for women in the mid-1980s. The clinic brought reproductive care to women who were "reluctant or unable to attend standard services, or for whom services were inappropriate, or did not meet their needs." The program grew rapidly and is now based at the Princess Royal Maternity, offering outpatient care in a number of community-based city-wide services that are offered to pregnant women—those who use drugs and those who do not. The clinic recognizes that maternal drug use is one "of a range of social problems and is managed in that context."[95] Thus, even though drug use is viewed as a risk, it is considered to be a manageable one. Social workers become involved early on to provide economic and social support, not crisis intervention. They recognize that illegal drug use in itself does not equal bad parenting. In fact, abstinence does not in itself guarantee good parenting. The women are treated with respect and find the services acceptable.[96]

At the program, heavy-handed attempts to reduce drug use and to achieve abstinence is avoided; rather, stabilization is the goal. Women who use drugs may discontinue use during pregnancy (antenatal detoxification) and stabilize on methadone maintenance (the dose may vary throughout the pregnancy). Unlike most services in the U.S. and Canada, although antenatal care and delivery are obstetrically led,

95. Hepburn 2002: 250–251.
96. Hepburn 1999, 2002.

midwives are a component of the multidisciplinary service. Mothers are not routinely separated from their infants after birth and they are encouraged to breast-feed to minimize withdrawal symptoms in the infant. It is recognized that "maternal HIV infection is a contraindication because of increased risk of vertical transmission. The evidence suggests that hepatitis C is not transmitted by breast feeding but there is no absolute proof of this."[97] Dr. Hepburn concludes that for this group of vulnerable infants, the benefits outweigh theoretical risk, and breast-feeding is recommended. She also asserts that confidentiality is essential, and it is not uncommon for service workers to assume they know what women need, when in fact they do not. Ninety-five percent of the babies go home with their mothers.[98] Women who use illegal drugs and attend their services have comparable birth outcomes to nondrug using women. However, the combination of older drug-using women and long-term use of drugs may culminate in poor health, which could have a negative impact on maternal outcomes.[99]

Liverpool

Catherine Siney created the first drug liaison midwife post at the Liverpool Women's Hospital in 1990 to coordinate maternity services for women who use drugs and for those who are HIV, or hepatitis C, positive. She trained medical and service staff, and stressed that there is a "difference between drug use and drug dependence," and that infants should not be given unnecessary treatment.[100] In that program today, reducing women's tobacco smoking continues to be a central concern, because cigarette use, rather than illegal drug use, is one of the main factors contributing to low birth weights.[101] Women are offered methadone maintenance throughout their pregnancy. Women who use illegal drugs are cared for alongside nondrug users, and their infants are not labeled or taken to a special care unit, nor are they tar-

97. Hepburn 2002: 258.
98. Hepburn 1999.
99. Mary Hepburn (personal communication, April 20, 2003).
100. Siney 1999: 11.
101. Siney, Kidd, Walkinshaw, Morrison, and Manasse 1995.

geted by social workers. Women are also not subjected to drug testing. Siney states that assessment charts for infant withdrawal are often subjective, thus problematic. Similar to the Glasgow program, the Liverpool program claims that severe withdrawal symptoms in infants will usually develop within seventy-two hours, and if no effect is demonstrated by then, it is unlikely that they will develop them later. Infants are released with their mothers after three or four days even when they have mild symptoms of withdrawal.[102] As early as 1993, it was noted that the birth outcomes of women who use illegal drugs (and/or methadone) are similar to nondrug using women. Siney concludes that services provided by midwives offer women a "memorable" birth experience "for all the right reasons."[103]

Manchester

In Manchester, Faye Macrory developed the first jointly funded position of Drug Liaison Midwife based on her volunteer work on a street-health project for sex workers. The post is supported by the maternity and drug services and is based within the drug treatment agency. The service provides "up-to-date, relevant and factual information in a non-judgmental and sympathetic manner" to women and their families about pregnancy, drugs, and parenting.[104] The liaison midwife is instrumental in creating and evaluating programs, publishing educational material, and ensuring that women who use illegal drugs are welcome into the maternity services. The premise of the program, which became official in 1995, is to create a noncritical environment where women can freely disclose and discuss their drug use without fear of punishment. While the role has enabled appropriate and effective service provision to become established, it also has uncovered a wide range of associated unmet needs. Subsequently, in April 2001, Faye Macrory was appointed as a Consultant Midwife to further develop services for women who use alcohol and drugs.

102. Walkinshaw, Shaw, and Siney 2002: 218.
103. Siney 1994: 24.
104. Macrory 2002: 242.

The Drug Liaison Midwife reports to her, as does the HIV Support Midwife. The service has adopted the SCODA guidelines that state:

> Drug use by parents does not automatically indicate child neglect or abuse. Automatic child abuse registration will deter parents from approaching drug dependence clinics or other professionals for help and should be avoided. In families where drug use is a factor, a comprehensive assessment of the relationship between parental drug use and child care is indicated. Each family should be assessed individually.[105]

Since the implementation of the service, infants are no longer separated from their mothers after birth or sent to the Special Care Baby Unit in the hospital. In the first year, 152 women used the services; by the second year, 177 women used the services and 57 babies were delivered at the hospital. The service does liaison with social services, although they are not automatically involved, and each case is assessed individually. Similar to the Glasgow program, breast feeding is encouraged, even when the mothers are still using illegal drugs, for this reduces withdrawal in the infant, and "the need for treatment." Faye Macrory states that it is vital that everyone work together to provide a service that is "free from prejudice, conflict, and confrontation."[106] She also reminds service workers that

> [by] focusing all their resources and attention on pregnant women, they may simply be reinforcing the already strong societal message women get—and internalise—that their primary or only value is in producing offspring, and that the only attention they will get is in their role as mothers. For women whose sense of self and self-esteem is already precarious, the feeling that they are only valued [when pregnant]...may increase their suspicion of health care, drug treatment and HIV/AIDS prevention advisors. They may feel often quite rightly, that once the baby is delivered or once the infant ceases to be followed for a research protocol, no one will continue to be interested in them. It must always be re-

105. SCODA, as cited in Macrory 1997: 15.
106. Macrory 2002: 245, 248.

> membered that the pregnant woman is a whole person and not just a uterus, and that pregnancy is only one part—and usually a very small part—of any woman's life.[107]

Drug use is only one factor that shapes a woman's life and her pregnancy. Drug use is also mediated by a woman's social environment, as is her pregnancy. The research has consistently demonstrated that the social environment is just as, or possibly more, important in relation to infant development than prenatal exposure to illegal drugs. Thus, we should strive towards providing women and their children with medical, social, and economic support that is user-friendly and appropriate to their needs.

Resistance in the U.S.

Although states have enacted legislation to extend the rights of the fetus and to prosecute pregnant women who use illegal drugs, many groups concerned with the welfare of children and women oppose these laws. Organizations like the American Academy of Pediatrics and the Association of Maternal and Child Health oppose prosecution of pregnant women. They claim that women are less likely to access treatment and that their children may be negatively labeled even when no health problems present themselves. Many medical groups in the U.S. oppose the prosecution of pregnant women and mothers who use illegal drugs, including the American Medical Association, the American College of Obstetricians and Gynecologists, and the American Nurses Association. Groups like the National Advocates for Pregnant Women (NAPW) seek to protect the rights of pregnant women and their children.

The National Advocates for Pregnant Women emerged in response to the persecution of pregnant women in the mid-1980s. The organization argues that policy and laws that punish pregnant women and new mothers who use illegal drugs drive them out of the healthcare and social service system and endanger their health. NAPW seeks to protect the rights of women and children and seeks full reproductive

107. Macrory and Crosby 1995: 17.

rights and services for women. Although many women have been writing about the infringement of women's reproductive rights and its intersection with the war on drugs, NAPW officially recognizes the need to create a comprehensive campaign that links reproductive issues, drug policy, and legal protection to women who are adversely affected by criminal and civil law. Lynn Paltrow, the Executive Director, has been active in several cases defending the rights of pregnant women and new mothers. In 2002, NAPW brought together women from Britain, Canada, and the U.S. to forge coalitions between abortion-rights and anti-drug war activists. NAPW and other advocacy groups recognize that since the mid-1980s, women's bodies have become the new terrain for advancing the war on drugs.

Conclusion

In the 1960s and 1970s, as women gained more control over their reproduction, challenged gender roles, and sought equality in the home and in the workplace, maternal-state conflicts arose. The danger of maternal drug use to the fetus, especially crack, has justified proposals, legislation, and programs that seek to limit women's reproductive autonomy. Most often, these policies, proposals, and laws impact poor women and women of color disproportionately. As well, their children suffer when they are medically treated for NAS or apprehended by the state. In order to challenge these interventions, we need to expose the myths about maternal fitness and mothering. State and medical intervention is not static; rather, it shifts historically. Poor women are less protected than middle-class and wealthy women from state and nonstate intervention—for women's experiences of reproduction and illegal drug use are mediated by their race, class, and gender. Thus, women who use illegal drugs are not homogenous, and their diversity should be acknowledged by activists, writers, and policy-makers.

Criminal and civil laws that seek to punish women suspected of using illegal drugs during pregnancy will only further marginalize them and their children. These laws ignore the fact that poverty negatively affects maternal outcomes. It is well established that by offering women nonjudgemental prenatal and infant care, economic and social support, maternal outcomes improve. Further, midwives have been successful in providing this care as they attempt to normalize pregnancy and birth for those mothers who use drugs.

Chapter 3

The Welfare Regulation of Women

Welfare Regulation

As noted earlier, the legal, medical, and social service regulation of women overlap and often compete with one another. Women suspected of using drugs, and infants identified and labeled NAS, have come under surveillance by social services. New civil and criminal legislation in the U.S. equates maternal drug use with child abuse, and women suspected of using illegal drugs have had their infants taken away from them after birth. Child apprehension is one of the most punitive tools that social workers wield when a woman is perceived as unfit and/or a child abuser. All single mothers on welfare are at risk of losing their children, especially those identified as being illegal drug users. Historically, the majority of state apprehension of children falls under the category of neglect, rather than physical and sexual abuse, and this holds true today.[1] Canadian child neglect researcher Karen Swift asserts that

> state apprehension of children under the category of neglect is often a punitive measure against mothers who live in poverty. Mothers in poverty, especially those who are racialized, are vulnerable to child welfare authorities because they are living under conditions of deprivation imposed by the

1. Swift 1995.

> state–inadequate food, substandard shelter, inadequate child-care, inadequate clothing, and generally impoverished environments–that make parenting extremely challenging.[2]

Historically, welfare assistance has failed to meet the monthly living expenses of women receiving benefits. Today, cutbacks in social assistance in Britain, Canada, and the U.S. render more women, especially those labeled illegal drug users, vulnerable to child apprehension, as do new civil and criminal legislation equating maternal drug use with child abuse.

In addition, women suspected of using illegal drugs can be denied welfare benefits. Today, women on welfare are forced into drug treatment programs, anger management, parenting, and life skills classes, as well as subjected to drug testing. These punitive policies are linked to larger political and economic shifts which demonize single mothers in order to justify cutbacks and neoliberal economic agendas.

U.S. poverty researchers Judith Goode and Jeff Maskovsky write that today "the state's new role is to regulate the poor through surveillance and incarceration, not through supportive services."[3] They note that over the last thirty years the welfare state has been replaced by the law-and-order state which will contribute to greater poverty in the U.S. and abroad. They explore how policy that serves global capitalism has been advanced since the 1970s, and how public education, health, and social services have been cut back as privatization is proposed. Programs initiated during the war on poverty have been constructed as creating welfare "dependency." Welfare dependency, rather than poverty, is depicted as "the evil destroying people's lives."[4]

Today, poor bashing has taken on a new viciousness and any woman who is suspected of using illegal drugs is depicted as especially deviant. Rather than look at the roots of their poverty, poor women are constructed as not wanting to improve themselves and are seen as reluctant to join the free market and engage in entrepreneurship. The deserving poor are those who embrace the ideology of the

2. B.C. CEDAW Group 2003: 18.
3. Goode and Maskovsky 2001: 6.
4. Ibid.: 5.

market, while those who remain dependent on the state are viewed as undeserving.[5] Thus, women who are reluctant to leave their children alone or in the care of others are deemed undeserving. Women who use drugs are also viewed as reluctant to embrace the work ethic, for it is assumed that their immoral lifestyle and "addictions" interfere with employment.

Women and children have felt the full impact of the new welfare reforms. Their experiences differ from region to region, but there are similar concerns voiced by women in the U.S., Britain, and Canada as social services have been cut back. Single mothers, especially women of color, are viewed as the most dependent and deviant. Images of black women as promiscuous bad mothers, welfare queens, and matriarchs continue to inform welfare policy. "By blaming these women for their own poverty and, indeed, for the economic ills of the entire nation, attention is diverted from the injustice of the racial and gendered labor market and from the 'savage inequalities' increasingly characterizing U.S. society."[6] Attention is also diverted from tax cuts that favor wealthy people and from tax breaks, corporate welfare, and other government assistance that subsidize the business sector.

Most importantly, women who apply and attempt to receive welfare benefits are subjected to gendered forms of social control. Social workers label women "deserving" and "undeserving," and the assessment of mothering and the proper feminine role is central to welfare policy. When women apply for welfare they become subject to both surveillance and a host of interventions and punishments by social workers.[7] Those women who do not conform to gendered notions of mothering and the family are punished. Child apprehension and the denial of benefits are tools that the welfare system wields when a woman is deemed "unfit." Since the 1980s, single mothers on welfare have been depicted by political reformers and the mainstream media as a "danger" to their children.[8] Rather than viewing poverty, racism,

---

5. Ibid.: 8.
6. Mullings 2001: 47.
7. See Chunn 1995; Edwards 1988; and Maher 1992.
8. See Gomez 1997; Humphries 1999; and Greaves et al. 2002.

colonialism, and gender bias as detrimental to families' well-being, mothers alone are constructed as solely responsible. Poor mothers who use illegal drugs are constructed as being more deviant and dangerous than their nondrug using counterparts.

Fitness to Parent

One of the most contentious areas related to womens' illegal drug use is their "fitness" to parent. Rarely are fathers' fitness to parent considered. In fact, they are basically absent from the discussion. Women who use illegal drugs are viewed as incapable of caring for their children because it is believed that their compulsion to use drugs supercedes their parenting role. Most often, mothers who use illegal drugs are seen as out of control and as a risk to their children. The media has consistently portrayed them as failing in their role as mothers.[9] In contrast to these negative images, significant research studies by Colten; Dreher et al.; Hepburn; Jackson and Berry; Kearny et al.; Klee, Jackson, and Lewis; Leeders; Rosenbaum; Siney; and Taylor provide evidence that not only can women who use illegal drugs provide adequate parenting, especially when they are offered social and economic support, but they also employ a host of strategies to protect their children.[10] This research is significant and most often it includes ethnographic studies, in-depth interviews, and research conducted at programs which offer nonjudgmental social, medical, and economic support to women over a long period of time.

Much of the negative research about mothers who use illegal drugs stems from animal research, and risk assessment, child abuse potential, and childrearing attitude studies. Interestingly, mothers are com-

---

9. Rosenbaum et al. 1990.

10. Boyd 1999; Colten 1980, 1982; Dreher et al. 1994; Hepburn 1993; Jackson and Berry 1994; Kearney et al. 1994; Klee, Jackson, and Lewis 2002; Leeders 1992; Lewis, Klee, and Jackson 1995; Lief 1976; Murphy and Rosenbaum 1999; Rosenbaum 1981; Rosenbaum et al. 1990; Siney 1999; Sowder and Burt 1980; Sterk-Elifson 1996; Talylor 1993; Zarin-Ackerman 1976.

pletely absent from these studies, as are their children. Many of these studies are conducted prior to women giving birth (i.e., risk assessment surveys), and animal studies assume that the behavior of rats subjected to repeated injections of cocaine in a clinical setting is similar to women's behavior in their natural social environment. These studies mistakenly assume that there is a correlation between women's illegal drug use and poor parenting.[11] Diana Hogan's 1998 review of the existing research on the social environment of children of drug users and the developmental outcomes for these children argues that illegal drug users are diverse and the concentration of research that includes only children in foster care, court cases, and parents in treatment skews the results. She argues that researchers extrapolate findings from studies on alcohol and parenting and apply them to children of illegal drug users. She also suggests that researchers often fail to distinguish between mothers on heroin and cocaine, and mothers on methadone. She argues that the illegality of specific drugs, the drug of choice, duration of use, and personal history may shape parenting differently. She also notes that social support appears to be crucial in relation to mothers' abilities to care for their children. Social and economic deprivation, isolation, and stress often shape family life in negative ways. Thus, research findings cannot be generalized to the general population of illegal drug users.[12]

One of the most striking findings across the board in Britain, Canada, and the U.S. is women's assertion that mothering is viewed as their central role. They feel responsible for their children and any harm that may come to them. As early as 1980, a large U.S. study by Sowder and Burt of 160 "addict" families and 160 "nonaddict" families discovered that there was no difference between the two groups in relation to their parenting, expectations, and reports of abuse and neglect.[13] In the same year, Mary Ellen Colten argued that rather than suffering from abuse and neglect, children may suffer because of the

11. Johns et al. 1994; Vernotica et al. 1996; Williams-Peterson et al. 1994.
12. Hogan 1998.
13. Sowder and Burt 1980.

limited social and economic resources offered to mothers who use illegal drugs, and the disdain and marginalization they are subjected to. In 1981, Marsha Rosenbaum discussed her findings from her ethnographic study of women who used heroin in San Francisco. Most of the women she interviewed viewed themselves as solely responsible for their children.[14] Women who use illegal drugs in Canada, England, Scotland, the Netherlands, and the U.S. have similar attitudes and hopes related to their mothering as nondrug using women. Women also employ harm-reduction strategies in order to protect their families from their drug use and violence, and voice their distress when they fail.[15]

Drug researchers Sheigla Murphy and Marsha Rosenbaum highlight that the social conditions of poor women who use illegal drugs, including crack, are more harmful to mothers' and children's "well-being, and safety than drug use."[16] However, rather than offered support, women are subjected to criminalization in the U.S., and to child apprehension, intervention in the family, and denial of benefits to various degrees in Britain, Canada, and the U.S. In Britain, Suzan Lewis, Hilary Klee, and Marcia Jackson note in their 1995 study on illegal drug use and experiences of pregnancy that

> female drug users are not an homogenous group. However, there is little support for the stereotype of drug-using pregnant women as self-centered, rejecting social norms and unconcerned about the well-being of their unborn children. On the contrary, all have to some extent internalized dominant social constructions of the ideal mother-to-be and recognize that they do not fit this image.[17]

The ideology of mothering ignores the plight of mothers, especially those deemed to be "deviant." Most significantly, it ignores the

---

14. Rosenbaum 1981.
15. Kearney et al. 1994; Theidon 1995.
16. Murphy and Rosenbaum 1999: 12.
17. Lewis, Klee, and Jackson 1995: 225, 226.

constraints placed on mothers due to racism, class bias, and gender inequality.

Most studies on women who use illegal drugs focus on poor women. Similar to the studies on maternal drug use and the impact on the fetus and birth outcomes, we mistake the effects of poverty with the effects of drugs. As well, much liberal and conservative research fails to analyze how punitive law (including drug law) and social policy shapes women's lives in very negative ways. Rarely do we discuss how global capitalism, the restructuring of the workplace that creates more low-paying jobs, and short-term contracts may impact family life in a negative way. Or how lack of national medical coverage, education, and housing impact women and their children. Rather, conventional studies blame women and offer criminological and psychological individualistic explanations of deviance, abuse, and neglect. We need to strip away the moralism that colors our view of women who use illegal drugs. Negative labels like "addict" and "unfit mother" do much to obscure the political, social, legal, and economic factors that shape women's lives, and their inequality. There are inadequate parents from all walks of life. We also need to avoid falling into the trap of measuring women's mothering capabilities as prescribed by Western ideologies. Women's roles as caring mothers may be central to many women who use illegal drugs, but not all women can, or want to, measure themselves against Western ideologies and standards concerning good parenting. We need to broaden our analysis of mothering and view it as a social responsibility rather than just as a woman's role. In addition, we need to problematize contemporary welfare reform and the accompanying demonization of single-parent mothers.

Welfare Reform in the U.S.

Social policy researcher Slyvia Bashevkin notes that welfare reform in the U.S. followed similar trends in Britain initiated by the conservative governments of Margaret Thatcher and John Major. Ronald Regan and George Bush Sr. pointed to the moral failings of women on welfare, and the modern welfare state was called into question for producing an underclass of dependent single mothers. The conservative government of Brian Mulroney was less ideological in his claim that social programs were no longer "affordable." He opened Canada's borders to free trade and the supremacy of the market above all other national concerns. In addition, he opened up "the adoption of U.S.-style welfare rhetoric by Canada's provincial leaders." In all three nations, conservative rhetoric was replaced by moderate voices. However, the 1990s elections of Jean Chrétien in Canada, William Clinton in the U.S, and Tony Blair in Britain did not reverse earlier trends. In fact, the opposite occurred. All three federal leaders were instrumental in dismantling the modern welfare state. Their policies have been "*more* punitive, more restrictive, and more obsessed with paid work than those of their predecessors (italics in the original)."[18]

It took the election of a Democratic president, considered to be more moderate, to usher in more punitive welfare reforms in the U.S. Former President William Clinton, stated in 1992 that he would "end welfare as we know it." He made good on his election promise by dismantling the welfare state and enacting the Personal Responsibility and Work Opportunity Reconciliation Act of 1996 (PRWORA), which "remoralized" welfare and limited assistance to five years in one's lifetime.[19] Workfare, rather than cash assistance was imposed, and women were required to abandon their children at home in order to work in low-paying community service jobs that offered little training and supervision and displaced other workers. Women who needed cash assistance were considered as dependent on the state and unwilling to participate in the workplace.[20] PRWORA also banned legal immigrants from receiving food stamps and left Temporary Assistance for Needy Families to each state's discretion. Social policy researcher Sylvia Bashevkin notes that contemporary changes in welfare policy in the U.S., Britain, and Canada "demeaned the unpaid caring work of millions of adults, overwhelmingly mothers, at the

18. Bashevkin 2002: 21, 9.
19. Baumohl and Schram 2000: 213.
20. See Piven 2001.

same time as they diminished the citizenship status of people without children."[21]

As welfare policy becomes "leaner and meaner," poor women are told they are personally responsible for their poverty. The gap between the rich and the poor widens in the U.S., and the restructuring of the workplace continues as full-time union work decreases, replaced by low-paying, part-time, contract, nonunion, and workfare labor. As large corporations like Bell Atlantic and Federal Express hire workfare recipients for a pittance, a host of corporations employs prisoners for even less. These workers cannot strike nor collectively address workplace injustices. These practices contribute to corporate profit at the expense of workers' wages and safety and push wages down, which contributes to all workers' vulnerability and inability to collectively stem the tide of free market forces (which are not free wheeling at all but shaped by state policies such as workfare and deregulation of corporate activity), and the restructuring of labor to benefit corporate profit. Significantly, workfare ideology renders all women's work in the home invisible. Caring for children, the elderly, and the home is not considered "work." Moving women into poorly paid jobs in the public sphere leaves unquestioned the private/public divide and how women's unrecognized and unpaid work (which is essential to the running of the marketplace) is devalued.

Today's poor bashing is part of the discourse of neoliberalism and the market which situates women in the domestic sphere, caring for children and the elderly without state or federal economic and social support. Rather, domestic duties are viewed as women's individual responsibility. Childcare and healthcare are not constructed as "work" that contribute to society, rather they are viewed as women's responsibility. The cutbacks in economic and social support for women and children, and greater surveillance of and punitiveness towards women, are best understood against the backdrop of global capitalism and the law-and-order ideology that accompanies it. Workfare programs ensure that employment rather than car-

21. Bashevkin 2002: 9.

ing for children is central to welfare policy. Furthermore, workfare punishes women for being widowed, abandoned, and divorced, and it assumes that they are solely responsible for their children at the same time that it demeans the unpaid work of mothering. While state and welfare policies renege on their commitment to provide some assistance to women and their families, drug arrests, race profiling, and prison time leave many fathers and mothers unable to provide for their own families. Negative stereotypes and myths about women who use illegal drugs have fueled neoliberal cutbacks and denial of welfare benefits, and children exposed to maternal drug use are constructed as diverting already strapped funding to welfare agencies.

Women Regulating Women

Feminist writer Barbara Omolade notes how black women in the U.S. supervise each other, black professionals regulate black clerks who serve black clients. Black women who work in welfare services find themselves enforcing the rules rather than helping their sisters.[22] Most welfare workers, regardless of their race/ethnicity, view their clients with the same disdain as policy-makers. Woman welfare workers serve as the "gatekeepers" to services, and because they are overworked, underpaid, and at the bottom of the hierarchy, they too have few resources to address structural inequality.[23] However, they have tremendous power over their welfare clients. Too often, they make distinctions about the women who come to them for help, categorizing them as "deserving" and "undeserving" poor. Those who are deemed as problematic, and who do not fit the stereotype of the welfare client, can be punished and denied services.

Caroline Kingfisher profiles a conversation between two social workers and their supervisor and herself during her ethnography of a welfare office in Michigan. The social workers (F & S) and their supervisor (E) state:

22. Omolade 1994.
23. Kingfisher 2001.

E: You have to know when to be empathetic and when to, get out your whip.

F: I already know THAT, see? I'm, I'm empathetic to all my clients 'til they LIE to me, once they LIE to me I HATE them and I won't give them ANYthing. (laughs)

E: WHOA. (laughs)

S: (sarcastic tone) Not REVENGE (oh yeah).

F. Yes it IS (laughs).[24]

The social workers go on to express how they make women "jump more ropes" and wait for services when they are categorized as undeserving. Kingfisher states that the relationship between poor women and their social workers is very personalized and that workers actively regulate and punish their welfare clients. Given the fact that welfare rules make it nearly impossible for women to be "truthful" about their lives, most women can be constructed as liars, which has negative consequences for them. Those who are illegal drug users have even more reasons to fear being truthful.

Women, Welfare, and Illegal Drugs in the U.S.

Due to the belief that illegal drug use equals poor parenting, thirty states have enacted or amended child welfare statutes so that infants who test positive for drugs, or who show signs of NAS, are defined as "neglected" and/or "abused" and can be apprehended by the state.[25] These U.S. statutes often focus on illegal drugs rather than legal ones although a few include alcohol and specifically address concerns about FAS. Civil child abuse statutes and criminal child abuse laws assure that hospitals will create policy to drug-test pregnant women and their infants after birth. It also assures that positive tests for illegal drugs will be reported. In addition, the U.S. federal changes to welfare in 1996 authorized states to issue random drug tests of welfare recipients. However, Michigan was the only state to adopt it. The

24. Ibid: 274.
25. Paltrow, Cohen and Carey 2000a.

Michigan law was immediately challenged as unconstitutional. In October 2002, the U.S. Court of Appeals in Cincinnati unanimously held that the law is justified because the state has an interest in preventing crime- and drug-related child abuse.

Due to changes in federal welfare policy, civil child abuse statutes, and criminal child abuse laws, thousands of children have been apprehended by the state and placed in foster care. As noted earlier, some women have been charged in criminal court with child abuse. However, the majority of women suspected of using illegal drugs are vulnerable to civil child abuse statutes, welfare intervention, and child apprehension. Hospital staff notify welfare workers when women and/or infants test positive for drugs. As discussed in Chapter 2, women are tested without their consent and testing is highly subjective. Poor women and women of color in public hospitals are tested more often than those who deliver in private hospitals.[26] Drug testing cannot predict which infants will experience NAS or which parents may abuse their children. Policy *assumes* that testing positive for illegal drugs equals abusive parenting. This situation has led to a dire situation in an already overburdened foster-care system in the U.S. Prior to these changes in civil child welfare statutes, the number of children in foster care in the U.S. was actually on the decline, but since the mid-1980s, it has soared and this increase is due to "the perceived drug epidemic."[27]

By the end of the 1980s, the number of children in foster care had skyrocketed, and California and New York were responsible for over half of the increase. Furthermore, of those children in care, the majority were black children. In the Spring of 2000, 38 percent of the children in foster care in the U.S. were black children (down from 1999 when 42 percent were black children), even though they make up less than 17 percent of the general population.[28] However, in New York City at the end of 1997, 73 percent of the children in foster care were black.[29] Dorothy Roberts argues that the foster-care system in

26. Humphries et al. 1992; Noble 1997.

27. Noble 1997: 183.

28. U.S. Department of Health and Human Services 2002a; U.S. Department of Human Services 2002b.

29. Roberts 2002: 9.

U.S. cities functions as "an apartheid institution." She draws attention to the fact that foster-care case loads have tripled in some U.S. cities, and black children are taken from their parents with little thought for their well-being or consideration of the pain and dislocation they and their parents experience.

Since prenatal drug use was defined as child abuse and neglect, children have been taken from their mothers and placed in inadequate care. In New York City, infants have been confined to hospital wards for months then moved to temporary shelters, and some have been confined to cribs lined up like army barracks, where "once the infants learned to walk, the tops of their cribs were covered with bars in order to control them."[30] Amanda Noble argues that it is impossible to tell what negative psychological effects these punitive practices may have on them. In many states, a child's custody may rest on his or her mother's ability to complete a drug treatment program. Thus, the child remains in the state's custody until his or her mother completes treatment. Similar to drug court treatment programs, women are subjected to mandatory drug testing, 12-step programs, and very strict rules for up to a year. When women do not "do well" in programs and fail to complete them, they are punished and lose custody of their children. Amanda Noble describes how women who were charged with child abuse and forced to enter drug treatment are pathologized, and their experiences of race, class, and gender inequality are ignored. Not only are women viewed as having the disease of "addiction," they are now perceived as "child abusers as well."[31]

Additionally, women who are HIV-positive are being punished for failing to follow medical advice during their pregnancies and after the births of their infants. Women who refuse to take toxic anti-HIV drugs are also viewed as endangering the fetus. Mandatory testing of newborns for HIV in states like New York is a controversial ethical and legal issue. HIV-positive women who refuse to follow the AZT regime set up for their infants are threatened with child apprehension. Activists note that some studies demonstrate that infants prenatally exposed to AZT

30. Bussiere and Shauffer, as cited in Noble 1997: 185.
31. Noble 197: 187, 189.

are sicker than those not exposed. Other studies find that HIV-positive infants who were given AZT were more likely to develop AIDS than those infants who were not given the medication.[32] Mothers Opposing Mandatory Medicine (MOMM) are challenging medical and legal practices that limit women's choices regarding their own care and the care of their infants.[33] Women of color in the U.S., and Native Indian women in Canada, have the highest rates of HIV/AIDS, thus, they face greater risk of medical, social service, and legal intervention than other mothers. MOMM also provides information and contacts to people who want information about alternative medical care for HIV-positive infants and pregnant women. They have educational material and guidelines for HIV-positive women so that they can "exercise informed choice" and avoid legal complications, especially child apprehension.

Section 15

In the U.S., thousands of women suspected of using illegal drugs have lost their rights to welfare benefits, cash assistance, and housing. Since 1996, new welfare legislation seeks to punish them. Section 15 of the Personal Responsibility and Work Opportunity Reconciliation Act of 1996 prohibits anyone convicted of a state or federal felony offense associated with the use or sale of drugs from receiving federally funded cash and food stamps for life (Congress tried to have the law extended to misdemeanants, too). This legislation applies only to those convicted of drug offenses; thus, people convicted of murder are still eligible for welfare benefits. All states have the right to either modify section 15 or to opt out all togther. Patricia Allard points out that as of 2002, forty-two states have enforced the ban, twenty-two in full, and twenty have modified it. This policy impacts women and children disproportionally. However, Allard explains that women of color are especially affected because of race profiling in enforcement and drug policies, and as a result of "race and gender-based socioeconomic inequalities" that shape poverty and overrepresentation in the welfare system.[34]

---

32. Gerhard 2001.
33. Ibid.: 46.
34. Allard 2002: 2.

Of the twenty-one states Allard reviewed, 48 percent of the women affected by the ban were Latina and African American. She estimates that, in total, 92,000 women were no longer eligible to receive benefits for life and that 135,000 children were affected by the ban. The ban eliminates benefits for mothers; "in other words, a single-mother of one will receive cash assistance and food stamps to cover the expenses of her child, but not her."[35] Obviously this would have a negative impact on the whole family, not just the mother. These types of practices support the ideology that mothers and children are separate (just as the fetus is viewed as separate from the mother), when in fact they are not. In Patricia Hirch's 1999 study of women in Pennsylvania, twenty-two of the twenty-six mothers she interviewed were disfranchised from federal cash assistance and food stamps.[36] These women had been convicted of possessing very small amounts of drugs (U.S.$5–10 worth). For these nonviolent acts, women are denied financial support when needed and punished for life.

Interestingly, although moral reformers are quick to point out that women who use illegal drugs are a risk to their fetus and their children, they fail to see how welfare policy places children at risk. For any women leaving prison, or just attempting to raise their children, the ban assures that they will be permanently disadvantaged. Reintegration into the community will be severely limited, and maybe impossible. Many women will be unable to care for their families on such limited income and benefits, and loss of custody and family break up will result. Some states have modified the ban so that women who participate in drug treatment can be eligible for benefits; however, this ignores the facts that, nationally, drug treatment programs for women are scarce and waiting lists are long, especially for mothers with children. As well, it deflects attention away from the fact that Supplemental Security Income (SSI) is no longer available to people diagnosed with alcohol and drug addiction.

35. Ibid.: 8.
36. Hirch 1999.

Denial of welfare benefits is not restricted to those women who have been convicted of a drug offense. In some states, women who are identified as having a drug problem or whose infants test positive for drugs at birth may lose their benefits, too. For example, since 1995, any woman in South Carolina who has been identified as needing alcohol or drug treatment, gives birth to an infant showing NAS symptoms, or whose infant tests positive for drugs is ineligible for financial benefits. However, financial assistance may be reinstated if a woman agrees to random drug tests and/or drug treatment.[37]

HUD Housing

The U.S. Department of Housing and Urban Development (HUD) allows the Public Housing Authorities (PHAs) and Residence Management Corporations (RMCs) across the U.S. to deny "suspected" and convicted illegal drug users and sellers public housing. Residents of public housing, most often single mothers, can be evicted if suspected of using/selling illegal drugs and a criminal conviction is not necessary to establish proof. Residents can be evicted through civil procedures, which use a "a less stringent standard" than the criminal courts.[38] The Anti-Drug Abuse Act passed by Congress in 1988 allowed public housing leases to state that tenants can lose their apartments if guests or family members engage in drug-related criminal activity. By 1994, the Act was amended to include drug-related activity on or off public housing property. On March 26, 2002, the U.S. Supreme Court voted unanimously to overturn the 9th Circuit Court of Appeals' decision on *Department of Housing and Urban Development vs. Rucker,* which struck down the law allowing public housing tenants to be evicted if family members are suspected of illegal drug use/selling. Pearlie Rucker was the lead plaintiff in this case. Pearlie Rucker is a 65-year-old grandmother who was evicted from her apartment after her grandson was found with marijuana outside her public housing apartment. The Supreme Court ruling upholds the fed-

37. Ibid.: 57.
38. BJS 1992: 184.

eral act and gives public housing authorities the go-ahead to continue evicting families if they or their guests are suspected of using or selling illegal drugs.

HUD also works hand in hand with the Department of Justice to use asset forfeiture laws to seize the leasehold of those residents suspected of drug dealing. Residents can be easily evicted because they have no right to remain in their home without a lease. Residents are not allowed to run a business in their homes, and "suspected" drug dealers can be evicted for violating their public housing lease. In order for suspected drug users and sellers to be evicted quickly, public housing evictions have been expedited in forty-four states; the grievance procedure requirements for lease termination and eviction actions have been waived.[39] Thus, suspected drug users and dealers cannot appeal public housing decisions on lease termination and eviction actions. This policy disproportionately impacts women and their families, for it is women, especially poor single mothers, who make up the majority of those who live in HUD housing.

HUD's Public Housing Drug Elimination Program (PHDEP) provides funds to public housing. These funds have been used "to fight crime by increasing police coverage and security... to employ security personnel and investigators; to contract with private security services; to reimburse local law-enforcement agencies for above-baseline services." Although PHDEP funds are to provide "alternatives to crime and violence,"[40] HUD housing has done little to achieve this goal and has increasingly become the arm of state oppression.

Catherine Fitts, a former Deputy Assistant Secretary for HUD, states that the agency has become an enforcement operation that grants access to SWAT teams throughout the U.S. and polices neighbourhoods. Police raids are coordinated with HUD through a program called Operation Safe Home, and HUD has petitioned the U.S. government "for independent powers of seizure, so that the HUD can profit directly from seizures of drugs, and suspected drug-related

39. Ibid.: 185.
40. ONDCP 2001: 52.

cash."[41] In the presumed service of the drug war, HUD coordinates with SWAT teams to terrorize the poor, especially black women, and often their families are torn apart. Fitts also believes that the war on drugs is a means for SWAT teams to round up the poor and move them into private prisons where they become a financial resource; for the poor are worth more to corporations when they are in prison working for 10 cents a day "than when they are free."[42]

Welfare in Canada

Similar to the U.S. and Britain, Canada's welfare system has undergone massive restructuring since the 1990s. Much has been written about the cutbacks in the provinces of Alberta, Ontario, and British Columbia, where conservative governments have gutted the welfare state and moved toward privatization. However these changes were made possible after the Progressive Conservative government of Brian Mulroney pushed for greater integration with the U.S. and imposed a cap on increases in federal transfer payments to wealthy provinces. The limit imposed on the Canada Assistance Plan allowed provinces to reduce social spending and limited the federal government's ability to "impose" national welfare standards. Consequently, welfare policy became more individualized under the control of provincial governments. Some provinces began to cut social welfare benefits and introduced new definitions of employability that limited single mothers eligibility.[43] More drastic changes were made possible after the Liberal federal government, under the leadership of Jean Chrétien, discontinued the Canada Assistance Plan (CAP) and replaced it with the Canada Health an Social Tranfer (CHST) in 1996. The earlier CAP provided unlimited cost-shared funding for welfare to the provinces. Margaret Little[44] explores how the criteria for federal funding assured that some historical punitive welfare practices

41. Damuzi 2001: 56.
42. Ibid.
43. Bashevkin 2002: 21.
44. Little 2003.

would be abandoned. With CAP, the provinces had to provide assistance based solely on financial need, with no residential requirements, and appeal boards protecting recipients rights had to be established. She explains that workfare and employment-tied programs were prohibited. With the emergence of CHST, drastic changes occurred as national standards were discontinued. Thus, provinces could create their own criteria, refusing anyone they chose regardless of financial need. It also paved the way for workfare programs and the increased surveillance of women.

In Ontario, women saw cutbacks, from already inadequate monthly benefits, of up to 21.6 percent after welfare was changed under the Mike Harris government, which swept into power in 1995. Similar cutbacks occurred after Gordon Cambell's Liberal government was elected in B.C. in 2001. Some single mothers saw their benefits reduced by about Can$370 a month, a 46 percent reduction of benefits that covered only 45 to 65 percent of the minimum monthly cost of living.[45] From 2000 to 2002, 15,000 women have been removed from welfare assistance in B.C. Although some of these women may have found employment, the majority have not.[46] Welfare is no longer about helping the poor; rather, it is intent on ending what is labeled "welfare dependency."[47] Welfare dependency is a political construct that ignores the employment history of women, for most women on welfare have worked. It also ignores the struggles of single-parent mothers who hold down two and three low-paying jobs in order to provide for their children, including mothers participating in workfare programs.

The restructuring of welfare falls on mothers with children. Social researchers from all three nations—Pat Carlen in Britain; Slyvia Bashevkin, Margaret Little, and Jean Swanson in Canada; and Judith Goode and Jeff Maskovsky in the U.S. (to name a few)— note that "poor bashing" has become a national sport of which single mothers are the target.[48] In Britain, Canada, and the U.S., cutbacks are de-

45. B.C. CEDAW Group 2003: 14–15.
46. Reitsma-Steet and Prentice 2002.
47. Morgen and Weigt 2001.
48. See Bashevkin 2002; Carlen 1998; Goode and Maskovsky 2001; Little 2003; and Swanson 2001.

picted as necessary because of single mothers' immorality and their refusal to work. In Ontario, former Premier Harris, furthered rationalized intrusive welfare interventions by claiming that women on welfare were drug users. He proposed that all welfare recipients undergo drug testing and abstain from drugs, and those who refused would risk losing their benefits.[49] This policy was depicted by the provincial government as

> common sense—you can't get off welfare and hold a job if you're addicted to drugs. That's why we'll provide mandatory treatment for welfare recipients who use drugs. We'll help them get off drugs, off welfare and back on their feet again. Those who refuse treatment or who won't take tests on request will lose their benefits.[50]

Harris also cut back extra allowances provided for pregnant women and mothers with young children. He claimed that they were spending their allowances on beer, which they gave away to their boyfriends. The gutting of the welfare system was accompanied by reform focusing on neglect and child protection at the expense of family unity. New ideologies concerning "dangerous mothers" and technologies to monitor them have emerged.[51]

Similar to concerns in the U.S. about women who are present in drug-production operations, B.C. social workers have recently targeted marijuana growers. In March 2000, forty-two children were apprehended by the state during marijuana raids, even though, there was no evidence of abuse. The police consistently construct marijuana production as the domain of foreigners and motorcycle gangs, outsiders to the "Canadian way of life." Canadian journalist Denny Launders notes that all but four of the children apprehended by the state were Vietnamese.[52] Racial profiling of "grow" operations deflects attention away from the numerous marijuana grow operations run by white working- and middle-class people who supplement their in-

49. Macdonald et al. 2001.
50. Etsten 2000: 8.
51. Chen 2003.
52. Launders 2000.

comes in the lower mainland and in depressed areas of B.C. It also deflects attention away from the fact that marijuana production contributes to the provincial economy. Launders explores how race and drug prohibition share an overlapping history in B.C., and that the apprehension of Vietnamese children is a form of cultural genocide.

Native Indian children are also at risk of child apprehension in B.C. and other provinces in Canada.[53] Even though First Nations people represent 3–4 percent of the population in B.C., the Report of the Aboriginal Committee in 1992 found that over half the children in foster care were First Nations;[54] in 2002, 44.3 percent of the children in care were First Nations.[55] Social work researcher Ben Carniol notes that colonization and racism shape social work practice in Canada, and he calls for structural and policy changes.[56] However, in provinces like Ontario and British Columbia, welfare policy has become more repressive, especially in relation to women suspected of drug use.

In B.C., the Ministry of Children and Family Development has developed the "Protocol Framework and Working Guidelines between Child Protection and Alcohol and Drug Services."[57] The protocol claims that "substance misuse is a significant variable in a number of harms to children including but not limited to: Sudden Infant Death Syndrome; pre-natal harm resulting in Fetal Alcohol Syndrome or Effects or Neonatal Abstinence Syndrome (FAS, FAE and NAS); emotional abuse and neglect, physical abuse and family violence." Alcohol and illegal drug use are associated with child abuse in the protocol; however, there is no evidence provided to support the claim or any of the other claims listed. Social workers are required to assess twenty-three risk factors to determine whether children need protection. The gender-neutral language employed deflects attention away from the fact that most parents being assessed are mothers. The abuse and neglect of the mother when she was a child, and alcohol and drug use are identified as risk factors. Similar to risk assessment protocols

53. Monture 1989.
54. Report of the Aboriginal Committee 1992: 1.
55. British Columbia Child Protection Division 2002.
56. Carniol 2000.
57. British Columbia Ministry of Children and Family Development 2003

for women in Canadian prisons, these assessments are "individualized instruments" that exclude social and economic factors. Most women who have suffered class, gender, and race inequality could be assessed as at risk.

The sharing of information is central to the protocol, and social workers have access to the addiction service assessments of their clients and to information about their ongoing treatment. They can request drug screening to monitor mothers' abstinence. Abstinence and behavioral changes are the stated goals for mothers with little attention being paid to economic and social factors such as lack of affordable housing, inability to earn a living wage, insufficient welfare rates, and institutionalized racism that shape the lives of women and their children in negative ways. Mothers assessed as having harmful alcohol or drug use are expected to participate in "therapeutic work during the day, evening and/or weekend sessions over a period of weeks." Only those women who "have stable living arrangements, may have supportive employment, support of friends, family and who are not subject to overwhelming pressures, problems and inducements to resume substance misuses" can undertake drug treatment in a nonresidential setting.[58] The narrow criteria laid out in the protocol will assure that most mothers who are assessed as "at risk" will be forced to attend residential treatment programs. There is no discussion how their absence from their children may negatively impact them or their children. Nor is there any discussion about the failure of drug treatment programs to offer women realistic alternatives in relation to their drug use and the social and economic factors that shape their lives. Rather, women who are constructed as "at risk" are forced to follow narrow criteria and standards of behavior that most nondrug using mothers would be unable to achieve. Thus, mothers are set up for failure, and those who are able to comply with the criteria set out by both social workers and addiction services do so against almost insurmountable odds.

In practice, children in B.C. have been apprehended when their parents have been arrested for the sale or production of illegal drugs, suspected of using drugs during their pregnancy, or in relation to

58. Ibid: 2, 17.

their drug history. Studies from the 1950s on demonstrate that poor women in the province who are visible, illegal drug users are vulnerable to child apprehension by the state, especially First Nations women. For women who have been suspected of using illegal drugs during pregnancy, the labeling of their infants NAS has assured that they would be apprehended by the state.[59]

Sunny Hill Hospital

In 1983, a special program for children labeled NAS was developed in Vancouver, B.C., at Sunny Hill Hospital for Children. In the first ten years, an estimated 372 children were treated at the inpatient NAS program. These infants were subjected to experimental treatment based on "'hunches' lacking in scientific validity," and these 'hunches' "were based on ideological assumptions concerning mothering," illegal drugs, and poverty.[60] It was believed by the director, and many of the staff, that mothers who used illegal drugs did not have the same "maternal instincts" as other mothers. The infants were isolated in tiny darkened rooms and subjected to sensory deprivation, and light, touch, and sound were limited for anywhere up to one to six months. Mothers and nurses were not allowed to touch the babies except briefly when feeding, bathing, or changing them. The infants were not rocked, cuddled, or spoken to, because it was thought that this would overstimulate them. It was believed by the staff at Sunny Hill that the infants needed a low-stimulation environment to reduce the symptoms of NAS. Thus, they lay in cribs, with blackout curtains around them, all day and night in the darkened rooms.

All of the mothers of the infants admitted into the program in the first ten years were on welfare, and 60 percent were Native Indian. As well, two-thirds of all the infants were permanently apprehended by the state and never returned to their mothers. At Sunny Hill, the director of the program and support staff worked hand in hand with

59. Boyd 1999.

60. For a more in-depth discussion of the Sunny Hill NAS program see Boyd 1999, chapter 3.

social services. The director often gave evidence in family court proceedings that NAS infants had special needs and were at risk for short- and long-term problems (according to criteria they developed). Until recently there was no oppositional medical opinion. Of those 372 infants who were "treated" at the Sunny Hill NAS inpatient program in the first ten years, many never demonstrated any NAS symptoms; nevertheless, they were kept in the darkened room for long periods of time (two weeks to three months) because of a lack of foster-care placement openings.

In addition to the experimental treatment the infants were subjected to, the program was hostile toward the mothers and, while their infants were in the inpatient program, failed to provide mothers with clear guidelines and protocol that would ensure their children would return home. In contrast, those few women who were able to bring their infants home from the program had to follow strict NAS follow-up care policy that further limited touch, sound, and light for the first year, and social workers and public health nurses visited to make sure that mothers followed the medical protocols provided after their inpatient stay. Follow-up medical examinations at the NAS outpatient program were also expected. The restrictions almost guaranteed that mothers would find it difficult to maintain custody. One woman spoke about her life after her baby was allowed to come home:

> They gave you these rules and regulations when you bring him home. How to care for him, how to approach him, how to touch him, how to keep him wrapped tight. To avoid the noise, the TV and vacuum cleaner and stuff like that . Loud groups of people and stuff like that. I was just scared. Everything the paper told me to do for NAS, it was like I can't just go out, I can't take my son out, I can't go visit my family... I was just so afraid because I couldn't go anywhere, I had no transportation. I couldn't take my baby on the bus, couldn't do anything. Take him to the store, I mean, it was like I was locked in this place, and the place I had was...one little bedroom, one little livingroom with a kitchen.[61]

---

61. Ibid.: 97–98.

Although a number of hospitals in B.C. developed similar programs, outside the province, NAS treatment was very different. Programs advocated mothers' participation and the touching and massaging of infants. Breast feeding was encouraged, and unless there were other medical conditions that needed treatment, infants who experienced NAS symptoms went home with their mothers after a short stay in the hospital ranging from three to fourteen days.

The NAS program at Sunny Hill has changed significantly since the founding director left and innovative programs have been developed for pregnant women and new mothers in Vancouver. A new postpartum unit was opened in January 2003 at B.C. Women's Hospital in Vancouver. The program is designed to keep mothers, and newborns exposed to drugs, together after delivery. However, the legacy of Sunny Hill continues and should be viewed as a cautionary lesson for future programs.

Apprehension of the Fetus

Social workers in Canada have also extended their domain of regulation through the surveillance of drug use, including maternal drug use. A number of legal cases emphasize their concern and shifting practices to "apprehend the fetus" in order to protect it from suspected illegal drug use by pregnant women. There were a number of legal cases in the 1980s and 1990s where women's reproductive autonomy was severely limited.[62] What is most significant about these cases is the attempt to apprehend a child that was not yet born, for the term "child" under the Family and Child Service Act refers to one that has been delivered, and the fetus cannot become a ward of the court. Thus, these cases challenged the legal construct of the term child and opened it up to debate and possible redefinition. Attempts to redefine the fetus as a child needing protection undermines women's reproductive autonomy. These cases are also significant as women labeled deviant and unfit or who fail to follow medical or social service advice could be subject to involuntary detention, forced Caesarean sections, drug treatment, and prison.

62. Lorna Turnbull 2001 provides a good overview.

In 1996, the Winnipeg Child and Family Services brought forward an application to the court to force a young Native Indian woman who was pregnant to enter treatment. Social services claimed that she was addicted to solvents and they sought to protect the unborn child. The Manitoba court ordered the young woman into treatment until her baby was born. The media sensationalized the case and depicted this woman as already having two children who were brain damaged due to her maternal solvent use. The media, social services, and the court assumed that there was a causal link between maternal solvent use and damage to the fetus, when in fact there is not. A review of the literature, including forty-three studies, on solvent exposure during pregnancy highlights that a "definable foetal solvent syndrome" has not been demonstrated.[63] On appeal, the Manitoba court made it clear that child welfare officials cannot force pregnant women into drug treatment and the fetus is not a legal person, thus the pregnant woman's right's take precedence. The young woman gave birth to a full-term, healthy child. However, the case went to the Supreme Court of Canada, and in 1997, it ruled that the courts cannot detain and order treatment for pregnant women to protect the fetus and that the unborn child does not possess legal rights (*Winnipeg Child and Family Services [Northwest Area] v. G. [D.F.]* 1997). This ruling has not stopped legal challenges from occurring; however, it did send an important message to social services and moral regulators that strive to "protect the fetus" at the expense of women's rights. Women who use illegal drugs in Canada have not experienced the same level of intervention as their counterparts in the U.S.

Welfare and Illegal Drug Use in Britain

Margaret Thatcher, representing the Conservative Party, promised to restructure the welfare state if she was elected. In 1979, her party won the election and proceeded to dismantle the welfare state. One of the ways this was accomplished was to limit eligibility for welfare

---

63. Addiction Research Foundation 1997: 2; Medrano 1996.

benefits and to cut back on rates. Thatcher was especially appalled by teenage mothers and claimed that an underclass of dependent mothers had emerged. The welfare state was to blame. Thatcher's emphasis on greater self-sufficiency was realized as tighter social welfare policy and lower benefits were imposed. The market was viewed as the answer to welfare dependency. John Major's conservative government followed in Thatcher's footsteps and initiated policy that granted incentives for women on welfare assistance to work, restructured unemployment insurance (lowering benefits and limiting eligibility), and followed-up with a crackdown on perceived welfare fraud. However, the Labour Party's return to majority power after the election of Tony Blair in 1997 has not countered the conservative restructuring of social welfare policy. Rather, policy has become more punitive and benefits to single parents have been reduced. Blair has cited U.S. workfare programs as the wave of the future and, in 1998, voluntary workfare programs were set up under the New Deals programs for single parents on assistance. However, compared with the U.S. and Canada, the British welfare system is still more generous.[64]

British researchers Julian Buchanan and Lee Young state that the government legitimized cutbacks by constructing the welfare recipient as dishonest and unwilling to work. The welfare recipient that was singled out was the single mother. In Britain, rather than provide support to mothers with children, "surveillance of problem families" became central.[65] They note that the Children Act 1989 and the NHS and Community Care Act 1990 restructured social work so that it became more closely entwined with the police and the medical community. Because social workers were already a profession under siege, due to conservative ideology and policy shifts, they shifted from being advocates of the poor to child protection workers. The focus on child protection rather than on caring for families further marginalized mothers who used illegal drugs. They note that often the decision to register or take a child into care had more to do with protecting the

64. See Sylvia Bashevkin 2002, *Welfare Hot Bottons*, a comparative study of contemporary social policy change in Britain, Canada, and the U.S.

65. Buchanan and Young 2002: 202.

social worker than the child. Women noted that social workers failed to offer support when they were in need; however, when clients were arrested on drug charges or sent to prison, social workers were quick to intervene and apprehend their children.[66]

Even with the demonization of single mothers on welfare by the press, accompanied by welfare reform and increased regulation of women, there are significant differences in policy in Britain, compared with the U.S. and Canada, especially in the area of maternal drug use. For example, the Standing Conference on Drug Abuse (SCODA) and the Local Government Drugs Forum (LGDF), which sets out guidelines for interagencies, make it clear that drug use in itself does not warrant separating a child from its mother. As early as 1986, the Clinical Social Workers Group, which was established by SCODA, recognized that drug use in itself does not "indicate child neglect and abuse," and "it is not automatically the case that parents are more capable without their drugs."[67] This policy is quite radical compared with social welfare legislation in the U.S. that equates maternal drug use with neglect and abuse, and Canadian social work policy that views illegal drug use as a risk factor and probable evidence of neglect and abuse. British researchers Marcia Jackson and Hilary Klee note that many of the social workers they interviewed in their study stated that they were aware of the negative image of social workers and worked hard to change it by communicating better and by offering support rather than crises intervention to their clients.[68] In addition, overrepresentation of children of color in care is less than in the U.S. and Canada. Of those children looked after by local councils in Britain in 2001, black children (including Foreign Nationals) accounted for 7 percent, mixed ethnic children accounted for 6 percent, Asian children accounted for 3 percent, and white children made up 80 percent.[69]

66. Wolfe 1999.
67. Shapiro 1992: 36, 38.
68. Jackson and Klee 2002.
69. Department of Health 2001.

Conclusion

The changes in British, Canadian, and U.S. medical, social service, and legal policy over the last thirty years to identify, regulate, and punish women suspected of using illegal drugs are linked to larger political shifts. Little attention is given to the fact that state law increasingly accommodates the interests of global capitalism and the wealthy. Corporations receive tax breaks and incentives that contribute to national debt loads, unsafe workplaces, and downsizing. Rather than examine corporate welfare, the state focuses on single-parent mothers and constructs them as a drain on social services. The perceived danger and immorality of women who use illegal drugs legitimize punitive economic cutbacks and social policy that promote further neoliberal agendas. Furthermore, attempts to regulate maternal drug use and the war on drugs intersect with movements that seek to limit women's reproductive autonomy. The regulation of women often centers on her ability to reproduce and on her central role as a mother.

Chapter 4

A Sociological Perspective of Drug Use and Treatment

Today, women in the U.S. who use illegal drugs are being punished by social service and legal agents and are increasingly subject to civil and criminal sanctions related to maternal drug use; however, voluntary drug treatment services have not expanded proportionately. Drug treatment is often viewed as an alternative to criminal sanctions, yet not all drug treatment is voluntary. A number of civil child abuse and civil commitment laws in the U.S. force women who use illegal drugs to enter drug treatment programs. Further, few alternative options outside of drug treatment or prison have been developed for women who use illegal drugs.

Drug treatment can refer to long-term residential centers, individual and group counseling, day-treatment centers, and self-help groups such as Alcoholics Anonymous (AA) and Narcotics Anonymous (NA). Drug treatment can be voluntary or coerced. President Bush Jr.'s drug strategy for 2003, which calls "upon the power of faith" to "create a new climate of 'compassionate coercion'" uses the criminal justice system to force people into drug treatment.[1] Conventional ideology defines alcohol and drug use as a medical and/or legal problem. The legal perspective sees the drug user as a criminal and the medical perspective is premised on an "addiction as disease" philosophy. Although these two models appear incompatible at first glance, the criminal justice system and drug treatment programs deal with

1. Drugscope 2002.

this contradiction by merging both models into a disease (medical)/criminal model of addiction.[2]

Historical Background

In the mid-1800s, the field of "addiction" became a new "growth area" for doctors. Reporting the physical symptoms of addiction and later attempting to define nonmedical and medical use took a backseat to psychological emphasis. The woman addicted to morphine was viewed as a "morphinomaniac" who "did not really want to be cured and had therefore to be treated like a lunatic." Morality, moral weakness, and personal responsibility have been important elements in the medical theory of addiction. Early on, opium eating was "medicalized; but failure to achieve a cure was a failure of personal responsibility, not medical science."[3] Similar to today, medical treatment was advocated for the white middle- and upper-class user, and prohibition and criminal sanctions were advocated for poor and working class users. The adoption of the disease model narrowed other options and understanding of drug dependence and treatment options. The historical, political, social, and economic environment were ignored in favor of disease theories, and the medical profession adopted much of the moral discourse espoused by the anti-opium and temperance movements.

Throughout the 1800s and 1900s, opiates and other drugs were "literally taken away from the people" and became the property of doctors,[4] and, of course, the criminal justice system. By the 1800s, the suppression of altered states of consciousness was aided by the emergence of positivism and the dominance of "objective" knowledge. Positivism heralded the "romanticization of the rational" over the subjective experience.[5] In Western society, altered states of consciousness (including mystic, ritual, and meditative) were considered as unsci-

2. Alexander 1990.
3. Berridge and Edwards 1981: 152, 153, 156.
4. Ibid. 242.
5. Noonan 2002: 119.

entific and subjective, and were often associated with pathological states.[6] In the mid-1800s, as drug use became medicalized and criminalized, the medical profession was quick to establish itself as the leader in the identification and treatment of drug/alcohol "addiction." Charles Terry and Mildred Pellens confirm that doctors themselves constructed narcotic addiction as their domain from this period into the early 1900s, and have contributed to much of the misinformation about it.[7] Their review of the early medical literature on narcotic addiction leads them to assert that the evidence is incomplete and confused. They claim that treatment most often consisted of separating the user from drugs, and that doctors were dogmatic in their adoption of withdrawal as the primary treatment option. They state that doctors assumed that withdrawal and abstinence brought about some type of cure. The authors have warned against using such "arbitrary procedures" on the general population; however, their warnings have not been heeded by most moral reformers. The disease model of addiction dominates in many Western nations today, and it is "an individualistic, privatizing ideology"[8] which continues to shape drug policy. The disease model "has always existed with earlier notions about free choice and moral culpability."[9] Thus, people addicted to drugs are held personally responsible for their failure to abstain.

The disease model of alcoholism has become the template for drug treatment in the U.S. and Canada. Alcoholics Anonymous (AA), which emerged in the mid-1930s, was premised on the disease model of addiction. However, the popularity of the disease model increased in the 1960s when I.M. Jellinek, a specialist on alcoholism, advocated the 12-step principle and the medical model/disease model of addiction in his book *The Disease Concept of Alcoholism*.[10] Critics claim that Jellinek's work has "no scientific value" and is methodologically flawed. His conclusions were drawn from a small self-selection of Alcoholics Anonymous members who were male. Although there is no

---

6. Deikman 1969; Tart 1969.
7. Terry and Pellens 1970.
8. Ibid. 229.
9. Reinarman 1988: 110.
10. Bufe 2000b: 30

scientific evidence to support biological or genetic explanations of addiction, the medical model advocates that addiction is biological, progressive, and permanent.[11] Therefore, abstinence and relapse management are central to drug treatment. In addition, continued surveillance is justified, regardless of sobriety, due to the risk of relapses. Drug treatment services, 12-step treatment (including AA and NA), self-help groups, and individuals have also adopted the premise that addiction is a biological, progressive disease that is predictable and irreversible and that culminates in loss of control if the individual continues to use drugs. They consider addiction to be permanent and believe that relapse may occur at anytime. Thus, abstinence is central to recovery.[12] Step one of the 12-step philosophy of AA states clearly that individuals are "powerless" over their drugs. Denial of addiction is a cornerstone of the disease model, and efforts to regard one's drug use in any other terms are perceived as evidence of denial.

Drug researchers Stanton Peele, Charles Bufe, and Archie Brodsky note that today over 90 percent of all drug treatment programs are 12-step programs in the U.S., and the recovery movement is a $10-billion-dollar-a-year industry, with little effect on rates of alcohol and drug addiction.[13] AA and NA dominate the addiction field—as voluntary treatment options decrease, especially for poor people, coerced participation in AA and NA increases. Charles Bufe explores how individuals are coerced into 12-step programs through criminal justice diversion programs (drug courts); condition of probation; prisons where attendance is linked to parole or release; employment programs; professional diversion programs for doctors, lawyers, and so on; teenagers being forced by parents; and welfare recipients being subjected to drug testing.[14] AA's 1996 survey of its membership revealed that roughly 40 percent of its participants were there involuntarily, while 50 percent of participants in NA were coerced.[15] Further,

11. Peele and Brodsky, with Arnold 1991.

12. The nicotine found in cigarettes and the caffeine found in soda-pop, coffee, and tea are curiously excluded from abstinence programs.

13. Peele, Bufe, with Brodsky 2000.

14. Bufe 2000b: 26.

15. Ibid.: 27–28.

the authors note that 12-step programs have a huge dropout rate, possibly over 90 percent.[16]

The dominance of 12-step programs and the disease model of addiction renders all other experiences of drug use and cessation of drug use invisible. Controlled use is the norm, but this reality is ignored as we are instructed daily to discipline ourselves in relation to our behaviors, which are personalized. In this way we participate in ruling ourselves.[17] However, those who fail to self-govern their drug use are constructed as "social problems," justifying more intrusive interventions by family members, professionals, and the state.

The debate on the nature of addiction colors law, policy, and practice. Treatment advocates often seek to replace or limit criminal justice with therapeutic social control. The drug court movement exemplifies this point. However, the philosophy of the drug courts in the U.S., and to a lesser extent in Britain and Canada, is "the same philosophy underlying civil commitment and the notion of *parens patriae*, namely, that the state has the obligation to divert into treatment certain defendants who pose a threat to themselves or others, in the process circumventing due process."[18] Conventional advocates of the therapeutic drug court movement in the U.S. claim that an addict's condition "is closer to insanity (in some of its forms) than to corruption of character in the usual sense."[19] As definitions of insanity have expanded, illegal drug users are viewed as sick, in need of treatment, and, curiously, in need of punishment. James Chriss critiques the drug court movement and argues that medicalization of illegal drug use will not "alleviate the problems associated with" it, and possibly it will make it worse. He also notes that the growing tendency in the U.S. to include marijuana "under the umbrella of addictive substances is dubious."[20] Regardless of the critics' views and the evidence about the harm caused by both the medicalization and criminalization of illegal drug users, treatment programs, like prisons, have become growing industries.

16. Bufe and Peele 2000: 44–70.
17. Cruikshank 1996: 248.
18. Chriss 2002: 202.
19. Shell 2002: 183.
20. Chriss 2002: 204, 205.

Alternative Views

Central to the debates surrounding illegal drug use is the negative and addictive quality of specific drugs, especially heroin and cocaine. But these drugs are not as dangerous or as "addictive" as generally believed, and numerous studies demonstrate that controlled use is not only possible but frequent.[21] People have been able not only to control their illegal drug use but also to stop using drugs without the aid of drug treatment professionals of self-help groups like AA and NA.[22] Although drug users may lose control of their use, it is not "impossible" to regain control again or to stop using without professional help.[23] There is a wealth of research that demonstrates how programs that focus on controlled use of alcohol and drugs are more effective than abstinence programs.[24] In fact, as sociologist Norman Zinberg notes, most people who consume alcohol and drugs regularly employ their own control mechanisms and drug use rituals. For many, especially among youths, loss of control is followed by control.[25]

The "war on drugs" discourse claims that self-controlled use of illegal drugs is impossible, which has a negative impact on illegal drug users who may have no, or little, access to alternative information. Dan Waldorf, Craig Reinarman, and Sheigla Murphy state that one of the reasons that the participants in their 1991 study on cocaine were able to control their use was that they believed it was possible and that cocaine was not as addicting as U.S. government

---

21. Alexander 1990; Blackwell 1983; Boyd 1999; Cohen 1989; Decorte, 2000; Erickson, Adlaf, Murray, and Smart 1987; Hanson et al. 1985; Robins 1975; Waldorf, Reinarman, and Murphy 1991; Winick 1962; Zingberg 1984.

22. Blackwell 1983; Boyd 1999; Decorte 2000; Erickson et al. 1987; Matthews 1995; Reinarman 1979; Waldorf et al. 1977; Waldorf et al. 1991; Winick 1962.

23. See Alexander 1990; Biernaki 1986; Blackwell 1983; Boyd 1999; Decorte 2000; Erickson et al. 1987; Matthews 1995; Peele and Brodsky 1991; Peele, Bufe and Brodsky 2000; Stevenson et al. 1956; Waldorf et al. 1991; Winick 1962.

24. Gamble and George 1997; Marlatt and Baer 1997; Peele, Bufe, with Brodsky 2000; Plant 1997; Zinberg 1984.

25. Zinberg 1984.

and media propaganda suggested.[26] Depictions of illegal drugs as overwhelming, powerful, and instantly addictive contribute to people's fear of them, and of themselves, rather than to drug treatment regimes and policy. These images also contribute to the glamorization of illegal drugs.

Political leaders and residents often cry out that drugs such as crack and heroin are destroying their communities. Of course negative drug use can be harmful, but critics of the disease model of addiction point out that people have a wide range of experiences in relation to drug use, and drug use is not static. It is not the drug that compels its use, rather it is the relationship with specific drugs that may shape an individual's pattern of drug use. Most people who use drugs, both legal and illegal, are able to use them recreationally without fear of escalated use or negative addiction. The majority of people who engage in the ritual and recreational use of illegal and legal drugs have described their experiences as positive.[27] However, current drug policy denies the existence of such a phenomenon, and the "war on drugs" attempts to wipe out all memory of "sensual enjoyment of drugs."[28] Although some people use drugs for fun, others use drugs to heal, "to work longer hours, enhance work or school performance... [to] alleviate hunger, reduce physical or emotional pain, fend off sleep, help to induce sleep... and as a strategy to cope" with political and economic factors such as war and violence.[29]

A person's relationship with drugs can be either negative or positive and this may vary according to "set and setting." Set refers to a person's attitudes and expectations about a specific drug and can be more important than the pharmacology of a drug in shaping a user's long-term relationship with a particular drug; and setting refers to the physical, cultural, and social environment where the drug is

26. Waldorf et al. 1991.

27. Alexander 1990; Boyd 1999; Davis 1996; Decorte 2000; Hadaway, Beyerstein, and Youdale 1991; Trebach 1982; Weil and Rosen 1998; Wodak 1992.

28. Larsen 1998: 10.

29. Gruskin, Plafker, and Smith-Estelle 2001: 1955.

taken.[30] Norman Zinberg explored how social sanctions, social controls, and rituals also shape drug use.[31] Social sanctions include informal social controls as well as formal social controls such as the law. Rituals may include waiting till after five to have a drink, never "bogarting" a joint (refusing to share), and using specific drugs for spiritual purposes. When new drugs are introduced for mass consumption, such as gin and other cheap distilled alcohol in the 1700s or crack in the mid-1980s, norms and rituals around their use do not exist. However, over time, users create informal social controls to regulate their own use and to mitigate harm to themselves. The state often reacts to perceived drug threats by enacting formal laws to prohibit use. Thus, the pharmacology of a drug, set and setting, and informal and formal social controls shape drug use.

In addition, history, race, class, and gender mediate one's drug use. A number of researchers have noted that alternative cultures, including street culture, and illegal drug use can sometimes be viewed as an act of resistance and a search for dignity in the face of economic marginalization, gender inequality, and racism.[32] However, criminologist Neil Websdale states that we should be cautious of looking at the illegal economy in poor neighborhoods as an "entirely oppositional culture." He notes that "such a conceptualization masks many similarities" between those who engage in street crime and "so-called noncriminal members of their communities."[33] In addition, sometimes drug use is labeled negative and self-destructive when, in fact, it is the opposite; it is more a belief in one's indestructibility.

Negative Drug Use

Many researchers, including feminists, have noted that trauma, including sexual abuse and exposure to trauma, may be a predictor to

30. Weil and Rosen 1998; Zingberg, 1984.
31. Zingberg 1984.
32. Bourgois 1995.
33. Websdale 2001: 178.

women's legal and illegal drug use.[34] However, drug researcher Lisa Maher challenges the idea that there is a casual relationship between early victimization and later drug use. Her ethnographic study of women who use and sell crack highlights women's agency and how women's lives are shaped in a patriarchal, racist, and class-based environment. She warns that any casual link between women's early victimization, such as child abuse, reduces drug use to a "mere psychological effect."[35]

Bruce Alexander, a Canadian psychologist and drug researcher, defines addiction as an "overwhelming involvement with the use of a drug" or other activities.[36] However, addiction is not necessarily good or bad, because being addicted to coffee, heroin, or reading may not harm a person or society. In contrast, "negative" addiction refers to destructive types of behavior, "where in the absence of achievable, healthy possibilities... lifestyles [are] built around... violence and excess." Alexander writes that negative drug use is not really a "drug problem," rather it is "part of a much larger pattern of social response to prolonged dislocation."[37] He broadly defines dislocation as poverty of the spirit, "the absence of that essential integration and identification with family, community, society and spiritual values that makes 'straight' life bearable most of the time and joyful at its peaks."[38]

Alexander states that "the link between the new economy and addiction is called 'dislocation,'" and argues that dislocation emerges in global market-driven societies where traditional culture, economies, and social relationships are destroyed. He claims that the "historical correlation between severe dislocation and addiction are strong."[39] Free market economies contribute to the dislocation of individuals (familial abuse) and groups (state violence against Aboriginal people) contributing to self-destructive behaviors.[40] Alexander is describing

34. MacKinnon 1991; Sanders-Phillips 1998.
35. Maher 1995: 5.
36. Alexander 1990: 104.
37. Alexander 1998: 29.
38. Ibid.: 28, 29.
39. Alexander 2001: 3, 13.
40. Alexander 1998: 28, 29.

the impact of global market forces, continued colonization, and alienation. Negative drug use and dislocation are linked to early capitalism and the dislocation of the poor in Ireland and Scotland, increased immigration to cities in England, the wretchedness of work and living conditions for the masses of poor, and disorderly gin use in England and in the new colonies in the 1700s. In addition, drawing from Frantz Fanon, I would argue that dislocation, which can derive from the colonial experience,[41] includes the institution of slavery, reserves and reservations, residential schools, and more recently, racial profiling which has led to an increase in child-welfare apprehensions and to the build up of the prison-industrial complex. Alexander notes that *negative drug use is only one type of response to dislocation.* In addition, negative drug use is not just a determined response; rather, it is sometimes a response to multiple social factors. Just as drug use varies, so too does negative drug use. People within the same social, cultural, and economic environment may use drugs differently and for different reasons.

Alexander also argues that the debates about whether illegal drug use and addiction are criminal or medical problems are misguided, for they are neither. Rather, "in a free market economy, the spread of addiction is primarily a political, social, and economic problem."[42] Dennis Sullivan and Larry Tifft, advocates of restorative justice, state that in a free market economy, hierarchal structural conditions and social arrangements shape people's lives and make it difficult for them to have their needs met.[43] Thus, drugs are not destroying our communities; it is the social, economic, and political inequality that is contributing to community disintegration. Norwegian criminologist, Nils Christie refers to "killed neighborhoods,"[44] those sections of cities throughout the United States and elsewhere that have been economically devastated. Economic violence coupled with race and gender inequality corrode the social fabric of families, communities, and nations. Since the 1980s, public housing has been cutback in Britain,

41. Fanon 1967; Monture-Angus 2000.
42. Alexander 2001: 19.
43. Sullivan and Tifft 2001.
44. Christie 1993.

Canada, and the U.S., and gentrification has thrived in this climate of privatization.[45] Local, state, and federal political and economic policies shape the lives of people in inner cities in the U.S. as it does in Britain and Canada. Negative drug use and selling may be one response to social-structural violence. The larger question which is rarely asked is how can violent social conditions be transformed, rather than how can zero tolerance for drugs be achieved?

Criminogist Neil Websdale describes the "blatant apartheid" that defines U.S. inner cities in his book *Policing the Poor: From Slave Plantation to Public Housing*. He notes that

> there are remarkable and disturbing homologies among the control of African slaves in the American colonies, the regulation of freedmen and freedwomen during nineteenth-century Reconstruction and Redemption, and the close surveillance and punitiveness directed at blacks in postindustrial inner cities.[46]

Other critical writers like bell hooks also explore how social factors such as internalized racism and white supremacy shape women's drug use.[47] However, most drug treatment programs are not interested in hearing about "individualized and systemic colonialism"[48] that affects individuals, families, and communities and that may precipitate negative drug use and conflict with the law. As bell hooks notes, it is "sex, race and class as factors which *together* determine the social construction of femaleness."[49]

Women's experience of illegal drug use is also shaped by social factors such as colonization, the law; race, class, and gender oppression; and social service and medical regulation. A Native Indian woman from B.C. who works in the field of drug treatment, describes negative addiction to alcohol as stemming

45. Smith 1996: 87.
46. Websdale 2001: 8.
47. hooks 1993.
48. Monture-Angus 2000: 57.
49. hooks 1989: 23.

> from a loss of sense of self, which happened with the outlawing of ceremony a hundred years ago. Ceremony brought meaning to life—ceremonies for birth; ceremonies when girls had their first menstruation and became a woman and her body was something to be honoured; ceremonies when young boys became men; ceremonies based on names; ceremonies dealing with death and pain...and the outlawing of ceremony was done just before the really big push for residential school. The whole structure of relationships within the community was devastated with that first law outlawing ceremonies and with residential school. I think three groups were responsible [the Church, the Canadian government, and the Canadian people].[50]

First Nations activist and scholar Patricia Monture-Angus writes that colonization makes it difficult for communities, families, and individuals to be healthy and functional.[51] Rather than focusing solely on the dysfunction of the individual or the dysfunction of the family, it is worth our while to acknowledge the historical and gendered nature of violence inflicted on Aboriginal women that is significantly different than the violence inflicted on women of European descent in North America. Violence against Aboriginal women in North America is entrenched in law, as well as in "the criminal justice, child welfare, and residential school experiences."[52] For many black women in Britain, Canada, and the U.S., the historical legacy of slavery shapes their lives. Women of color in colonized nations are viewed as less deserving of rights and protection and are more vulnerable to state violence and intervention. As bell hooks notes, "by perpetuating and upholding domination, society invests, so to speak, in the ill health of certain groups, all the better to oppress them."[53]

---

50. Maracle 1993: 219.
51. Monture-Angus 2000.
52. Monture-Angus 1999: 141.
53. hooks 1993: 70.

Dennis Sullivan and Larry Tift write that in today's world of global capitalism, where social structural violence reigns supreme, it is impossible for many people to

> survive economically, emotionally, and even physically in such arrangements, people begin to engage in a process of identity-editing, of self-falsification. They work on dismantling their authentic self and in its stead begin to forge an alias self, a meta-identity, if you will, through which they come to live an abstracted existence.... There is little hope of getting to that core part of ourselves where we discover who we are and how we are connected to others.[54]

Few people's needs are met in the face of structural violence and hierarchal power relations that destroy their lives and their relations with one another.[55] Negative drug use may be one of many varied responses to this violence.

Feminism and Drug Treatment

Rather than challenge the central tenets of the disease model of addiction, early feminist writers and activists in North America sought to remodel drug treatment services and 12-step programs so that they would better service women and recognize social factors that shape women's lives. In the 1970s, feminist researchers called attention to women and focused on heroin users and drug treatment for women.[56] The effects of poverty were often mistaken for the effects of drugs; however, most conventional research studies only included poor women, women in prison, and women in drug treatment in their samples. In addition, the most problematic illegal drug use was viewed as the norm. Many critical researchers have questioned the

54. Sullivan and Tift 2000: 22, 23.
55. Ibid.
56. Rosenbaum 1997.

practice of using captive participants, for it is often unethical and may skew results[57] and subsequent policy recommendations.

Feminists challenged specific conventional ideas about the female illegal drug user, and alternative women-centered treatment models began to emerge, models which most often recognized how patriarchal societies and gender inequality affected women. In addition, they spoke to violence against women and the need for services that acknowledged women's role as mothers and their unpaid work in the home.[58] They also focused on women's legal use of tobacco, alcohol, and prescribed drugs.[59] It became obvious, as it was in women's consciousness-raising groups of the 1970s, that women's stories about drugs and life and the social factors that shaped them were often very different than men's. Rather than the "man about town" and the "way of life" presented in books like William Burrough's *Junky*, women who used illegal drugs were often tied to their home and their children and were stigmatized for transgressing conventional gender roles.

Men who use illegal drugs are given quite a bit of latitude in fiction, and in real life, that women are not offered. Rather, women continue to be pathologized and seen as needing serious criminal, medical, and social service intervention when it comes to light that they are using illegal drugs. Even the best intentioned ethnographic research on women who use illegal drugs has tended to perpetuate negative stereotypes.[60] Alexander Liazos notes that sociologists continue to emphasize the "deviant" and the "problems," rather than linking the "phenomena of deviance" to larger historical, political, social and economic contexts, and it is those who are marginalized rather than those who make efforts to control and regulate "deviance" who are investigated.[61]

57. Waldorf et al. 1991.

58. Bepko 1991; Ettorre 1992; Kasl 1992; MacKinnon 1991; Sleeth and Barnsley 1989.

59. Ettoree 1992.

60. For a critique of research see Boyd 2001; Campbell 2000.

61. Liazos 1972.

Women's Experience of Treatment in North America

Women note that they have little access to women-only and women-centered drug treatment. In fact, in North America, they have little access to any kind of drug treatment and waiting lists are long (especially for poor women waiting for publicly funded drug treatment). Today, as in the past, women are reluctant to go to drug treatment for several reasons. Women claim that drug treatment does not serve their needs, especially if they are mothers. Researchers note how women are doubly stigmatized for participating in illegal drug use (breaking the law) and for transcending conventional gender roles. Thus, they are often treated by drug treatment staff, and male drug users, as more pathological and deviant than male users. My own 1999 research with female drug users in Western Canada indicates that they are rarely offered the same supports as male drug users, and the women themselves note that drug treatment services, including methadone clinics, are sexist. Other research verifies this as well.[62] For example, Claire Sterk notes that several women in her 1999 study of crack users in Atlanta stated that a double standard exists in drug treatment and that women are subject to more restrictions than men. Her study showed that in order to protect women from the unwanted advances and harassment of men, they had to be in by 10 p.m. In contrast, the men in the drug treatment program had no curfew.[63]

Additionally, drug treatment centers rarely take in women who are pregnant and rarely allow children to accompany their mothers.[64] Residential treatment is not an option for most women because they have children and other family commitments. Treatment, whether it is residential, an intensive day program, or nightly NA meetings, is less accessible to women, especially the poor, because childcare is often not provided. Furthermore, many residential programs are

62. Boyd 1999; Friedman and Alicea 1995; Rhoads 1983; Sterk 1999.
63. Sterk 1999: 138.
64. Boyd 1999; Rosenbaum 1997; Sales and Murphy 2000; Sterk 1999.

long, requiring women to stay from one month to a year and there are no accommodations for their children.[65] Poor women who are under the surveillance of social workers are fearful of child apprehension when entering drug treatment because their drug use, and quest for help, may be viewed by their workers as evidence of their maternal unfitness.[66] Women note that their children are their central concern and separation from them makes it difficult to see drug treatment as the top priority, as treatment workers wish them to.[67]

Drug treatment for pregnant women is even more problematic, for most programs in North America will not admit them, nor are service providers trained to work with them. This is problematic for several reasons. First, in the U.S., pregnant drug users are stigmatized and subjected to punitive medical, social, and criminal interventions. Rather than voluntary treatment, pregnant women who are suspected of using illegal drugs are more likely to be subjected to state interventions in the form of "apprehension of the fetus," imprisonment, and forced drug treatment. Pregnant women in Canada receiving financial assistance find their past and/or current drug history being assessed by social workers and addiction services in order to determine whether they are a risk to their children.

Aboriginal women and women of color note how they experience racial/ethnic and religious and spiritual conflicts in drug treatment.[68] Hispanic and black women in drug treatment have criticized the confrontation techniques used in therapy, and Aboriginal women have noted that Christian theology that underlies much drug treatment is a barrier[69] and may be reminiscent of residential school. AA, NA, and all 12-step treatment programs are predominantly Christian.[70] Further, Aboriginal women note that "mistrust" of services and programs and the fact that services are developed by "outsiders" are barriers to

65. Sales and Murphy 2000.
66. Boyd 1999; Rosenbaum 1998; Sterk 1999.
67. Boyd 1999.
68. Alegria et al. 1998; Boyd 1999; Jumper-Thurman and Plested 1998.
69. Alegria et al 1998; Boyd 1999; Sterk 1999.
70. Bufe 2000a.

reaching out for help.[71] An Afrocentric drug treatment paradigm drawing on black feminist theory and black family perspectives is proposed by some writers to address issues relevant to these women in the U.S. The paradigm would challenge and dispel myths about black women as mammies, matriarchs, welfare moms, and Jezebels, and offer culturally sensitive treatment.[72] bell hooks notes that 12-step programs tend to attract mostly white participants and black women often feel marginalized. She also explores how the myth of the strong black woman is internalized by women themselves, making it difficult for them to recognize their negative addiction.[73]

Treatment Goals

Women-centered treatment is limited if it does not offer diverse avenues to stability and support. Exploring and recognizing cultural differences in itself is not sufficient, for white women and upper-class women often assume that they know best and move toward solutions that favor their own worldview and privilege.[74] Thus, class, white privilege, and their associated practices need to be addressed. It is also essential to explore how imperialism, capitalism, colonization, racism, and patriarchy shape and constrain individuals, families, and communities. At the same time, we need to recognize the lived experiences of women who seek help and of those who organize to help themselves and others in relation to their drug use.

Other services for women need to implement policy and admittance for women who use illegal drugs. Traditionally, battered women's shelters, safe houses, and residential treatment had policies that mandated that women be abstinent prior to using their services. For many women, this is impossible and unnecessary. Paloma Sales and Sheigla Murphy explore how poor pregnant drug users in the San Francisco Bay Area survive homelessness, child apprehension, poor

---

71. Jumper-Thurman and Plested 1998: 560.
72. Roberts, Jackson, and Carlton-Laney 2000.
73. hooks 1993: 67–77.
74. Razack 1998.

health, stigmatization, violence against them by male partners, and street violence (such as rape and verbal harassment). They state that the more violence the women interviewed experienced, the more drugs they used, and the more drugs they used, the more violence they experienced; as well, the violence they experienced was directly associated with their gendered roles as mothers, girlfriends, and wives.[75] These women have traditionally been barred from women-centered programs and shelters.

Counselors at drug treatment services often lack training.[76] This may have to do with hiring in the field, for the drug treatment industry tends to employ its own,[77] recruiting only those ex-addicts who are fully indoctrinated in the disease model of addiction. However, women wish to have more than just 12-step models of treatment available, and often state this model is not effective for them.[78] Women note that though they may discontinue using illegal drugs, poverty, racism, and sexism remain unchanged and thus the conditions of their lives remain the same.[79] What is often labeled "client resistance" to treatment is often a resistance to counselors and their attitudes and practices.[80] Twelve-step programs are numerous because governments in the U.S. and Canada have been reluctant to fund programs that are not abstinence-based. Another important factor is that 12-step programs, such as AA and NA, are free, and, theoretically offer access to everyone regardless of their class. This is significant in a nation like the U.S. that does not have universal medical coverage and where waiting lists for publicly funded drug treatment are long.

The all-or-nothing quality of abstinence-based treatment often places failure at the clients' feet instead of its own program rigidity. As one woman noted:

75. Sales and Murphy 2000.
76. Sterk 1999.
77. Peele 1989.
78. Boyd 1999; Sales and Murphy 2000; Sterk 1999.
79. Bourgois 1995; Boyd 1999; Sterk 1999.
80. Shearer et al. 2001.

> It is all set up to make you feel like a failure, because when there is only one method of treatment, if you don't fit in there. Well, that is the reason that... one of the reasons that you became addicted in the first place.[81]

Although abstinence-based treatment is effective for many participants, it should not be the only treatment model available to women.

When seeking support, women have had their children apprehended by the state while they are in treatment. In addition, they have been denied privileges, medical care, and visits from family and friends; subjected to body searches, religious instruction, arbitrary rules and policy; and experienced race, class, and gender bias. Furthermore, women are punished when they are unable or unwilling to remain abstinent or to abide by the rules imposed on them in treatment.

Drug services should include a broad spectrum of user-friendly services that address the needs of women and their children. Detox; medical, social, and counseling services; maintenance programs; residential and day services; abstinence and self-management programs; needle-exchange; and safe injection sites are needed. However, rather than just offering treatment programs, a broad range of support services should be available to women, such as affordable housing, safe houses, universal medical and dental care, day care, access to education, living wages and guaranteed incomes. The focus on drug use in itself is faulty, for women's lives and their drug use, are shaped by cultural, political, social, and economic factors. The focus on individualized behavioral and cognitive therapy to curtail drug use is also limited. Women need support that derives from their own individual, family, and community experience. It is difficult for many women working in the "helping" professions to believe that other women are knowledgeable about the conditions of their lives and may have some idea of their own needs, and most important that those needs may be different from those identified by the "expert."

81. Boyd 1999: 161.

The Drug Treatment Industry and Diversity

Drug addiction and treatment is a billion-dollar industry and many authors have explored the marketing of addiction in the U.S. and elsewhere.[82] Some writers have referred to it as the "substance abuse industrial complex" which is fueled by the war on drugs.[83] The drug court movement, which originated in the U.S. but is quickly spreading to other Western nations, further expands the drug-addiction industry. The disease model of addiction denies structural oppression and all problems are viewed as "internal." Similarly, the recovery movement is premised on the disease model of addiction and 12-step programs, and it is reactionary. It espouses to adopt feminist ideas when in reality it depicts addiction as an expression of women's own "internal weaknesses," including overeating, compulsive shopping, and drug use. Any behavior can be viewed as a disease, thus women no longer need to look at the socioeconomic factors that shape their lives.[84] The recovery movement encourages women to individually govern themselves and to participate in the moral regulation of others.

We should be cautious of individualized pathological notions of drug use because they ignore the multiple social factors that shape women's drug use. Drug use is not static and problem use is often situational and drifts into controlled use. Interestingly, many women discount their own recreational experiences of drugs as anomalies. Although a small minority of women may "crave" drugs, these desires are rarely "ungovernable," and for the majority of people, drug use is spiritual, recreational, pleasant, and celebratory.[85] Criticism of the disease model of addiction and 12-step programs does not mean that abstinence in itself is negative or not a worthy quest. For some people, 12-step programs have been beneficial; for many, abstinence has been coupled with a more fulfilling life. Negative addiction can be a very painful event for

82. Peele 1989; Peele and Brodsky, with Arnold 1991; Rapping 1996.
83. Woodiwess 2001.
84. Rapping 1996.
85. Denton 2001.

women and their families. The absence of legal drug maintenance, controlled-drug use programs, and user-friendly services limits what choices women have. The institutionalization of one model negates diversity and constructs all those women who fail to conform, or who refuse to conform, as deviant and responsible for their own failure.

Harm Reduction

Until the harm reduction movement emerged in the 1980s in the Netherlands and Britain, few alternatives to Alcohol Anonymous and Narcotics Anonymous existed in North America. In contrast to the disease model of addiction, harm reduction offers practical programs that focus on minimizing drug-related harm to both the individual and society. Programs such as needle exchanges, methadone services, and self-management training programs (i.e., controlled alcohol use) are seen as practical programs that can help to minimize harm. One of the most important philosophical differences between the disease model of addiction and harm reduction is that harm reduction recognizes that historically people have always sought ways to change consciousness through the use of drugs, and that drug use ranges from positive to negative experience; therefore, abstinence is unnecessary and, in many cases, unrealistic. Harm reduction does not reject abstinence; rather, it is viewed as one option among many.

The reasons people use drugs are complex and shaped by many social factors; thus, programs should reflect the diversity of drug-using patterns rather than promoting abstinence as the goal for everyone. Harm reduction recognizes that drug-use patterns are not static and that legal and illegal categories of drugs are social constructions that have nothing to do with dangerousness. Harm reduction attempts to offer pragmatic interventions that make drug use safer, rather than interventions based on morality.[86] One of the most important premises advocated by the first harm reduction advocates and drug user union in the Netherlands, the "Junkiebond," was the acceptance

---

86. O'Hare 1994.

of drug use and the drug user. The Junkiebond was responding to a policy that would have forced those addicted to illegal drugs to abstain.[87] Dutch drug researcher van de Wijngaart notes that to accept that the reasons for drug use are normal necessitates a different response to drug use. It is accepted in the Netherlands that recreational use does not lead to addiction. He states that the assumption behind drug policy in the Netherlands is that "people take drugs because they want to, that drug use serves some function, gives them some satisfaction in some area of their lives, and that they will stop taking drugs or use less if they find a (better) alternative that will serve somewhat the same function."[88]

In the late 1960s, a public health rather than a disease model was adopted in the Netherlands and the government rejected "the idea of compulsory treatment."[89] Harm reduction is fully accepted in the Netherlands and to lesser degree in the U.K. (There have been serious challenges since Tony Blair's government came into power). However, in the U.S., harm reduction has barely gained a foothold in official policy. Programs such as needle exchanges are still illegal in many states, and every day people risk arrest in many cities by supplying clean needles. Harm reduction has been accepted in many areas of Canada, especially in British Columbia. In Vancouver, the 2002 election for city council and mayor brought harm reduction to the forefront, making safe injection sites (also referred to as supervized injection rooms) and harm reduction the major topics of debate. Because of the high rates of injecting drug use, HIV/AIDs and hepatitis C infection, drug overdose rates, and lack of private space, the Vancouver Area Network of Drug Users (VANDU)[90]

---

87. van de Wijngaart 1991.

88. Ibid: 85.

89. Ibid.: 34.

90. In 1997, a group of people got together in Vancouver, B.C., to form a user-run organization. VANDU emerged out of this group. VANDU is a group of users, former users, and non-users who work to improve the lives of people who use illicit drugs through user-based peer support and education. They have been the most vocal voice in the Downtown Eastside representing visible illegal drug users.

spearheaded the opening of safe injection sites in the Downtown Eastside of Vancouver, and former mayor Philip Owen eventually came to agree that they were worth implementing. In 2001, the Vancouver City Council approved a drug strategy (four pillars approach) that outlined the necessity of harm reduction, prevention, treatment, and enforcement. Safe injection sites were recommended in the drug strategy. Philip Owen's successor, Larry Campbell, also advocated for safe injection sites. The opening of the "official" safe injection site was delayed and an interim safe injection site and drop-in center was opened by poverty activists, street nurses, and the Harm Reduction Coalition which includes VANDU. The site opened at the same time that the city of Vancouver implemented a high-profile police operation in the Downtown Eastside. A May 2003 Human Rights Watch report documents evidence of police misconduct and abuse toward illegal drug users in the Downtown Eastside. Social and health providers and illegal drug users state that they are unable to access services in the area due to the heightened police presence, which contradicts the goals of harm reduction strategies.[91] Against this backdrop, in September 2003, the "official" safe-injection site opened.

Canada's new drug law, enacted in 1997, advocates harm reduction while also sanctioning harsh criminal sentencing. One has to ask how effective harm reduction can be while certain drugs continue to be criminalized and while punitive police presence and legal penalties such as imprisonment continue to be used. Criminalization contributes to the very factors that harm reduction advocates wish to minimize—harm due to adulterated drugs, overdoses due to uncertain quality, transmission of diseases, drug trade violence, and illegal markets. Expanding police powers and crack downs do little to minimize harms related to drugs. Studies in Australia, Britain, Canada, and the U.S. highlight that targeted police operations and conventional drug-control strategies have no impact on drug prices, purity, and supply. However, criminal justice interventions "has worsened the health and social consequences of drug

---

91. Csete and Cohen 2003.

use."[92] The term "harm reduction" has been used by conservative reformers to justify locking up drug users, to assess parents and their risk to their children, and to argue for compulsory drug treatment schemes in order to reduce harm to society.

Furthermore, conservative and liberal harm reduction advocates ignore the ways that continued colonization, imperialism, and race, class, and gender oppression figure into the social construction of drug users. In North America, many professions and the public continue to perceive illegal drug users as immoral, sick, criminal, and in need of social, legal, and medical control. It is difficult for many to throw off the mantle of moralism that pervades drug policy. Similarly, it is a struggle to let go of punitive medical and social service practices and punishment industries which compete, overlap, and benefit, from the social control of illegal drug users. Regulating drug users fuels the drug treatment industry and contributes to the prison-industrial complex. The social control of drug users also contributes to expanded budgets for other criminal justice professionals (including drug court employees). Thus, moral reformers and professionals have a stake in the regulation of drug users. Domestic police would suffer a major blow to their budgets if drugs were decriminalized or legalized and if the more radical ideas that inform harm reduction were realized.

Advocates of drug treatment and the medical model ignore how public health mandates have also exaggerated drug issues. Punitive legal and medical practices often "draw sustenance from each other,"[93] and often work hand and hand with harsh social service practices. In fact, the perceived negative health consequences of criminalized drugs are used as justification for expanding police powers and imposing severe legal penalties such as imprisonment. Framing illegal drug users and "addicts" as having no "control" over their drug use justifies medical, legal, and social service regulation. Bruce Alexander notes, and I would agree, that liberal reform programs such as harm reduction will

92. Best et al. 2001; Drucker 1999; Maher and Dixon 1999; Wood et al. 2003b: 134.

93. Davies and Shewan 2000: 237.

do little to stem the tide of negative addiction because they fail to address the larger issues of neoliberal ideology and dislocation.

However, harm reduction programs can provide effective, practical interventions and services. Harm reduction programs to reduce HIV/AIDS and hepatitis transmission and to prevent drug overdose have been at the forefront of the advocates' agenda. HIV-positive black and Hispanic women are overrepresented given their relatively small percentage in the U.S. population compared with white women. For example, whereas black women make up about 13 percent of the female population, they make up about 57 percent of women diagnosed with AIDS; Hispanic women who make up about 11 percent of the female population, make up about 20 percent of all women diagnosed with AIDS. Women are most at risk for HIV/AIDS through injecting drug use (IDU) (42 percent); however, heterosexual contact is their second largest risk (40 percent). In contrast, men are only at a 4 percent risk of infection through heterosexual contact.[94] It is estimated that black and Hispanic women account for 75 percent of all women in the U.S. "with injection-related AIDS in 2001."[95] In Canada, roughly 39 percent of "all new HIV infections in 2000 were related to injection drug use." As early as 1997, it was noted that in Vancouver, women injection drug users had a higher prevalence of HIV than their male counterparts.[96] The Downtown Eastside of Vancouver, where the 18 percent annual HIV incidence rate remains the "most rapid infection rate ever documented in the developed world," poor young women and Aboriginal women are vulnerable to infection.[97]

In 1999, injection drug users in the general population of London had an HIV prevalence rate of 2.3 compared with .3 percent in the rest of England and Wales. Hepatitis C prevalence rates for injection drug users in England and Wales were 32 percent in 1999, with higher rates in London.[98] These rates are much lower than rates in Canada

94. West 2001: 21.
95. Day 2002: 14.
96. Spittal et al. 2002: 894.
97. Wood et al. 2003a: 3.; Spittal et al. 2002.
98. Aujean et al. 2001: 58.

and the U.S. Harm reduction programs such as needle exchanges emerged in the mid-1980s and were successful in limiting the transmission of both HIV and hepatitis in Britain.

HIV/AIDS should be understood as part of a broader set of social conditions. Drug researcher Lisa Maher notes that for some injecting drug users "HIV and other blood-borne viruses are just one of many risks to be negotiated on a daily basis: the risk of arrest, death, withdrawal, overdose, being attacked, robbed or ripped off, losing your children, losing a limb and losing your dignity. These are not individual and isolated but rather, connected and cumulative."[99] Furthermore, women injecting drug users are high risk to blood-borne infections due to the fact that many are "second on the needle." Many women do not inject themselves and rely on their partners to do so, while others need assistance because of collapsed veins.[100] Compounding their risk of contracting HIV/AIDS is late detection and diagnosis and delays in treatment, all of which can have significant negative consequences for them.

Alternative-Treatment Options

As noted earlier, the ritual use of peyote and other drugs in spiritual healing has long been recognized in the Americas. Aboriginal people have continued to honor plants and value their use in ritual practice, even when these ceremonies have been criminalized by the state. To see all drug use as similar and all addiction as negative ignores the historical evidence that some plants and drugs can have positive qualities. Aboriginal people who belong to the Native American Church—given official recognition in the U.S. in 1918—have long acknowledged the spiritual potential of peyote. The church has recently been offering a treatment using peyote medicine to women and men who are addicted to alcohol. It is believed that the psychedelic experience helps them to discover their "spiritual core and to break from their addiction."[101]

99. Maher 2002: 322.
100. Kerr 2003; Spittal et al. 2002.
101. CBC 2001.

In Brazil, Ayahuasca (a powerful hallucinogen) has been in legal use for spiritual practices since the mid-1980s.[102] Members of the Ayahuasca Church noticed that many people addicted to alcohol over a long period of time were able to stop drinking and others were able to give up tobacco and illegal drugs after participating in religious ceremonies where ayahuasca was offered in the form of a tea. It is believed that ayahuasca opens the window to one's future and past. Teenagers as young as fourteen drink ayahuasca tea with older church members guiding their visionary experiences. The church claims that the "tea" acts as a deterrent against addiction and illicit drug-taking.[103] However, it is the ritual context and the knowledge that plants can communicate that are emphasized when hallucinogens are used for therapeutic purposes. These practices are directly opposed to our modern-day medical model, which labels all phenomena it cannot observe as unscientific.

Latin American researchers and journalists have made it clear that the traditional use of coca differs greatly from how cocaine is used in many Western nations. They advocate the use of coca tea and coca tablets for cocaine addiction and argue that maintenance and detox programs could use the plant in place of refined drugs since the coca leaf has no negative physical effects. In addition, we might consider introducing opium tea to heroin and methadone users, as well as those addicted to a host of other legally prescribed narcotics.

Although there has been little interest in maintenance programs that provide liquid opium and coca products, a number of programs in different countries provide legal heroin to users. It has been demonstrated that heroin maintenance stabilizes clients and reduces criminal activity; however, Rachel Lart notes that British psychiatrists were reluctant to prescribe it to their clients at the clinics.[104] She discusses a study conducted in England during the late 1970s, which changed prescribing practices from heroin to methadone. The study, conducted by Hartnoll and his colleagues, included a sample of ninety-six "confirmed heroin addicts." Half of them were offered

102. Tupper 2002.
103. CBC 2001.
104. Lart 1998.

heroin maintenance, and half were offered methadone maintenance. Their progress was followed for twelve months. The drug users who had been offered methadone dropped out of the program at a much higher rate than those who had been prescribed heroin; however, the abstinence rates were higher for those who had been prescribed methadone. Those who had been offered methadone also had higher rates of illicit drug use and criminal activity than those who had been offered heroin.[105]

The researchers concluded that offering methadone was more confrontational and offered more avenues for change (i.e., abstinence), whereas heroin maintenance maintained the status quo and addicts did not change their lifestyle. The authors discussed the choice between policy that strives for abstinence (methadone maintenance) and one that maintains chronic heroin addicts. Their logic limits other ways of thinking about the issue. Continued heroin maintenance was considered to be less challenging than methadone maintenance because it was perceived as less therapeutic; to "cure" the addict was admirable, but to provide prescriptions for heroin was tolerated only in the face of a growing epidemic of injection heroin use in England.[106] Thus, if doctors could not transform "immoral" drug users, they showed little interest or support in the practice.

Methadone maintenance programs are available to narcotic users in Britain, Canada, and the U.S. (as well as other countries), although program policy and access is varied. Methadone maintenance has remained controversial since it emerged in the 1960s; due to the whims of doctors and governments, clients have been subjected to experimentation and fluctuations in policy and delivery of services. Drug testing and daily attendance at methadone clinics are routine practices in Canada and the U.S. Although methadone maintenance is "perceived" as offering the illegal drug user the possibility of a more stable life, many women drug users in Canada use it as a last resort because of its rigid policies. Thus, only a small fraction of illegal drug users benefit from methadone maintenance pro-

105. Hartnoll et al. 1980: 883.
106. Lart 1998: 68.

grams there. In the U.S., public funding for methadone maintenance has been cut back and many women are unable to afford to stay on the program. [107] In Canada, doctors in B.C. are charging extra-billing and counseling fees. Rebates are available to women on welfare but only after the receipts are sent into the Ministry of Health. Paying up front and waiting for one's rebate is an unnecessary hardship on women and this may deter some women from using the program.

Women on methadone in North America are often described as failing in their roles as daughters, wives, and mothers. The women who use the clinics note that doctors and service providers are sexist and look at them as being immoral and criminal.[108] Women who are mothers are especially vulnerable because program providers are often misinformed about maternal drug use and parenting, and most women are subjected to humiliating rules in order to obtain their prescriptions. One of the most contentious rules is drug testing during which women are forced to urinate in front of nurses and other medical staff. Drug testing, recommended doses, and daily pick-up often appear arbitrary; as well, there are no rewards for compliance with the rules. In fact, long-term clients find that they are subject to a host of new rules whenever a new government is elected or when the media and individual politicians create a "new" moral panic about methadone users. Methadone services have always been about social control, which is unfortunate because women benefit in many ways when they are able to stay on methadone and when they encounter user-friendly services. Women on methadone speak about their increased sense of stability, lessened criminal activity, improved health, and increased distance from the drug trade.[109]

Illegal drug users have consistently made it clear, however, that they would prefer heroin maintenance programs, or at least a range of narcotics to chose from. All of the women who had been on methadone in my 1999 Canadian study would have preferred legal heroin main-

107. Rosenbaum and Murphy 1987.
108. Boyd 1999.
109. Rosenbaum and Murphy 1987.

tenance programs. Women who use illegal drugs point out that methadone is more difficult to withdraw from than heroin and have further concerns about its toxicity.[110] Others note that they should be able to access their drug of choice rather than substitutes. Several nations have heroin maintenance programs, including Switzerland, Britain (although methadone has virtually replaced heroin prescribing), and the Netherlands. In addition, pilot projects have been proposed in Canada, Australia, Germany, and Spain. Research findings related to heroin programs have been positive. The Swiss heroin trial began in 1994 and took place in sixteen different locations, including large cities like Zurich. The retention rates were high in Switzerland (about 69 percent), and clients' physical and mental health improved as their criminal and illegal drug use decreased. [111]

Drug Courts

Feminist research and activism have shown more interest in providing drug treatment for women rather than imposing criminal sanctions on them. There is no doubt that women, especially poor women, have not had the same access to drug treatment as men. In addition, lower-class women have had less access to drug treatment than middle- and upper-class women in Britain, Canada, and the U.S. Women argue that conventional 12-step treatment services have not traditionally addressed their needs. Consequently, advocates of drug treatment call for women-centered models of treatment, quicker and easier access, and more treatment programs for women. Often, the rallying call for more drug treatment lacks a critique of the disease model of addiction and abstinence. Nor does it question the more recent movement to create drug courts, which are seen as an alternative to traditional criminal court proceedings. Drug courts offer mandatory drug treatment rather than incarceration to some offenders.

---

110. Boyd 1999; Rosenbaum and Murphy 1987.
111. Uchtenhagen et al., as cited in Kuo, Fisher and Vlahov 2000.

History of the Drug Courts

Since the 1980s, there has been strong approval for drug courts, especially in the U.S. Some authors refer to the U.S. model of drug courts and international expansion as the "U.S.-led drug court movement."[112] Although drug courts are a U.S. phenomenon, they have recently been initiated in Britain and in Canada. Professionals, ranging from judges, social workers, psychiatrists, doctors, nurses, drug treatment and family counselors, are ready to carve out a place for themselves in these courts. Social workers claim to see new opportunities for themselves. They believe they are qualified to work with the "new" drug court offenders, arm in arm with the criminal justice system.[113] Researchers have rushed to herald the drug court's effectiveness and many advocates view them positively as a "humane" alternative to the traditional criminal justice system, one that will appease both law-and-order advocates and liberals alike.

Drug courts vary across the U.S., with the first special drug-case courtrooms appearing in New York City and Chicago in the 1950s. In response to the harsh Rockefeller drug laws enacted in the 1970s, New York City set up "Narcotic Courts." The Dade County, Florida drug court was the first to integrate mandatory drug treatment in 1989. The drug courts divert some non-violent offenders to treatment rather than prison. However, failure to comply by the rules established by the judge may result in being sent to prison. The drug court model includes criminal justice and drug treatment services working together by using the "coercive power of the court to promote abstinence and pro-social behavior."[114] The goal of the drug courts is to reduce illegal drug use and to lower associated criminal behavior and recidivism rates. By 2003, over 1,380 drug courts were in operation or in the planning stage in the U.S. In 2004, the U.S. Department of Justice proposes to provide U.S.$68 million in funding to drug courts (in contrast to U.S.$50 million in 2001 and U.S.$30 million in 1997).[115]

112. Nolan 2002: 89.
113. Jenkins 1995.
114. Belenko 1998: 4.
115. ONDCP 2003

The drug court model entails several components, including judicial supervision in mandatory drug treatment; quick identification and processing of drug defendants and referral to drug treatment; close supervision and status hearing with a judge to monitor treatment; the incorporation of sanctions and awards; and mandatory drug testing. The judge's role is quite different in drug courts and, although the judge works with a team consisting of prosecutors, defense attorneys, drug treatment counselors, and a host of other practitioners, his or her role is central to monitoring the offender's progress in drug treatment. Drug court participants spend a minimum of one year in community drug treatment programs; those unable to complete the program are sent to prison. The percentage of those unable to complete the program is high. Even though drug court participants are screened before being accepted to the program, about half of all participants in drug courts are sent to prison, and some programs have even higher rates of failure. The claims of success, then, are overstated—a 50 percent failure rate is significant.[116]

Cost Effectiveness of Drug Courts

One of the selling points of drug courts is that they are cheaper than traditional criminal justice responses to drug offenders. However, this overly optimistic claim does not hold up under scrutiny. Drug courts cost more per participant than traditional probation,[117] although drug court advocates state there are savings to be made due to reduced recidivism, job creation, and earnings.[118] However, critics note that participants in drug court programs spend more time under supervision than nondrug court offenders, and that access to employment has not been a central feature of the majority of drug courts.[119]

116. Belenko 1998: 5; Belenko 2001: 1.
117. Makkai 1998.
118. Belenko 1998.
119. Anderson 2001; Miethe, Lu, and Reese 2000.

One of the most amazing omissions in the information about drug courts is an analysis of the completion and failure rates for drug offenders from different class, gender, and ethnic/race backgrounds. Additionally, other social factors that may influence the effectiveness or failure of the drug court are absent from much of the discourse.

Gender and Cultural Factors

It has been noted that there is little research about women moving through the drug courts in the U.S., although women make up 18 percent of drug court participants.[120] Nevertheless, research rarely addresses the gender-specific needs of women and ignores the fact that they might have different priorities and life experiences than men. However, the Women's Drug Court in Kalamazoo, Michigan, is gender specific. It offers counseling, drug testing, day-care, transportation, drug treatment, and court supervision to women eligible for the program. An in-house publication about the program notes that women who are identified as "substance abusers" and are nonviolent felony offenders are eligible. From its inception in 1992 until 1998, 1,071 women were referred to the Women's Drug Court; however, only 399 women were accepted. Of those women accepted, 43 percent had no prior felonies and 43 percent (163 women) were discharged from the program before completion. In addition, 2 percent (16 women) chose to discontinue the program prior to completion. Of the 16 percent of the women in the program who used only one drug, 25 percent used marijuana and 21 percent used alcohol. Fifty-six percent of the 399 women referred to the Women's Drug Court had never received drug treatment prior to the program. Of the total women referred, 251 waived their right to an attorney.[121]

Other in-house publications note that the National Association of Women Judges claims that drug courts are a "viable" alternative to im-

120. Beckerman and Fontana 2001: 48

121. Kalamazoo County Statistical Report.

prisonment for pregnant women.[122] It is thought that over 450 "drug-free babies" were born to women moving through the drug courts in the U.S. prior to 1997.[123] Family drug courts are also seen as an initiative that can "improve access" to drug treatment, "strengthen families, increase rates of family reunification, and improve child placement decision." All of the participants, mostly women, are subject to drug testing, court appearance, and drug treatment. Social workers are considered the most appropriate professionals to identify and refer women and their families to family drug court. As of 1998, there were only sixteen family courts running, although there were plans for ten more.[124]

It has been noted that when day-care and gender-specific programs are offered to women moving through the drug courts, their completion rate is higher than mens. Further, it is argued that these programs are more successful in helping women regain custody of their children once they complete treatment.[125] It is difficult to assess in-house publications about gender-specific drug court programs, for like most drug court information, they are not peer reviewed and they are often methodologically flawed. Adela Beckerman and Leonard Fontana attempt to rectify this problem in their article "Issues of Race and Gender in Court-Ordered Substance Abuse Treatment." They note that little attention has been given to the diversity of drug court participants and that issues of race and gender are ignored. They state that mandatory drug treatment through the drug courts does not assure client engagement and completion of the program. Rather, they conclude that even though researchers acknowledge that retention in drug treatment is one of the most important predictors of positive outcomes (abstinence and graduation), few program facilitators and researchers have examined "strategies to enhance" retention and treatment outcomes.

In addition, they argue that "addiction" is viewed as the primary problem in most programs rather than poverty, racism, and gender discrimination—for example, black people often view addictions as

122. Drug Strategies 1998.
123. Drug Court Survey Report 1997: 6.
124. Drug Strategies 1998.
125. Drug Court Survey Report 1997.

secondary to social and economic factors that negatively affect their lives. Therefore, programs need to address the cultural context of black women's and men's lives. For example, programs that focus on black women must recognize that many women's addictions are "associated" with histories of sexual and emotional victimization. Further, "small-single-gender group sessions" for black women and men make it easier to address the social factors that shape their lives. Mandatory drug treatment, they conclude, is insufficient to engage and retain drug court participants and to reduce drug use and criminal behavior. Rather, these expectations are "simplistic," and more attention must be given to strategies to retain participants, such as providing access to housing and medical care. They state that failure to complete mandatory drug treatment may not be "defiance of judicial authority," but may signify a failure in the program's design. For when cultural specific programs are integrated into treatment, retention rates are higher.[126]

Widening the Net of Social Control

Those women who are eligible for drug courts are subject to greater supervision and drug testing than drug offenders on probation. Over half of the drug courts require that mandatory drug testing occurs twice a week in the initial stages, whereas over 50 percent of drug defendants on probation are subject to drug testing once a month.[127] Marc Mauer of the Sentencing Project says that drug courts "seem to me to be a very structured and cumbersome mechanism to get what we know is needed, which is education, health and job services for the ex-offender. If the courts work well, much of the success will just replicate what a good parole officer would have done 25 years ago."[128]

One thing that everyone agrees on, advocates and critics alike, is that the drug courts monitor offenders more closely—they are

126. Beckerman and Fontana 2001: 45–61, 58.
127. Belenko 1998: 14.
128. FAMM 2000: 13.

under greater and longer surveillance by judges and by drug treatment providers than nondrug court offenders who are under other types of community supervision like probation and electronic monitoring. The supervision of drug court offenders is regarded as being more intrusive than offenders who received no prison time or shorter sentences.[129] In addition, the surveillance of drug offenders moving through the drug courts consists of several overlapping professionals, including drug treatment providers, social workers, medical staff, and criminal justice workers. The alliance between these professionals may not always be a comfortable one because the judge, representing the criminal justice system, will dictate to the other professionals how an offender's treatment will evolve, including the penalties, sanctions, and rewards they will be subject, for both noncompliance and "success." However, punishment rather than rewards are the norm.[130]

Researchers Terance Miethe, Hong Lu, and Erin Reese explain how drug courts are "actually more stigmatizing than conventional courts." Participants are subject to verbal abuse, shaming, and public disapproval by hostile judges who pay little attention to delabeling, forgiveness, and reintegration. Instead, participants are seen as being "deviant" rather than having "criminalized behavior," and from their first appearance in drug court they are subject to very degrading ceremonies. The drug court system believes that participants will benefit from frequent contact with the judge, but research demonstrates that "offenders" have little respect for judges.[131] As well, judges with absolutely no training are acting as pseudo-therapists who revert to their conventional judicial role when offenders do not comply with the judge's expectations of them. Judges who encourage public displays of emotion have been criticized. Critics note that the cult of personality infuses the drug court and there is little monitoring of a judge's behavior (benevolent or sadistic), nor is there adequate research on sentencing disparities. Furthermore, critics argue that offenders are forced to view their life circumstances through the lens of

129. Makkai 1998.

130. Burdon 2001.

131. Miethe, Lu, and Reese 2000: 522.

individual pathology and disease rather than through social factors such as economic exclusion or racial profiling.

Several issues related to offenders' and patients' rights have also emerged in response to the drug courts. Conflicts exist between prosecutors and defense attorneys concerning sanctions for noncompliance with drug treatment and relapse,[132] one being that the majority of drug court judges are prosecutors, who still see their role as striving toward law and order and sending anyone who has infractions (i.e., positive drug tests) back to prison. Their law-and-order stance is suppose to be tempered by the other members of the team, but this is difficult to do when even counselors and drug treatment practitioners have become "informers" for the state instead of professionals who provide care. Confidentiality is eroded when drug treatment is no longer voluntary but becomes coerced in order to reduce criminal activity and recidivism.

Drug Courts in Canada

The first drug court in Canada emerged in 1998 in Toronto, Ontario, which was funded by the federal government as a four-year pilot project. In 2000, former justice minister Anne McLennan announced plans to open drug courts in all of Canada's major cities by the year 2004.[133] To date, only the Toronto and Vancouver courts are operating. The following section focuses on the drug court in Toronto in detail because there are several factors specific to the program that offer an interesting contrast to the U.S. courts.

The Toronto drug court is thought to be "a product of a Canadian environment."[134] It is run differently than its U.S. counterparts because Canada does not have the same legal structure to facilitate drug courts. For example, mandatory minimum sentences for drug offenses do not exist and all illegal drug legislation is federal. Nor do

132. Belenko 1998.
133. Skelton and Ovenden 2000.
134. Bentley 2001: 20.

judges have the power to send drug offenders back to prison if they break the rules established by the drug court. The judge presiding over the drug court in Toronto can only revoke the drug offender's bail when an infraction has occurred. Other important differences that distinguish the Canadian drug court from drug courts in the U.S. include offering methadone maintenance where it is deemed appropriate; not requiring abstinence to be mandatory at the initial stages of treatment; and recognizing relapse as an integral part of the recovery process. Continued drug use, therefore, does not necessarily lead to expulsion from the program; rather, it may lead to increased court attendance, counseling, performing community service, or revocation of bail (a return to prison for a few days). However, the Catch 22 of this system is that drug offenders who do not take responsibility for their continued drug use—or who deny using despite positive urine screens or admissions in counseling—are not allowed to continue the program and are sent to prison. Furthermore, the program insists that participants be drug-free for at least four months prior to completing the program. [135]

The program in Toronto provides court-supervised treatment for nonviolent offenders addicted to heroin and/or opiates. Unlike many U.S. programs, people charged with trafficking small amounts are eligible for the program, as are those who have prostitution-related offenses. These offenders will most likely be women, as prostitution is constructed as a gender-specific activity in Canada, and elsewhere.

The federal prosecutor has exclusive jurisdiction to determine eligibility into the program.[136] Critics note that this gives the prosecutor immense power, especially since a review process by a judge is not available to offenders, even though judges have the power to exclude people from the program once they have been recommended by the prosecutor. Critics note that those offenders who must plead guilty in order to become eligible to enter the program must sign a consent form to dispense of Crown disclosure and delay sentencing. By doing so, they lose

135. Ibid.: 20.
136. Ibid.

their Charter rights to speedy sentencing and speedy trial—"they basically give up all their legal rights as we know them."[137] In addition, they must consent to the sharing of information between the drug court and the treatment team. These contracts are signed in the presence of a lawyer. However, defense lawyers are not present in the drug court.

Women and men in the program must attend treatment and court sessions regularly (twice a week initially), their progress is addressed by the judge and his or her team, and a system of incentives and sanctions are applied to encourage the participants to maintain abstinence. All participants who attend court on the assigned day must sit through the entire court session, as it is believed that they will benefit from being present as the other participants in the program are addressed. Stories of success and failure are voiced and heard in court, but it is debatable whether participants benefit from these public displays of moral regulation. In addition, court attendance ignores the reality that in order to attend participants must be absent from work and their homes; there is no acknowledgment that women are primarily responsible for their children and may have difficulty attending court all day. Little of the literature I reviewed on the Canadian or U.S. drug courts addresses providing childcare or compensation for childcare while women attend court. Nor does it address how attending court for several hours a day contributes to the well-being of families when mothers are absent. Both in Canada and the U.S., the drug courts view participants as unattached individuals responsible for their own well-being, nor is the gender-specific dynamic of the court where women are publically disciplined by male judges addressed.

In the first evaluation period of the Toronto program (eighteen months after it began), 46 percent of the participants who had entered the program had either graduated or were still participating. This adds up to a 54 percent drop-out or expulsion rate, which is very similar to U.S. rates. Similar to the U.S., participants in the Toronto drug court are under intensive supervision and in treatment

137. Mulgrew 1999: A16.

for at least one year, and under reduced supervision for another six to twelve months. K. Barnes, the drug court prosecutor, states that the "participant is easily the most supervised non-incarcerated offender in Canada."[138] Furthermore, participants in the program must demonstrate "improved skill development, stable and appropriate housing, and educational and vocational success" within the allotted time.[139] That is a tall order. Can you "fix" a lifetime of poor education and marginalization in one and a half years? Why is housing and education relegated to the criminal justice system? The criteria and measurements of success used in the program bring up further questions about middle-class values and the regulation of morality that shape the expectations and policy that drive the drug courts.

Although the Toronto drug court is believed to be an alternative to prison for non-violent drug offenders, it has adopted a "tough on crime" policy, which requires that participants be responsible for all of their actions, and its "supervision is rigorous and consequences for non-compliance with program objectives are immediate."[140] Barnes states that criminal law involvement in the program is essential. Judge Paul Bentley notes that the drug court "shifts the emphasis…from legal to therapeutic" by using what is labeled "smart punishment," meaning the "imposition of the minimum amount of punishment necessary to achieve the twin sentencing goals of reduced criminality and drug usage."[141] Classical theory assumes that everyone responds to punishment in similar ways and that people make rational choices and should be held accountable for them. There is no analysis of race, class, gender, or the many other social and economic constraints that shape people's lives. However, as Canadian writer Sherene Razack states, "[W]omen live a collective reality of oppression in which their individual choices are seriously constrained in ways related to race,

---

138. Barnes 2001: 3, 2.
139. Bentley 2001: 9.
140. Barnes 2001: 1, 2.
141. Bentley 2001: 3.

class, sexuality, and disability. We ought to use with care any rhetoric that does not begin there."[142]

Coerced-Treatment Replaces Voluntary-Treatment Options

A number of researchers have questioned the role of the drug courts and the "convergence" of the "medical and legal model" as a "united program of therapeutic jurisprudence."[143] Drug treatment money is now being funneled through the criminal justice system and treatment is no longer voluntary. James Chriss, a critic of the drug courts in the U.S., asks who gains from diverting criminal justice federal funds into drug courts. He states that judges, and various helping professions including AA, 12-step programs, social workers, and therapists benefit economically.[144] In addition, funding is diverted from voluntary drug treatment to coerced treatment. Critics question the "psychotherapeutic ethos" that imbues the drug court, and the lack of due process. As the disease model of addiction is central to drug court philosophy and practice, Chriss argues that, in the U.S., "a whole new group of citizens—most of whom are nonviolent marijuana or alcohol users" are constructed as "sick" or "ill" needing intervention. The drug court philosophy is the same as civil-commitment philosophy and *parens patriae*. The state diverts individuals deemed as a threat to themselves and to society into treatment. "In drug court the rules of evidence are largely suspended, along with other procedural rules."[145] The judge sets the tone and style of each drug court. Philip Bean, a British drug researcher, notes that "the cult of personality has from inception been close to the drug court culture." The judge acts as a maternal or paternal figure who punishes

142. Razack 1998: 35.
143. Nolan 2002: 95.
144. Chriss 2002: 197.
145. Bean 2002: 237.

offenders for their own good. He states that "as an exercise in social control it is masterly; rarely has a social control system been better packaged, or presented in such an effective and sophisticated way."[146]

Critics of drug courts note that coerced treatment is problematic when voluntary treatment is unavailable for most women in the U.S. and in Canada. Long waiting lists in both countries and limited space in treatment programs for those on welfare benefits limit their access. We might ask why voluntary treatment is not provided to women prior to their involvement with the criminal justice system. The drug court system has done nothing to stem the tide of drug arrests and imprisonment for women in the U.S. Imprisonments for drug arrests continue to rise while more women and men are diverted into the drug courts. Consequently, a widening net of regulation has resulted. In the U.S., abstinence-based treatment is the foundation of the drug courts. Although the Toronto drug court states that it is not primarily an abstinence-based program, dirty tests are cause for sanctions (including marijuana), and all participants must be drug-free by the end of the program. Drug testing is an integral tool of social control in the Canadian, British, and U.S. drug courts, even though drug testing is unreliable and offers very little information about the circumstances of use.[147]

One of the most problematic aspects of the drug courts is the sharing of information between treatment service providers and the court. The confidentiality usually provided to patients in relation to their healthcare providers is terminated. Critics argue that coerced drug treatment "violates one of the sacred tenets of the therapeutic alliance, namely, that persons must enter into treatment voluntarily."[148] In Britain, harm reduction practices still inform drug treatment and not all illegal drug use is viewed as problematic. Critics of the two new West Yorkshire drug courts and the Drug Treatment and Testing Or-

146. Ibid.: 236, 237.
147. Humphries et al. 1992.
148. Chriss 2002: 199.

ders (DTTOS) program (convicted drug offenders are offered court-monitored drug treatment) note that those offenders who fail risk being sent to court to "face tougher sentences." Coerced treatment and "the institutionalization of the therapeutic ethos can also be interpreted as the constitution of a regime of social control." Social problems such as illegal drug use are viewed as individualized "psychological pathologies needing therapeutic treatment."[149] In fact, identified social problems such as unemployment, addiction, and poverty are increasingly viewed as mental-health issues rather than structural issues related to globalization, and to race, class, and gender inequality.

Mental health researcher John Anderson asks how the proposed drug court in Vancouver (which is now running) will address the needs of users there. This question can be extended to other drug courts running or being proposed outside of Canada. He asks how drug courts will address the needs of Vancouver's illegal drug users in the Downtown Eastside where many users are homeless, unemployed, and inject heroin and cocaine, which places them at the risk of contracting HIV and hepatitis C and of taking a lethal overdose. He successfully argues that "there is no evidence that drug courts are effective at reducing the incidence of either of these serious health problems."[150] As well, drug courts will do little to limit the impact of poverty, violence against women, drug laws, racial profiling, and federal and local social and economic policy that shape the Downtown Eastside.

Although it is evident that drug courts have been viewed by many as a more humane alternative to drug offenders, treatment should never be linked to lowering criminal activity; the premise that drug use is linked to crime is flawed. Rather, our current drug laws contribute to punishment industries that create criminals out of a wide range of people who wish to alter their consciousness with an illegal

149. Furedi 2002: 217, 229.
150. Anderson 2000: 473.

rather than a legal drug. Drug court and drug treatment referral should not be the only option for women who wish to escape prison. Critics note that coerced medical control of drug users can be as coercive and as damaging as legal control, and the combination of the two can be even more oppressive.[151] In both the United States and Canada, voluntary drug treatment for women has been in short supply and funding is inadequate. In addition, publicly funded drug treatment is even more difficult to find in the U.S. Anderson asks why we would sabotage access to, and efforts to expand, voluntary treatment in favor of the criminal justice system as a "point of entry."[152]

Many studies demonstrate that recidivism rates are actually higher for drug court participants,[153] and others note that "reductions in recidivism are so small that if they exist at all they are statistically meaningless."[154] First-time offenders and casual users are in danger of becoming enmeshed in the criminal justice system and sent to prison if they cannot complete drug court programs. Drug court offenders may spend more time in the criminal justice system than their counterparts sentenced to probation or prison. In addition, those offenders are subject to being sent to prison for infractions of the rules, even though there is no evidence demonstrating that prison is therapeutic. As drug court critic Philip Bean argues, "The offender sent to prison for three days, three weeks, or three months is being punished, and a clear recognition needs to be made of that."[155]

In many programs in the U.S., participants have to pay for their treatment and this affects women disproportionately, given their lower economic status when compared with men. Given the concerns about unlawful convictions in relation to drug offenses, we should be wary of drug court procedure. Drug treatment may look more benign than prison, but for those women who will not successfully complete the program, prison is ultimately their destination. And for those women who do not have the economic means to fight their

151. Boyd 1999; Cohen 1985; Davies and Shewan 2000; Smart 1984.
152. Anderson 2001: 473.
153. Meithe and Reese 2000.
154. Hoffman 2000: 1533.
155. Bean 2002: 250.

drug conviction, including unlawful convictions, or who fear even harsher sentencing if they plead not guilty and go to trial (a reality in the U.S.), drug court and mandatory treatment is not a "choice." Rather, it is coerced social control of women who may have few resources to protect themselves from police profiling, the arm of the law, and the "helping" professions.

There has been little attention given to the needs of poor women and women of color—day-care provisions, job training, and education are not common components of the drug court programs. What, then, do drug courts have to offer women that they cannot achieve through voluntary treatment and increased social and economic support? How can social workers and drug treatment professionals working for the criminal justice system offer women anything more than further social control? Any pretension related to "care" will surely be tempered by their collaboration with punishment industries. As women move through the criminal justice system, some will be diverted to drug courts. The debate about whether to sanction drug courts seems immensely flawed given that no one should be criminalized for drug use or threatened with prison or mandatory treatment. In many ways, the debate obscures this fact. Critics point out that illegal drugs are criminalized, and drug courts offer a more humane avenue than traditional criminal justice sanctions. This is faulty logic. Channeling funding to the ever-expanding criminal justice system rather than providing more funding for voluntary treatment and economic and social services is detrimental to women and their families. Drug courts can do little to address the structural oppression that shapes their lives.

There is no evidence that criminal justice efforts, including drug courts, will reduce drug use, but this has not stopped us from granting the state and agencies working for the state, more and more powers to regulate drug users. Our reliance on punishment industries—in the forms of the adversarial rights-based criminal courts, prisons, drug courts, and supervision—is misguided and irrational. The practice of drug courts maintains and perpetuates the idea that drug users are out of control and in need of intrusive and punitive intervention and surveillance by the state, social services, and nongovernment agencies such as the medical profession. The female drug user is constructed as an individual with choices who lacks self-discipline, thus justifying punitive state, social service, and medical regulation. As funding for education, health, economic and social services for women and children are cut, criminal justice funding expands. Drug courts are simply criminal courts wrapped up in new clothing. Drug policy alternatives should challenge the status quo and address the many issues important to women, rather than maintain legal and medical coercion.

Conclusion

As we continue to ignore the lived realities of women who do not "fit" the medical model of addiction, and public health models, efforts to understand drug use and treatment is limited. The astonishing arrogance of some Western scientists becomes quite evident when we open our eyes to oppositional knowledges and practices. By viewing negative drug use as an individual pathology, we lose sight of cultural differences and of people's diverse experiences. As long as we claim that illegal drug users are compelled to use drugs, are individually responsible for their failure to abstain, and that these drugs are dangerous, women drug users will never be given full adult status. Criminalization and medicalization diminishes women's experiences with drug use and ignores social factors that shape drug use.[156]

Pathologizing and criminalizing women who use illegal drugs silence those stories that challenge conventional myths about users and treatment options. Instead of listening to the wealthy and the privileged who sell their stories to *People* magazine, or to advocates of programs such as DARE and Scared Straight, we might listen to those who ritually use plants to alter their consciousness—medicinal users of plants such as marijuana and opium, recreational users who have pleasant experiences, and users who are addicted to drugs, all of whom have different stories to tell. If we did so, this dialogue would

156. Davies and Shewan 2000.

be very different from the one we are having today. Anti drug-war groups and drug user unions throughout the Western world are attempting to turn the tide and are challenging conventional ideologies and practices which advocate that illegal drug users are in need of medical, legal, and social service control.

Critics are questioning why social problems such as poverty and addiction are linked to low self-esteem rather than to social factors, and are critical of the language of therapy rather than social change that is emphasized by politicians, judges, and those coerced into being "helped."[157] Our drug law and treatment ideology and practice fail to challenge the structural and interpersonal factors that impact women's lives in very negative ways. As we volunteer to govern ourselves in relation to our personal lives, those who refuse, or fail, are constructed as deviant, justifying professional and criminal justice interventions. Advancing self-control and sobriety as the template for citizenship is problematic, especially when coerced therapeutic intervention and prison are the alternatives for those women who fail to conform.

157. See Furedi 2000.

Chapter 5

Women in Conflict with the Law

More women are moving through the criminal justice system than previous generations in Britain, Canada, and the United States. In Britain and the U.S., drug convictions account for much of this increase. For many women, prison time will be their sentence. In the United States, disenfranchisement laws and restrictions on benefits, housing, and employment restrict women who have been criminalized for drug offences and block them from re-entering conventional society upon their release from prison. Today, as in the past, women's drug use is constructed as more deviant and dangerous than men's, for not only have they committed a crime, they have also transgressed their conventional gender role; in addition, they are blamed for the breakdown of the traditional nuclear family and for abandoning their maternal role. Poor women and women of color are especially vulnerable to legal regulation. British writer Kalunta-Crumpton argues that black women are viewed as aggressive and a threat to order, "racial images [which] are as old as the slave trade."[1]

In Britain, Canada, and the U.S., repressive prison policy and intrusive techniques have been implemented in order to fight the "war on drugs" in the prisons. Subsequently, women in prison are subject to increased surveillance. Arbitrary rules and punishments make an already unbearable environment worse. Conventional discourse about dangerous drugs, users, and traffickers promotes punitive practices

1. Kalunta-Crumpton: 1999: 199.

and deflects attention away from the erosion of civil rights, the tearing apart of families and communities, and the increased moral regulation and punishment of women. The prison-industrial complex presents real dangers to women and the goals of social justice. This chapter analyses these issues by examining sentencing, drug law, conflict with the law, and routes to arrest. In addition, the emergence of the prison, the pains of imprisonment, the restructuring of prison as a result of the war on drugs, and prison release for women in Britain, Canada, and the U.S. are explored.

Arrest Rates and Imprisonment of Women in Britain, Canada, and the U.S.

Women in Britain

Today, the Medicines Act 1968 (which regulates medicinal products) and the Misuse of Drugs Act 1971 (which regulates nonmedical use of drugs) regulate the use of drugs in Britain. Drug penalties are similar to Canada's drug laws: they are not lenient yet not as harsh as those in the U.S. The maximum sentence for possession of Class A drugs such as cocaine is seven years, and for Class B drugs such as cannabis and sedatives, five years. The highest penalty for trafficking in Class A drugs is life imprisonment. However, in 2004 the government reclassified cannabis from a Class B to a Class C drug. In practice, rather than on arrest, emphasis will be on warnings and confiscation of the drug.

In 1999, 90 percent of all drug offenders in Britain were found guilty or cautioned for possession. Similar to the U.S. and Canada, marijuana charges were significantly more frequent than cocaine and heroin charges. In 1999, 74 percent of all drug offences were for marijuana. In addition, in 1999, 11 percent of drug offenders in Britain were women.[2] By 2000, 39 percent of women in prison were serving

2. Corkery 2001: 31, 35, 30.

time for nonviolent drug offences (2 percent higher than 1998), compared with 15 percent of men.[3]

Similar to increasing prison rates for women in Canada and the U.S., the number of women in prison in Britain has doubled over the last decade. Not since the end of the nineteenth century have so many women been imprisoned; in fact, only 988 women were imprisoned in 1970, compared with 4,370 in 2002. Between April of 2001 and April of 2002, the number of women in prison increased by 22 percent (compared with a 7 percent increase in males held). In fact, women made up 6 percent of the prison population in 2002.[4] Claims that women in Britain are becoming more violent and criminal are unfounded. Women's offending in Britain, Canada, and the U.S. continues to be less violent and serious than men's (most common crimes are drug offences, theft and handling of stolen goods, forgery and fraud), posing little risk to the public. In fact, over a third of the women prisoners have had no previous convictions, and the remaining have a much lower conviction rate than men. Over half of the increase in the 1990s resulted from an increase in the number of women convicted of drug offences—between 1996–97, drug convictions accounted for 68 percent of the increases.[5] In 2002, drug convictions continued to account for increases in the female prison population; women sentenced to prison for drug charges increased 18 percent since 2001. Where men were more likely to be in prison for a violent offence, of the women in prison, the largest proportion were convicted for drug offences.[6] This is significant for several reasons. First, similar to men in Canada and the U.S., British men use more illegal drugs than women; however, women were overrepresented in prison in relation to drug convictions, and sentencing for drug offences were much longer than other crime categories. "For example, in 1997 the average sentence for a drug offence was 30 months compared with 10 months for theft."[7]

3. Elkins and Olagundoye 2001: 1.
4. Ibid.:1; Chad and Simes 2002: 1; Wedderburn 2000: 1.
5. Wedderburn 2000: 3.
6. Chad and Simes 2002: 10.
7. Wedderburn 2000: 3.

Over 25 percent of the female prison population in 1999 were ethnic minorities, and of those, 15 percent were foreign nationals. Black women made up 19 percent of the prison population and 2.5 percent of the general population in 2000.[8] In 2000, of the 39 percent of the female prison population who were serving time for a drug offence, 70 percent were foreign national women, and over half of these women were black.[9]

Carol Hedderman and Loraine Gelsthorpe's 1997 study, "Understanding the Sentencing of Women," included a sample of 332 female drug offenders in Britain (as well as a sample of male offenders for the same offence) in 1991, and interviews with lay magistrates and a few stipendiary magistrates in 1995.[10] They found that women convicted of drug offences were often older and more likely to be charged at Crown Court than their male counterparts, which is partially due to their vulnerability as "drug mules" (people who transport drugs). Furthermore, there was some evidence that magistrates categorized women offenders into "good" and "bad" women and expected "higher morality" from them than men. The authors noted that most magistrates were intolerant of drug and alcohol use, viewing them as "self-inflicted" problems.[11] Since the early 1990s, risk assessments for re-offending women have influenced sentencing. Poor women, black women, foreign nationals, unconventional women, women identified as illegal drug users, and women with children in care are constructed as being at "risk" of re-offending. Therefore, women who "suffer extreme social deprivation" and who have repeat offences for property crime and/or drug offences are more vulnerable to imprisonment today than in the past.[12]

Women in Canada

Unlike the U.S., all drug offences in Canada fall under federal jurisdiction that is regulated under the Controlled Drugs and Substance

8. Elkins and Olagundoye 2001: 3.
9. Ibid.:1–4; Wedderburn 2000: 12–13.
10. Hedderman and Gelsthorpe 1997.
11. Dowds and Hedderman 1997: 18; Gelsthorpe and Loucks 1997: 33.
12. Hudson 2002: 38–40. See Carlen 2002.

Act (CDSA) of 1997. Sentencing is less punitive than in the U.S. Still, the maximum penalty for possession of cocaine and heroin is seven years, and the maximum penalty for trafficking is life. The attempt to separate marijuana from "hard" drugs like heroin in the CDSA has culminated in a maximum penalty of five years less a day for trafficking 3 kilograms or less. Prolonged incarceration for drug offences is less common than in the U.S.; however, women arrested for transporting drugs receive harsh sentencing, and an accumulation of minor offences and parole violations can lead to prolonged imprisonment for some women.

Between 2000 and 2001, women made up 5 percent of federal prison admissions and 9 percent of provincial prison admissions.[13] In 2001, there were roughly 870 federally sentenced women (385 incarcerated) and 900 women serving time in provincial prisons. Eighteen percent of all adults charged with a criminal-code violation are women. Although First Nations women represent about 1 to 2 percent of the Canadian population, they make up 20 percent of female federal prisoners.[14] In many provincial prisons, the percentage is even higher. In addition, black women are overrepresented in the prisons of Nova Scotia and Ontario; in 1995, the Commission on Systemic Racism in the Ontario Criminal Justice System noted that since 1992 black women were affected by tough drug policy more than white women in their province.[15] Similar to Britain and the U.S., in Canada, drug offences are both racialized and gendered and poor women are most vulnerable to drug arrests and conviction.

The female prison population has tripled since 1970, even though the majority of female crime is made up of minor offences such as property offences. Statistics Canada 2000 states that 27 percent of federal prisoners and 13 percent of provincial female prisoners are serving time for drug-related offences. And though there has been much discussion about how women are given more lenient sentences than men (even though their crimes are less serious than men's), women

13. Hendrick and Farmer 2002: 10.

14. Correctional Services Canada 2002.

15. Commission on Systemic Racisim in the Ontario Criminal Justice System 1995.

who are convicted of drug trafficking serve more time in prison than men (median six months for women, four months for men).[16]

Similar to Britain and the U.S., the majority of drug offences in Canada in 2000—56 percent—were for possession, although the rate is considerably lower than both the U.S. (81 percent) and Britain (90 percent).[17] In 2001, 75 percent of drug offences were for cannabis and over 70 percent of these were for possession.[18] Even though Canada is not as committed to locking up drug offenders as the U.S., it has the "highest number of drug arrests per capita of any nation other than the United States."[19] Furthermore, *drug offences rose 9 percent from 1999 to 2000 and 6 percent from 2000 and 2001 due to increases in cannabis charges.*[20] A higher percentage of women in provincial and federal prison are serving time for drug offences than their male counterparts. In 1996, 27 percent of women in federal prison were serving time for a drug offence compared with 8 percent of men.[21] In addition, since 1997 there has been a 20 percent increase in the number of women serving time for drug-related sentences in federal prisons.[22]

Women in the U.S.

In the year 2002, there were over one million women moving through the criminal justice system in the U.S. Of these approximately 146,600 were in federal and state prisons and in county and city jails,[23] the remainder were on probation or on parole.[24] At the end of 2002, women made up about 7 percent of the state and 8 percent of the federal prison population.[25] Of the total women in federal

16. Statistics Canada 2000: 177, 174.
17. Gannon 2001: 10.
18. Savoie 2002: 11.
19. PASAN 1994: 153.
20. CCJS 2001: 10; Savoie 2002: 1.
21. Statistics Canada 2000: 186.
22. Correctional Service Canada 2002–03.
23. Fitzgerald 2000: 11.
24. CANY/WPP 2002b.
25. U.S. Federal Bureau of Prisons 2002: 52.

prison in 2003, 67 percent were drug offenders (compared with 56 percent of men in federal prison).[26] The U.S. imprisons ten times more women than Western European countries whose combined population is similar to the U.S.[27] Women of color make up two-thirds of the female prison population[28]—black women are five times more likely and Hispanic women twice as likely to be incarcerated than white women.[29] It is estimated that the number of women entering prison has risen 400 percent, double the rate of men since the 1980s.[30] In addition, the rates of female detention for the Immigration and Naturalization Service doubled between 1995 and 1998.[31]

Women are most often imprisoned for nonviolent crimes such as property crimes and drug offences; however, since the 1980s, drug offences have accounted for much of the rise in the female prison population. In fact, women's drug-related incarceration has increased at a faster rate than men's.[32] Compared with one in ten women serving time in prison for a drug offence in 1979, one out

---

26. Ina Winn, Federal Bureau of Prisons (Personal communication, February 13, 19, 20, 2003).

27. Amnesty International 1999. The United States incarcerates more people than any other Western democracy, the majority being nonviolent drug offenders. Drug-law violators make up 60 percent of all federal prisoners; the rate has doubled from 31,300 sentenced drug offenders in 1990 to 63,011 sentenced drug offenders in 1998,1 and 23 percent of all state prisoners (see USDJ 2000a: 6, USDJ 1999: 3). To put this in perspective with the rest of the world, the U.S. has "100,000 more persons behind bars *just for drug offenses*... than the European Union has *for all offenses*... even though the EU has 100 million more citizens than the U.S" (see Beatty et al. 2000: 4). As disturbing is the fact that two out of three people entering prison in Texas in 1998 did so because of parole or probation violations, and half of these were for technical violations. More people in Texas are moving through the criminal justice system than any other state, for one out of twenty Texans are either in prison, jail, parole or probation, comprising 5 percent of the population. And despite its punitive imprisonment policy, Texas has a much higher crime rate than the national average (see Kaplan et al. 2000: 2).

28. CANY/WPP 2000.

29. Harrison and Beck 2002: 12.

30. CANY/WPP 2000a.

31. Bhattacharjee 2002: 4.

32. Amnesty International 1999.

of three women in prison are serving time for a drug offence today.[33] Although the war on drugs has been noted as a "war on women," not all women are impacted similarly, for the war on drugs targets the poor and black and Latino women. The report, "Gender and Justice: Women Drugs and Sentencing Policy," states that in 1995, Hispanic and black women made up 91 percent of the drug sentences in New York, even though they represented 32 percent of the general state population. Over 70 percent of drug offenders, in contrast to all offenders (50 percent), in New York faced second felony charges and were subject to mandatory sentencing, where judges were required to sentence defendants to prison. [34] Since the Rockerfeller Drug laws were passed in 1973, the female prison population has increased from 400 women in state prison to over 3,133 by 2002.[35]

In California, drug sentencing was shaped by the 1994 "three-strikes out" legislation, and mandatory minimums that limit judicial discretion. Three-strikes out convictions evoke a mandatory life sentence with no parole eligibility for twenty-five years, and two-strikes out convictions result in mandatory double sentencing for the offence. In California in 1995, black and Hispanic women made up 54 percent of the women's prison population sentenced for drugs even though they only made up 38 percent of the state's female population. Arrests grew significantly more for white women (48 percent increase) than for black (6 percent increase) and Hispanic (20 percent increase) women between 1986 and 1995. Nevertheless, black women are still overrepresented in terms of drug arrests (27 percent arrest rate, though they only make up 7 percent of the female population).[36] In November 2000, the Substance Abuse and Crime Prevention Act (Proposition 36) was passed by California voters. This initiative grants first- and second-time offenders for nonviolent drug possession to be diverted to drug treatment rather than sent to prison.

33. Bloom et al. 1994; Amnesty International 1999: 5.
34. Mauer et al. 1999a: 3, 7.
35. CANY/WPP 2002b.
36. Mauer et al. 1999a: 3, 9.

At the end of 2000, women convicted of drug offences in the U.S. accounted for a significantly larger portion of the growth in female prisoners (33 percent) than male prisoners (12 percent).[37] Of the specific categories listed by the Uniform Crime Reports (excluding traffic violations), there are more drug arrests in the U.S. than in any other arrest category (11 percent of all arrests, much more than larceny thefts, simple assault, and so on).[38] Since the 1970s, the penalty for possession of small amounts of marijuana has been reduced to a misdemeanor in twelve states. However, in 2001 almost half of all drug arrests in the U.S. were for marijuana and 80.6 percent of all drug arrests were for possession.[39] Thus, the drug "king pins" are rarely arrested. It is the poor, visible, nonviolent illegal drug "user" who is most at risk of imprisonment. It is difficult to assess how many women sentenced to federal prison are foreign nationals, for government statistics fail to differentiate between illegal aliens, legal residents, and visitors. Nevertheless, federal statistics state that in 2003, 29.3 percent of men and women in federal prison were non-citizens, and 16.1 percent of them were from Mexico.[40] Criminologist Michael Welch notes that "under the Illegal Immigration Reform and Immigrant Responsibility Act and the Antiterrorism and Effective Death Penalty Act passed by Congress in 1966, the Immigration and Naturalization Service has enjoyed new and expansive powers that allow the agency to detain and deport any legal (and illegal) immigrant who has been charged with or convicted of a drug offense."[41] However, deportation usually occurs after prisoners have served their time in prison, for the majority of states refuse to abide by international treaties signed by the U.S. to transfer foreign-born prisoners to serve their prison time in their country of birth. After serving their sentence, many prisoners have been deported to their birth countries, where they no longer have family or connections. The Patriot Act (and the proposed Vital Interdic-

37. Harrison and Beck 2002: 13.

38. USDJ 2000d: 2.

39. Oziewicz 2003; U.S. Department of Justice 2002: 232.

40. U.S. Federal Bureau of Prisons 2003; Ina Winn, Federal Bureau of Prisons (Personal communication February 13, 19, 20, 2003).

41. Welch 2002: 2.

tion of Criminal Terrorist Organizations [Victory] Act of 2003 and the Patriot II Act) has increased racial and religious (e.g. Muslim) profiling, incarceration, and deportation.

Conflict with the Law

Women, Prostitution, and Drug Dealing

Women suspected of using and/or selling drugs come into conflict with the law in numerous ways. Illegal drug users are stereotypically depicted as poor and belonging to ethnic/racial minority groups, and there is much speculation about how they can afford to buy drugs in the illegal market (especially when drugs are sold at inflated prices). Unlike pharmaceutical companies, which can advertise their products to consumers, the criminalization of "specific" drugs places many women in a precarious situation because they are at risk for arrest if they use, buy, sell, or produce illegal drugs. They are also at risk of arrest if they associate with others involved in the illegal drug market. Most women in Britain, Canada, and the U.S. are arrested for drug possession rather than for drug dealing. I want to make this fact clear, as it is often lost in the drug war rhetoric. In addition, marijuana arrests make up the largest category of drug arrests. Rather than focus on this phenomenon, most researchers have been curious about how women users of illegal drugs such as cocaine and heroin finance their drug use.

For example, prostitution and the exchange of sex for drugs, especially what has been labelled the "sex-for-crack phenomenon," has been explored.[42] Much of the academic writing from the U.S. on the sex-for-crack phenomenon has been exploitive, even though the authors claim it to be otherwise.[43] Other researchers have challenged sexualized stereotypes and the direct link between prostitution and illegal drug use. Many studies demonstrate that women have not turned to prostitution, or have done so infrequently, to support ille-

---

42. Bourgois and Dunlap 1993; Inciardi, Lockwood, and Pottieger 1993; Ratner 1993.

43. See Inciardi et al. 1993; and Ratner 1993.

gal drug use.[44] Furthermore, in many cases illegal drug use did not precipitate prostitution; rather, poverty most often initiated an interest in prostitution,[45] although over time drug use may have increased for those women who worked as street prostitutes.[46] In countries such as the Netherlands and Belgium, where there are more adequate social supports than in the U.S., women rarely report engaging in sex for drugs.[47] In Barbara Denton's 2001 study of female drug dealers in Australia, prostitution played a very small role, nor was it a "natural" option for those women using illegal drugs.[48]

Lurid stories about "crack whores" tend to ignore the fact that, historically, some women and men have exchanged sex for goods. The criminalization of specific drugs, such as heroin and cocaine, fuels high prices on the illegal drug market. Some researchers suggest that exchanging sex for drugs is one response to "poverty, ethnic segregation, and polarized gender relations" in the U.S. where women and children "suffer the most."[49] Conventional research constructs female drug use through the lens of victimization and pathology and fails to see how drug use is shaped by class inequality and how it is gendered and racialized. Criminologist Neil Websdale points out that poor women living in public housing in the U.S. often need to supplement their incomes in order to care for their children because their welfare benefits are inadequate. Thus, some women may engage in illegal activities to survive.[50] They might sell drugs or associate with men who do so. In addition, some women might supplement their incomes through prostitution, which can result in lengthy criminal records due to their increased visibility.

Outside of legitimate employment, drug dealing tends to be women's most common choice for financing their illegal drug use and

44. Boyd 1999; Denton 2001; Morgan and Joe 1997; Taylor 1993.
45. Boyd 1999; Rosenbaum 1981; Taylor 1993.
46. Lowman and Fraser 1995.
47. Cohen 1989, 1991; Decorte 2000.
48. Denton 2001.
49. Bourgois and Dunlap 1993: 129.
50. Websdale 2001: 64.

supplementing their inadequate incomes.[51] Not all illegal drug users participate in the illegal drug market in terms of cultivating, selling, or transporting drugs. Nor are all drug dealers illegal drug users. People who engage in the cultivation, selling, and transportation of illegal drugs also have legal employment.[52] In fact, in a study that included both women and men in Antwerp, Belgium, 73 percent of the participants had *never* engaged in an illegal activity to secure money to buy cocaine.[53] In addition, Peter Cohen's two sociological studies of male and female cocaine users in Amsterdam demonstrate even lower levels of illegal activity used to obtain money to buy cocaine.[54] Outside of legitimate employment, selling cocaine was the preferred criminal activity for men and women in the Amsterdam and Antwerp studies. In Dan Waldorf, Craig Reinarman, and Sheigla Murphy's 1991 study of 228 women and men who used cocaine in California, three out of five had never been arrested in their lives for any crime. In addition, one in five had been arrested for drug possession (although less than half were convicted), and only one in twenty was arrested for drug selling (again, less than half of these were convicted).[55]

Most women do not set out to become drug dealers; rather, they "drift" into drug dealing to support themselves and their families. By pooling money with friends, they are able to pay lower prices for higher quality drugs in larger quantities.[56] Many studies have focused on poor, marginalized illegal drug users and sellers whose low-level dealing reflected their subordinate social status in society. Criminologist Lisa Maher notes that for poor black and Hispanic women in Brooklyn, selling crack in the 1990s did not provide "equal opportunity employment;" instead, they were stigmatized more than men and subjected to risk and violence.[57] Similarly, anthropologist Philippe

51. Ibid.; Morgan and Joe 1997.

52. Bourgois 1995; Boyd 1999; Decorte 2000; Fields and Walter 1985; Hagedorn 1994; Waldorf et al. 1991; Waterston 1993.

53. Decorte 2000: 89.

54. Cohen 1989; Cohen and Sas 1993.

55. Waldorf et al. 1991: 294, 295.

56. Ibid.

57. Maher 1995.

Bourgois notes that Hispanic women in East Harlem—El Barrio—were also attempting to gain more "autonomy and rights" but their quest was limited to the streets of El Barrio.[58]

The reasons, women use and sell drugs are diverse. For example, the women in Denton's study were not drug-driven and drug use was not an all-consuming activity. They saw their drug dealing and property crime as "work," and, like many people in the conventional workforce, it was a source of pride, excitement, self-esteem, and of course monetary reward. These women were not "passive" players or "driven" into crime; rather they were capable and successful in their trade and provided financially for their family and friends.[59]

Shoshana Pollack's 2000 study of Caribbean-Canadian women in prison also breaks many stereotypes about women who come into conflict with the law. All of the women she interviewed stated that the "primary motivation for breaking the law was money." They discussed how their independence was constantly undermined by low wages, "government and social services, gender inequities and systemic racism."[60] Although some of the women were serving time for drug importation charges, none were illegal drug users. Patricia Morgan and Karen Ann Joe's 1997 research on women who sold methamphetamine in three U.S. cities demonstrates how women engage in drug selling and transporting in order to avoid dependency and in order to provide for their children in a world where there is little social support for them. They also explore how race, class, and gender inequities shape the conditions of women's lives and limit their choices. Morgan and Joe challenge stereotypes about women who are involved in the illegal drug trade; they state that, "most women who use and sell illicit drugs are not from minority disenfranchised populations living in large inner-city communities; most women who use and sell illicit drugs have not, and likely never will, engage in prostitution or felonious acts apart from illicit drug sale."[61]

58. Bourgois 1995: 213, 241.
59. Denton 2001.
60. Pollack 2000: 77, 76.
61. Morgan and Joe 1997: 107.

Drug dealing can bring women status, dignity, power, self-esteem, fulfilment, financial stability, and material goods that are unavailable to them in the legal market. Bourgois notes that in poor neighborhoods in East Harlem, drug dealing is normalized. However, drug dealing is not limited to the poor—it is a normalized activity in families and extended families who are not members of the urban poor.[62] Thus, we need to expand our analysis and popular misconceptions to understand how female drug dealers, whether lower, middle-, or upper-class, derive positive rewards (including monetary) from their work. Furthermore, we need to explore whether we are examining the impact of poverty, racism, and patriarchal violence in the lives of women, or whether we are describing the effects of drug dealing. When we begin to expand our analysis, many of our well-worn stereotypes about the "drug dealer" fall short.

However, race and class factors come into play for women who sell drugs in terms of police profiling, arrest, and conviction. Women of color and poor women are the most vulnerable to arrest and conviction and are often situated at the lowest level of the drug economy, mirroring their status in society. Many women working on the streets who sell small amounts of illegal drugs are exposed to both police and male violence. Poor women of color from Third World countries have been recruited to transport drugs into Western nations; these women, labeled "drug mules," are subject to long prison terms in countries where they often have little knowledge of the criminal justice system. British writer Pat Carlen notes that many women agree to transport drugs because they are poor and struggling to make ends meet. For those women who do transport/sell illegal drugs and are arrested, prison is often another arena of inequality and injustice.[63]

Although most drug couriers are men, the media has focused on reports that construct women as "drug traffickers."[64] It is often believed that all illegal drug users engage in criminal activity to support

62. Boyd 1999; Morgan and Joe 1997.

63. Carlen 1998.

64. Green 1996.

their drug use. In addition, as discussed above, it is believed that women most often finance their illegal drug use through prostitution. In fact, the majority of women and men who use illegal drugs in Western societies never engage in violence or in any crime outside the buying of their drug of choice. For the small percentage that do engage in criminal activities, it usually consists of nonviolent, low-level drug dealing and nonviolent crime such as cheque forgery, prostitution, and theft.[65] In fact, alcohol use is more closely associated with violent crime in Western societies.[66] Illegal drugs in themselves do not cause violent behavior and most drug-related violence can be attributed to the "illegal drug market *system*" (italics in original).[67] The illegal market is a direct result of drug prohibition.

Racial Profiling

Police and federal agents in Britain, Canada, the U.S., and in other Western nations assume that drug dealing is an illegal business solely run by people of color.[68] In fact, Drug Enforcement Agency (DEA) agents in the U.S. have claimed that drug couriers are often black females and that Hispanic and black people in general fit their profile of the drug dealer.[69] This type of racial profiling is evident in the practice of customs agents in U.S. airports where people of color are more likely to be searched by customs agents than are white people. A study of the U.S. customs service found that of the 102,000 people subjected to personal searches in the fiscal years of 1997 and 1998, 52 percent were people of color. Of these travelers, 31 percent were Hispanic, 13 percent were black, and 8 percent were Asian. In contrast, 25 percent of searched travelers were white. Furthermore, black women were more likely to be strip-searched than all other women and male travelers. Black women were also more likely to be

65. Alexander 1990.

66. Mumola 1999: 2.

67. Goldstein et al. 1997: 123.

68. HRW 2000a; Kalunta-Crumpton 1999; Mauer and The Sentencing Project 1999b; Mosher 1998.

69. Weich and Angula 2000: 3.

subjected to the most intrusive personal searches. In 1998, black women were nine times more likely to be x-rayed and two times more likely to be strip-searched than white women. In addition, all minority women (Hispanic, black, and Asian) were almost three times as likely as minority men to be strip-searched. There were no differences in the likelihood of being strip-searched between white men and women.[70]

Equally disturbing as the rate of strip-searches and x-rays of minority women was the finding that women, especially black women, who were strip-searched were less likely than their male counterparts to have illegal contraband on them. Black women were almost half as likely as white women to be carrying any contraband.[71] However, law-enforcement agents believe that drug couriers transporting marijuana, referred to as "marijuana mules," tend to be black women who are U.S. residents on welfare.[72]

Of the total personal searches at the JFK Airport in New York, *96 percent were failures, and unjustified, as no illegal contraband was found.* Only 4 percent of the personal searches were successful. However, there is no breakdown of what types of contraband were found and what percentage were illegal drugs. The profiling of all women for personal searches demonstrates how race and gender profiling (no class information was provided in the U.S. customs service study) and stereotypes about drug users, dealers, and drug couriers inform the practice of custom agents. Women, especially women of color, are targeted by customs agents even though they fail to deliver up the illegal drugs and contraband that customs agents search for. Race is one of the most important determining factors in the drug war, even though studies demonstrate that black and Hispanic people have the same, or lower, rate of drug use than white people. Racial profiling stemming from the institutionalization of racism and white-supremacist colonial ideology and policy, informs all criminal justice and customs practice. Since September 11, 2001, customs budgets have increased in Britain,

70. Ekstrand and Blume 2000: 49, 12, 40, 49.
71. Ibid.: 49, 10.
72. Huling 1992: 11.

Canada, and the U.S., and more agents have been deployed to guard "the nation" from suspected "foreign terrorists."[73]

Gendered Drug Law in the U.S.

Drug Conspiracy and Drug Couriers

Minorities and the poor are especially vulnerable to harsh sentences based on the class, and race, and gender profiling conducted by the police and federal agents; drug convictions and prison populations confirm this. Poor women of all racial and ethnic backgrounds are subjected to harsh sentencing because they rarely have evidence, which might reduce their sentence, to offer prosecutors after they are arrested for drug violations. It is usually the higher-level dealer who provides the names of people below them to prosecutors in order to reduce their own sentence. This situation of giving evidence against others is exacerbated by conspiracy laws, rigid mandatory sentencing and the elimination of parole for federal drug offences. The only way drug offenders can reduce their own sentence is to provide state evidence—to snitch on friends, family, and business associates. U.S. federal law permits the use of uncorroborated testimony in conspiracy cases; thus, no physical evidence of drugs is needed, only the testimony of others. And while drug defendants snitch on others (some who are innocent), they often walk free and receive much more lenient sentences than those they expose. Given the long sentences that drug defendants face, and the coercion they experience at the hands of prosecutors who pressure them to cooperate, it is not surprising that snitching has become an essential component of the U.S. legal system. Drug defendants who don't cooperate know that the full weight of the criminal justice system will be utilized and they will be severely punished for failing to provide evidence. Consequently, women have been imprisoned merely due to

73. Even though an American citizen was responsible for the Oklahoma bombing and naturalized residents were involved in the World Trade Center and the Pentagon attacks.

their association with their sons and boyfriends who have been arrested for drug violations.

Dorothy Gaines, a black women, and mother of three children, was sentenced to prison for nineteen years and seven months for two counts of conspiracy to possess and distribute crack cocaine. Allegedly, she possessed over one and a half kilograms of crack; however, the exact amount is vague because, even though Dorothy's home was searched by law officials, the drugs (material evidence) were never found. Nor was money or drug paraphernalia. Dorothy Gaines was arrested and later convicted because she had dated a man who used crack. He and others were implicated in a drug arrest and defendants gave evidence against her in order to lower their own sentences. The Alabama state court rejected the case against her due to lack of evidence. However, the case was moved up to the federal level in 1994.[74] Whether a case is tried in state or federal court is important to the female drug defendant for four reasons. First, parole was abolished in 1987 for federal cases; second, sentencing in federal court for drug cases is most often shaped by harsh mandatory sentences; third, federal prosecutors can forbid plea bargaining, which limits alternatives to imprisonment and severely limits drug treatment opportunities; and fourth, judges have little discretion in federal drug cases.[75]

Dorothy Gaines assumed that she would be found not guilty by the jury, so she did not plea bargain. At the trial, she was painted as an essential player in the men's crack-dealing enterprise and the jury found her guilty. Even though she was a first-time offender, her sentence was not reduced because she had refused to cooperate by giving evidence or taking a plea bargain. Of the two male defendants tried at the same time as Gaines, and who gave evidence against her, one has already been released, and the other's release date is set for 2004. Dorothy Gaines earliest release date was set for 2012; however, as a result of international and national pressure, President Clinton pardoned her in 2000 and she was able to rejoin her family.[76] Nevertheless, Dorothy Gaines's prison time was deeply felt by both her and her family.

74. Stewart 1998.

75. Weich and Angula 2000: 12.

76. FAMM 2000.

Women smuggling drugs into the U.S. are also subject to harsh sentencing and there is concern that some of these women are innocent, having been tricked or threatened into carrying drugs. Data from Tracy Huling's study, "Injustice Will Be Done: Women Drug Couriers and the Rockefeller Drug Laws," shows that of the total women arrested at the JFK Airport and charged as drug couriers (A-I drug charges) between January 1990 and December 1991, 93 percent plea-bargained to reduce their sentencing, and only 5 percent went to trial. Of those women who plea-bargained, 96 percent had no prior criminal record. She questions the extensive use of plea bargaining from women who face A-I felony drug charges. Case studies of women charged as drug couriers demonstrates that the New York criminal justice system is incapable of determining many women's guilt.[77]

Huling raises several disturbing issues about the cases in her study. First, the data demonstrate that black and Hispanic women are victims of racial profiling by custom agents. There is evidence to suggest that not only are some women coerced into carrying drugs but they are also used as "decoys." and custom agents are tipped off about them. These decoys are used to deflect attention away from other more experienced drug couriers on the same flights who are also carrying illegal drugs. Second, many women arrested as drug couriers cannot afford bail; thus, they are detained in jail. Huling notes that she was not aware of any woman arrested as a drug courier who was released on bail. Third, women in prison who are denied bail are unable to develop an effective defense, for they have little access to phones and cannot visit their defense lawyers. Most are poor and unable to hire costly investigators, and court-appointed lawyers have huge caseloads and limited budgets. As well, visiting women in jail presents numerous problems for defense lawyers because visits often take up many hours. In addition, most women are advised by their lawyers to plea bargain, which is an admission of guilt, in order to reduce their sentences, regardless of their innocence or guilt. Finally, many of the women interviewed in Huling's study never saw the illegal drugs that they were accused of carrying. In several cases, the coats and bags that the illegal drugs were reported to be in were taken from the women when

77. Huling 1992.

they were detained, and they did not reappear when the drugs were "discovered" by customs authorities. When a woman plea-bargains, the case does not go to trial and the drugs are not required as evidence.

Feminist researchers note that throughout the world women's participation in the drug trade is shaped by international and national political, social, and economic factors that have an impact on the lives of women. They note that poor and racialized women who work as drug couriers are at the lowest echelon of the drug economy, mirroring their status in society. Poor and racialized women are motivated by poverty and familial concerns and are also the most visible of workers in the drug economy and thus vulnerable to arrest, conviction, and imprisonment.[78]

Plea Bargaining

Draconian drug laws, including mandatory minimum and three- and two-strikes out legislation, have led to the widespread use of plea bargaining and the entry of guilty pleas in the U.S. Female drug defendants are warned by prosecutors that they will pay the price if they proceed to trial. Innocent women and men have entered a plea bargain, fearful that they will receive longer sentences if their cases go to trial.[79] Improper police activity, which is "tested" at trial, cannot be scrutinized when drug offenders plea bargain (and there is a tremendous amount of police corruption related to drug law enforcement). And the right to due process of law is jeopardized because people fear that they will not be given a fair trial.[80] Drug offenders who plead not guilty and who are later convicted at trial can expect to spend even more time in prison than violent offenders and other drug war prisoners who plea bargain. In 1997 and 1998, drug violators convicted at trial were sentenced to 188.4 months on average, compared with those convicted by a guilty plea who were sentenced to seventy-one months on average.[81]

78. Green 1996, 1998; Joshua 1996; Wedderburn 2000.
79. DPTF 1996; SenGupta and Peterson 1999.
80. DPTF 1996.
81. USDJ 2000a: 62.

Drug offenders tend to be serving more time than non-drug offenders, and this has a negative effect on them and on their children, their families, and their communities. In fact, nonviolent drug offenders serve similar prison sentences as people convicted of murder and kidnapping, and more prison time than those convicted of rape, manslaughter, and assault.[82] Furthermore, black and Hispanic people are overrepresented in federal courts. Due to racial profiling and more punitive sentencing for crack than powder cocaine, black and Hispanic people made up almost all crack prosecutions (96.5 percent) in the period between 1992 and 1994.[83] In the face of mounting evidence of unlawful convictions, and lack of evidence in conspiracy trials, these statistics are revealing in their punitive nature against suspected drug law violators.

Asset Seizures and the Impact on Women

Women in the U.S are vulnerable to civil forfeiture law. The U.S. Comprehensive Crime Control Act of 1984 contributed to the rise of seizures by allowing federal agencies to keep most of the assets (property, money, and goods) of suspects. Both state and local agencies are offered up to 80 percent of the assets they seize if they bring their case to federal court. In 1984, only eight states had asset forfeiture laws; however, by 1991, forty-three states had them. There are huge incentives for local, state, and federal agents to seize assets. Many of these seizures are conducted under civil rather than criminal law. Under civil law, the presumption of innocence until proven guilty does not exist. Therefore, many innocent people have had their property seized, and it is rare for them to go to trial to recover their assets because they no longer have the financial means to do so.[84]

Women who live with men suspected of producing and selling illegal drugs are also at risk. Civil forfeiture impacts women in very gender-specific ways as a result of the "innocent owner" concept, which refers to women who own, share, co-own, or lease property

82. Ibid.: 62.
83. Weich and Angula 2000: 13.
84. Redden 2000: 201, 202.

with male partners whose property has been seized by the government. Researchers James Massey, Susan Miller, and Anna Whilhelmi examined fifty-three federal court cases between 1986 and 1995 that involved women who wished to reclaim property seized through civil forfeiture.[85] Most of the women in these cases were wives, although some were mothers, girlfriends, and daughters. What makes innocent-owner claims problematic is that their property may be targeted for forfeiture even though there are no criminal proceedings; thus, property can be seized if there is "probable cause" that the property was engaged in the commitment of a crime. Claimants must initiate the process to recover their property and to challenge government claims to the property.

The court consistently views women as culpable in their partners' "suspected" crimes. In *U.S. v. 755 Forest Road* 1993, the court ruled that the wife was willfully blind to her husband's drug use. In *U.S. v. Sixty Acres* 1990, a wife claimed that she lived in fear of her husband and was unaware of his drug dealing, and although the appellate court had evidence that he had threatened her and had "beaten to death his previous wife,"[86] she was denied her claim because the court felt that harm was not imminent or immediate; thus, it could not have affected her "duress" nor her knowledge of her husband's activities.

The link connecting all of the civil forfeiture cases examined by Massey, Miller, and Whilhelmi was the judge's belief that the wife must have known about her husband's drug use and/or selling because she was not only intimate with her partner but she lived with him, and yet did little to stop his behavior. Judges construct women as inherently more moral than men and as responsible for the regulation of the home and of male behavior. Judges fail to recognize the many social factors that shape women's lives, including violence against women by men, unequal power relations, exclusion from decision-making in the home, and economic deprivation at the hands of their partners and the larger society. The children of female claimants also suffer when the government seizes property perma-

85. Massey, Miller, and Wilhelmi 1998.
86. Ibid.: 24.

nently, and when women are technically "married to the government" and lose their right to will their property to their children.

Some of the civil forfeiture abuses of the past in the U.S. have been addressed in the Civil Asset Forfeiture Reform Act of 2000. However, it is only a small step, and it does little to rectify local, state, and federal agencies directly benefiting from the assets they seize, nor the gender bias and victimization of women who live with men suspected of using, producing, or dealing drugs.

Drug War Refugees

Woman activists fighting the war on drugs have been subject to police harassment and persecution. Even though Canada has legalized medical marijuana (although it is highly restricted) as have some states, many well-known marijuana activists, organizers, and patients of "compassion clubs" have been subjected to persecution.[87] The first compassion club opened in San Francisco and since then they have emerged in Britain, Canada, and elsewhere. At the club, marijuana is available to people suffering from diseases that can be treated with it. Marijuana is used today by people suffering from nausea and vomiting due to cancer chemotherapy and AID's wasting syndrome (marijuana stimulates the appetite); glaucoma; epilepsy; multiple sclerosis; muscle spasms and tremors in paraplegia and quadriplegia; migraines; rheumatic diseases; premenstrual syndrome; menstrual cramps; labor pains; chronic pain; depression; and mood disorders.[88] The harassment and arrest of compassion club activists has been a priority of the DEA in the U.S. as federal agents defy state law that has legalized medical marijuana use.

In 1998, Renee Boje escaped to Canada from California after she was arrested and charged by federal agents who informed her that state laws, specifically Proposition 215, contravened federal law. Renee had been hired by Todd McCormick, a cancer sufferer who grew marijuana at his home, to illustrate a book he was writing about

87. Damuzi 2000; WAMM 2003.

88. For a more comprehensive discussion, see Grinspoon and Bakalar 1997: 23–162, from which this list is drawn.

medical marijuana. Following her arrest, the DEA pressured her to testify against McCormick and his publisher. She refused. Although her charges were eventually dropped, the DEA has pursued her case and representatives of John Walters, the drug czar in the U.S., have publically claimed that they wish to make an example of her and will continue to aggressively pursue her extradition from Canada.

Renee Boje is one of a handful of U.S. citizens who are seeking asylum in Canada as a drug war refugee. In the U.S., Renee could be subject to a mandatory minimum sentence of ten years to life if she is found guilty. The U.S. government is intent on having her extradited from Canada because they fear that her case may be precedent-setting; they also seem irked that Renee is defying them. If Canada accepts Renee as a drug war refugee, it is believed that it will pave the way for other U.S. medical marijuana users, cultivators, and organizers of compassion clubs who face arrest to flee to Canada, just as Vietnam draftees and deserters did in the 1960s and early 1970s.[89] On February 9, 2000, a B.C. Supreme Court judge ordered Renee to surrender herself to the authorities for extradition. She was then released on bail and is now appealing to the Canadian public and the Minister of Justice to intervene.

During the seventy-two hours Renee Boje was detained after her arrest in the U.S., she was strip-searched fifteen times, twice in front of male officers who made "lewd and threatening remarks." Canadian lawyer Eugene Oscapella and other supporters have asked that the minister of justice in Canada support Renee Boje's claim for refugee status, and that she not be extradited to the U.S. Given U.S. reports of sexual and physical abuse of women in prisons, drug laws and sentencing which are disproportionate to penalties in Canada, and Canada's federal medical marijuana policy and public support for decriminalizing marijuana possession, it is argued that Renee should be allowed to stay in Canada.[90]

Since the terrorist attacks on the World Trade Center and the Pentagon in 2001, the White House has made a point of arresting medical marijuana users and compassion club organizers in the U.S. In California, the DEA has targeted compassion clubs and hospices even

89. Damuzi 2000.
90. Oscapella 200l: 14.

though they are protected under state law. Valerie Corral, the founder and director of Wo/Men's Alliance for Medical Marijuana (WAMM) in Santa Cruz, and her husband, Michael, were arrested in September 2002. WAMM is a non-profit collective which helped mostly terminally ill patients control pain and other symptoms. Challenging the federal government, on December 10, 2002, the City of Santa Cruz's city council voted unanimously to give Valerie Corral and her husband Michael "authority to cultivate, distribute, and possess medical marijuana."[91] On April 23, 2003, the City of Santa Cruz, WAMM, and seven patients filed the first lawsuit by the public against the federal government (*County of Santa Cruz et. al. V. Ashcroft et. al.*) requesting that the federal government cease their raids and respect California law.[92] In August 2003, the San Jose District Court dismissed the lawsuit. Valerie Corral, Renee Boje, and others are victims of the war on drugs and of the contested area between U.S. federal and state law.

Prison and the Regulation of Women

The war on drugs has not only impacted sentencing and increased prison rates, it has also contributed to the restructuring of the prison system, and many argue that a new punitiveness towards women has emerged. Given the increased prison rates for women largely to non-violent drug convictions in Britain and the U.S., and the overrepresentation of women compared with men who are sentenced to prison for drug offences in Britain, Canada and the U.S., it is worthwhile examining the emergence of the prison and the penitentiary system as the major form of punishment in Western nations that contribute to the social control of "unruly" women.[93] Feminist researchers in Britain, Canada, and the U.S. note that punishment remains central to prison strategy. Many of the past issues and concerns of women prisoners are relevant today. It is interesting to note that the regula-

91. Drug Policy Alliance 2002.

92. WAMM 2003.

93. See Karlene Faith's 1993 book, "Unruly Women: The Politics of Confinement and Resistance."

tion of unruly women during the witch hunts was central to the creation of the criminal justice system as we now know it. The regulation of altered states of consciousness and the sexualization of women's crimes stems from this era.

The Emergence of the Prison

Historically, the rich and powerful in Western nations (who were primarily white men), have viewed the poor and colonized groups as dangerous and thus more likely to be criminal than the rich. Throughout history, the rich have also been able to escape punishment for many of their actions.[94] Prior to the 1800s, offenders were incarcerated for short periods of time while they awaited trial or transportation. Fines, transportation, and corporal punishment were the preferred punishments. It was not until the 1800s that reformers sought to curtail public executions and other forms of corporal punishment, and prison construction and long-term incarceration began as we know it today. Jeremy Bentham's panopticon was the idealized construction for the new prison regime. This shift signifies the movement from corporal punishment to the regulation of both the body and the soul. The shift in penal practice was not humanitarian reform; rather, prison construction and prison administrators rushed to ensure that their prisoners were subject to "surveillance" at all times.[95] Quaker social reformers saw the penitentiary as a place to do penance, and the construction of the prison assured this for it offered a site of total surveillance, enforced solitude, religious instruction, penance, and the redemption of the prisoner's soul. There is no substantial evidence that the caging of people in prison for long periods of time reduces crime, but this has not deterred governments from building more prisons and housing more prisoners since the 1800s. Michel Foucault states, "Prison is the only place where power is manifested in its naked state, in its most excessive form, and where it is justified as moral force."[96]

94. Rennie 1978.
95. Faith 1994: 21.
96. Foucault 1977: 210.

Penance and religious instruction fell out of favor in the 1950s and was largely replaced by the psy-profession's emphasis on treatment. However, since the 1970s there has been a return to law and order and punishment in the U.S., and to a certain degree in Britain and Canada. The law-and-order attitude that has emerged in the U.S. since the 1970s culminated in mandatory minimums, fixed, three- and two-strikes out legislation, and a new punitiveness towards women. Since 2000, the U.S. has been implementing policy that is reminiscent of earlier prison regimes based on religious instruction, salvation, and redemption. President Bush Jr.'s initiative to offer prison management (and other services such as halfway houses and drug treatment) to religious organizations signifies a return to earlier prison regimes.

Historically, women were treated severely in prison. Female prisoners in the 1800s and early 1900s were considered to be fallen and depraved women. Matrons, unheard of in male prisons, were used as role models and guides for these wayward women. Matrons and moral reformers offered them gender-specific programs to mold them into proper Victorian women. White middle-class women sought to control their lower-class sisters who challenged conventional standards of femininity. Criminologist Nicole Rafter notes that white middle-class women viewed themselves as more moral than men in the 1800s, thus criminalized women were seen as being doubly deviant—more "depraved" than male prisoners and less deserving.[97] Therefore, they not only had to follow prison rules, they also had to conform to conventional standards of femininity.[98]

Two separate prison systems emerged for women in North America—the reformatory and the penitentiary. Rafter examines how sentencing and the reformatories maintain a double sexual standard for women and the degree to which the state will go to socially control and criminalize female sexuality. Although these laws have been repealed, new laws (especially in relation to illegal drugs) have emerged to regulate women.

---

97. Rafter 1990.
98. Ibid. 1990.

The War on Drugs and the Restructuring of Prisons

The rising female prison populations have exacerbated existing prison conditions for women, compounded by overcrowding, budget cuts, and lack of resources. In addition, security measures developed in response to male prisoners are enforced on female prisoners in Britain, Canada, and the U.S., although female prisoners pose little risk.[99] In Britain, Canada, and the U.S., both prison staff and prisoners have noted that the "war against drugs" has changed the face of prisons. The logic and the organization of the prison have shifted in order to wage the war. Security changes that have been implemented, but are not limited to, include the searching of staff and visitors (even children), mandatory treatment and drug testing, and search teams. The war against drugs justifies an even more intense regime of surveillance at the expense of women's dignity and rights.

Search Teams

In Britain, Canada, and the U.S., intimidating search teams have been given broad powers to search women and their cells for illegal drugs. Women (and men) in prison are not protected as those in the outside community from unreasonable search and seizure. Women who have never used drugs are subjected to drug testing, searches of their rooms, and strip-searching of their bodies. A female prisoner in Britain notes:

> On every cell search that I've seen they [Dedicated Search Teams] all dressed in black combat gear. They looked a bit like karate people. Once the prison was closed down for three days because some drugs had gone missing, and they searched every single cell, did these people. They did strip searches, too. They were very humiliating.[100]

---

99. Faith 2000; Wedderburn 2000: 22–23.
100. Carlen 1998: 122.

One British reporter wrote that women have "been made to bend over, spreadeagled and naked, while officers carry out vaginal inspections."[101] Whether women have used illegal drugs or not, strip-searching, drug testing, and search teams do little to protect the public and rehabilitate women in prison. Instead, these techniques remind women that their bodies are not their own, nor are the spaces that imprison them. In the U.S., male correctional officers can watch over female prisoners while they shower, dress, and use the bathroom, and they can invade their bodies when conducting searches for drugs.[102] Given the high percentage of women in prisons who have experienced sexual assault, strip-searching can be experienced as another assault.[103]

In addition, women in prison have little protection from their jailers. Women throughout the U.S. are mostly guarded by men (unlike Canada); however, investigations of sexual abuse are rare. Female prisoners find it difficult to have unlawful conduct stopped, for correctional officers are rarely held accountable for their actions.[104] Although there is no causal link between rape and violence against women and subsequent negative addiction, activists have pointed out that drug use, whether legal or illegal, may become one way for women to escape the terror of male violence in prison.

Drug Testing in Prison

A governor in Britain discusses the random urine drug testing introduced in 1995. He states:

> The sample testing of 10 percent per month is done by computer, and personally a lot of us think it is a farce.... The prisoners are absolutely aware that cannabis stays in the blood stream for a lot longer than hard drugs, so there are some anecdotal stories of people switching from cannabis to hard drugs,

---

101. *The Observer*, 24 November 1996, as cited in Carlen 1998: 7.
102. Amnesty International 1999.
103. Carlen 1998; 1993.
104. Amnesty International 1999; Faith 1993; HRW 1998; HRW/WRP 1996.

> because there is less risk of being caught.... It isn't cost effective because we test an awful lot of people who would never touch it. It's also the indignity of all that. We're saying, 'We're treating you with respect—now, come and pee in a bucket.'[105]

Drug testing means that women must urinate in full view of prison staff. Pat Carlen notes that prisoners and staff recognize how ineffective random drug testing is and how it contributes to women's distress in prison. Punishing women for positive drug tests may deflect attention away from the fact that there is no national detox or drug treatment program available for women in prison and that drug use and trafficking is not as prevalent in women's prisons as in men's.

In keeping with the war on drugs philosophy, random drug testing programs have also been initiated in prisons in Canada and the U.S. Prison administrators argue that drug testing is necessary to reduce illegal drug use, the sale of drugs, and violence associated with these activities.[106] However, drug testing has very limited use in actually lowering drug-use rates in prison and has no impact on reducing HIV/AIDS, hepatitis C, and deaths due to drug overdose. Also, those who test positive for drugs may not have drug treatment programs provided to them.

Urine analysis is quite limited in what it can tell prison staff. First, it is highly unreliable. False positives are common, and over-the-counter medications, herbal teas, and poppy seed cake can give a positive result. Drug testing can only tell us about the drugs that were used during a narrow period of time and cannot distinguish between first-time users and regular users.[107] Drug tests are done in-house in the prisons, and critics note that they are far from accurate. What is most significant from a harm reduction practice is that drug-testing programs in prisons may contribute to women switching from marijuana to heroin and cocaine. Marijuana, our most benign drug—unlike alcohol, cocaine, and heroin (which can

105. Carlen 1998: 119.
106. Riley 1995.
107. Humphries et al. 1992.

only be detected for one to three days)—can be detected in the urine for about thirty days after use.[108]

It has been suggested that drug testing may reduce violence in prison, but this is misleading. Illegal drug use does not lead to violent behavior; rather, it is the illegal trade of all commodities, including drugs, that lead to turf wars and violence, which are not characteristics of women's prisons.[109] Selling drugs in prison is shaped by prohibition, as is drug use. Ironically, as the prison regime becomes more oppressive, using drugs may become more attractive if only to escape for a few hours. It is interesting to note that women are offered an array of "legal" drugs like Prozac and Valium by prison staff.

Canadian researcher Michael Jackson discusses drug testing and the loss of liberty by highlighting several cases of urinalysis and drug contraband in his book *Justice Behind the Walls*. These cases are quite telling because they illustrate how drug testing is flawed, how people imprisoned are subjected to random drug testing and to administrative policy and punishment if they refuse the tests. Punishment is often severe and arbitrary, and even illegal if it were to happen on the outside. In one case, a bottle with liquid that looked like heroin in it was confiscated from a male prisoner after a cell search. Although he argued it was legal medication, he was taken to segregation. The liquid tested positive for heroin at the prison. With the help of his lawyer, he was successful in having the liquid retested and it came back negative for heroin. It was determined that the liquid was camphor. By then he had spent a week in segregation on false charges.[110] This is not an isolated case, nor is it specific to male prisoners. Women suspected of using, possessing, and dealing illegal drugs in prison (including homebrew) are also dealt with swiftly, with little concern for due process and the disparity in punishments meted out to them.

Canadian researcher Joane Martel notes that segregation is fraught with isolation and a list of forbidden things such as "tele-

108. Riley 1995.
109. Alexander 1990; Riley 1995.
110. Jackson 2002.

phone calls, cigarettes, personal belongings, undergarments, grooming items (i.e., a toothbrush, shampoo, toilet paper)."[111] However, these restrictions are mild compared with some of the environments women are forced to live in for twenty-three hours a day. For example, the segregation "hole," with a bare mattresses and wet blankets on the floor competing with bugs and mold, can be damp and cold in the winter and boiling in the summer with little ventilation. Women in the hole have to endure additional humiliations. They are often denied sufficient quantities of sanitary napkins, and are often forced into segregation in male units where they are subjected to sexualized behaviors from the male prisoners, such as masturbation and indecent exposure. For all prisoners, one of the most enduring features of the hole is loneliness. The damaging effects are evident through both psychological and physical harm, which are documented through reports of anxiety and panic attacks, hallucinations, suicides and self-mutilation.[112]

Martel found that in 1999, women in Canadian provincial prisons were sent to the hole more often than women in federal prisons. This is revealing since women are sentenced to provincial prisons for minor offences, thus the use of solitary confinement is an established punishment practice. In addition to drug violations, women are sent to the hole for minor infractions such as being "argumentative," being in possession of a "deck of cards," "swearing, tattooing or self-injurious activities."[113] For those who cannot display, or resist displaying, white-middle-class gender norms in prison, discipline can be swift and brutal.

British researcher Margaret Malloch highlights in her recent book, *Women, Drugs and Custody*, that prison officials view drug users as more problematic than nondrug users. Over 63 percent of the prison officials she interviewed in England and Scotland claimed that drug users in prison were "more aggressive, violent and/or disruptive than the other women." They were also viewed as anti-authoritarian and

---

111. Martel 2000: 130.
112. Amnesty International 1999; Martel 2000.
113. Martel 2000: 129, 130.

devious. Ninety-one percent of the prison officials interviewed stated that women drug users were also more of a discipline and security problem. Consequently, women drug users are disciplined and sent to isolation more often than their nondrug using counterparts.[114]

Since the 1990s, the U.S. has been intent on building "super-maximum security"prisons and units, or what have been labeled "super-max" prisons, whose environments are similar to the conditions in the hole or in solitary confinement. Although most of these prisons are for men, the states of Arizona, California, Colorado, Oklahoma, and Mississippi have units for women that fit the description of a "supermax."[115]

Health Care and Legal Drugging

Female prisoners in the U.S. report having serious health problems. In a study of imprisoned women in California, Connecticut, and Florida, almost half of the women surveyed stated they had health problems that interfered with their lives.[116] Incarcerated women in Canada, more often than men, suffer from "chronic health conditions resulting from lives of poverty, drug use, family violence, sexual assault, adolescent pregnancy, malnutrition, and poor preventive health care."[117]

Although women in prison in Britain, Canada, and the U.S. must be provided medical care free of charge, in reality they have rarely received the medical attention they require. Since the expansion of the pharmaceutical industry in the 1950s, legal drugs are often used as a way to control women in prison rather than to treat illness.[118] Women in prison are prescribed antidepressants, sedatives, and tranquilizers two to ten times more often than are their male counterparts.[119] In the U.S., both psychologists and correctional officers have ordered

114. Malloch 2000: 113, 114.
115. Amnesty International 1999: 2.; HRW 2000b.
116. Acoca and Austin, as cited in Amnesty International 1999.
117. Correctional Service Canada 1994.
118. Auerhahn and Leonard 2000; Faith 1993.
119. Auerhahn and Leonard 2000.

drugs for female prisoners even though they are not qualified to do so. Although they are vulnerable to the overprescribing of psychotropic drugs, they are often denied medication for chronic illnesses.[120] In Britain, drug treatment is not always readily available for women in prison, but they are prescribed "unacceptable dosages" of legal drugs known to be addictive. The Prison Reform Trust recommends that protocols be set up and audited for drug prescribing in collaboration with the National Health Service.[121]

Male prisons have historically been, and continue to be, more violent than women's prisons. Perceived female violence in prison is exaggerated and acted upon swiftly by prison guards. Unruly and angry women are seen as "unfeminine" and pathological, whereas male violence is normalized and viewed as a rational act of asserting control and reclaiming power.[122] Consequently, in Britain, Canada, and the U.S., unruly women are pathologized and subjected to drug therapy to modify their moods, which is revealing given that such a significant portion are serving time for "drug" offences. We fail to see that women's unruly and at times violent behavior is rooted not in their biology or sick minds, but that like men, it is the outcome of social events.[123]

The case of Jane Benson highlights the legal drugging of women in prison. Jane Benson was involuntarily drugged while in custody both before and during her 1988 murder trial in California. She was in severe back pain from a broken shoulder injury and was given combinations of Elavil, Valium, Vistaril, Tylenol with codiene, and Robaxin by prison staff. Except for Elavil, all of the drugs given to her are central-nervous-system depressants. Taken together they can induce mental confusion, sedation, disorientation, and physical debilitation. When Jane Benson refused the medication, she was threatened with solitary confinement. Her requests for an outside doctor were also refused. In 2001, she petitioned the court in California for a reversal of her 1988 conviction for second-degree murder and for a new trial. She

120. Amnesty International 1999.
121. Wedderburn 2000: 21.
122. Shaw 2000.
123. Faith 1993; Shaw 2000.

claimed that the "consumption of prescription medications while jailed in Lake County in 1988 was not voluntary" and rendered her confused and impaired during her trial.[124] Therefore, she was not "fit" to stand trial because she was drugged by the medical staff in the jail and feared reprisal if she did not continue the medication.

Elizabeth Leonard's 2002 book, *Convicted Survivors: The Imprisonment of Battered Women Who Kill*, documents how the use of psychotropic drugs to "chemically restrain" female prisoners is common in the U.S. She examines the past use of major tranquilizers, such as Thorazine, and current prescribing practices to chemically restrain women. A number of the women she interviewed in California prisons were legally drugged (similar to Jane Benson), and this interfered with their "self-presentation in the courtroom" and ultimately with their defense. One woman notes:

> The jail psychologist or psychiatrist put me on drugs in jail. I was too distraught to make a rational decision about medication. During the trial I was on both a tranquilizer and an antidepressant. I was not able to testify well—I was a zombie. They said I was cold and remorseless, not showing any emotion. I'm articulate—a college graduate with a graduate degree—the meds made me inarticulate.[125]

As well as being subjected to legal doping and having a difficult time getting the drugs that they need while in prison, women have also been subjected to drug experiments. Between the 1950s and 1970s, pharmaceutical companies developed relations with prison doctors and an array of prison testing programs were developed. Prisoners' health was jeopardized in order to test new drugs, products, and surgical procedures. In Britain, Canada, and the U.S., the government used prisoners for many dangerous experiments, including sensory deprivation, electric shock, and pain tolerance. Pharmaceutical companies were given contracts to test their new drugs on prisoners. These experiments were not therapeutic and most prison-

---

124. *Jane Ellyn Benson, Petitioner, v. Cal Therhune, Jr. 2001.*
125. Leonard 2002: 98.
126. Hornblum 1998.

ers did not give their informed consent.[126] In the 1950s and 1960s, CIA doctors administered massive doses of LSD to prisoners and psychiatric patients without their consent in Canada and the U.S. Twenty-three women in the Kingston Prison for Women, a federal prison in Canada, were given high doses of LSD in 1961, some while in solitary confinement. Dorothy Proctor was given LSD while in segregation in 1961 and her experience was horrifying.[127] She has spoken out about her experience and has launched a suit against the Canadian government. The impact of being forced to have her mind altered with high doses of LSD without her consent has led to long-term problems.

Drug Treatment

Critics note that health services in women's prisons in Britain, Canada, and the U.S., are not equal to the care provided to people on the outside. Although women in prison in all three nations have significant alcohol and drug problems, drug treatment and withdrawal treatment is also not as available to them. A U.S. survey in 1997 discovered that of fifty-two departments of corrections surveyed, only twenty-seven had drug treatment services designed specifically for women.[128] When prison programs are available, including therapy, they often have time-caps such as twenty-one weeks of therapy per prisoner in Canada. Therefore, women serving lengthy terms, including life sentences, are left to their own resources, and in prison these resources are limited.

The quality and availability of drug treatment also vary, and when treatment does exist abstinence is the primary goal. Most often treatment in Canada and the U.S. is premised on 12-step programs that view addiction as a disease. Having drug treatment in prison is wrought with problems for those women who are not sentenced for drug-related offences. They may be hesitant to access services for fear

127. Blanchfield 1998.
128. Amnesty International 1999: 3.
129. Boyd and Faith 1999.

that their "drug problem" may then be perceived by prison authorities as a reason to delay their release or parole.[129] As well, confidentiality in prison rarely exists so women are wary (for historically good reasons) of addressing issues of any significance in drug treatment programs—disclosure may lead to punitive action, especially in relation to illegal drug use or other criminal activity.[130]

In Canada, similar to Britain and the U.S., "substance abuse" is constructed as a "risk/need" that is linked to involvement in criminal activity. These risk assessments are "individualized instruments" that exclude structural factors such as the effects of poverty and colonization.[131] Because women are viewed as having more needs than men, they are now constructed as being more at risk for involvement in criminal activity, which impacts their level of security while in prison and their plans for release. One of the core Correctional Service Canada (CSC) programs is "Substance Abuse." This program, similar to other core programs, was created to provide women with ways to make "responsible choices" in a supportive environment so that they can be "empowered." Canadian criminologist Kelly Hannah-Moffat describes how the substance abuse programs offered to women is based on a "model of self change" rather than therapy.[132] Therefore, it is up to women who are identified as having "drug problems" to take responsibility and enrol in the programs offered, but if they do not, they are viewed as being in denial, uncooperative, and at risk of engaging in criminal activity.

Women in Canadian prisons who do enroll in substance abuse programs must agree to regular drug testing. Dirty drug screens can lead to "institutional charges, segregation, revocation of privileges, cancelled visits or, in the case of community supervision, return to prison."[133] If women contest the policy, they are seen as attempting to hide their illegal drug use. This circular reasoning ensures that women will have difficulty contesting drug policy. Thus, punish-

130. Hanlon et al. 1999.
131. Monture-Angus 2000: 56.
132. Hannah-Moffat 2000: 33.
133. Ibid.: 33.

ment remains central to prison practice, and empowerment ideology and policy facilitate social control. In addition, the self-esteem movement informs prison programs which promise "to deliver a technology of subjectivity that will solve social problems from crime and poverty to gender inequality by waging a social revolution, not against capitalism, racism and inequality, but against the order of the self and the way we govern ourselves."[134] Female prisoners are asked to participate in their own "empowerment" and to discipline and rule themselves while they are subjected to increased surveillance and penal subjugation. Self-esteem is a new technology used to "prevent" crime and to punish and supervise women already in prison.

Caribbean-Canadian women who were interviewed in the 1990s in a federal prison in Ontario, did not seem to be suffering from poor self-esteem, and they found that their attempts to remain self-sufficient were consistently undermined by race, class, and gender inequalities as well as state services. Other women imprisoned around the world, including political prisoners (and many drug offenders in prison view themselves as political prisoners), do not fit the stereotype of the dependent female prisoner lacking self-esteem. Dependency must be understood as a "social relation of subordination" rather than as an individualized pathology and a personality disorder.[135] In fact, resistance to state and male dependency is often perceived as "law breaking" within and outside the prison. Prisons are totalitarian institutions that are arranged so that women have no independence. In fact, independence is punished and the "'independent woman' does not do well in prison."[136] By deeming women as dependent and lacking in self-esteem, we legitimize programs and policy that maintain their continued marginalization. In addition, women in conflict with the law are seen as emotional and childlike rather than rational like their male counterparts.

Because a large majority of female prisoners in North America and in Britain have alcohol and drug problems prior to imprisonment,

---

134. Cruikshank 1996: 231.
135. Pollack 2000: 76, 80.
136. Boyd and Faith 1999: 2000.

addiction and correctional providers believe that treatment is essential. Although it has been advocated by some that coerced criminal justice treatment is as effective as voluntary treatment, critics note that mandating offenders into drug treatment extends their prison time; and those referred by the courts to drug treatment often remain there longer than other clients who entered voluntarily.[137]

In Britain, Canada, and the U.S., offenders can be ordered by the courts to undergo drug treatment during their incarceration, in lieu of incarceration, or upon their release. There are many names for this practice, ranging from coerced treatment, court-ordered treatment, and compulsory treatment. Because drug treatment is rarely voluntary in prison nor confidential, women are resistant, not to treatment per se, but to correctional staff who run the programs and who use punitive policy and practices.[138] Correctional staff and counselors in Canada and the U.S. are often unqualified and inexperienced. The building of prisons in impoverished rural areas in the U.S. and Canada to boost the economy of these regions has led to a lack of services for prisoners. Not only are there a limited number of professionals to choose from in remote rural areas but there are also few resources already in existence (such as halfway houses, universities, prison groups) that could be used as resources. Thus, staffing problems, unqualified staff, and high turnover due to low wages have a negative impact on drug treatment services for women.[139]

In Britain, women prisoners state that most of the prison staff have little training related to illegal drug use. Similar to Canadian programs, drug addiction is believed to be the result of faulty thinking rather than associated with structural and familial oppression and therefore psychologists are central to the delivery of cognitive behavioral programs.[140] However, women in British prisons state that prison medical staff are unsympathetic to drug users and this affects drug treatment in a negative way.[141] As in Canada and the U.S., drug

137. Farabee et al. 1999: 159; Shearer et al. 2001.
138. Shearer et al. 2001.
139. Farabee et al. 1999.
140. Kendall 2002: 195.
141. Malloch 2000: 127.

rehabilitation focuses on abstinence and gender-specific programs such as assertiveness training to promote self-esteem, which emphasize that women are somehow inadequate.[142]

Advocates of drug treatment state that it is critical that clear sanctions for noncompliance be set up and that the "program's authority and integrity" be maintained by removing rule breakers, otherwise programs will fail. Given that correctional drug treatment is within a prison, it would be naive to think that it would function less coercively than the prison itself. Thus, the question one may ask rests on the ethics and legality of coerced treatment, especially given the lack of funding for voluntary treatment outside the prison.

HIV and Prison

Worldwide, prisoners have higher rates of HIV/AIDS infection than the general population. However, not all individuals sentenced to prison use illegal drugs while others may become drug users.[143] Certainly, the prison experience in many ways lends itself to self-prescribed and medically prescribed medication. Prisoners are at high risk for HIV/AIDS and hepatitis C infection because of the scarcity of needles, which leads to the sharing of unclean needles. However, for many drug users, prison is the first place where they ever share needles.[144] Critics note that being sentenced to prison should not be a sentence to HIV/AIDS infection. Drug laws that criminalize drugs such as marijuana, cocaine, and heroin can be blamed for the high rates of HIV/AIDS infection among prisoners.[145]

Rates of HIV/AIDS infection vary from prison to prison and from region to region. However, there are some significant differences from nation to nation. The highest rates of infection for Western societies are in the U.S.—of those women tested in state prisons in 1997, 3.5 percent were HIV positive, which are much higher than those of male

142. Ibid.: 149.
143. Boyd and Faith 1999.
144. Jurgen 2000.
145. PASAN 1994; Riley and Oscapella 1996; Jurgens 1997.

prisoners (2.2 percent). About 75 percent of people imprisoned in the U.S. though, have never been tested for HIV, so we can assume that these are quite conservative statistical projections.[146] What is significant, even with such a small sample and poor representation, is that black and Hispanic people in prison report a higher rate of HIV infection, and women have higher rates of infection than men in every state and region except the western states. In addition, the rate of AIDS in prison is five times higher than in the general population in the U.S.

New York and Connecticut state prisons have the highest HIV/AIDS rates for women in the U.S., 20.7 percent and 13.1 percent, respectively. The rates for men in these states are 4.6 percent and 10.3 percent, respectively. There was no breakdown by gender for HIV/AIDS-related deaths in prison; however, in 1997, one out of five deaths in state prison was attributed to AIDS-related causes, down from one and three in the early to mid-1990s.[147] In federal and state prisons, Hispanic women (4.2 percent) have the highest rate of HIV infection in prison, followed by black women (3.9 percent); white women's rates (2.3 percent) are followed by white men (1.4 percent).[148]

In Canada, one of the most urgent health-related concerns in women's prisons is the transmission of HIV and hepatitis C. Women in Canadian prisons have a higher rate of infection than men in prison.[149] At the Burnaby Correctional Centre for Women in British Columbia, 78 percent of 69 women tested were positive for hepatitis C in 1996.[150] However, prison administrations have been slow in acknowledging the high rates of HIV/AIDS and hepatitis C infection in prison and in implementing harm reduction practices.[151] Throughout the world, women both inside and outside prison suffer as a result of late detection and diagnosis, and delays in treatment are key problems.

146. Maruschak 1999.
147. Ibid.: 1, 5.
148. Maruschak 1999: 9.
149. Jurgens 1996.
150. Canadian HIV/AIDS Legal Network 2001a.
151. Toepell 1997.

Overall, Britain has had much more success in curtailing HIV and hepatitis transmission. British researcher Margaret Malloch states that since the mid-1980s, injecting drug use both in and outside prison has become a concern. However, several studies conducted in the late 1980s and 1990s noted that prisoners shared needles while in prison, and it was feared that they would transmit disease to the general population. Similar to Canada and the U.S., British initiatives to provide education and treatment to lower drug use and HIV and hepatitis transmission in the prison were accompanied and overshadowed by mandatory drug testing, closer surveillance of prisoners and their visitors, body and strip searches, and the use of sniff dogs.[152] In addition, abstinence rather than harm reduction has been the main focus of prison policy.

In countries such as Switzerland, Germany, Spain, and Austria, sterile needles have been available in some prisons since 1993 without any problems.[153] Yet, clean needles are not available to women in prison in Britain, Canada, and the U.S. Harm reduction practices in prison vary greatly throughout the world. In Canada, condoms have been available in men's prisons since 1992, and bleach, for cleaning needles, since 1996. Unfortunately, these harm reduction practices are not available evenly across Canada, and their implementation relies on the medical staff and administrators of each prison.

Methadone in Prison

Many women in Britain, Canada, and the U.S. who are sentenced to prison are already addicted to drugs, regardless of whether they are charged for a drug, theft, or prostitution offence. Yet many jails and prisons lack adequate health services for women in drug withdrawal. Women's experience of cold-turkey regimes (withdrawal without medical aid) is rarer than it used to be, but support varies from prison to prison. In addition, women's drug use is not confined to heroin and cocaine; rather, many women are addicted to drugs such as Val-

152. Malloch 2000.
153. Jurgens 2000.

ium and Ativan. Outside of prison, detox services for women may be limited but they have a wider range of programs to choose from than when they are in prison.

In Canada, 15–20 percent of people who are addicted to narcotics use methadone services.[154] In 1996, British Columbia created the first methadone program located in the prison system in Canada. In 1997, the federal prison system implemented a similar program. The Catch 22 is that even though women may have been addicted to narcotics on their arrival to prison, their eligibility often rests on whether they were on a legal methadone program at the time of their arrest.[155] Even though methadone services have expanded in B.C., many illegal users are still wary of the service and perceive it as being more punitive than helpful.

In Britain, some women who are already on methadone in the community and are deemed "stable" by treatment providers can remain on the program when in prison. However, Margaret Malloch notes in her 2000 study on the experiences of women drug users in prison in England and Scotland, that only 3 percent of women on methadone who entered prison were deemed "stable." Most often, women were given tranquillizers and painkillers and sometimes women were given diazepam to withdraw from temazepam when they entered prison. However, this treatment was not a standardized practice so that in some prisons women had no access to withdrawal or methadone treatment.[156]

In contrast to restrictive access to methadone in British and North American prisons, other countries are implementing alternative and more accessible programs. A pilot project in Switzerland has provided heroin prescriptions to prisoners who have been dependent for more than two years and who have failed other drug treatment regimes. Clean needles, as well as harm reduction education, has been offered to women at Hindelbank prison since the mid-1990s. Nells and his colleagues discussed the success of the harm reduction programs, reporting that drug use did not increase and that both staff and women prisoners felt positive about heroin prescriptions

---

154. Kuo et al. 2000.
155. Canadian HIV/AIDS Legal Network 2001b; Rothon 1997–1998.
156. Malloch 2000: 80–84.

and clean needles being provided. However, the researchers note that about a third of the women in prison had little information about drugs and that harm reduction education in prison was vital in reducing the risk of infection, disease, and death. The researchers argue that prisons should always be viewed as part of the community, for people enter and leave prison regularly. They conclude that relationships between prison staff and prisoners must shift in order for harm reduction practices to be successful. Instead of prison staff viewing their central role as incarcerating people, they must begin caring for people in prison.[157]

Although Britain and Canada have accepted the principle of harm reduction and practice to varying degrees, the use of harm reduction in prison is still very controversial and limited. It has been suggested by some that initiating harm reduction programs in prisons—providing condoms, bleach, clean needles, and methadone to prisoners—encourages drug use and sexual activity among prisoners. In addition, it has been argued that providing bleach and needles increases drug use and puts the staff at risk of infection and injury.[158] However, when harm reduction programs have been implemented in prison, they have not increased drug use nor have they endangered staff.

It is impossible to keep illegal drugs out of prison, just as it is impossible to make people on the outside refrain from illegal drug use. Prisons have not acted as a deterrent to drug use, and total abstinence is unachievable within and outside the institution. In most societies, prisoners eventually go home. Critics of current prison policy note that female prisoners are guaranteed the right to receive health care, which includes preventative measures, similar to the outside population. It has been argued in the U.S. that denying prisoners condoms, bleach, needles, and methadone is unconstitutional because it is "cruel and unusual punishment."[159] Prisoners around the world are directing their attention to legal action against the state for failing to provide medical services and for failing to protect them from infection.

157. Nells et al 2000.
158. Ibid.
159. Jurgen 2000.

Pregnancy and the Use of Restraints

Women in prison are subjected to a host of controversial prison practices, including the use of restraints even when pregnant and in labor. Many women who are sentenced to prison are pregnant. Amnesty International has documented the use of restraints on pregnant and sick female prisoners in the U.S. Maria Jones, convicted of a drug offence, was incarcerated at Cook County jail in Illinois and, although her prior offence was shoplifting, she was categorized as dangerous. She described her baby's birth to Amnesty International:

> I was placed on a monitoring machine with the leg shackles still on. I was taken into the labour room and my leg was shackled to the hospital bed. The officer was stationed just outside the door. I was in labour for almost twelve hours. I asked the officer to disconnect the leg iron from the bed when I needed to use the bathroom, but the officer made me use the bedpan instead. I was not permitted to move around to help the labour along.
>
> I was given an epidural, and I carefully moved into a sitting position while dealing with the leg iron. While the needle was still in my back, I felt a strong contraction and I knew that the baby was coming. When I told the nurse, she told me not to push and said that the baby wasn't coming yet. I asked for the doctor and worked the leg chain around so that I could lay down again.
>
> Finally the officer came and unlocked the shackles from my ankles. My baby was born then. I stayed in the delivery room with my baby for a little while, but then the officer put the leg shackles and handcuffs back on me and I was taken out of the delivery room. I was in the hospital for about three days, with one hand and one foot shackled to the bed. There was a heavy blue box connecting the cuff with the bed, which left me no room to move. My handcuffs were removed when I was eating or holding my baby, but the leg irons were always on. My leg was disconnected from the bed only when I

> used the bathroom. Otherwise I was handcuffed and shackled, with one hand and one foot shackled to the hospital bed. Since I went back to the jail, every visit with my baby has been through the glass. I have not been permitted to hold my baby since my release from the hospital.[160]

Outside of the fact that women giving birth hold no security risk and therefore should not be restrained, having women shackled during birth presents numerous medical complications for both the mother and the child. Women need to be mobile during labor so that they can assume different positions in order to find comfort, and in case of an emergency.[161] Women are shackled even though a correctional officer is present throughout the labor and birth. In 1997, over 2,200 pregnant women were sentenced to prison in the U.S., and over 1,300 babies were born on the inside.[162] Amnesty International argues that the routine use of shackling of pregnant women violates international human rights standards.

An increase in punitiveness by the staff in British women's prisons has also been discussed by writers such as Pat Carlen. The increase in strip-searching and use of restraints were noted in the mid-1990s, and a widely publicized case of a woman handcuffed in labor brought about a statement in 1997 by the Prison Service that "women admitted to NHS hospitals to give birth should not be handcuffed from the time of their arrival until they leave."[163]

Mothering

Probably the most significant difference between women and men in prison relates to mothering and caregiving and the feelings of despair that women experience being separated from their children.[164]

---

160. Amnesty International 1999: 2, 3.
161. Amnesty International 1999.
162. Paltrow, Cohen, and Carey 2000b: 6.
163. H.M. Prison Service, as cited in Wedderburn 2000: 23.
164. Boyd 1999; Boyd and Faith 1999; Dodge and Pogrebin 2001; Faith 1993; Mauer et al. 1999a.

Separation from children ranked as the primary concern of mothers in prison, and the short- and long-term impact of imprisonment on children is immense. It was estimated that in 1999, two million children in the U.S. had a parent in prison— of these children, 1.5 million were under eighteen and two hundred thousand had a mother in prison.[165] In addition, black children were nine times more likely, and Hispanic children were three times more likely, to have a parent in prison than white children.[166]

In 1999 in the U.S., 64 percent of mothers in state prison and 84 percent of mothers in federal prison lived with their children prior to arrest. In contrast, only 44 percent of fathers in state prison, and 55 percent in federal prisons lived with their children prior to arrest. Even though both fathers and mothers experience the pain of separation from their children when they are incarcerated, mothers are more likely to be single parents (more than half the mothers in federal prison were single parents compared with 14 percent of fathers, and 46 percent of mothers in state prison were single parents compared with 15 percent of men). Women also have less support from male partners and families on the outside.[167]

When fathers are incarcerated in the U.S., it is most likely that the mothers on the outside will care for their children. Almost 90 percent of the children whose fathers are imprisoned are in the care of the mothers. Women are not afforded the same support by their male partners. Only 28 percent of children whose mothers are imprisoned are in the care of the fathers. Overwhelmingly, the care of a mother's children resides with grandparents (52.9 percent), other relatives (25.7 percent), and foster care (9.6 percent). In contrast, only 1.6 percent of the children of fathers are in foster care.[168]

Similar to their U.S. and Canadian counterparts, British women lose custody of their children when in prison. Toby Wolfe's 1999 study notes that over 60 percent of women in prison are mothers, and 25

165. Peugh and Belenko 1999: 33; U.S. Department of Justice 2000: 3.
166. U.S. Department of Justice 2000c.
167. Doge and Pogrebin: 2000.
168. U.S. Department of Justice 2000c.

percent are single parents (a significantly lower rate than in the U.S. and Canada). The majority of children are cared for by their mothers when men are sentenced to prison; in contrast only 5 percent of women can rely on the father to care for their children during their imprisonment.[169] Although about one hundred thousand children are separated from their fathers when they are imprisoned, another eight thousand children are separated from their mothers for the same reason.[170] The numbers could be even higher—as many women are reluctant to reveal that they have children for fear that their children will be apprehended by the state. These fears are grounded, given that 8 percent of mothers lose custody of their children and 10 percent state that they do not expect to live with their children upon release, even though they did so before their imprisonment. Eighty-five percent of mothers have never been separated from their children for a long period of time prior to imprisonment,[171] whereas only 35 percent of men in prison lived with their children prior to their imprisonment.[172] Wolfe reveals how women in prison are often known to social services prior to their imprisonment, and sometimes one or more of their children has already been apprehended by the state. One woman describes her difficulties with social services:

> Do you know, before I went to jail, for four years I tried to get a social worker— I was on a drugs rehab—couldn't get one. As soon as I went to jail, they come straight in, out with my kids, taking the kids out the home and everything... If I hadn't done anything about it, my kids would've been put in care.[173]

While in prison, many mothers strive to keep in touch with their children through phone calls, mail, and visits. In the U.S., mothers report more weekly contact with their children than their male counterparts.[174]

---

169. Wolfe 1999.
170. Lyon 2002: 3.
171. Wedderburn 2000: 9
172. Wolfe 1999: 18.
173. Ibid.: 17.
174. U.S. Department of Justice 2000c.

Few prisons have nurseries and facilities for overnight visits with children.[175] In fact, it is often prisoners themselves and family members who have created programs that facilitate visiting. The criminal justice system fosters alienation rather than family unity. Women's attempts to keep contact with their children are severely limited because of financial concerns and punitive prison practices that range from a lack of parent-child programs, prohibitive collect-call policies (that cost more in prison than collect calls on the outside), restrictive visiting, censorship of phone and mail communication, and the remote locations of prisons.

Historically, because there are so few prisons for women compared with men's prisons, women have often been incarcerated in prisons located in remote areas that are long distances from where their children live (up to one thousand miles in Canada and five hundred miles in the U.S.). In many states and provinces, prisons are located in rural areas that compete to have prisons in their communities in order to increase employment and profit. In fact, 54 percent of mothers in state prison and over 40 percent of mothers in U.S. federal prison have never been visited by their children.[176] Visiting parents is difficult for both underage and adult children because of the cost of transportation and lodging. Although most women are sentenced to prisons far away from their families and children, foreign national women are sent even greater distances. It is more difficult for their children and families to visit, making it difficult for their families to lend them support. Language and cultural barriers may also contribute to a sense of isolation and make it difficult to negotiate with guards and the criminal justice system.

Mothers like Dorothy Gaines, who unjustly served time in the U.S. for drug conspiracy, are deeply distressed by the plight of their families after being sentenced to prison. Dorothy said this about her struggle to keep her children together after she was imprisoned:

> Because I was determined that Chara and Phillip not go into foster care, Natasha [Dorothy's oldest daughter] dropped out of college to support her younger siblings. Phillip is struggling

175. Collins 2002: 317.
176. U.S. Department of Justice 2000c: 1–14.

> the most, though. He went from being on the honor roll to getting failing grades. He has tried to commit suicide twice and was arrested recently for petty offenses, like shoplifting. He says he wants to go to prison so he can be with me.[177]

Dorothy's story is all too familiar to women in prison and their families. It is well documented that imprisoning mothers has a very negative influence on their children. Most important, they no longer have access to their mothers and to their love, protection, and care. Lack of contact with their mothers and the "forced" separation can lead to psychological and behavioral problems, anxiety, depression, and sleep problems.[178] Many children are present at the time of their mothers' arrest and this can be especially traumatic for them. Anyone who has witnessed the DEA dressed to intimidate, using unjustified force (both in terms of human power and military trappings), smashing down doors, throwing people to the floor, their guns pointed and ready to shoot can understand how children and adults may be traumatized by such an event. It is estimated that in the U.S. one in five children have witnessed their mothers' arrest.[179]

Children whose mothers are arrested are often sent in to foster care, even though it is well documented that children in care are often victimized both physically and sexually by their caretakers. Many women in prison were themselves raised in foster care. Thus, for many women prison is viewed as an extension of welfare policy and other punitive practices. As law-and-order advocates pontificate about saving the family and upholding family values, they seem intent on destroying the families of the poor and of people of color.

Mothers in all three nations have real fears that their partners on the outside will not provide for their children and that they will be unable to maintain custody on their own while they are in prison and when they are released.[180] Trying to coordinate visits from children

---

177. FAMM 2000: 6.
178. Snyder-Joy and Carlo 1998.
179. CANY/WPP 2002a: 3.
180. Boyd 1999; Faith and Boyd 1999; Dodge and Pogrebin 2001; Rafter 1990.

who are in foster care is extremely difficult, and yet any loss of contact is treated as evidence of the mother's noncompliance, thus she risks permanently losing custody. Women in prison who are known to have drug problems or have been ordered by the courts to attend drug treatment have great difficulty in keeping custody of their children, because they are seen as unfit parents by the courts. Further, the court expects mothers to demonstrate that they have been rehabilitated.[181] Because so few male parents provide a home for their children, mothers in prison worry about their children's care with relatives and foster placements. For women who are imprisoned for drug-related offences, the fear of loss of custody is often realized, for it is mistakenly assumed that their compulsion to use drugs is stronger than their commitment to their children.

The ramifications of imprisonment fall disproportionately on black and Hispanic women who are overrepresented in prison in the U.S. for drug crimes. The three states that have the greatest increase of incarceration for black women (California, New York, and Pennsylvania) also have the most children in foster care.[182] In Canada, First Nations and black women are overrepresented in prison, which also correlates with the overrepresentation of First Nations and black children in foster care.

The enactment of the 1997 Adoption and Safe Families Act (ASFA) in the U.S. also hinders mothers from regaining custody of their children. The justification of the legislation was to limit the amount of time children reside in foster care and to encourage their permanent adoption. Children in care for more than fifteen consecutive months in a period of twenty-two months may be adopted, at which time the rights of the biological parent are terminated. However, the ASFA negatively effects women in prison for drug offences who generally serve terms longer than fifteen months. Therefore, a woman sentenced to prison for a drug offence loses "the right to reunite with her children."[183]

181. Boyd and Faith 1999; Henriques and Manatu-Rupert 2001.
182. Collins 2002: 315.
183. Hagan and Coleman 2001: 359.

Tearing Apart the Family and Community, and Visiting Prisons

Almost all women in prison leave behind families and friends. Nevertheless, conventional research tends to only consider families and communities in relation to how they may support or deter criminal activity. In contrast, critical writers note that the war on drugs fuels race, class, and gender disparity, and persecution has had a tremendous impact on the lives of the poor. In addition, when people are imprisoned, their families and communities are seriously harmed. The burden of childcare and financial support most often rests with the women of the community. Most prisoners in Western societies are men, and men make up the vast majority of adults charged with drug offences. Regardless of similar drug-use rates, black men are almost seven times more likely than white men to be imprisoned in federal and state prisons in the U.S.[184] Since 1995, it is estimated that 35 percent of all black males aged twenty-five to thirty-five move through the criminal justice system as prisoners, parolees, or probationers.[185] At the end of 2001, almost 7 million adults were under correctional supervision in the U.S.; over 2 million adults were held in prison; and 4.7 million adult men and women were on probation or parole.[186] When women who are mothers are sentenced to prison, the family is torn apart. Furthermore, high conviction rates for men of color are having a devastating impact on families and communities throughout the U.S. When men are absent from the home, they can no longer support women and their children.

It is estimated that 85 percent of prison visitors are female relatives of prisoners.[187] Although women make up the bulk of prison visitors, woman prisoners do not receive as many visitors as men. Women outside of prison are taking care of the children, the elderly, and the home; they are working outside the home and supporting and main-

---

184. U.S. Department of Justice 1999: 9, 11.
185. Drucker 1999: 14.
186. BJS 2002b: 1.
187. Saxakali 1997.

taining contact with family members in prison. Keeping contact with prisoners can be a full-time job. Involuntary transfers to new prisons, restrictive visiting, visiting prisons located in rural areas far from the homes of urban dwellers, costly collect calls (as mandated by prisons), and supplying the necessities that are not provided in prison keep mothers, wives, and daughters busy and financially strained. The prison-industrial complex shapes the lives of everyone, not just those imprisoned. Women visiting prisons are often shocked to find out that prison administration and guards construct them as guilty through association. Their status can suddenly shift from mother, wife, girlfriend, sister, and daughter to suspect.

Privileged guests who may have offered services to prisoners or participated in tours of prisons are often surprised by how differently they are treated once they are visiting as a friend or family member of a prisoner. Visitor questionnaires must be submitted and verified prior to visiting. Upon arrival at the prison, visitors are subjected to intrusive and humiliating practices. As early as 1990, 93 percent of U.S. federal prison staff checked visitors' belongings for drugs. In order to search for drugs, 92.5 percent of visitors at federal prisons had to submit to a clothing exchange, 27.5 percent were subjected to a body cavity search, and 51 percent of visitors were patted down for drugs. By 1990, 69 percent of visitors to state prisons were patted down for drugs, 87.4 percent had to submit to a clothing exchange, and 22.4 percent were subjected to a body cavity search.[188] These humiliating practices remind visitors that they, too, are suspect in the eyes of the prison authorities.

British writer Joe Levenson explains how the rights of visitors are sacrificed and how family ties are severed as a result of the implementation of war-on-drugs strategies.[189] Although he is discussing prisons in Britain, these same drug strategies are used in Canada and the U.S. In 1998, the Prison Service in Britain reiterated its goal to reduce the flow of drugs into prisons. Over 89 percent of British prisons use dogs to detect drugs on incoming visitors, however their suc-

188. U.S. Department of Justice 2000b: 8, 9.
189. Levenson 2001: 12–13.

cess rate is low and their track record is unreliable. The dogs are unable to distinguish legal drugs from illegal drugs. Nevertheless, visitors are picked out by dogs and then subjected to strip-searching or to closed visits.

When the Prison Reform Trust visited Parkhurst prison in 1999, they found that in the prior eighteen months, only *three people out of five hundred* visitors picked out by the dogs and strip-searched actually had drugs on them. Children were also subject to strip searches, although no drugs were found on them. To date, there is no central monitoring of strip-searching of visitors at the prisons. A governor at a women's prison in Britain states that "women will say they don't want their children to visit because they don't want them searched."[190]

Only half of the women in British prisons who lived with their children or were in contact with them have ever been visited by their children while in prison.[191] Humiliating and repressive drug surveillance and search techniques serve several purposes: they make clear that visitors are viewed as suspects; they intimidate and demonstrate the coercive power of the state; they assure that children, family, and friends are humiliated; and they are applied to the least powerful. This type of surveillance affects women in prison who hope to protect their children from coercive displays of power by the state, and many may decide to limit family visits.

IONSCAN machines have also been installed at the entrance of most prisons, and they are used on visitors to detect traces of drugs on their hands, clothing, money, and wallets. Prisoners returning from supervised visits outside the prison are also subjected to the machines, as well as to dogs. One important fact that is often ignored by advocates of greater drug surveillance of prisoners and visitors is the fact that the guards themselves bring drugs and contraband into the prison, and they can get away with it because they are not constructed as "suspects." Some guards have offered drugs and contraband in exchange for sex, although we hear little about this phenomenon in the mainstream media.[192]

---

190. Ibid.: 118.
191. Wedderburn 2000: 22.
192. Kilroy 2003.

The financial and emotional cost is high for family members and friends who keep in touch with women in prison. Intimidation by guards, costly calls, transportation, and providing the necessary needs, including legal services for prisoners, takes its toll. The longer a woman's sentence, the less likely she will be visited by family and friends as time goes by.[193] In fact, prisoners note that prisons and prison policy are constructed so that families will eventually have to abandon their loved ones. Others realize that, given the emotional and financial cost of contact, their family's support may end after the first few years. In one study of women in prison in the U.S., over half of the women interviewed had lost touch with their families, which meant they had to fend for themselves in prison and upon their release.[194] Many women note that they purposely pull back from their families because of the financial and emotional hardships their imprisonment places on them, especially when serving the long sentences handed out for drug offences.

Release

For women who leave prison after serving their time for drug violations, the punishment does not end. For one thing, employment prospects are severally limited. For another, friends and family may no longer be there to offer them support and housing. Women's lack of skills and education, which is not addressed in prison in any meaningful way, coupled with their prison record often limit what employment may be available to them. Most often women are looking at "low-paying, dead-end employment."[195] Job training in women's prisons consists of dog training, flower arranging, and service jobs that do little to change the conditions of women's lives. Prisoners who have enrolled and completed BA's have a much better chance of making it on the outside. Recidivism rates are much lower for those women who obtain a BA than for the general prison population.[196]

193. Farrant 2001.
194. Dodge and Pogrebin 2001: 51.
195. Ibid.: 50.
196. Faith 1993.

Until women are offered more meaningful ways to change the social conditions of their lives, they will continue to face multiple obstacles upon release.

The same social factors that bring women into conflict with the law affect their release back into the community and their success in staying clear of the criminal justice system in the future. It has been recognized that women who are arrested for drug-related offences are often caught up in a revolving door phenomenon.[197] Most women find that men abandon them while they are in prison.[198] Thus, women's time in prison and their eventual release into the community are compounded by their loss of partners and children. When mothers are able to maintain child custody during their imprisonment and after their release, they rarely receive any type of support (financial or emotional) from their childrens' fathers.[199] For those mothers whose children are in foster care, upon release they are expected to follow strict criteria set out by social services, which are often unachievable, before they can see their children. For example, they might have to enter a drug treatment center for six months, then find a job and housing, take anger management classes, and provide urine analysis regularly to prove that they are abstinent before possibly being granted visitation rights. These obstacles to the reunification of mothers with their children ignore the social constraints that limit women's choices. The same social factors, including race, gender, and class inequalities, that shape women's conflicts with the law await them when they are released.

Many children who are put in care when their mothers are sent to prison remain there after their release. Women in Canada and the U.S. have also noted that social workers have little to offer them in terms of support but are quick to intervene and take their children when they are perceived as transgressing the law or their role as a "good" mother. Tony Wolfe notes that how long a child stays in care after a mother's release from prison is determined by the social work-

197. Hanlon et al. 1999.

198. Henriques and Manatu-Rupert 2001; Stanton 1980.

199. Dodge and Pogrebin 2001.

ers' attitude and the availability of housing. Many mothers in Britain are caught in a Catch 22 situation, for it is difficult to secure long-term public housing until they have custody of their children.[200]

When mothers are not able to succeed in following the criteria set out by their probation officers and social services, they are personally blamed for failing. One mother in the U.S. talks about the difficulties she faced with social services after her release from prison:

> I wrote and stuff but they won't tell me where they are. My social worker said once I get on my feet and keep a job for 6 months we can see about visitation. What she doesn't understand is for the past year I have been trying to find a job, but no one wants to have someone who was in prison for 6 years. They [my children] are the only good thing that has ever happened to me, and I want them back. I didn't even know where they are.[201]

Mothers also experience problems when they are reunited with their children after release. One Canadian mother explains:

> I spent time for drug-related crimes.... They affected me a lot. With both my children, with my first child... that was when I had to go to jail, I was gone almost three years and we were separated. And I had a lot of problems with my child due to the separation.... And a lot of problems with myself.[202]

Women often feel personally responsible for failing to provide for their children when they are in prison, which fuels their despair both inside and upon release.

Further Obstacles

Having a permanent criminal record can prevent women from entering certain professions and from obtaining employment. In addi-

200. Carlen 1998.
201. Dodge and Pogrebin 2001: 47.
202. Boyd 1999: 176.

tion, drug offenders in the U.S. are subject to harsher penalties upon release from prison than other prisoners. The 1988 Anti-Drug Abuse Act authorizes state and federal judges to deny specific federal benefits to people convicted of drug possession or trafficking. Federal benefits that can be denied include, student loans; small-business loans; medical, scientific and academic research grants and fellowships; physicians' prescription-writing authority; and radio and television broadcast licenses. Rather than viewing drug laws as problematic and burdensome, the U.S. Department of Justice explains why drug offenders should be denied benefits:

> Drug offenders place an extraordinary burden on the criminal justice system. Correctional institutions are filled with serious drug offenders. Probation alone is most often inadequate for dealing with drug offenders. However, lower-level drug offenders are not routinely incarcerated unless they also commit a serious offense or have multiple drug-related convictions. To close the gap between incarceration and probation, DOJ has explored numerous intermediate steps or punishments, including civil penalties, license suspension and revocation, boot camps and shock incarceration, halfway houses, electronic monitoring, and drug testing...The denial of federal benefits is another sanction that address individuals found guilty of violating the Controlled Substances Act. The denial of such federal benefits as grants, contracts, purchase orders, financial aid, and business and professional licenses will, at the very least, ensure that they forfeit their claims to most taxpayer-supported economic benefits and other privileges.[203]

In contrast to the U.S. Department of Justice's rhetoric, many women are serving time in prison for drug possession and low-level dealing. Punishing them after they are released from prison guarantees that their re-entry will be difficult. The policy also makes certain that those women who are granted probation will also be negatively effected.

In addition, the U.S. Department of Housing and Urban Development (HUD) allows the Public Housing Authorities (PHAs) and

203. Bureau of Justice Assistance 2002: 2.

Residence Management Corporations (RMCs) across the U.S. to deny housing to those who have been convicted of a drug offence and to those "suspected" of these offences. This policy disproportionately impacts poor women with children who might benefit from subsidized housing, and who make up the majority of those dwelling in public housing.

In addition, the U.S. federal government can revoke passports of those convicted of drug offences who have crossed international borders, and as of 1990, twenty-seven states have the right to suspend the driver's licences of drug offenders. As with other laws that punish drug offenders, the federal government offers each state an incentive to comply. Those states that do not enact legislation to suspend the driver's licenses of drug offenders lose 10 percent of specific federal highway funds each year for noncompliance.[204]

Anyone convicted of a drug felony in the U.S. can be prohibited for life from receiving federally funded cash, or near cash, assistance (Congress tried to have the law extended to those convicted of misdemeanors too).[205] In 1996, federal welfare reform legislation banned all those convicted of drug felonies from receiving Temporary Assistance for Needy Families (TANF) benefits and food stamps. Although the definition of a drug felony varies from state to state, twenty-three states have complied with the federal legislation; however, twenty-seven states have chosen to enact state legislation that modifies or eliminates the ban. Where enacted upon, the 1996 federal legislation disproportionately affects poor single mothers.

Finally, the right to vote, the bedrock of a democratic society, has been denied to convicted criminal offenders in the U.S.[206] Forty-six states and the District of Columbia deny the vote to all adult prisoners; thirty-two states deny the vote to those on parole; twenty-nine

204. BJS 1992: 185.

205. Hirsch 1999.

206. Critics point out that Bush Jr. stole the vote in Florida because of the number of people disenfranchised. Many of the people on the "official" disenfranchised list in Florida had never been arrested or convicted of a crime and had never been convicted of a felony. However, they were denied the right to vote in the election.

deny the vote to all those on probation; and fourteen disenfranchise ex-offenders for life. As a result of the war on drugs and racial profiling, nonviolent drug offenders are vulnerable to disenfranchisement. In Alabama and Florida, one out of three black men is permanently denied the right to vote. Over 3.9 million U.S. citizens have temporarily or permanently been disenfranchised because of a felony conviction; however, almost three-quarters of these people are not in prison but are on "probation, parole, or have completed their sentence."[207]

Unfortunately, the 1998 study "Losing the Vote" by The Sentencing Project and Human Rights Watch did not include women who have lost their right to vote.[208] However, the report speculates that given the racial disparity for black men in relation to disenfranchisement, black women are probably overrepresented, too. The overrepresentation of black women in prison supports their claim. The authors note that no other Western democracy disenfranchises ex-offenders for life, and many nations allow people to vote while in prison (for example, Canada, Denmark, France, the Netherlands, Peru, and Japan).

The Prison Industry

Mona Danner claims that harsh laws and three-strikes out legislation does not protect women from crime, nor does it reduce crime; instead, it further impoverishes families and communities. She also claims that corporations and politicians benefit from harsh law-and-order agendas. She writes that women are used by law-and-order advocates who claim to be defending women from dangerous criminals in order to pass punitive crime-control bills. These laws actually harm women who have to pay for them through taxation. As family cap laws (which limits financial assistance according to the number of children in the family) and cutbacks in education, welfare and health

207. Fellner and Mauer 1998: 1, 2, 8.
208. The Sentencing Project and Human Rights Watch 1998.

care are initiated, crime-control budgets expand. Women on benefits are more likely to lose them, and women employed in the helping professions such as social workers are likely to lose their livelihood.[209] Curiously, there seems to be no lack of U.S. government funding for punishment and military defense industries in which men are traditionally employed.

Harsh drug laws have increased women's risk for imprisonment since the mid-1980s in Britain, Canada, and the U.S. On any given day in California, you are no more than forty minutes away by car to a prison, California's fastest growing industry. Drug laws provide the human bodies that fill the prisons, creating a system of class and racial apartheid.[210] Over the last ten years, more prisons for women have been constructed in Britain, Canada, and the U.S., even though there is no evidence to suggest that women are more criminal than they were in the past. Nevertheless, lobby groups have pressured the U.S. government to pass new repressive laws, such as the three-strikes out legislation.

The U. S. now imprisons a higher proportion of its population than any other nation in the world. The ever-expanding prison-industrial complex is further exacerbated by private prisons, which also exist in Britain and Canada, and by prison labor. Making prisons profitable has terrible consequences for prisoners. Feminist writer Emily Aspinwall states that private prisons wish to expand the laws that adjudicate what is considered criminal because more crime means more criminals and more prisons,[211] thus, more profit. Even though the rate of violent crime has fallen over the last decade, the prison population has increased.[212] The Corrections Corporation of America (CCA) and Wakenhut own approximately 75 percent of the global private-prison market. Women are especially vulnerable to increased imprisonment because as poverty increases, women's options decrease. Furthermore, as more states enact laws to regulate women's behavior during pregnancy, including maternal drug use, more women will be sentenced to prison.

209. Danner 2000.
210. Davis, Estes, and Schiraldi 1996.
211. Aspinwall 2001: 8.
212. Schlosser 1998.

As many critics have argued, the prison-industrial complex is an expanding enterprise.[213] Nils Christie and others note that the war on drugs in all Western nations has become a tool to strengthen control by the state over "dangerous" and "marganilized" classes of people. The new punitiveness towards women, coupled with the war against drugs and terrorism, provides the human bodies from which the prison-industrial complex derives its profits.

Resistance

In the 1800s and early 1900s, political writers such as Peter Kropotkin and Emma Goldman questioned state law and authority and called for the abolition of prisons. Emma Goldman wrote that prisons were a social crime and a failure. She and many others had first-hand experience with being imprisoned for their political beliefs and actions. Goldman was also critical of moral regulation and prohibition, and criticized socialists of her time for patting prohibition on its back in order to win votes.[214]

The contemporary abolitionist movement calls for an end to all "punishment regimes" whether they be prisons, community service orders, house arrest, or drug testing.[215] The movement is international and intersects with prison rights, anti-drug war, anarchist, and transformative justice groups. The International Conference on Penal Abolition (ICOPA) was founded by grassroots activists in Canada in 1983 to highlight the plight of prisoners around the world. Prison abolitionists do not attempt to "reform" the prison, rather they wish to "transform the conditions that first produce injustices and then justify selective incarceration for victims who offended."[216] Groups like Strength in Sisterhood (SIS), which emerged in 1994 in Canada, align themselves with this perspective and challenge prison policy and practices through their activism, research,

213. See Christie 1993; Schlosser 1998; and Sullivan and Tifft 1980.

214. Shulman 1972: 85.

215. Hudson 1997.

216. Faith 2000: 2.

and writing. They also lend support to women in and out of prison. Decarceration for drug offences is advocated as is decarceration for all other nonviolent offences.[217] Critical Resistance, a national grass-roots organization in the U.S., advocates for the elimination of prisons and punishment industries. In Britain, the Prison Reform Trust advocates for prison reform. They were responsible for initiating and publishing an inquiry into sentencing and prison conditions for women in 2000. Organizations in the U.S., such as Drug Policy Alliance, Legal Services for Prisoners with Children Justice Works, the November Coalition, and Families Against Mandatory Minimums (FAMM) also advocate for women (and their children) imprisoned for drug offences. Decriminalization and legalization of drugs, can be viewed as one step toward social justice. Many see marijuana reform as the first step towards decarceration.

Following the lead of other European nations, in 2003, the Home Office in Britain announced that marijuana users will no longer be targeted for arrest. In addition, a recent report by the Joseph Rowntree Foundation in Britain noted the tendency for marijuana users to grow small amounts for their own use and friends makes them less dependent on drug dealers and international criminal enterprises; thus, they recommend "on-the-spot" warnings for sole-use growers rather than a caution or a criminal conviction.[218] In 2002 the Senate Special Committee on Illegal Drugs recommended the legalization of marijuana in Canada. In the same year a special parliamentary committee recommended that possession and cultivation of marijuana under 30 grams be decriminalized. Justice Minister Martin Cauchon announced that Canada would move toward decriminalization of marijuana in 2003. This move has been met with severe criticizm by the U.S. government and by opponents in Canada. Ignoring the recommendations of the Senate, special parliamentary committee, and the public, the justice minister put forth a new proposal in May 2003 to impose fines on people caught with 15 grams or less of marijuana. In contrast to British recommendations to issue warnings to sole-use

217. Ibid.
218. Utting 2003.

growers, this Canadian proposal doubles the penalty for marijuana growers. A Can$240-million federal anti-drug strategy to educate Canadians about the "harms" of marijuana has also been advocated.

When U.S. representatives criticize Canadian marijuana reform proposals, they ignore the fact that the penalty for possession of small amounts of marijuana has been reduced to a misdemeanor in twelve states. In fact, all but one of these state's laws have higher limits than the most recent Canadian proposal. For example, Ohio has a 100 gram limit; Maine, 35 grams.[219] Critics also note that U.S. federal representatives continue to regard marijuana as a dangerous drug and they fail to accept these state laws regarding the drug.

219. Oziewicz 2003.

Chapter 6

U.S. International Policy and the War in Colombia

It is impossible to fully understand drug policy in the U.S., and in Britain and Canada, without examining foreign policy. The preceding chapters focused on the impact of drug policy on women in these nations. This chapter will explore how Western drug policy and free trade impact Third World Nations. More specifically, it will examine U.S. drug policy in Colombia, which has been accompanied by increased violence, militarization, and privatization. Although all people in Colombia are affected by U.S. drug policy, women and Indigenous people have been the most vulnerable to its implementation.

Colombia, a former Spanish colony, is located at the northwestern tip of South America, a country of forty million people that is rich in natural resources. But poverty prevails, especially for women and children. The country has been severely damaged by domestic armed conflicts and the war on drugs. According to human rights advocates, the U.S. war on drug's initiative, Plan Colombia, has increased violence in Colombia, and a number of women's peace organizations have drawn our attention to how the war, poverty, and Plan Colombia has affected them. Although some may believe that U.S. international drug policy and the civil war in Colombia have little to do with women, activists disagree. Women's groups both inside and outside Colombia argue that the militarization of the country has increased violence against women.[1] They point out how the regulation of drugs in Western liberal societies is linked to violence in Colombia and other Third World nations.

1. Lloyd 1998.

Feminist writer Susan Caulfield explores how "criminal justice has become the institutionalization of militarism in U.S. culture."[2] She points out that militarism is a key source of violence in the U.S. and that there is a connection between militarism and violence against women. Caulfield also notes that when nations go to war against crime—or drugs—and use military models against their domestic population and other nations, they legitimize the use of force and violence becomes acceptable. There has been little "official" recognition of how Plan Colombia affects women; the lives of women and children are often shaped by events that are not of their own making as decisions are most often brokered by groups of men. The lack of representation of women in government in the United States and Colombia also assures that women's interests are ignored. In addition, powerful corporate interest groups like Occidental Petroleum, Elli Lilly, and the Corrections Corporation of America influence national and international policy, including drug policy.

The following sections provide background information on U.S. intervention in other nations, the Central Intelligence Agency (CIA), the national drug strategy, Plan Colombia, the civil war in Colombia, and the effect of these agents, policies, and struggles on Indigenous people and women.

U.S. and CIA Intervention and International Drug Policy

The U.S., like many nations, is committed to eradicating illegal drug use, trafficking, and cultivation throughout the world; however, the demand and use of drugs has not diminished at home. In fact, illegal drugs are cheaper and readily available today.[3] Although the war on drugs has not reduced drug use, trafficking, and cultivation, it has allowed the U.S. to extend its political and economic power internationally. U.S. military aid and intervention, including CIA covert ac-

2. Caulfield 2001: 131.
3. United Nations report, as cited in Woodiwess 2001: 381.

tions related to drug cultivation and trafficking in Laos, Burma, Thailand, Afghanistan, Pakistan, Bolivia, Peru, Colombia, and Mexico (to name a few), have contributed to violence and the support of anti-democratic practices and human rights violations in these countries.

Britain also plays a significant role in international drug control. The British government is active in linking aid and the implementation of drug policy in foreign nations. It is the third largest donor to the United Nations International Drug Control Program, whose central goals are reducing drug production and crop eradication. It is also a member of the European Union. Similar to U.S. foreign drug policy, there is little evidence demonstrating that British programs to eradicate crops and reduce drug production are successful. British drug researcher Penny Green notes that drug-related aid is little more than "window dressing for governments wishing to demonstrate their commitment to the international war effort." In addition, she argues that Britain and Europe have been negatively affected by the Americanization of drug policy.[4]

The Americanization[5] of drug policy has partially been accomplished through international law. The United Nation's Single Convention on Narcotic Drugs in 1961 brought together most of the international agreements related to the drug trade. Researcher Michael Woodiwess notes that it was the first time "a global drug prohibition regime constructed on the U.S. model" was enacted.[6] In the same year, the U.S. was instrumental in shaping United Nation initiatives for drug control, which most countries around the world abide by today. Woodiwess notes that the United Nations "ironically, considering its mission, had thus encouraged the rapid expansion of drug-control bureaucracies in more that a hundred countries in order to perpetuate an American crusade that, as we have seen, was overtly racist in origin and covertly racist in operation."[7] Critics of U.S. drug policy have written about the Americanization of international law

---

4. Green 1998: 37.

5. Ethan Nadelmann 1993 also refers to the "Americanization" of drug enforcement and criminal law around the world as "harmonization."

6. Woodiwess 2001: 379.

7. Ibid: 380.

enforcement over the last few decades. Drug researcher Ethan Nadelmann states:

> I must stress the dominant role that drug enforcement has played in the evolution of U.S. international law enforcement since the late 1960s...the modern era of international law enforcement is one in which U.S. criminal justice priorities and U.S. model of criminalization and criminal investigation have been exported abroad. Foreign governments have responded to U.S. pressure, inducements, and examples by enacting new criminal laws regarding drug trafficking, money laundering, insider trading, and organized crime and by changing financial and corporate secrecy laws as well as their codes of criminal procedure to better accommodate U.S. requests for assistance.[8]

He also notes that the Americanization of criminal law has been achieved through a wide range of developments, including unprecedented use of the military to fight the war at home and abroad, and the practice of hiring "privateer mercenaries."

Alfred McCoy was one of the first writers to document the CIA's complicity in the drug trade and trafficking. He wrote about the U.S. shipping of arms to guerrilla fighters in Afghanistan to fight off Soviet invaders from 1979–89. The U.S. government ignored drug trafficking in Pakistan and Afghanistan and funded CIA covert operations that supported and protected drug traffickers. During the ten years of CIA covert support for the resistance movement, out of which the Taliban emerged, the U.S. government and the media were silent about the role of leading Afghan and Pakistan military in heroin trafficking. Today, there is little attention given to the fact that the U.S. could have arranged to back a wide array of resistance leaders, but instead chose to back Gulbuddin Hekmatyar who was known to be both brutal and corrupt, and who opposed secular reforms and advocated punishing women students who refused to wear veils by throwing vials of acid on their faces.[9]

8. Nadelmann 1993: 466, 469, 470.
9. McCoy 1991: 450.

Backed by U.S. funding, the Pakistan border was opened in order to accommodate the CIA and millions of Afghan refugees during the war. McCoy notes that the Pakistan military also controlled $2 billion in CIA covert aid and arms "which they distributed to Afghan guerrillas during the war. The aid also supported training camps for Afghan guerrillas run by the Pakistan military. It was here that many Afghan men first came into contact with Taliban fundamentalists' Islamic beliefs."[10] After ten years of war against the Soviets and U.S.$2 billion in CIA covert funds, Afghanistan guerillas and the Pakistan military had emerged as proficient drug traffickers. In the 1970s, Pakistan did not have a large heroin problem, but by the 1980s that would change as more and more people used and became addicted to heroin. The heroin trade flourished during the war, even though seventeen DEA agents were stationed at the U.S. embassy in Islamabad. During that time, they never made one major arrest.[11]

The U.S. ignored the heroin trade because it served its own purposes. In fact, writers Peter Dale Scott and Jonathan Marshall point out that "heroin was shipped out in the same Pakistani army trucks that brought in covert U.S. aid to the Afghan guerrilla."[12] The CIA was able to protect their allies in Afghanistan and Pakistan, and the DEA ignored drug trafficking in the area. As noted by several critics of CIA policy, the war against the Soviets and the civil war was funded by the sale of opium, which was then converted to heroin and sold on the European and American market. Women's groups in Afghanistan were ignored by the U.S. government in their opposition to the Taliban; the U.S. quest to limit Soviet expansion was deemed more important than the rights of Afghani women. By 1990, the U.S. was trying to establish distance from the "monster" it had created and had become "embarrassed by the widely bruited connections between the drug trade and elements of the insurgents," especially since it was aggressively pursuing the war on drugs at home.[13] After Afghanistan successfully expelled the Soviet Union, the U.S. government abandoned them when civil war broke out.

10. Boyd 2002: 400.
11. McCoy 1991: 460.
12. Scott and Marshall 1998: 187.
13. Time (Australian edition), as cited in McCoy 1991: 459.

Many writers have painstakingly documented the CIA's covert operations and toleration and protection of drug trafficking throughout the world since the 1950s, and how the U.S. government has supported right-wing groups in order to further its political goals.[14] Consistently, the CIA has denied these charges but investigations have told another story. CIA covert activities in Burma, Loas, and Thailand in the 1950s fueled U.S. heroin use in the 1960s. Covert CIA activities in Pakistan and Afghanistan from 1979 to 1989 increased heroin production and sales in Pakistan, Europe, and the U.S., and the cocaine trade in South American since the 1980s has contributed to greater availability and lower prices in the U.S.[15] Many readers may be familiar with the contra-drug scandal under President Regan which exposed the U.S. government, its Justice Department, and the Central Intelligence Agency (CIA) for their complicity in supporting anti-democratic Nicaraguan contra factions and drug trafficking in the 1980s. CIA covert operations have contributed not only to growing drug use and its associated problems but also to human rights abuses, violence against women, and the arming and support of right-wing paramilitary forces, death squads, assassinations, and corruption.

Narcoterrorism

Jim Redden wrote in 2000, that the "War on Crime, the War on Drugs, and the War on Terrorism in the U.S. are essentially one massive domestic law enforcement initiative."[16] I believe that he would agree that these three "wars" are more than domestic law-enforcement initiatives but have become global in their reach. As early as 1986, President Reagan was claiming that "these twin evils—narcotics trafficking and terrorism—represent the most insidious and dangerous threats to the hemisphere today."[17] Nation states throughout the world

14. See Chomsky 2000; McCoy 1991; Mendez 1990; Naiman 1996–98; Scott and Marshall 1998; Redden 2000; Woodiwess 2001.

15. Scott and Marshall 1998.

16. Redden 2000: 206.

17. Scott and Marshall 1998: 23.

have bowed to pressure by enacting new legislation that follows U.S. interests in relation to its continued battle against the "red scare" (which included but was not limited to sabotaging and breaking labor organizations and movements, challenging socialist movements, and funding death squads to fight left movements). When the "red scare" became outdated, the U.S. government popularized the term "narcoterrorism" as a way to refer to Communist forces believed to be linked to drug traffickers who support their cause, and to drug cartels that use terrorist methods.[18]

The fear of narcoterrorism deflected attention away from U.S. support of foreign drug trafficking and organized crime and created support for intervention against "leftist regimes"[19] and groups thought to be linked to terrorism. Today, the White House is linking individuals and groups, especially those they identify as fundamentalist Muslims, to drug trafficking. International governments have been restrained after they were warned by President Bush Jr., following the terrorist attacks on September 11, 2001, that they "are either for us or against us." The U.S. and its allies, including Britain and Canada, are not willing to scrutinize their "colonial imposition of 'modern' formal criminal codes in most Third World states."[20]

Then in early 2002, the White House delivered a message to the American people as they watched the Super Bowl. In an ad that cost American taxpayers $4 million in total,[21] President Bush Jr. warned viewers that "[t]errorists use drug profits to fund their cells to commit acts of murder. If you quit drugs, you join the fight against terror in America."[22] The message, which was also placed in popular U.S. magazines, constructs illegal drug users as supporting terrorism. Marijuana smokers (the most popular illegal drug in the U.S.) may ask themselves how that might be? We might also ask when CIA agents, who have pro-

---

18. Ibid.
19. Ibid: 25.
20. West 2000: 29.
21. See Saunders 2002 for a larger discussion about the two 30-second spots which cost American tax payers U.S.$3.4 million for the TV air time and U.S.$1.6 million in production costs.
22. Ibid.: A1.

tected and supported drug trafficking when it suits their political purposes, will cease their covert actions? This public message followed in the wake of the President's State of the Union Address less then a week earlier, in which he divided the world into good and evil and defined, in his terms, the "axis of evil," which consisted of Iran, Iraq, and North Korea. He also referred to these countries as "rogue nations" whose non-cooperation could threaten U.S. interests. Capturing Bin Laden and other members of al-Qaida, who are held responsible for the September 11 terrorist attacks, had become a secondary concern.

Over the course of 2002 and into 2003, the U.S. government steadily deployed military troops on Iraq's border. It justified its "pre-emptive" invasion of Iraq on March 17, 2003, as a mission of the "willing" intent on destroying weapons of mass destruction and toppling Saddam Hussein's regime. Ignoring the protestations of millions of citizens around the world, and of national leaders and the United Nations, the U.S. and the "coalition of the willing" invaded Iraq. Tony Blair, Britain's prime minister, supported the invasion of Iraq and deployed British troops to the region. The alliance of Tony Blair (who is perceived by the public and members of his own party as a puppet of the U.S.) with President Bush Jr. over the invasion of Iraq has inadvertently strengthened U.S. power. Canada did not join the "coalition of the willing."[23] To date, weapons of mass destruction have not been discovered anywhere in Iraq, and the U.S. is busy rewarding companies that have links to the Republican Party with contracts for the "reconstruction" of the country.[24] In addition, President Bush Jr. is intent on following in his father's footsteps. He has publicly acknowledged the CIA's role in further covert actions and has increased military and drug war spending to new heights.[25] The proposed Vital Interdiction of

23. However, critics note that Canadian troops were deployed in Afghanistan and served with British and U.S. troops in Iraq.

24. Morgan and Vulliamy 2003.

25. A number of critics note that "what the Bush Administration has in mind is not the defense of the American citizenry against a foreign enemy but the protection of the American oligarchy from the American democracy" (Lapham 2003: 8).

Criminal Terrorist Organizations (Victory) Act of 2003 expands the U.S. Justice Department's powers to seek and punish drug traffickers "suspected" of funding alleged terrorist groups even when they are unaware of this fact. It also further erodes civil liberties and increases state power.

United States Federal Drug Policy

In 2001, the U.S. government published the *National Drug Control Strategy* (NDCS), which outlines its drug war policy. War metaphors are present throughout the document and law enforcement is presented as a collaboration between federal, state, local, and tribal organizations, reflecting its motto, "in unity there is strength."[26] However, these multi-level organizations are notorious for thwarting one anothers' efforts and failing to share information.[27] In addition, the NDCS praises drug enforcement agencies for their costly and timely operations, listing many of these costly undertakings; one example being Operation Impunity. These "operations," like the term "collateral damage," masks the violence that is inflicted on the environment and on people when they are carried out. By reading official government sources on national and international U.S. drug policy, one begins to understand the "moral righteousness of the war" that is advocated and supported by billions of U.S. tax dollars. Texts like the NDCS "provide for and sustain legality of the state. Indeed, texts and documents have become the general mode of ruling in advanced capitalist societies."[28]

The government of the U.S. promotes protecting the border from the "drug threat" as a top priority in their war on drugs. This is a con-

---

26. ONDCP 2001: 83.

27. The Homeland Security Act, signed into law by President George Bush Jr. in 2002, attempts to reorganize many of these agencies. Twenty-two separate agencies will merge into a single unit including immigration, customs, and the coast guard. However, critics note that the law challenges privacy protections and civil rights.

28. Ng 1988: 90–91.

venient policy, similar to the domino theory, and the subsequent foreign policy initiated to contain communism. Guarding the U.S. border means controlling drug policy in foreign nation states. Latin American countries as well as Mexico and Canada, have been very vulnerable to U.S. intervention. Both Mexico and Canada are seen as threats because their countries border the south and the north of the U.S., and their governments are considered incompetent in regulating illegal drugs at home. The U.S. has expressed its concern about Canadian marijuana being smuggled into the U.S. Since September 11, 2001, several U.S. government representatives have toured Canada warning that "plans to liberalize" drug policy "could rupture Canada-U.S. relations." U.S. drug czar John Walters, Special Assistant to the Office of National Drug Control Policy David Murray, and U.S. Ambassador Paul Cellucci have publicly expressed their disapproval of Canadian federal medical marijuana policy, the planned safe injection sites, and the reform recommendations to decriminalize marijuana.[29] However, as usual, the U.S. fails to mention that many states have already decriminalized small amounts of marijuana and that most imported marijuana still comes into the U.S. from Mexico. Nor do they mention the "many tons of cocaine flowing north to Canada" from the U.S.[30] The construction of unreliable drug-source countries by the U.S. detracts attention away from its own insatiable appetite for illegal drugs, its domestic illegal drug production, and its government's complicity in the drug trade.

The *National Drug Control Strategy* clearly states, "We must stop drugs everywhere they enter our countries."[31] The Carribean, Mexico, and Latin America are represented as key drug-source countries, but little mention is made of U.S. amphetamine producers, and marijuana growers. Marijuana growing is a large national business that supports economically depressed communities throughout the U.S. Up to a third of marijuana consumed in the U.S. is home grown.[32]

---

29. Armstrong 2003: A8; Canadian Press 2003; Matas 2002.

30. Damuzi 2001: 68. They also fail to mention the U.S. trafficking of handguns to Canada (O'Hanlon 2003).

31. ONDCP 2001: 94.

32. NACLA 2002: 17.

Although the U.S. government has been intent on arresting marijuana growers, it has failed to contain or cease its domestic marijuana cultivation at home; nevertheless, it maintains its stance that it will eradicate coca cultivation in Colombia, Peru, and Bolivia.[33]

The U.S. has been active in exporting their drug policy to Third World countries. However, its interest in South America and its militarized response to drug control there stems from its official stance that drug control is an issue of national security. After World War II, the U.S. foreign policy in South America was shaped by its interest in containing the spread of communism and encouraging a free market economy. In order to achieve these goals, it initiated "counterinsurgency tactics" to fight left-leaning groups and governments.[34] Since the war, the U.S. has exploited and contributed to the economic and social instability of Latin America, and since 1969, the drug war has been used to secure U.S. control over Latin America.[35] Rather than eradicating poverty or implementing quality education and health care inside and outside its own borders, the U.S. has made eradicating illegal drugs its priority, especially in source countries.

By linking U.S. economic aid with drug policy, Latin American nations are in a difficult situation. They have often had to accept that instability is the price to pay for U.S. benevolence. Social movements (including those of peasant and Indigenous groups) throughout Latin America (in Bolivia, Brazil, Colombia, Ecuador, Mexico, and Venezuela) oppose free trade agreements that threaten their livelihood, independence, and resources and that prevent the equitable redistribution of wealth and land which would allow them to restructure their political, social, and economic environment. For example, the agreements of the International Monetary Fund ensure that receiving-countries comply with U.S. economic standards and requirements.[36] However, complying with U.S. requirements and the

33. Scott and Marshall 1998.
34. Chomsky 2000; Walker III 1996.
35. Walker III 1996.
36. Woodiwiss 2001.

Americanization of the global economy (partially driven by Western consumerism) has done nothing to improve the lives of most people in the world, who continue to live in poverty and who are deprived of basic human rights and protections.

The Civil War in Colombia

In order to understand the lives of women in Colombia today, it is necessary to examine the roots of the ongoing civil war and its links to Plan Colombia. Writer Hector Mondragon says that Colombian history "is a history of systematic violence in the interests of multinational exploitation," which exploits the campesino, Afro-Colombians, and Indigenous people and claims their land.[37] The roots of the civil war can be traced to the peasant movements of the 1920s and 1930s.[38] Most peasants lived and worked under terrible conditions on large coffee-producing estates, and their concerns about labor and property rights culminated in a movement that advocated labor and political reforms. The Colombian government called on the military to crush the movement, and by the 1940s, in order to protect their lives, some peasants began to arm themselves. As the peasant movement grew, it was influenced by socialist and communist thought and they used both self-defense and guerrilla warfare to advance its goals. *La Violencia*, which began in 1948, was a ten year war between the government and the armed peasants. Out of this historical precedent, armed struggle "became a part of a broader political strategy to capture state power."[39] Military attacks on peasant organizations killed many people and drove two million off their lands. These displaced peasants became the supporting base for the Revolutionary Armed Forces of Colombia (FARC), which emerged in 1964.

The exclusionary National Front coalition, which was established in 1958 (and lasted until 1974) by the Liberal and Conservative Par-

---

37. Mondragon 2001b: 2. See Guizado 1996; Hargreaves 1992; Marshall 1991; Morales 1996; and Ryes 1996.

38. Meza 1998.

39. Ibid.: 23.

ties, also contributed to the strengthening of the peasant movement. Until 1991, the Liberal and Conservative Parties dominated the political scene and attempted to crush the peasant groups and all other social protest and political dissent. In 1965, the government granted the military the power to arm civilians to fight against guerilla groups, including FARC, the National Liberation Army (ELN), the Popular Liberation Army (EPL), and the April 19th Movement (M–19), which had emerged in the 1960s and 1970s. Researcher Ricardo Vargas Meza notes that in the 1970s FARC had little political or military power, in fact it saw its role as mainly a political one.[40]

It was not until the 1980s when the Colombian government began to crack down on legal opposition that FARC emerged as the military leader of the revolutionary movement; it distanced itself from the Communist Party while seizing power in many regions. A cease-fire approved by the Belisario Betancur (1982–86) government and FARC, and the later accords of La Uribe signed fourteen months later, led the way for a potentially peaceful solution to the conflict. Many of FARC's social, economic, and political demands were addressed in the accords of La Uribe. FARC formed the Patriotic Union (UP) in order to establish itself in the legal political process at the local, regional, and national levels. Its efforts to obtain a peaceful solution were severely hampered by the state's assassination of two hundred UP leaders in 1988; by 1998, three thousand UP members had been killed.[41]

The conflicts between the military and paramilitary groups and the guerilla groups were slightly contained until the mid-1980s. However, after the cease-fire was signed by FARC, M–19, ADO, and the EPL, the military's hands were tied in countering guerilla sympathy and legal political advances in Colombia. Thus, they began to aid and arm paramilitary groups to halt guerrilla political advancement.[42] New allies were forged with the large landowners, many of them newly wealthy drug traffickers. By the end of the 1980s, drug traffickers were

40. Ibid.

41. Ibid.: 25.

42. Chernick 1998.

the largest landowners in Colombia who were interested in funding the paramilitaries to protect their land and power, which were being threatened by the guerilla forces. There was little outcry against the activities of the paramilitary groups; however, when the paramilitaries began to target judges, politicians, and presidential candidates, attitudes and policy changed. In 1989, the Supreme Court of Colombia overturned the 1965 law which allowed the military to arm civilian forces. This did not, however, effectively curb the paramilitary groups, and in 1994, President Sampler authorized the creation of the Convivir, civilian defence groups in rural areas.

Several writers note that a shift occurred when the Colombian state and the military began to disengage from the civil war in the mid-1980s and began supporting, through aid and assistance, an expanding paramilitary force to fight the war against the guerillas. However, the paramilitaries are not fully accountable to, or controlled by, the military or the state. In addition, paramilitary violence has been increasingly directed at the civilian population rather than at guerrilla forces.[43] Although FARC has grown and the territory it controls has expanded, it has continued to be denied a legitimate avenue to political power. FARC claims that the Colombian and U.S. governments fail to distinguish between the drug trafficker and the guerillas, and they consider Plan Colombia a declaration of war against the guerilla groups. FARC notes that the regions targeted for militarization and fumigation in Plan Colombia are under FARC control. In its view, the paramilitaries are agents of "state terror."[44] The use of paramilitaries make it increasingly difficult to perceive a peaceful solution to the roughly forty year conflict, which continues to be fueled by the war on drugs.

U.S. policy is supported by some segments of the Colombian population, mainly investors and large landowners (many of whom are drug traffickers). These two groups benefit from the suppression of labor disputes, land seizures, the opening of trade markets, the privatization of national industries, and state terrorism against anyone

43. Ibid.
44. Ibid.: 32.

in their way—including women, union leaders, peasants, students, human rights workers, teachers, and Indigenous people.

The large landholders in Colombia have benefited from neoliberal economic policy and have increased their political power at every level of government. Privatization and neoliberalism have led to further misery for the poor. The masses of poor, especially women, gained little through privatization and promises of investment, for employment and growth did not materialize.[45] Rather, the poor have experienced a mounting reign of terror against them, sanctioned by the state, as they have been forced off their land, terrorized, and murdered. The current conflict has resulted in over two million peasants being displaced by violence.[46]

Privatization and neoliberal economic policy are directly linked to the increase in coca cultivation and drug trafficking in Colombia.[47] The Colombian elites, the U.S., and the World Bank and International Monetary Fund encourage privatization and neoliberalism in all economic spheres except drug trafficking. Overborrowing by governments in the1960 and 1970s, which was welcomed by creditors, and high interest rates led to the debt crisis of the 1980s. The economic policies of the World Bank and the International Monetary Fund were structured on an unlimited free market, and their adjustment programs put into place to ensure that countries pay off their debt created recession and poverty for most people. In Colombia, similar to other Latin American nations, the majority of the people were cut off from legitimate paths of survival. Considering the demand for drugs in both the United States and Europe, many turned to coca cultivation and trafficking as a source of income. In many Latin American countries a large portion of export income goes toward servicing IMF debt, and it is argued that drug revenues enable Colombia to sustain its foreign debt obligations. Susan George, author of *The Debt Boomerang*, highlights how the drug-debt link is ignored by the IMF.[48]

45. Tokatlian 1996.
46. Colombian Support Network 2001; Mondragon 2001a.
47. George 1992; Mondragan 2001b.
48. George 1992.

It is evident that over the last thirty years, Colombia's drug trade has also been shaped by U.S. policy. In the 1970s, Colombia's drug trade was largely confined to marijuana, but by the late 1970s, it had become active in transporting refined cocaine to Western nations. It was not until U.S.-funded eradication programs eliminated the coca crop in Peru and Bolivia and targeted the transportation of coca paste to Colombia, however, that cultivation and production of cocaine began. Since the 1990s, Colombia's drug trade has been further diversified and opium poppies are now being cultivated.[49]

Plan Colombia

In the U.S. today, approximately U.S.$18.8 billion a year is allocated to federal drug programs to continue the war on drugs, double what it was in 1992.[50] In 1999, Colombia became the recipient of the largest amount of U.S. military and economic assistance outside of Egypt and Israel.[51] Plan Colombia consists of a U.S.$1.3-billion initiative above the regular federal budget. Coupled with the additional funding to fight the "war on terrorism," U.S. federal agencies and police have expanded their power base both domestically and internationally. Contrary to U.S. propaganda about winning the global war on drugs, the heavily funded Americanization of drug policy throughout the world has not led to a decrease in drug use, trafficking, and cultivation. Instead, coca production and consumption has remained stable, prices are down, and illegal drugs such as marijuana and cocaine are readily available to consumers in the U.S.[52]

Overlooking human rights violations, the U.S. Andean Initiative was announced by President Bush Sr. in 1989 to fight the war on drugs in Colombia, Peru, and Bolivia. Additional military aid was received thereafter. In 1990, U.S. military aid to fight the war on drugs in Colombia

49. NACLA 2002: 13.

50. ONDCP 2001: 119.

51. Chomsky 2000. In 2003, the U.S. war budget for Iraq far exceeded this amount.

52. Drucker 1999: 16; Woodiwiss 2001.

totaled U.S.$93.2 million dollars, and only U.S.$2.1 million was slotted for economic assistance. Anti-drug aid, training, and equipment was also provided by the European Union, Canada, and Japan. Plan Colombia, which was approved in 2000, has also increased militarization in Latin America. Of the U.S.$1.3 billion allocated for Plan Colombia in 2000, 83 percent was earmarked as military aid for Colombia and its neighbors—Bolivia, Ecuador, and Peru—but Colombia was the primary recipient. The initiative was passed as an "emergency aid package," which allowed the U.S. government to spend over the amount already allotted for aid programs in Colombia. It is anticipated that the plan will cost about U.S.$7.5 billion dollars over six years to fight the war against drugs. President Bush Jr. has also expanded funding through the Andean Counterdrug Initiative. He may also attempt to expand the scope of the existing programs to fight against terrorism. His administration requested an additional U.S.$98 million to train and equip a special brigade of the Colombian Army to protect oil pipelines owned by Occidental Petroleum from the ELN and FARC,[53] which have been identified by the U.S. as terrorist groups.

The Colombian initiative is seen by the U.S. government as "helping to decrease drug production and trafficking and diminish the corrosive influence of drug-related corruption."[54] Over 80 percent of Plan Colombia is intended to provide military aid to Colombia's military, police, and fumigation programs, including helicopters, radar systems, planes, patrol boats, and intelligence and training. The bulk of U.S. funding will finance further law enforcement through interdiction support, arms, training, intelligence support, and policing.[55] In addition, U.S.$6 million is to be provided by the Colombian government, the European Union, the IMF, and the World Bank, which will be directed to social and economic programs; however, to date little attention or planning of these programs by the Colombian govern-

53. WOLA 2002.

54. ONDCP 2001: 100.

55. In addition, the Bush Jr. administration withheld U.S.$5 million in aid in 2003 and threatened to withhold more if Colombia (and 34 other nations) does not exempt "Americans" from prosecution by the newly formed International Criminal Court (*Guardian Weekly* 2003: 32)

ment is evident.[56] The human rights component was waived earlier by former President Bill Clinton, because, he claimed it interfered with U.S. national security interests.[57]

For approximately forty years, Colombia has been ravished by civil war, and the political violence has risen steadily as U.S. military funding has increased in the region. The Colombian Commission of Jurists report that the killings attributed to the paramilitaries have increased from 46 percent in 1995 to 80 percent in 1999, between "5,000 and 7,000 unarmed peasants have been slaughtered by them."[58] An average of ten people were killed every day between 1988 and 1997; however, by the year 2001, the killings had increased to thirty-eight a day.[59] In addition, over two million people, in a country of forty million are displaced, the majority being women and children, and Indigenous and Afro-Colombian people. FARC is also responsible for kidnaping and killing, as well as taxing, drug traffickers. Some critics note that it has abandoned its original political goals as the civil conflict has progressed. However, both Amnesty International and Human Rights Watch claim that in Colombia, the U.S. is arming the military and the police which are connected to paramilitary groups, and they are responsible for the majority of human rights violations in the region. As well, some military units and the police are identified as human rights abusers.[60]

Human Rights Watch has been investigating and exposing human rights violations in the Americas since the early 1980s. They have compiled detailed evidence of ties between the Colombian Army and paramilitary groups which are responsible for deaths, torture, and other human rights violations.[61] The Colombia Support Network states that the paramilitaries are responsible for at least 70 percent of

56. Chomsky 2000.
57. Amnesty International 2001.
58. Chomsky 2000: 65.
59. WOLA 2002: 1.
60. Amnesty International 2001; Human Rights Watch 2000c.
61. HRW 2000c.

the human rights violations in the country.[62] They have also documented the existence of close links between drug traffickers, paramilitary groups, and the army. The money raised by drug trafficking is used to buy arms and to support paramilitary actions such as the formation of death squads that carry out human rights violations, massacres, and assassinations. Further, they point out that the U.S. trains Colombian army intelligence officers who are linked to paramilitary groups. Thus, Plan Colombia supports and strengthens the ties, and the military might, of these groups.

In May 2001, Jineth Bedoya Lima, a journalist, was kidnaped by paramilitaries and physically and psychologically tortured for twelve hours. The paramilitaries threatened to kill her and four fellow journalists who had reported human rights violations.[63] Her story is all too common in Colombia, and attacks have increased since Plan Colombia was initiated.[64] Human rights activists note that Plan Colombia has fueled the conflicts in Colombia and that violence and killings doubled between 1998 and 2001.[65]

Plan Colombia represents a major break from past U.S. intervention in the region. Prior to 1999, the Colombian National Police were the major recipients of U.S. aid. With Plan Colombia, the army and three new battalions are receiving the majority of the funding. The military is being brought into the game because the U.S. claims that FARC and other leftist groups occupy designated areas to be fumigated in the south; therefore, it is too dangerous to leave these activities to the local police.[66] The three new counternarcotics battalions (each with about nine hundred men) in the Colombian army are in effect trained and equipped by the U.S. Their "official" role is to secure and clear the area of "suspects" who may attempt to shoot at U.S. contractors, pilots, and their police escorts, while fumigating coca crops.[67]

---

62. Colombia Support Network 2001.
63. Amnesty International 2001.
64. Ibid.
65. Isacson 2001a.
66. Ibid.
67. Isacson and Vaicius 2001.

The U.S. employs hundreds of "contract employees through U.S. corporations to carry out its policies in Colombia and in other countries."[68] The hiring of private corporations is referred to as "outsourcing." Critics note that U.S. citizens are largely unaware that they are "funding a private war with private soldiers" in the Andean region because "the law does not require the state and defense departments to make information public" about outsourcing.[69] DynCorp, which has been around since 1946, is one of the primary private mercenary corporations that the U.S. government employs for intervention in Latin America. The company assists in drug interdiction, eradication missions (including aerial spraying of coca), and training, among other activities. Critics of the privatization of the drug war question whether DynCorp and other private corporations are accountable for their employees' actions and suggest that they have been involved in not only drug-fighting but in repressing leftist groups in Colombia.[70] In Bolivia, the company was implicated in both buying and selling prostitutes. DynCorp was also a major financial backer of President Bush Jr.'s presidential election, and its subsequent reward is a contract to police the reconstruction of Iraq.[71]

Critics note that the paramilitaries are agents of state terrorism in Colombia. After the September 11 attacks, the State Department identified FARC and ELN as terrorist organizations that will be targeted in the global anti-terrorist campaign. The United Self-Defense Forces of Colombia, a paramilitary group is also on its list. Critics note that in the past the U.S. has repeatedly stated that it is not in Colombia to fight against the guerilla groups. Thus, the intention of Bush Jr.'s administration to expand the scope of the programs in Colombia to fight terrorism and to protect oil interests marks a clear shift in public policy. These new initiatives, Plan Colombia, and earlier military aid to Latin America to fight the war on drugs are seen by many people, including the guerillas, as a war against them.

---

68. Bigwood 2001: 1.
69. Bigwood 2001: 2; Isacson 2001b: 8.
70. Tamayo 200l.
71. Beaumont 2002: 2.

The Displacement of Indigenous Peoples

The Indigenous peoples of Colombia have been subjected to violence and displacement as a result of the appropriation of the natural resources on their land. Early in the twentieth century, Colombian and British merchants drove Indigenous peoples from their land in order to extract latex from rubber plants. The people who inhabited those lands, and the fragile ecological stability of the tropical rain forest, were of little concern to early corporate entrepreneurs. Some estimate that over forty thousand Indigenous peoples were killed during the period rubber was extracted.[72] As late as 1970, the killing of Indigenous peoples in Colombia went unpunished because, as in North America, white colonizers saw them as nonpersons.[73] Many areas in the south were solely inhabited by Indigenous peoples until the 1960s when the civil war brought settlers (campensinos) into the "agricultural area." Although the Colombian government encouraged the settlement of small plots of land, it did not provide an adequate infrastructure; consequently, the cost of transporting crops to market and bringing in goods could not yield a sustainable living. Thus, many of the campesinos turned to growing coca for their livelihood.

Today, the continued displacement of campensinos and Indigenous peoples, and the destruction of the Amazon Rainforest in Colombia, is linked to Plan Colombia and free trade initiatives. Armando Valbuena, the president of the National Indigenous Organization of Colombia, points out that the Indigenous peoples understand that the Plan Colombia has little to do with eradicating drug production and trafficking. Rather, they know it is a strategy to eradicate leftist social movements, to displace Indigenous peoples and peasants, and to exploit their natural resources.[74] The fumigation of the coca leaf plays an important role. The U.S. claims that the chemicals used in aerial fumigation are not toxic; however, the manufacturers of glyphosate recommend that livestock be kept out of the area

72. Valbuena 2001.
73. Ibid.
74. Ibid.

for two weeks and humans should stay away until the chemical dries.[75] When Agent Orange was sprayed indiscriminately on civilians and food sources in Vietnam, the U.S. government also denied harm.

Human rights groups and people living in these areas note that people are suffering from the defoliant chemical. Aerial fumigation of the coca leaf destroys their livelihood because it destroys the food crops of small farmers, their livestock and water sources, and the soil. The peasants and Indigenous peoples who live in these areas report higher incidences of respiratory and skin problems, miscarriages and birth deformities, and gastrointestinal disorders such as vomiting and diarrhea. The spraying kills all plant life in its path. In the town of La Concordia, "food crops, people's houses, the school, the soccer field, the road itself" were sprayed.[76] Valbuena says that when food security is destroyed, campesinos are both threatened and undermined; therefore, the aerial fumigation is a war against the peoples of Colombia and its environment. Nor have crop substitution programs been successfully used; most farmers report that they have never been approached by the Colombian government or compensated for growing food crops rather than coca.[77]

The illegal market in coca paste has also contributed to deforestation and the toxic dumping of harmful chemicals.[78] Chemicals used to make coca paste include sulfuric acid, kerosene, and ammonia, all of which are dumped into the soil and water, destroying the fragile ecosystem. British drug researcher Penny Green criticizes the hypocrisies of Western drug control strategies for failing to restrict the chemical agents needed for drug refinement. These chemicals are mostly manufactured in Western nations.[79]

Nevertheless, Hector Mondragan states that the corporations are the worst enemies of the Indigenous peoples because they covet their natural resources, including oil, minerals, and agriculture. Since

75. Borger and Hodgson 2001.
76. Isacson and Vaicius 2001: 15.
77. Ibid.; Podur 2001.
78. George 1992.
79. Green 1998: 41.

1999, the number of oil contracts in Colombia held by the U.S., Canada, Britain, and Spain has increased.[80] However, the primary companies originate in Britain and the U.S. In 1999, Colombian president Andres Pastrana met with George Bush Jr., then governor of Texas, and the heads of oil and electric companies. He promised privatization, contracts, and concessions for oil and electric development. Not surprisingly, Occidental Petroleum lobbied the U.S. congress to support Plan Colombia. Al Gore, who was vice president at the time, was a stockholder in its company. And Canada Oxy has contracts to exploit oil in two areas where Plan Colombia will unfold.[81] Furthermore, British Petroleum Amoco is Colombia's largest foreign investor. The London-based corporation has been linked to paramilitaries and was active in training them in the early 1990s.[82]

The 2002 announcement that the Bush Jr. administration has allocated U.S.$98 million to train and equip a special regiment of the Colombian army to protect the oil pipeline belonging to Occidental Petroleum raises further fears about finding a peaceful solution to the civil war and ending the displacement of Indigenous peoples. It also provides further evidence that U.S. intervention is related to economic and political concerns, rather than the pretext of the war on drugs and terrorism. Other writers note that international banking corporations are thriving in Colombia, earning money off the profits gained in the illegal market, most of which leaves the country and lands up in banks in the U.S., Asia, and the Europe Union. As well, Philips Morris, the cigarette producer, has been implicated in the contraband laundering system in Colombia.[83]

The U'wa people claim that their lands have been militarized since Plan Colombia was initiated in an attempt to guarantee Occidental Petroleum's rights to their natural resources and land.[84] As well, Afro-Colombians are on land destined for oil development and the construction of canals and dams; thus, they have become targets of vio-

80. Mondragon 2001a.
81. Ibid.
82. Guevera 2002: 37.
83. Mondragon 2001a.
84. Valbuena 2001.

lence and displacement.[85] Writer and activist Justin Podur notes that only 8 to 9 percent of the Colombian population is black; however they make up about nine hundred thousand of the displaced peoples.[86] The regions that are targeted for economic development of oil and mineral deposits are the same areas that are being militarized since the inception of Plan Colombia.[87] Vast regions of land are being expropriated by the Colombian state in the countryside so that its economic agenda can move forward—an agenda which is imposed on the people through the different free trade agreements and the proposed Free Trade Area of the Americas (FTAA).

The genocide and displacement of campesinos and Indigenous peoples in Colombia and elsewhere have led to violence and a loss of languages, knowledge, and cultural traditions. Militarization and global capitalism have also led to massive destruction of the environment and biological diversity. The campesinos and Indigenous peoples in Colombia know that Plan Colombia and free trade agreements are used to "wipe out and eliminate all of our spiritual relationship and link to the land." Armando Valbuena explains that free trade and Plan Colombia will destroy the

> traditional orchard, the way that we take care of the environment, the way that we care for the water sources, and the delicate balance between production and the eco-system, the link between the harvest and the universe, the way that we control pests in our agriculture with natural spraying, food like beans and all of its different strains, corn in all its varieties,...the vegetable, beans, and all types of medicinal plants...all of this diversity are among the worst enemies of the multinationals."[88]

Ethnobiologist Wade Davis concludes that "[we] are living in the midst of an ecological catastrophe" where economic and government policies are blind to past and current destruction. "All memory is convulsed in an upheaval of violence."[89]

85. Podur 2001a.
86. Ibid.: 46.
87. Monbiot 2001.
88. Valbuena 2001.
89. Davis 1998: 231.

Women's Resistance to Violence in Colombia

It is often overlooked that of the two million people who have been displaced in Colombia, the vast majority are women and their children who are forced to leave regions where conflict occurs, abandoning their homes, land, and sustenance. Women are also forced to flee if they are identified as being sympathetic to or a collaborator with any of the warring factions. However, activists and human rights groups note that people have been falsely accused as collaborators and sympathizers as an excuse to forcibly remove them from their lands and, in this way, vast regions have been expropriated. Although FARC has a minor role in the displacement of people, the paramilitaries are largely responsible. Women and children in Colombia are not protected by the state and are at increased risk at the hands of the paramilitaries. The Women's Commission for Refugee Women and Children (WCRWC) notes that over 58 percent of displaced people in Colombia are women and almost 40 percent of displaced households are headed by women. Although the Colombian government and the U.S. have increased military aid, little humanitarian support has been contributed by national and international agencies. Many women have fled with their children to shantytowns outside urban centers where they live in makeshift homes constructed of cardboard, tin, and plastic. There they often care not only for their own children, but also for those they have adopted and for their elderly parents. Their homes have no electricity or running water, and the shanty towns are without roads or schools.[90]

Women in Colombia have spoken out about their increased vulnerability in the face of militarization of the region. They have recorded many human rights violations, including kidnapings, murders, and torturing of people. They also note that although kidnapings, murder, and torture are usually reserved for men by men, women have also been victims. Furthermore, the killing of men is often accompanied by the assault of the women in their families, and

90. WCRWC 1999: 2.

the destruction and looting of their homes.[91] Women are vulnerable to violence and are used by all sides of the military conflict in their vendettas against one another, and rape is used as a tool of revenge.[92] Because of the numerous conflict zones, armed factions, and risk of violence, women's movements are restricted, yet they are forced to leave their homes within hours after being attacked, "traumatized and terrorized." Women are often fearful to use their real names and their identity card for fear of retaliation, which later limits the services they can obtain. Others have had to flee without their identity cards and do not know how to obtain another one. After fleeing from her home, a woman "will be lucky to count on the help of a friend or relative for immediate, temporary shelter, whether it is a corner of a shack in an outlying barrio or a covered corridor in a downtown building. Just as likely, she will find no support whatsoever and will have to scramble to find a foothold in the barrios or at the edges of smaller towns." Other women and their children end up in public buildings converted into shelters such as the coliseum in Turbo. There, "hundreds of beds and cots are pressed together in the coliseum's entryway, a cavernous concrete room, with peeling paint and dusty floors. They cook and wash outside the coliseum, in makeshift kitchens."[93] Lack of adequate shelter, water, and food plague the women and their families.

The displacement of the campesinos and Indigenous peoples in Colombia is a war against their food security—families who were once self-reliant and grew their own food are now dependent and suffering. In 1998, 68 percent of the displaced children in the camps in Turbo were malnourished, and malaria was commonly reported.[94] Most of the children who have been displaced are not in school. Medical services and day-care for the children are inadequate, and many are left alone as their mothers attempt to find work. Further, many of the children have witnessed attacks on their parents or have been attacked themselves. As the paramilitary, army, police, and guerilla groups target civilians, children also become victims of the conflict.

91. Ibid.
92. Podur 2001b.
93. WCRWC 1999: 4, 6.
94. Ibid.: 7.

Young girls are especially vulnerable to rape and abduction, and the WCRWC notes that some of them have joined military groups in order to protect themselves. WCRWC also notes that dislocation and the breakdown of the community and family places young girls at risk of exploitation. It is not uncommon for young girls to agree to relationships that provide them with shelter and security. Young boys and girls have little access to education or secure employment. Concerns for young boys differ, though, because they are more actively recruited into military service by the various factions, and becoming a soldier can be appealing in the face of few alternative options.

Women also have few options in Colombia. They can flee conflict zones and join the many displaced peoples or they, too, can align themselves with men and paramilitary groups which may provide some security at the expense of their autonomy. These decisions are often based on fear and need, not choice. To a lesser extent, women are invited into guerilla groups. When women do flee conflict zones, they are deprived of housing, food, and economic security, and increased poverty is almost a given. Employment opportunities are rare and when jobs are secured, incomes are low. Furthermore, women are stigmatized for being displaced. Some women have resorted to begging and prostitution in order to care for their children and themselves.[95] When the Women's Commission for Refugee Women and Children sent a delegation to Colombia in 1998, they noted that the women they interviewed found it difficult to obtain any type of emergency assistance from Colombian and international agencies. Others did not know assistance was available.

Women have also spoken out about being excluded from the peace process. They have been verbal about the fact that women do not hold senior government positions nor do they have positions on human rights and humanitarian agencies which deal with the conditions of being displaced. Although women are not included in the "official" peace process, they have made their presence known in Colombia and at the international level. The ANMUCIC (*Asociacion Nacional de Mujeres Campesinas e Indigenas de Colombia*) consists of

95. Ibid.

one hundred thousand rural women throughout Colombia. They have been active in assisting displaced women, providing shelter, and applying for aid from the government and various agencies. *Profamilia* (*La Asociacion Probeinsestar de la Familia Colmbiana*) is an independent chapter of the International Federation of Planned Parenthood. They have forty-seven women's clinics and eleven youth centers throughout Colombia, providing reproductive health care for women, men, and youth. Their clinics, including their mobile units, have been visited by displaced women. In addition, two other women's groups have risen to international prominence, the *Organizacion Femenina Popular* (OFP) and the *Ruta Pacifica de Mujeres*. Both groups speak out about the impact of the war on women and demand that they be part of the peace process.

The OFP orginated in Barrancabermeja in 1972. It was founded by the Catholic Church, but broke away in 1988. Since then, it has opened other OFPs, or women's houses (*casas de la mujer*), in working-class neighborhoods in the Magadalena Medio region. They provide for the women and children who are displaced, and offer shelter and food, public kitchens, education (such as teaching material, publications, and scholarships), job training, economic aid in setting up co-operatives, legal advice and aid for victims of human rights violations, and youth and health services. They are at the forefront of the ongoing conflict with the paramilitaries in Colombia. Similar to other independent unarmed and peaceful independent groups in Colombia, the OFPs are "the only force left standing" in the way of the paramilitaries, as they forge into new urban areas being taken over by the conflict.[96]

Operations under Plan Colombia, where the military and police "set up a temporary presence" in the city, is accompanied by "hundreds of paramilitary fighters" who move into the neighborhoods; and when the military and police move on, the paramilitaries remain and the violence begins. As the paramilitaries move into urban centers, neighborhoods are closely supervised, people are stopped and interrogated, and their mobility is restricted. Residents fearful of the

---

96. Isacson 2001b.

paramilitaries remain indoors as much as possible.[97] Meanwhile, FARC and groups like ELN plan their counterattack. But it is the men, women, and children and organizations such as OFP, caught between the crossfire, that are most at risk.

On January 27, 2001, paramilitaries visited the OFP women's house run by Yolanda Becerra's in Barrancabermeja and demanded that she hand over her keys to the center. She explained that the paramilitaries want to get rid of the directors of the centers and their organizers so that they can take over their "food, health, and other services" that neighborhoods rely on.[98] The paramilitaries returned the following day and the police were called, but since then Yolanda has been threatened again. She notes that the paramilitaries are not only targeting the OFP but also their social base of support, for women are being warned that they will be a target if they support the OFP.

On August 15, 2001, a plenary event organized by the OFP for the international women's mobilization for peace was blockaded by paramilitaries in Barrancabermeja. The paramilitaries held signs that accused the women's groups of working with and recruiting youths for the guerillas. It is standard practice for the paramilitaries to accuse human rights and peace activists as being "tools of the insurgency.... It is an attempt to instill fear and to justify violent action against peaceful, unarmed members of civil society who are working for social justice." The women involved in the international women's mobilization for peace are unarmed and represent those "who have suffered war and injustice and who seek to be authors of peace."[99] Despite the blockade and threats by the paramilitaries, the women's groups met and when the blockades were lifted on the following day they took to the streets and held vigils outside of the OFP's offices located in neighborhoods that have been targeted by paramilitaries. The vigils were viewed as "part of a symbolic retaking of the city from the paramilitaries. The war and violence close public space—the mobilization is to take that public space back."[100]

97. Ibid.
98. Ibid.: 11.
99. Leal, Rozental, and Podur 2001: 1.
100. Ibid.

Nevertheless, the paramilitaries continue to threaten women's groups and those who use their services. On November 10, 2001, paramilitaries were responsible for demolishing an OFP community center *Casa de la Mujer del Nororiente.* Two OFP activists, Dora Guzman Gonzalez and Gloria Amparo Suarez, had agreed to officially identify the man in charge of the paramilitary action. On November 19, 2001, two armed men representing the paramilitary group *Autodefensas Unidas de Colombia* (AUC) went to Dora's home asking for her, and fifteen minutes later, five armed men arrived at the OFP women's center looking for both women. The armed men told the women at the center that "if they pick him out in the identity parade they will find themselves in serious trouble, or more serious than they are in already."[101] The paramilitaries in the region continue threatening to attack and kill the members of the OFP center and continue to keep women in the region away from it. Although OFP is not aligned or linked to guerilla groups, it has been left alone by the groups to do their work.[102] In contrast, paramilitary hostility has led OFP, and other human rights defenders in Colombia, to be accompanied by foreign volunteers from Peace Brigades International (PBI) when they go out in public. PBI is a non-profit organization that accompanies human rights defenders in many nations who are under threat. Without their aid, many human rights defenders would be unable to speak out about the current violence and hostility and to continue providing services for the women, men, and children of Colombia.

Women's associations have also been very active in helping other women and their families hide and relocate. The Colombian government has failed to protect and provide for women and children during the ongoing conflicts. The women's groups in Colombia note that women are not only victims of war, they suffer poverty and domestic, public, and political violence.[103] In Colombia, poor women have little access to education, employment, health care and day-care. Activists note that "women suffer more than men from the conflict and Indigenous and African women suffer even more." Rural women are

---

101. Urgent Action Network, Amnesty International USA, 2001.
102. Isacson 2001a.
103. Podur 2001b.

especially vulnerable, and activists note that it is dangerous for women because they become "a military objective" in the ongoing conflict.[104] Both paramilitary and guerilla groups attempt to repress independent organizations. However, the women have not been silenced; instead, they continue to make their stories known at home and internationally, aid women and their children, protest against violence and neoliberal economic plans, and work toward peace.

Activists working toward democracy and peace state that violence will continue to escalate in Colombia until women's, Indigenous, peasant, and neighborhood concerns are addressed, giving them jurisdiction and power and acknowledging the problems that are rooted in colonization. They note that the participation of all people, including women, the campesinos, Afro-Colombians, Indigenous, and urban neighborhood organizations is needed to reorganize the territories. Women's peace organizations have been developing a political agenda for women "to recover sovereignty, and create an international strategy for anti-war intervention. Women are fighting not only for humanity but the basis for life itself, in the biodiversity and ecology."[105] Activists stress that it is the responsibility of the state to protect women and their human rights and that it is very important that mobilizations, peace rallies, delegations, murders, and violence against the people are made visible; otherwise their struggle will be limited. Activists assert that when women are invisible, they "are vulnerable to violence."[106] The OFP echoes this when it says it is campaigning against fear, for "it is better to act with fear than to cease to act because of fear."[107]

Groups that visit Colombia and maintain a presence there to publicize the ongoing struggle include Peace Brigades International, Canada-Colombian Solidarity Campaign, Amnesty International, Washington Office on Latin America, Colombia Support Network, and Women's Commission for Refugee Women and Children. They are also active in mobilizing international support for the peace

---

104. Ibid.
105. Podur 2001b: 2.
106. Leal, Rozental, and Podur 2001.
107. Canada-Colombia Solidarity Campaign 2001.

groups and activists in Colombia. Women's groups like OFP appeal to the international community to show their concern about the violence against them by pressuring the Colombian and U.S. government to take accountability for their actions and inactions that contribute to human rights abuses. In addition, they ask that foreign peace groups continue to offer a physical presence and to continue accompanying human rights defenders in Colombia.[108]

In Colombia, some peace efforts have been linked to support for the legalization of drugs. Legalization debates are not new. Ever since the 1970s, influential Colombians have seriously debated the merits of whether legalization of drugs would reduce drug trade violence. However, the White House opposes all debate leaning toward decriminalization or legalization. Nevertheless, the debate continues. In the spring of 2001, at the Summit of the Americas which met in Quebec City, over one hundred top Latin American leaders (who included both female and male religious ministers, Nobel Laureates, political and cultural leaders) called on President Bush Jr. to halt Plan Colombia in an open letter. They pointed out several key concerns—the increased massacres of civilians, often in areas designated for fumigation of coca plantations; that Plan Colombia fuels internal conflict, which undermines both the government and civil society; and that the U.S.-backed aerial defoliation of coca plantations seriously harms subsistence farmers and their families because it destroys food crops and families have been forced to leave their land. The leaders argued that Plan Colombia will fail because social and economic factors are not addressed and once people are forced off their land, new suppliers will emerge to meet the needs of U.S. illegal drug consumers. Instead of Plan Colombia, they called for peaceful resolutions and economic development.[109]

In June 2002, the OFP and the Women's Path for Peace called for an end to war in Colombia and criticized the end of the peace talks earlier in that year. They noted that women will continue to suffer for a number of reasons:

---

108. Isacson 2001b.
109. Lindesmith Center-Drug Policy Foundation 2001.

> They face retaliations for the way in which and with whom women fall in love, killing them for being the "enemy's" girlfriend, friend, mother, sister, the lover of police, army, paramilitary or guerilla personnel; being publicly harassed and ridiculed for the way they dress; being unable to walk the streets or neighbourhoods freely; being selectively assassinated and labeled as auxiliaries to one of the various armed actors; women of all ages being raped by the various armed actors; being internally and externally displaced; being forced out of their homes by the armed actors, who then use them for their own purposes; not being allowed to retrieve and bury their dead; the closing of schools due to heavy violence thereby increasing women's domestic responsibilities. These are the daily realities that millions of women in Colombia face by virtue of living in a country of war.[110]

The women in Colombia call for civil responses and for increased participation by women as a more meaningful way to address the social problems and conflicts in Colombia, rather than military ones. They argue that the war economy and the militarization of Colombia increases women's impoverishment and unemployment and reduces spending on social programs, which "were all gains made by the women's social movement."[111]

Further Justification for Foreign Intervention

The peace talks with FARC and former President Pastrana ended in February 2002. In May 2002, hard-line presidential candidate Alvaro Uribe Velez won the election in Colombia. He began his four-year term in August 2002. Velez promises to increase the size of the army and police, and has begun to set up an organization of a million informers to provide the state with information about armed groups. Critics state that Velez is sympathetic to the right-wing para-

110. The Second Women 2002: 1.
111. Ibid.

militaries, and that attacks on and harassment of human rights workers and women's groups will increase. Velez's family is also connected to a very high-profile drug dealing family, the Ochoa family, and he has associations to military members who are linked to human rights abuses.[112] The paramilitaries campaigned strongly to bring Velez into office. He is calling for more U.S. aid and claims that increased militarism is the only way to stop the war in Colombia from spilling into other South American countries.[113] He also claims that the left-leaning groups like FARC are responsible for the majority of the violence in Colombia. Critics worry that he will instigate further violence and that women and children will suffer even more. In addition, critics of Plan Columbia argue that violence and corruption will not disappear if the drug trade is eliminated; they claim that these abuses of power have much deeper roots and causes.[114]

The war on drugs masks and distracts from U.S. and Colombian governments, corporations, professionals, and respectable institutions (such as northern banks) that have been involved in violence, organized crime, terrorism, and drug trafficking. As Micheal Woodiwess points out, the U.S. government is "hardly likely to support any analysis that makes [it] part of the problem."[115] Rather, the U.S. government repeatedly reiterates, that organized crime, terrorism, and drug trafficking are the primary threats to the nation state and that global strategies are necessary to combat these evils.

Furthermore, poor women and men in Third World countries that cultivate plants (from which drugs are derived), such as poppies and coca, are most vulnerable to plant-eradication programs and violence associated with the drug war. The women and men who cultivate poppies and coca, and those who work as drug couriers, have little resemblance to the stereotype of the free-wheeling drug trafficker depicted by the state and the mainstream media. To date, the illegal market in cocaine benefits the consumer countries of the European Union, North America, and Japan in terms of profit more than the cultivating regions.

112. Knox 2002b: F3.
113. Knox 2002a: A9
114. Kawell 2002: 12.
115. Woodiwess 2001: 388.

As little as 5–8 percent of the illegal cocaine profit remains in countries such as Peru, Bolivia, and Columbia, and only 0.4 percent of profits remain with peasant producers.[116]

Researchers, the mainstream media, and governments identify organized crime and "drug cartels" as a threat to Western nations. The U.S. government claims that Colombian and Mexican drug cartels "control" the cocaine market, but there is little evidence to support these accusations. In fact, the majority of drug dealers are male, unorganized, and have no ties to organized crime and cartel-like organizations; instead, they are loosely formed organizations that are quite fluid.[117] In addition, the use of the term cartel is very misleading. Cartel refers to an illegal business that is intent on regulating the trade, dividing the market, restricting quantity, and increasing prices. These characteristics are not exhibited by organizations labeled cartels (e.g., Medellin). However, as many critics note, the myth continues and further marginalizes groups by associating them with criminal groups.[118]

Critics note that the U.S. government itself cannot claim innocence in relation to organized crime, terrorism, and drug trafficking. In fact, the U.S. government has a very long history of supporting and protecting all three criminal activities at home and abroad. For example, state-sanctioned terrorism and genocide were waged against Aboriginal peoples throughout what is now the United States. Terrorism and organized crime against black people were common during and after slavery when the Ku Klux Klan emerged and lynching became a standard practice in the South.[119] Violence against women in all its manifestations is systemic. And the war on drugs in the U.S. has been referred to as a war of terrorism against the population at home, evidenced by the persecution of drug users, racial profiling, the rise of the prison-industrial complex, police brutality and corruption, asset forfeiture, Draconian laws, unlawful convictions, and the persecution of pregnant women. Others have noted that U.S. imperialism and corporate downsizing are state-sanctioned terrorism against the masses of their own people.

---

116. Cubas 1996.
117. Dorn and South 1993; Woodiwess 2001.
118. Naylor 1995: 40.
119. Woodiwess 2001.

Contrary to the claims of the U.S. government and the media, the menace does not reside outside the U.S. Terrorism, drug trafficking, and organized crime are not the domain of "foreign hordes," rather they rest solidly with U.S. state-sanctioned practices at home and abroad. As Woodiwess notes:

> High-level politicians and respectable members of business and professional communities have gained more from organized criminal activity than any other group and, for the most part, stayed out of prison... the United States has allowed and even sometimes encouraged certain kinds of organized criminal activity, if this activity advanced American foreign policy objectives.[120]

Critics note that the most serious threat to the "nation" is not foreign drug cartels, but rather state, corporate, and professional crime.

Victim Nation

Historically the United States has viewed itself as a "victim nation,"[121] one that is under siege from "foreigners." After World War II, the fear of communism fueled the build-up of the military-industrial complex. With the end of the Cold War, a new enemy was needed. As early as 1969, President Nixon had declared war on drugs. But the battle took on new proportions when then Vice President George Bush Sr. announced that drugs were a national security threat and the government authorized an expanded military. In 1989, by then President Bush Sr. announced on national televison that he was going to speak about an issue that "was so important, so threatening that it warranted talking directly with you, the American people. All of us agree that the greatest domestic threat facing our nation today is drugs." He called for even more laws, enforcement, prisons, and funding to fight the war on drugs.

However, mounting opposition to the war on drugs at home and abroad emerged during the 1990s, and a new updated war now jus-

120. Ibid.: 12, 13.
121. Campbell 2000: 64.

tifies military spending and intervention. Today, the war on drugs, terrorists, narcoterrorists, and organized crime justifies U.S. militarization and imperialism. The Americanization of criminal law has been accelerated since the terrorists acts of September 11. The USA Patriot and Homeland Security Acts (and proposed Patriot II and Victory Act) expand government and police powers and authorize extended surveillance and intervention at home and throughout the world. The war on terrorism, which is linked to the war on drugs, is driven by U.S. vengeance and a political agenda (that British Labour leader Tony Blair continues to support),[122] which may not limit or eradicate terrorism, but it will certainly do much to destroy what little security and democracy Western nations provide and directly contribute to the senseless deaths of men, women, and children who have nothing to do with terrorist acts. "Whether engaged in the battle against terrorism" or in the "war on drugs," the U.S. occupies military bases throughout the world. U.S. troop and personnel remain in Germany, Japan, Bosnia, the Philippines, Afghanistan, Kuwait, Iraq, Qatar, Saudi Arabia, Colombia, El Salvador, Bermuda, Iceland, South Korea, and Italy, to name a few.[123]

U.S. negotiations, and "inter-government negotiations are typically between 'bands of men,' [but] it is women and children who suffer the consequences."[124] If the U.S. wished to act on its rhetoric of linking drug trafficking to terrorist groups, it could quickly eliminate their funding in one grand sweep by ending drug prohibition. The illegal drug trade

---

122. Prime Minister Tony Blair remained firm in his support of the call by President Bush Jr. for military intervention in Iraq. On February 15, 2003, the largest anti-war demonstration ever seen in London, (which was one of many anti-war protests throughout the world where millions marched), highlighted the public's dismay with Tony Blair's war stance and his continued support of U.S. policy. On February 26, 2003, deifying the party line, 122 Labour Party MPs voted against his proposed policy on Iraq. However, Blair remained defiant and refused to be deterred from his "moral" stance. In addition, as critics challenged evidence, new "proof" and "goals" were seemingly invented each week by President Bush Jr. and his representatives in support of war against Iraq.

123. Withington 2003: 5.

124. West 2000: 24.

would collapse. Since this initiative is not addressed, we can assume that the war on drugs and the war on terrorism is waged for other reasons.

Until the U.S. government looks at its own complicity in the violence, terrorism, killing, displacement of women and their families, environmental destruction, drug trafficking, and domestic demand for illegal drugs, it is difficult to imagine a shift in international and national policy. Noam Chomsky asks, What right does the U.S. have to carry out military intervention and crop eradication programs throughout the world in order to eradicate crops like coca? What right does the U.S. have to force countries to open the doors to "free" trade, which paves the way for the sale of U.S. produced legal drugs such as tobacco, which is more lethal than cocaine? He asks whether other nations, such as Colombia and China which are targets of U.S. free trade policies, also have the "right" to wage war against the U.S. through their own economic sanctions, military, chemical and biological warfare? Chomsky concludes "if not, why not?"[125]

Global capitalism, free trade, and the Americanization of drug law have not brought prosperity to women in the Third World; rather, they have experienced exploitation, poverty, violence, and destabilization. Similarly, low-income women in Britain, Canada, and the U.S. have not prospered; rather economic and drug policies have disadvantaged them. People throughout the world have implicated both state and corporate practices and drug laws as violence against them—there is no doubt that the war on drugs, Plan Colombia, and other militarized initiatives are wars against people.

Throughout the world, investigations into U.S. complicity and support of violence and antidemocratic regimes, drug trafficking, and the failure of the war on drugs, has culminated in growing dissent. Many women around the world oppose the war on drugs and consider military initiatives and criminal justice in direct opposition to peace and social justice goals.

---

125. Chomsky 2000: 79.

Chapter 7

The Road to Social Justice

The regulation of altered states of consciousness is not new, although the discourse and techniques used to do so shift historically. In the early 1900s, Emma Goldman, the famous anarchist, warned against state and legal attempts to safeguard people against "immorality." She also spoke about the limitless capacity of Puritanism "for evil."[1] Whether in the guise of state, religious, or nonstate regulation, the moral regulation of women who wish to alter their consciousness in ways that are not "state (and church) sanctioned" has fueled punitive practices that are race, class, and gender specific. Drug use is racialized, gendered, and class-based. Throughout Western history, illegal drug use has also been pathologized and criminalized.

Western imperialism and colonization were accompanied by the condemnation of plants used in spiritual and healing practices by Indigenous peoples in North and South America. Today, U.S. imperialism in Colombia also contributes to the genocide of Indigenous peoples and violence against women. It also ignores the fact that the coca leaf is chewed by millions in South America without any ill effect and has a significant role in healing and in spiritual beliefs there. In addition, prohibitionists have historically argued for harsh criminal sanctions by constructing men of color as corrupt traffickers who are intent on leading white moral women into addiction and sexual slavery. Men and women of color have been viewed by prohibitionists as a threat to Christian Anglo-Saxon life. Fears about the mixing of the races and race suicide have shaped drug policy, and drugs have been seen as the agent that promotes white women's downfall.

1. Goldman 1910: 180.

Women's transgressions against conventional gender norms are perceived as evidence of their immorality. Poor women, women of color, and unruly women who use illegal drugs are viewed as more immoral, pathological, and criminal than their conventional counterparts, and more deviant than men. The regulation of women's sexuality, reproduction, and parenting intersects with the war on drugs. It is here that drug war ideologies and the subordination of women's bodies culminate in a volatile mix.

In Britain, Canada, and the U.S. a new punitiveness toward women drug users, especially single parents, has emerged since the 1970s. These women are depicted as producing social problems and draining already strapped social, medical, and criminal justice services. Their perceived unwillingness to work, to follow doctors' orders, to refrain from using drugs not approved by the medical profession and justice agents, and their unfitness to parent justifies cutbacks in social and economic services and increased criminal justice spending. This book was written with the intention of drawing our attention to the plight of such women and their families and to illuminate how the war on drugs affects them in gender-specific ways. Women who are suspected of using drugs are vulnerable to interlocking and competing spheres of formal and informal control. However, not all women are impacted similarly, poor women and women of color are most vulnerable to state and nonstate intervention. In addition, although state and nonstate intervention is patriarchal, women are also instrumental in regulating and punishing other women constructed as "less moral" than themselves. Women in Third World nations such as Colombia and women of color and Aboriginal women continue to be negatively affected by colonization in all its diverse effects. The punishment of women who use illegal drugs, especially pregnant women, challenges the rights and reproductive autonomy of all women.

Legalization

Over the last thirty years, medical, social service, and criminal justice have been restructured to advance the war on drugs in Britain,

Canada, and the U.S. Billions of dollars are spent each year to regulate and punish people who use illegal drugs. In the U.S., domestic policy is linked to international drug policy that increases economic and civil instability and violence against women in nations such as Colombia. A practical response to the war on drugs is legalization. Legalization of drugs would end the militarization of drug policy and criminalization of drug users in the in the U.S., and in countries in which the U.S. war on drugs has intervened. Legalization around the world would also end the illegal market and drug trade. Thus, drug trafficking and turf violence would end. Groups could no longer be charged with profiting from the drug trade to further their political goals (including the CIA and suspected narcoterrorists). Further, legalization would limit overdoses due to the unknown quality and quantity of drugs bought on the illegal market, and lower HIV/AIDS and other infections such as hepatitis C because needles would be legal and accessible. In addition, legalization would strip illegal drug use of its pathologized, racialized, sexualized, and criminalized status. It would also remove drug use from punishment industries and would bring an end to intrusive techniques such as drug testing. Finally, women's bodies and reproductive autonomy would no longer be used as the newest terrain for advancing the war on drugs.

The war against drugs diverts funding from social, medical, and economic services for women and their families. It also diminishes the gains that women have made in relation to their legal and social rights and diminishes their autonomy over their own bodies. Women in Colombia, Britain, Canada, and the U.S. have all experienced threats to their social and economic rights which have been gained by the contemporary women's movements in each nation.

The movement opposing the war on drugs has been gaining momentum for a number of years. Today, coalitions between groups have been forged and broader links have been made to political and economic shifts in Britain, Canada, Colombia, and the US. Feminist, civil rights, anti-drug war and abolitionist activists, and drug user unions have emerged to stem the tide and to offer alternatives. Many of these groups emphasize social justice rather than criminal justice. Anti-drug war activists and advocates of abolition and transformative justice argue that militarization and criminal justice are not social justice goals. Anti-drug war efforts are linked to social and political movements that seek to transforms the world we live in. The movement to end the war on drugs domestically and internationally must be accompanied by goals for peace and social justice that include the elimination of militarization, criminalization, and race, class, and gender inequalities. Power hierarchies in all of their manifestations need to be replaced with alternatives to imperialism, colonization, capitalism, exploitation, and oppression.[2]

Writers have spoken out about the Americanization of drug policy. In addition, writers and activists warn about the Americanization of nations. These critics note that increased pressure by the U.S. and domestic politicians to further integrate a host of military, legal and social components—defense, border patrol, drug policy and enforcement, criminal justice, free trade, deregulation, privatization, and ownership of domestic companies— has increased U.S. power and global expansion, limited civil liberties and democracy, and threatened the sovereignty of less powerful nations.

Today, as the war on drugs advances, women have plenty to fear, but not necessarily from alleged terrorists or drug users and dealers, but from moral regulation in all its guises and from state, military, criminal justice, and corporate attempts to erode democracy to further their interests in Western and Third World nations. It is time to take a deeper look at the war on drugs and the harm it causes women. It is also time to acknowledge that altered states of consciousness has been sought after for millennia, and that drugs, in all of their diversity, are part of the social fabric of life.

---

2. Quinney 1997: 115.

References

Addiction Research Foundation. (1997). Solvent's effect on fetus unproven. *The Journal, 26*(1), 2.

Adlaf, E., Begin, P., Deguire, A., Garlick, R., Racine, S., Sawka, E., & Single, E. (Eds.) Canadian Addiction Survey (CAS): A national survey of Canadians' use of alcohol and other drugs: Highlights. Ottawa: Canadian Centre on Substance Abuse.

Albersheim, S. (1994, June). Practical management of infants of substance-using mothers, and their long-term followup. In *Effects of alcohol and other drugs in pregnancy: Issues for families and communities.* Speaker Materials for a Conference to Address FAS and NAS (pp. 151–167). Vancouver, BC: Sunny Hill Health Centre for Children & University of British Columbia, Division of Continuing Education in the Health Sciences.

Albertyn, C. (2000). Using rights and the law to reduce Women's vulnerability to HIV/AIDS: A discussion paper. Montreal: Canadian HIV/AIDS Legal Network.

Alegria, M., Vera, M., Negron, G., Buros, M., Albizu, C., & Canino, G. (1998). Methodological and conceptual issues in understanding female Hispanic drug users. In C. Wetherington and A. Roman (Eds.), *Drug addiction research and the health of women* (pp. 529–551). Rockville, MD: National Institute on Drug Abuse.

Alexander, B. (1990). *Peaceful measures: Canada's way out of the "war on drugs."* Toronto: University of Toronto Press.

Alexander, B. (1998). Reframing Canada's "drug problem." *Policy Options, 19*(8), 28–30.

Alexander, B. (2001). The roots of addiction in free market society. *Canadian Centre for Policy Alternatives*, 1–31. Retrieved September 15, 2002, from http://www.policyalternatives.ca

Allard, P. (2002). *Life sentences: Denying welfare benefits to women convicted of drug offenses*. Washington, DC: The Sentencing Project.

Amnesty International. (1999). *"Not part of my sentence": Violations of the human rights of women in custody*. Amnesty International: Rights for all: Amnesty International's Campaign in the United States of America.

Amnesty International. (2001). *Annual Report 2001: Colombia*. London: Amnesty International.

Anderson, J. (2001). What to do about "much ado" about drug courts? *International Journal of Drug Policy*, *12*, 460–475.

Anderson, K. (2000). *A recognition of being: Reconstructing native womanhood*. Toronto: Second Story Press.

Annas, G. (1997, August 7). Reefer madness: The federal response to California's medical-marijuana law. *The New England Journal of Medicine*, *337*(6). Retrieved October 5, 2001, from http://www.reneeboje.com/nejm.html

Armstrong, E. (1998). Diagnosing moral disorder: The discovery and evolution of fetal alcohol syndrome. *Social Science and Medicine*, *47*(12), 2025–2042.

Armstrong, E., & Abel, E. (2000). Fetal alcohol syndrome: The origins of a moral panic. *Alcohol and Alcoholism*, *35*(3), 276–282.

Armstrong, J. (2003, May 3). Shooting heroin, in a Vancouver storefront. *The Globe and Mail*, p. A8.

Aronowitz, S. (1984). When the new left was new. In S. Sayres, A. Stephanson, S. Aronowitz, F. Jameson (Eds.), *The 60s without apology* (pp. 11–43). Minneapolis: University of Minnesota Press.

Aspinwall, E. (2001). Prisons hit the stock market. *Kinesis*, p. 8.

Associated Press (2002). *Lawyers for Noelle Bush go back to court*. Retrieved October 15, 2002, from wysiwyg://25/http //www.floridatoday.com/topstories/100802 noelle.htm

Auerhahn, K., & Leonard, E. (2000). Docile bodies? Chemical restraints and the female inmate. *The Journal of Criminal Law and Criminology, 90*(2), 599–634.

Aujean, S., Murphy, R., King, L., & Jeffery, D. (Eds.). (2001). *Annual report on the UK drug situation.* London: DrugScope.

Baker, N. (2002, August 23). Arizona lacks law to protect crack babies, experts say after infant's death. *The Arizona Republic.* Retrieved November 18, 2002, from http://www.arizonarepublic.com/special46/articles/0823crackfolo.html

Barnes, K. (2001). The Toronto drug treatment court (DTC)—2000. Program summary (In-house publication prepared by K. Barnes, office of the drug treatment court prosecutor, Toronto, Ontario)

Basen, G., Eichler, M., & Lippman, A. (Eds.). (1993). *Misconceptions: The social construction of choice and the new reproductive and genetic technologies* (Vols. 1 & 2). Maple Pond, ON: Voyageur Publishing.

Bashevkin, S. (2002). *Welfare hot buttons: Women, work, and social policy reform.* Toronto: University of Toronto Press.

Baumohl, J., & Schram, S. (2000). Books: review/commentary. *Contemporary Drug Problems, 27*(1), 213–215.

B.C. (CEDAW). (2003, January 23). British Columbia moves backwards on women's equality. Submission of the B.C. Convention on the Elimination of all Forms of Discrimination Against Women (CEDAW) Group to the United Nations on the Elimination of Discrimination Against Women on the occasion of the Committees's review of Canada's 5th Report. Retrieved March 13, 2003, from http://www.povnet.org/resources/CEDAW.pdf

Bean, P. (2002). Drug courts, the judge, and the rehabilitative ideal. In J. Nolan (Ed.), *Drug courts in theory and in practice* (pp. 235–254). New York: Aldine de Gruyter.

Beatty, P., Holman, B., & Schiraldi, V. (2000). *Poor prescription: The costs of imprisoning drug offenders in the United States.* Washington, DC: The Justice Policy Institute.

Beaumont, P. (2002, November 28–December 4). Afghan president stripped of his elite bodyguards. *Guardian Weekly*, p. 2.

Becker, H. (1963). *Outsiders: Studies in the sociology of deviance.* New York: Free Press.

Beckerman, A., & Fontana, L. (2001). Issues of race and gender in court-ordered substance abuse treatment. *Journal of Offender Rehabilitation, 33*(4), 45–61.

Belenko, S. (1998). Research on drug courts: A critical review. *National Drug Court Institute Review, 1*(1), 1–42.

Belenko, S. (2001). *Research on drug courts: A critical review 2001 update.* Colombia University, NY: The National Center on Addiction and Substance Abuse (CASA).

Benson v. Terhune, 157 F. Supp.2d 1093 (No. C00–1360 PJH) (N.D. Cal. July 26, 2001).

Bentley, P. (2001). Canada's first drug treatment court. (In-house publication prepared by the Honourable Mr. Justice Paul Bentley, Toronto, Ontario)

Bepko, C. (1991). *Feminism and addiction.* New York: Haworth.

Berridge, V., & Edwards, G. (1981). *Opium and the people: Opiate use in nineteenth century England.* London: Allan Lane.

Best, D., Strang, J., Beswick, T., & Gossop, M. (2001). Assessment of a concentrated, high-profile police operation. *British Journal of Criminology, 41*, 738–745.

Best, J. (1995). Typification and social problems construction. In J. Best (Ed.), *Images of issues: Typifying contemporary social problems* (2nd ed., pp. 3–10). New York: Aldine de Gruyter.

Best, J. (1999). *Random violence: How we talk about new crimes and new victims.* Berkeley: University of California Press.

Bhattacharjee, A. (2002). Private fists and public force: Race, gender, and surveillance. In J. Silliman & A. Bhattacharjee (Eds.),

Policing the national body: Race, gender, and criminalization (pp. 1–54). Cambridge: South End Press.

Bianchi, H. (1994). *Justice as sanctuary*. Bloomington, IN: Indiana University Press.

Biernacki, P. (1986). *Pathways from heroin addiction: Recovery without treatment*. Philadelphia: Temple University Press.

Bigwood, J. (2001). DynCorp in Colombia: Outsourcing the drug war. *Special to Corpwatch*. Retrieved June 5, 2001, from http://www.corpwatch.org/issues/military/featured/2001/dyncorp.html

Birch, H. (1994) (Ed.). *Moving targets: Women, murder and representation*. Berkeley: University of California Press.

Blackwell, J. (1983). Drifting, controlling and overcoming: Opiate users who avoid becoming chronically dependent. *Journal of Drug Issues, 13*(2), 219–235.

Blanchfield, M. (1998, July 21). I was reduced to a lab rat. *Ottawa Citizen*, p. A1.

Bland, K. (2002, September 7). Prenatal exposure to crack killed baby. *The Arizona Republic*. Retrieved November 18, 2002, from http://www.arizonarepublic.com/special46/articles/0907crackbaby07.html

Bloom, B., Chesney-Lind, M., & Owen, B. (1994). Women in California prisons: Hidden victims of the war on drugs. In The Drug Policy Foundation (Ed.), *The crucial next stage: Health care & human rights* (Section G: 1–10). Washington, DC: Author.

Bond, T. (2001). Barriers between black women & the reproductive rights movement. *Political Environments, 8*, 1, 3, 4.

Borger, J., & Hodgson, M. (2001). U.S. drug war "aids Colombian paramilitaries." *The Guardian*. Retrieved June 6, 2001, from http:www.corpwatch.org/issues/military/background/2001/jborger.html

Bourgois, P. (1995). *In search of respect: Selling crack in El Barrio.* New York: Cambridge University Press.

Bourgois, P., & Dunlap, E. (1993). Exorcising sex-for-crack: An ethnographic perspective from Harlem. In M. Ratner (Ed.), *Crack pipe as pimp: An ethnographic investigation of sex-for-crack exchanges* (pp. 97–132). New York: Lexington Books.

Boyd, N. (1984). The origins of Canadian narcotics legislation: The process of criminalization in historical context. *Dalhousie Law Journal, 8,* 102–136.

Boyd, N. (1990). *Criminological perspectives on social problems: Study guide.* Burnaby, BC: Centre for Distance Education, Simon Fraser University.

Boyd, N. (1991). *High society: Legal and illegal drugs in Canada.* Toronto: Key West Books.

Boyd, N. (1998). Rethinking our policy on cannabis. *Policy Options, 19*(8), 31–33.

Boyd, S. (1999). *Mothers and illicit drugs: Transcending the myths.* Toronto: University of Toronto Press.

Boyd, S. (2001). Feminist research on mothers and illegal drugs. *Resources for Feminist Research: New Feminist Research, 28* (3,4), 113–130.

Boyd S. (2002). Media constructions of illegal drugs, users, and sellers: A closer look at *Traffic. International Journal of Drug Policy, 13,* 397–407.

Boyd, S., & Faith, K. (1999). Women, illegal drugs and prison: Views from Canada. *The International Journal of Drug Policy, 10,* 195–207.

Brecher, E., & The Editors of Consumer Reports. (1972). *Licit & illicit drugs.* Boston: Little, Brown.

Breines, W. (1982). *Community and organization in the New Left, 1962–1968: The great refusal.* New York: Praeger.

British Columbia Child Protection Division (2002). *Summary of trends in numbers of Aboriginal and non-Aboriginal children in care (CIC) June 2001–September 2002*. Victoria, BC: Child Protection Division, Ministry of Children and Family Development.

British Columbia Ministry of Children and Family Development (2003). *Protocol framework and working guidelines between child protection and alcohol and drug services*. Victoria, BC: Ministry of Children and Family Development. Retrieved June 20, 2003, from http://www.mct.gov.bc.ca/publications/privacy_charter/pfwg_toc.htm

British Columbia Provincial Health Officer (1998). *A report on the health of British Columbians: Provincial Health Officer's Annual Report 1997. Feature Report: The health and well-being of British Columbia's children*. Victoria, BC: Ministry of Health and Ministry Responsible for Seniors.

Buchanan, J., & Young, L. (2002). Child protection: Social workers' views. In H. Klee, M. Jackson, & S. Lewis (Eds.), *Drug misuse and motherhood* (pp. 195–210). London: Routledge.

Bufe, C. (2000a). 12-step groups as religious organizations. In S. Peele, C. Bufe, & A. Brodsky *Resisting 12-step coercion: How to fight forced participation in AA, NA, or 12-step treatment* (pp. 82–106). Tucson, AZ: See Sharp Press.

Bufe, C. (2000b) The nature of the problem. In S. Peele, C. Bufe, & A. Brodsky *Resisting 12-step coercion: how to fight forced participation in AA, NA, or 12-step treatment* (pp. 17–43). Tucson, AZ: See Sharp Press.

Bufe, C., & Peele, S. (2000). The efficacy of 12-step groups and 12-step treatment. In S. Peele, C. Bufe, & A. Brodsky *Resisting 12-step coercion: how to fight forced participation in AA, NA, or 12-step treatment* (pp. 44–81). Tucson, AZ: See Sharp Press.

Burdon, W. (2001). Drug courts and contingency management. *Journal of Drug Issues, 31*(1), 73–85.

Bureau of Justice Assistance. (July 2002). *Denial of federal benefits program*. Washington, DC: U.S. Department of Justice. Retrieved July 2002, from www.ojp.usdoj.gov/BJA

Bureau of Justice Statistics. (1992). *Drugs, crime, and the justice system.* Washington, DC: U.S. Department of Justice.

Bureau of Justice Statistics. (2000). *Drugs and crime facts. Drug use.* Retrieved July 2001, from http://www.ojp.usdoj.gov/bjs/dcf/du.htm

Bureau of Justice Statistics. (2002a). *Drugs and crime facts: Drug use in the general population.* Retrieved April 11, 2002, from http://www.ojp.usdoj.gov/bjs/dcf/du.htm

Bureau of Justice Statistics. (2002b). *Probation and Parole Statistics.* Retrieved April 18, 2003, from http://www.ojp.usdoj.gov/bjs/pandp.htm

Burkholder, M., & Johnson, L. (1990). *Colonial Latin America.* New York: Oxford Press.

Burroughs, W. (1977). *Junky.* New York: Penguin.

Callahan, J., & Knight, J. (1992). Prenatal harm as child abuse? In C. Feinman (Ed.), *The criminalization of a woman's body* (pp. 127–155). New York: Harrington Park Press.

Campbell, N. (2000). *Using women: Gender, drug policy, and social justice.* New York: Routledge.

Canada-Colombia Solidarity Campaign. (2001). November 2001 Colombia update. Retrieved November 26, 2001, from http://tao.ca/~ccsc/nov01.htm

Canadian Broadcasting Corporation Radio (CBC). (2001). Stoned Straight. *Ideas.* [Radio program].

Canadian Centre for Justice Statistics (CCJS). (2001). *Canadian crime statistics.* Ottawa: Statistics Canada.

Canadian HIV/AIDS Legal Network (2001a). *HIV/AIDS and Hepatitis C in prisons: The facts. Fact sheet 1: HIV/AIDS in Prison.* Montreal: Author.

Canadian HIV/AIDS Legal Network (2001b). *Prevention and treatment: Methadone. Fact sheet 7: HIV/AIDS in Prison.* Montreal: Author.

Canadian Press (2003, May 3). Cellucci repeats warning over decriminalizing pot. *The Globe and Mail*, p. A4.

Carlen, P. (1983). *Women's imprisonment.* London: Routledge.

Carlen, P. (1998). *Sledgehammer: Women's imprisonment at the Millennium.* London: MacMillan Press.

Carlen, P. (2002). New discourses of justification and reform for women's imprisonment in England. In P. Carlen (Ed.), *Women and punishment: The struggle for justice* (pp. 220–236). Devon, UK: Willan Publishing.

Carniol, B. (2000). *Case critical: Challenging social services in Canada* (4th ed.). Toronto: Between the Lines.

Caulfield, S. (2001). Militarism, feminism, and criminal justice: Challenging institutionalized ideologies. In P. Kraska (Ed.), *Militarizing the American criminal justice system: The changing roles of the armed forces and the police* (pp. 120–140). Boston: Northeastern University Press.

Cayley, D. (1997). *Justice as sanctuary.* Toronto: Canadian Broadcasting Corporation.

Cayley, D. (1998). *The expanding prison.* Toronto: Anansi.

Centre for Disease Control and Prevention (CDC). (2001). *Health consequences of tobacco use among women. Fact sheets.* "Women and Smoking, A Report of the Surgeon General-2001." Retrieved July 10, 2002, from http://www.cdc.gov/tobacco/sgr/sgr_forwomen/factsheet-consequences.htm

Centre for Reproductive Law & Policy (1996, February). *Punishing women for their behavior during pregnancy. Fact sheet.* New York: Author.

Chads, K., & Simes, J. (2002). *April 2002 Monthly Prison Population Brief.* London: Home Office.

Chasnoff, I. (1988). Newborn infants with drug withdrawal symptoms. *Pediatrics in Review,* 9(9), 273–277.

Chasnoff, I., Griffith, D., Freier, C., & Murray, J. (1992). Cocaine/Polydrug use in pregnancy: Two-year follow-up. *Pediatrics,* 89(2), 337–339.

Chasnoff, I., Landress, H., & Barrett, M. (1990). The prevalence of illicit-drug use during pregnancy and discrepancies in mandatory reporting in Pinellas County, Florida. *The New England Journal of Medicine, 322*(17), 1202–1206.

Chen, X. (2003). Constituting "dangerous parents" through the spectre of child death: A critique of child protection restructuring in Ontario. In D. Brock (Ed.), *Making normal: Social regulation in Canada* (pp. 209–234). ON: Nelson Thomson.

Chernick, M. (1998). The paramilitarization of the war in Colombia. *NACLA Report on the Americas, 36*(5), 28–33.

Chesney-Lind, M. (1999). Media misogyny: Demonizing "violent" girls and women. In J. Ferrell and N. Websdale (Eds.), *Making trouble: Cultural constructions of crime, deviance, and control* (pp. 115–140). New York: Aldine de Gruyter.

Chomsky, N. (1994). *World orders old and new*. New York: Columbia University Press.

Chomsky, N. (2000). *Rogue states: The rule of force in world affairs.* Cambridge, MA: South End Press.

Chriss, J. (2002). The drug court movement: An analysis of tacit assumption. In J. Nolan (Ed.), *Drug courts in theory and in practice* (pp. 189–213). New York: Aldine de Gruyter.

Christie, N. (1993). *Crime control as industry*. London: Routledge.

Chunn, D. (1995). Feminism, law, and public policy: "Politicizing the personal." In N. Mandell and A. Duffy (Eds.), *Canadian families: Diversity, conflict and change* (pp. 177–210). Toronto: Harcourt Brace.

Chunn, D., & Gavigan, S. (1991). Women and crime in Canada. In M. Jackson & C. Griffiths (Eds.), *Canadian criminology* (chap. 11). Toronto: Harcourt Brace Jovanovich.

Clover, C. (1999). "Her body, himself: Gender in the slasher film." In S. Thorman (Ed.), *A feminist film theory: A reader* (pp. 234–250). New York: New York University Press.

Cohen, P. (1989). *Cocaine use in Amsterdam in non deviant subcultures.* Amsterdam: University of Amsterdam.

Cohen, P., & Sas, A. (1993). *Ten years of cocaine : A follow-up of 64 cocaine users in Amsterdam.* Amsterdam: University of Amsterdam.

Cohen, S. (1985). *Visions of social control.* Cambridge: Polity.

Collins, C. (2002).The children of female African American prisoners. In C. Reasons, D. Conley, & J. Debro (Eds.), *Race, class, gender, and justice in the United States* (pp. 313–319). Boston: Allyn and Bacon.

Collins, P. (1991). *Black feminist thought: Knowledge, consciousness, and the politics of empowerment.* New York: Routledge.

Colombia Support Network (2001). To Colombia Support Network members, friends, allies and supporters. Retrived November 1, 2001, from http://www.zmag.ortg/crisescurevts/colobia/csn-message.htm

Colten, M. (1980). A comparison of heroin-addicted and nonaddicted mothers: Their attitudes, beliefs, and parenting experiences. In *Heroin-addicted parents and their children: Two reports.* (National Institute on Drug Abuse Services Research Report, pp. 1–18). Washington, DC: U.S. Department of Health and Human Services; Public Health Service; Alcohol, Drug Abuse, and Mental Health Administration.

Colten, M. (1982). Attitudes, experiences, and self-perceptions of heroin-addicted mothers. *Journal of Social Issues, 38*(2), 77–92.

Commission on Systemic Racisim in the Ontario Criminal Justice System (1995). *Report of the Commission on Systemic Racisim in the Ontario criminal justice system: A community summary.* Toronto: Queen's Printer for Ontario.

Controlled Drugs and Substances Act, S.C. 1996, c.19.

Cooperstock, R., & Hill, J. (1982). *The effects of tranquillization: Benzodiazepine use in Canada.* Ottawa: Health and Welfare Canada.

Corkery, J. (2001). *Drug seizure and offender statistics: United Kingdom, 1999.* London: Home Office Research.

Correctional Association of New York/Women in Prison Project. (CANY/WPP). (2000). *Women in prison. Fact Sheet.* New York: Author.

Correctional Association of New York/Women and Prison Project. (CANY//WPP). (2002a). *The Effects of imprisonment on families. Fact sheet.* New York: Author.

Correctional Association of New York/Women and Prison Project. (CANY/WPP). (2002b). *Women in prison. Fact sheet.* New York: Author.

Correctional Service Canada. (1994). *HIV/AIDS in prison: Final report of the Expert Committee on AIDS and Prisons.* Ottawa: Solicitor General.

Correctional Service Canada. (2003, June 10). *Basic facts about federal corrections.* Retrieved June 10, 2003, from http://www.csc-scc.gc.ca/text/faits/facts07-content05_e.shtml

Correctional Service Canada (2002–03). Departmental Performance Report (2002–03). Retrieved from http://www.csc-scc.gc.ca/text/pblct/dpr/2003/section_3_overview_of_changes_e.shtml

Cruikshank, B. (1996). Revolutions within: Self-government and self-esteem. In A. Barry, T. Osborne, & N. Rose (Eds.), *Foucault and political reason: liberalism, neo-liberalism and rationalities of government* (pp. 231–251). Chicago: Chicago University Press.

Csete, J., & Cohen, J. (2003). *Abusing the user: Police misconduct, harm reduction and HIV/AIDS in Vancouver, 15* (2B). New York: Human Rights Watch.

Cubas, H. (1996). *Commercialising coca: Possibilities and proposals.* (Narcotics and Development Discussion Paper No. 11). London: Catholic Institute for International Relations.

Culhane, D. (1998). *The pleasure of the crown: Anthropology, law and First Nations.* Burnaby, BC: Talon Books.

Damuzi, R. (2000). Cannabis concert in Vancouver. *Cannabis Culture, 28,* 30.

Damuzi, R. (2001). U.S. prison empire. *Cannabis Culture, 30,* 52–59.

Danner, M. (2000). Three strikes and it's women who are out: The hidden consequences for women of criminal justice policy reforms. In R. Muraskin (Ed.), *It's a crime: Women and Justice* (pp. 215–24). Upper Saddle River, NJ: Prentice-Hall.

Davies, J., & Shewan, D. (2000). The macro and micro logic of drugs and prisons. In D. Shewan & J. Davies (Eds.), *Drug use and prisons: An international perspective* (pp. 233–251). Amsterdam: Harwood Academic Publishers.

Davis, C., Estes, R., & Schiraldi, V. (1996). "Three strikes": The new apartheid. *Report.* San Francisco: Center on Juvenile & Criminal Justice.

Davis, W. (1996). *One river: Explorations and discoveries in the Amazon rain forest.* New York: Simon & Schuster.

Davis, W. (1998). *The clouded leopard: Travels to landscapes of spirit and desire.* Vancouver: Douglas & McIntyre.

Day, D. (2002). *Health Emergency 2003: The spread of drug-related AIDS and hepatitis C among African Americans and Latinos.* New York: Harm Reduction Coalition.

Decorte, T. (2000). *The taming of cocaine: Cocaine use in European and American cities.* Brussels: VUB University Press.

Deikman, A. (1969). Deautomatization and the Mystic Experience. In C. Tart (Ed.), *Altered states of consciouness* (pp. 25–46). Garden City, NY: Anchor Books.

Denton, B. (2001). Property crime and women drug dealers in Australia. *Journal of Drug Issues, 31*(2), 465–477.

Department of Health. (2001). *Children looked after by local authorities. Year ending 31 March 2001, England.* Retrieved March 14, 2003, from http://www.doh.gov.uk/public/cla2001.htm

DES Action Canada. (2000). *DES: What is it?* Montreal: Author.

Dodge, M., & Pogrebin, M. (2001). Collateral costs of imprisonment for women: Complications of reintegration. *The Prison Journal, 81*(1), 42–54.

Dorn, N., & South, N. (1993). After Mr. Bennett and Mr. Bush: U.S. foreign policy and the prospects for drug control. In F. Pearce and M. Woodiwiss (Eds.), *Global crime connections: Dynamics and control* (72–90). Toronto: University of Toronto Press.

Dowds, L., & Hedderman, C. (1997). Looking for "leniency" and explaining difference. In C. Hedderman & L. Gelsthorpe (Eds.), *Understanding the sentencing of women* (pp. 9–22). London: Home Office.

Dreher, M., Nugent, J., & Hudgins, R. (1994). Prenatal marijuana exposure and neonatal outcomes in Jamaica: An ethnographic study. *Pediatrics, 93*(2), 254–260.

Drucker, E. (1999). Drug prohibition and public health: 25 years of evidence. *The Drug Policy Letter, 40*, 4–18.

Drug Court Survey Report. (1997). *Who is the drug court client?* Retrieved December 16, 2002, from http://www.american.edu/academic.depts/spa/justice/publications/exec3.htm

Drug Policy Alliance. (2002, December 12). *Newsletter.* Retrieved December 12, 2001, from http://www.drugpolicy.org

Drug Policy Task Force. (DPTF). (1996). *Report and recommendations of the Drug Policy Task Force.* New York: New York County Lawyers Association.

DrugScope. (2001). *Drug abuse briefing: A guide to the non-medical use of drugs in Britain* (8th ed.). London: Author.

Drugscope. (2002). President Bush's drug strategy for 2003. *Drugscope News.* Retrieved December 3, 2002, from http://www.drugscope.org.uk/news_item.asp?a=1&intID=713

Drug Strategies. (1998). *Women and Drug Abuse: Court Innovations. Keeping Score 1998.* Retrieved December 16, 2002, from http://www.drugstrategies.org/ks1998/s_court.html

Eaton, M. (1983). Mitigating circumstances: Family rhetoric. *International Journal of the Sociology of Law, 11*, 385–400.

Edwards, A. (1988). *Regulation and repression.* Sydney, Australia: Allen & Unwin.

Ehrenreich, B. (1989). *Fear of falling: The inner life of the middle class.* New York: Pantheon Books.

Ehrenreich, B., & English, D. (1973). *Witches, midwives, and nurses.* New York: Feminist Press.

Ekstrand, L., & Blume, J. (2000). *U.S. Customs Service, Better targeting of airline passengers for personal searches could produce better results.* Washington, DC: General Accounting Office.

Elizabeth Fry. (2000). *Annual Report. Canadian Association of Elizabeth Fry.* Retrieved June 2002, from http://www.elizabethfry.ca/areport/ar2000e/htm

Elkins, M., & Olagundoye, J. (2001). The prison population in 2000: A statistical review. *Findings, 154,* 1–4. London: Home Office, Research, Development and Statistics Derectorate.

Erickson, P., Adlaf, E., Murray, G., & Smart, R. (1987). *The steel drug: Cocaine in perspective.* Toronto: Lexington Books.

Etsten, D. (2000). Controversial proposed legislation heightens stigma. *Journal of Addiction and Mental Health, 3*(6), 8.

Ettorre, E. (1992). *Women and substance use.* New Brunswick, NJ: Rutgers University Press.

Faith, K. (1993). *Unruly women: The politics of confinement and resistance.* Vancouver: Press Gang.

Faith, K. (1994). Resistance: Lessons from Foucault and Feminism. IN H. L. Radtke and H. J. Stam (Eds.), Power/Gender: Social Relations in Theory and Practice (p. 36–65). London: Sage Publications.

Faith, K. (2000). Seeking tranformative justice for women: Views from Canada. *Journal of International Women's Studies, 2*(1), 1–16. Retrieved March 12, 2003, from http://www.bridgew.edu/DEPTS//ARTSCNCE/JIWS/nov00/seeking.htm

Faith, K. (2001). *The long journey of Leslie Van Houten: Life beyond the cult.* Boston: Northeastern University Press.

FAMM/GRAM. (2000). Dorothy Gaines featured in *Marie Claire,* and cited in *Families Against Mandatory Minimums, 1*(10), 6.

Fanon, F. (1967). *Black Skin, White Masks.* New York: Grove Press.

Farabee, D., Prendergast, M., Cartier, J., Wezler, H., Knight, K., & Anglin, D. (1999). Barriers to implementing effective correctional drug treatment programs. *The Prison Journal, 79*(2), 150–162.

Farrant, F. (2001). Waiting for no-one. *Prison Report Magazine, 55*, 7–8.

Fellner, J., & Mauer, M. (1998). *Losing the right to vote: The impact of felony disenfranchisement laws in the United States*. New York.: Human Rights Watch and The Sentencing Project.

Ferguson v. The City of Charleston, South Carolina, No. 121 S. Ct. 1281 (S.C. 1999).

Fields, A., & Walters, J. (1985). Hustling: Supporting a heroin habit. In B. Hanson et al. (Eds.), *Life with heroin: Voices from the inner city* (pp. 49–73). Toronto: Lexington Books.

Fischer, B., Single, E., Room, R., Poulin, C., Sawka, E., Thompson, H., & Topp, J. (1998). Cannabis use in Canada: Policy options for control. *Policy Options, 19*(8), 34–38.

Fitzgerald, M. (2000). Women & children: Casualities of war. *The Drug Policy Letter, 46*, 10–12.

Foucault, M. (1977). *Language, counter-memory, practice* (Ed. Donald Bouchard). Ithaca: Cornell University Press.

Foucault, M. (1979). *Discipline & punishment: The birth of the prison*. New York: Vintage Books.

Fracassa, M. (1999). Medicating the self: The roles of science and culture in the construction of prozac. *Journal of Popular Culture, 32*(4), 23–28.

Frank, D., Augustyn, M., Knight, W., Pell, T., & Zuckerman, B. (2001). Growth, development, and behavior in early childhood following prenatal cocaine exposure. *Journal of the American Medical Association, 285*(12), 1613–1625.

Frank, D., & Zuckerman, B. (1993). Children exposed to cocaine prenatally: Pieces of the puzzle. *Neurotoxicology and Teratology, 15*, 298–300.

Friedman, J., & Alicea, M. (1995). Women and heroin: The path of resistance and its consequences. *Gender and Society, 9*(4), 432–449.

Furedi, F. (2002). Drug control and the ascendancy of Britain's therapeutic culture. In J. Nolan (Ed.), *Drug courts in theory and in practice* (pp. 215–233). New York: Aldine de Gruyter.

Gagnon, L. (2002). Rising drug costs in Canada. *Federations, 2*(4), 1–2.

Gallagher, J. (1989). Fetus as patient. In S. Cohen & N. Taub (Eds.), *Reproductive laws for the 1990s* (pp. 185–235). Clifton, NJ: Humana Press.

Gamble, L., & George, M. (1997). "Really useful knowledge": The boundaries, customs, and folklore governing recreational drug use in a sample of young people. In P. Erickson, D. Riley, Y. Cheung, & P. O'Hare (Eds.), *Harm Reduction: A new direction for drug policies and programs* (pp. 340–362). Toronto: University of Toronto Press.

Gannon, M. (2001). Crime comparisons between Canada and the United States. Canadian Centre for Justice Statistics, *Juristat, 21*(11), 1–13.

Gavigan, S. (1988). Law, gender and ideology. In A. Bayefshy (Ed.), *Legal theory meets legal practice.* Edmonton: Academic Printing and Publishing.

Gelsthorpe, L., & Loucks, N. (1997). Justice in the making: Key influences on decision-making. In C. Hedderman & L. Gelsthorpe (Eds.), *Understanding the sentencing of women* (pp. 25–44). London: Home Office.

George, S. (1992). *The debt boomerang: How the Third World debt harms us all.* London: Pluto Press with the Transnational Institute.

Gerhard, S. (2001). HIV-positive women birthing outside the system. *Mothering, 108*, 44–57.

Glenn, E. (1994). Social constructions of mothering: A thematic overview. In E. Glenn, G. Chang, & L. Forcey (Eds.), *Mothering: Ideology, experience, and agency* (pp. 1–29). New York: Routledge.

Globe and Mail (2001, July 7). Where Bush begins. Comment. *The Globe and Mail*, p. A12.

Goode, J., & Maskovsky, J. (2001). Introduction. In J. Goode & J. Maskovsky (Eds.), *The new poverty studies: The ethnography of power, politics, and impoverished people in the United States* (pp. 1–34). New York: New York University Press.

Goldberg, D., Abrahamson, D., & Waldman, A. (1999). *Amici Curiae. Ferguson v. The City of Charleston, South Carolina*, No. 99–936, U. S. Supreme Court, 1–30.

Goldman, E. (1910). *Anarchism and other essays.* New York: Mother Earth Publishing.

Goldstein, P., Brownstein, H., Ryan, P., & Bellucci, P. (1997). Crack and homicide in New York City. In C. Reinarman & H. Levine (Eds.), *Crack in America: Demon drugs and social justice* (pp. 113–130). Berkeley: University of California Press.

Gomez, L. (1994). *Processing and managing social problems: The institutionalization of pregnant women's drug use in the California legislature and criminal justice system.* Unpublished doctoral dissertation, Stanford University.

Gomez, L. (1997). *Misconceiving mothers: Legislators, prosecutors, and the politics of prenatal drug exposure.* Philadelphia: Temple University Press.

Goode, J., & Maskovsky, J. (2001). Introduction. In J. Goode & J. Maskovsky (Eds.), *The new poverty studies: The ethnography of power, politics, and impoverished people in the United States* (pp. 1–34). New York: New York University Press.

Graham-Mulhall, S. (1981). *Opium the demon flower.* New York: Arno Press.

Gray, M. (1999). Long day's journey into night. *The Drug Policy Letter*, *39*, 12–14.

Greaves, L., & Barr, V. (2000). *Filtered policy: Women & tobacco in Canada*. Vancouver: B.C. Centre of Excellence for Women's Health.

Greaves, L., Varcoe, C., Poole, N., Morrow, M., Johnson, J., Pederson, A., & Irwin, L. (2002). *A motherhood issue: Discourses on mothering under duress*. Ottawa: Status of Women in Canada.

Green, P. (1996). Drug couriers: The construction of a public enemy. In P. Green (Ed.), *Drug couriers: A new perspective* (pp. 3–20). London: Quartet Books.

Green, P. (1998). *Drugs, trafficking and criminal policy*. Winchester, UK: Waterside Press.

Greider, K. (1995). Quieting the crack-kid alarm. *The Drug Policy Letter, 27*, 16–17, 20–21.

Grinspoon, L., & Bakalar, J. (1976). *Cocaine: A drug and its social evolution*. New York: Basic Books.

Grinspoon, L., & Bakalar, J. (1997). *Marihuana, the forbidden medicine*. New Haven: Yale University Press.

Gruskin, S., Plafker, K., & Smith-Estelle, A. (2001). Understanding and responding to youth substance use: The contribution of a health and human rights framework. *American Journal of Public Health, 91*(12), 1954–1963.

Guardian Weekly. (2003, July 17–23). Colombia's new leader deserves better from the U.S. Editorial. *Guardian Weekly*, p.32.

Guevera, R. (2002). The political economy of a narco-terror state. *Z Magazine, 15*(10), 35–38.

Guizado, A. (1996). Drug trafficking and society in Colombia. In B. Bagley & W. Walker III (Eds.), *Drug trafficking in the Americas* (pp. 97–120). Miami: University of Miami, North-South Press.

Gupta, T. (1995). Families of Native peoples, immigrants, and people of colour. In N. Mandell & A. Duffy (Eds.), *Canadian families* (pp. 141–174). Toronto: Harcourt Brace.

Gusfield, J. (1972). *Symbolic crusade: Status politics and the American temperance movement*. Chicago: University of Illinois Press.

Hadaway, P., Beyerstein, B., & Youdale, J. (1991). Canadian drug policies: Irrational, futile, and unjust. *The Journal of Drug Issues, 21*(1), 183–197.

Hagan, J., & Coleman, J. (2001). Returning captives of the American war on drugs: Issues of community and family reentry. *Crime & Delinquency, 47*(3), 352–367.

Hagedorn, J. (1994). Homeboys, dope fiends, legits, and new jacks. *Criminology, 32*(2), 197–219.

Hanlon, T., Nurco, D., Bateman, R., & O'Grady, K. (1999). The relative effects of three approaches to the parole supervision of narcotic addicts and cocaine abusers. *The Prison Journal, 79*(2), 163–181.

Hannah-Moffat, K. (2001). *Punishment in disguise.* Toronto: University of Toronto Press.

Hannah-Moffat, K., & Shaw, M. (2000). Prisons for women-theory, reform, ideals. In K. Hannah-Moffat and M. Shaw (Eds.), *An ideal prison? Critical essays on women's imprisonment in Canada* (pp. 11–27). Halifax: Fernwood Press.

Hanson, B., Beschner, G., Walters, J., & Bovelle, E. (Eds.). (1985). *Life with heroin: Voices from the inner city.* Toronto: Lexington Books.

Hargreaves, C. (1992). *Snowfields: The war on cocaine in the Andes.* London: Zedbooks.

Harrison, P., & Beck, A. (July 2002). *Prisoners in 2001.* Bureau of Justice Statistics. Washington, DC: U.S. Department of Justice.

Hartnoll, R., Mitcheson, M., Battersby, A., Brown, G., Ellis, M., Fleming, B., & Hedley, N. (1980). Evaluation of heroin maintenance in controlled trial. *Archives of General Psychiatry, 37*, 877–884.

Hawley, T., and Disney, E. (1992). Crack's children: The consequences of maternal cocaine abuse. *Social Policy Report, 11*(4), 1–23.

Healy, D. (1997). *The antidepressant era.* Cambridge, MA: Harvard University Press.

Healy, D. (June 28, 2001). *Psychopharmacology & the government of the self.* Retrieved January 6, 2003, from http://www.nature.com/nm/voting/intro.html

Hedderman, C., & Gelsthorpe, L. (Eds.). (1997). *Understanding the sentencing of women.* London: Home Office.

Henderson, S. (1993). Luvdup and de-elited: Responses to drug use in the second decade. In P. Aggleton, P. Davies, & G. Hart (Eds.), *Aids: Facing the second decade* (pp. 119–130). London: Falmer.

Hendrick, D., & Farmer, L. (2002). Adult correctional services in Canada, 2000/01. *Juristat, 22*(10), 1–24. Ottawa: Canadian Centre for Justice Statistics.

Henriques, Z., & Manatu-Rupert, N. (2001). Living on the outside: African American women before, during, and after imprisonment. *The Prison Journal, 81*(1), 6–19.

Hepburn, M. (1993). Drug Use in Pregnancy. *British Journal of Hospital Medicine, 49*(1), 51–55.

Hepburn, M. (1999, May). Providing services to substance using mothers and their babies. Paper presented at the Justice Institute of British Columbia, New Westminister, BC.

Hepburn, M. (2002). Providing care for pregnant women who use drugs: The Glasgow Women's Reproductive Health Service. In H. Klee, M. Jackson, & S. Lewis (Eds.), *Drug misuse and motherhood* (pp. 250–260). London: Routledge.

Hinchliff, S. (2001). The meaning of ecstasy use and clubbing to women in the late 1990s. *International Journal of Drug Policy, 12*, 455–468.

Hirsch, A. (1999). *"Some days are harder than hard": Welfare reform and women with drug convictions in Pennsylvania.* New York: Center for Law and Social Policy.

Hoffman, M. (2000). The drug court scandal. *North Carolina Law Review, 78*(5), 1437–1534.

Hofmeister, F.J. (1971). Discussion. *American Journal of Obstetrics and Gynaecology, 109*(5), 722–723.

Hogan, D. (1998). Annotation: The psychological development and welfare of children of opiate and cocaine users: Review and research needs. *Journal of Child Psychology and Psychiatry, 39*(5), 609–620.

Hogshire, J. (1999). *Pills-a-go-go: A fiendish investigation into pill marketing, art, history and consumption.* Venice, CA: Feral House.

Home Office. (2000). *Statistics on race and the criminal justice system.* London: Research Development and Statistics Directorate.

hooks, b. (1981). *Ain't I a woman: Black women and feminism.* Boston: South End Press.

hooks, b. (1984). *Feminist theory: From margin to center.* Boston: South End Press.

hooks, b. (1989). *Talking back.* Boston: South End Press.

hooks, b. (1992). *Black looks: Race and representation.* Boston: South End Press.

hooks, b. (1993). *Sisters of the yam: Black women and self-recovery.* Boston: South End Press.

hooks, b. (1995). *Killing rage: Ending racism.* New York: Henry Holt and Company.

Hornblum, A. (1998). *Acres of skin: Human experiments at Holmesburg Prison.* New York: Routledge.

Hudson, B. (1997). Punishment or redress? Current themes in European abolitionist criminology. In B. MacLean & D. Milovanovic (Eds.), *Thinking critically about crime* (pp. 131–138). Vancouver: Collective Press.

Hudson, B. (2002). Gender issues in penal policy and penal theory. In P. Carlen (Ed.), *Women and punishment: The struggle for justice* (pp. 21–46). Devon, UK: Willan Publishing.

Hughes, R., & Brewin, R. (1979). *The tranquilizing of America: Pill popping and the American way of life.* New York: Warner Books.

Huling, T. (1992). *Injustice will be done: Women drug couriers and the Rockefeller Drug Laws.* NY: Correctional Association of New York.

Human Rights Watch (HRW). (1998). *No where to hide: Retaliation against women in Michigan state prisons, 10*(2). New York: Author.

Human Rights Watch (HRW). (2000a). *Punishment and prejudice: Racial disparities in the war on drugs, 12*(2). New York: Author.

Human Rights Watch (HRW). (2000b). *Out of sight: Super-maximum security confinement in the United States, 12*(1). New York: Author.

Human Rights Watch (HRW). (2000c). *The ties that bind: Colombia and military-paramilitary links, 12*(1B). New York: Author.

Human Rights Watch/Women's Rights Project (HRW/WRP). (1996). *All too familiar: Sexual abuse of women in U.S. state prisons.* New York: Author.

Humphries, D. (1999). *Crack mothers: Pregnancy, drugs, and the media.* Columbus: Ohio State University Press.

Humphries, D., Dawson, J., Cronin, V., Keating, P., Wisniewski, C., & Eichfield, J. (1992). Mothers and children, drugs and crack: Reactions to maternal drug dependency. In C. Feinman (Ed.), *The criminalization of a woman's body* (pp. 203–221). New York: Haworth.

Hunt, A. (1999). *Governing morals: A social history of moral regulation.* Cambridge: Cambridge University Press.

Hyatt, S. (2001). From citizen to volunteer. In J. Goode & J. Maskovsky (Eds.), *The new poverty studies: The ethnography of power, politics, and impoverished people in the United States* (pp. 201–235). New York: New York University Press.

Inciardi, J., Lockwood, D., & Pottieger, A. (1993). *Women and crack-cocaine.* Toronto: Maxwell Macmillan.

Isacson, A. (2001a). *Secretary Powell in Colombia: Some tough questions.* Washington, DC: Center for International Policy. Retrieved November 29, 2001, from http://www.ciponline.org/colombia/091003.htm

Isacson, A. (2001b). *The new masters of Barranca.* Washington, DC: Center for International Policy. Retrieved November 29, 2001, from http://www.ciponline.org/colombia/0401barr.htm

Isacson, A., & Vaicius, I. (2001). *Plan Colombia's ground zero.* Washington, DC: Center for International Policy. Retrieved November 29, 2001, from http://www.ciponline.org/colombia/0401putu.htm

Jackson, M. (2002). *Justice behind the wall: Human rights in Canadian prisons.* Vancouver: Douglas & McIntyre.

Jackson, M., & Berry, G. (1994). Motherhood and drug-dependency: The attributes of full-time versus part-time responsibility for child care. *International Journal of the Addictions, 29*(12), 1519–1535.

Jackson, M., & Klee, H. (2002). Practitioner views of pregnant drug users. In H. Klee, M. Jackson, & S. Lewis (Eds.), *Drug misuse and motherhood* (pp. 105–123). London: Routledge.

Jenkins, L. (1995). Pre-trial diversion strategies for drug involved offenders: Focus on social work involvement. *Journal of Offender Rehabilitation, 22*(¾), 129–140.

Johns, J., Noonan, L., Zimmerman, L., & Pedersen, C. (1994). Effects of chronic and acute cocaine treatment on the onset of maternal behavior and aggression in Sprague-Dawley rats. *Behavioral Neuroscience, 108* (1), 107–112.

Johnson v. State, 602 So.2d 1288 (Fla.: 1992).

Jumper-Thurman, P., & Plested, B. (1998). Health needs of American Indian women. In C. Wetherington and A. Roman (Eds.), *Drug addiction research and the health of women* (pp. 553–563). Rockville, MD: National Institute on Drug Abuse.

Jurgens, R. (1996). *HIV/AIDS in Prisons: Final report.* Montreal: Canadian HIV/AIDS Legal Network and Canadian AIDS Society.

Jurgens, R. (1997). Will prisons fail the AIDS test? In P. Erickson, D. Riley, Y. Cheung, & P. O'Hare (Eds.), *Harm reduction: A new direction for drug policies and programs* (pp. 151–173). Toronto: University of Toronto Press.

Jurgens, R. (2000). HIV/AIDS and drug use in prisons: Moral and legal responsibilities of prisons. In D. Shewan & J. Davies (Eds.), *Drug use and prisons: An international perspective* (pp. 1–26). Amsterdam: Harwood Academic Publishers.

Kalamazoo County Statistical Report. (2002). *Kalamazoo County substance abuse diversion program statistical report.* Retrieved December 16, 2002, from http://www.american.edu/academic.depts/spa/justice/publications/kal.htm

Kalunta-Crumpton, A. (1999). *Race and drug trials: The social construction of guilt and innocence.* Aldershot, UK: Ashgate.

Kandall, S. (1996). *Substance and shadow: Women and addiction in the United States.* Cambridge, MA: Harvard University Press.

Kaplan, D., Schiraldi, V., & Ziedenberg, J. (2000). *Texas tough? An analysis of incarceration and crime trends in The Lone Star state.* Washington DC: The Justice Policy Institute.

Kasl, C. (1992). *Many roads, one journey.* New York: Harper Perennial.

Kawell, J. (2002). Drug economies of the Americas. *NACLA Report on the Americas, 36*(2), 8–12.

Kearney, M., Murphy, S., & Rosenbaum, M. (1994). Mothering on crack cocaine: A grounded theory analysis. *Social Science and Medicine, 38*(2), 351–361.

Kelm, M. (2001). *Colonizing bodies: Aboriginal health and healing in British Colombia 1900–1950.* Vancouver: University of British Columbia Press.

Kendall, K. (2002). Time to think again about cognitive behavioural programmes. In P. Carlen (Ed.), *Women and punishment: The struggle for justice* (pp. 182–198). Devon, UK: Willan Publishing.

Kerr, T. (2003, January 25). Injection drug use, HIV/AIDS and safe injection facilities. Paper presented at Drugs & The Law: Examing Canada's Drug Policy conference of the Rational Drug Policy Association, University of Victoria, B.C.

Kilroy, D. (2003). Strip-searching: Stop the state's sexual assault of women in prison. *Journal of Prisoners on Prisons, 12*: 30–43.

Kingfisher, C. (2001). Producing disunity: The constraints and incitements of welfare work. In J. Goode & J. Maskovsky (Eds.), *The new poverty studies: The ethnography of power, politics, and impoverished people in the United States* (pp. 273–292). New York: New York University Press.

Klee, H., Jackon, M., & Lewis, S. (Eds.). (2002). *Drug misuse and motherhood.* London: Routledge.

Knox, P. (2002a, May 29). Facing a huge challenge, Uribe seeks world's help. *The Globe and Mail,* p. A9.

Knox, P. (2002b, May 25). He's "going to give it to the guerrillas." *The Globe and Mail,* p. F3.

Kohn, M. (1992). *Dope girls: The birth of the British underground.* London: Lawrence & Whishart.

Kolder, V., Gallagher, J., Parsons, M. (1987). Court-ordered obstetrical interventions. *The New England Journal Of Medicine. 316*(19), 1192–1196.

Koren, G. (1997). *The children of neverland: The silent human disaster.* Toronto: The Kid In US.

Kramer, H., & Sprenger, J. (1971). *The Malleus Maleficarum.* New York: Dove Publication.

Kunitz, D. (2001). On drugs: Gateways to gnosis, or bags of glue? *Harper's, 303*(1817), 91–96.

Kuo, I., Fischer, B., & Vlahov, D. (2000). Consideration of a North American heroin-assisted clinical trial for the treatment of opiate-dependent individuals. *International Journal of Drug Policy, 11*(5), 357–370.

Lapham, L. (2003). Light in the window. Notebook. *Harper's, 306*(1835), 7–9.

Larkin, R., & Foss, D. (1984). Lexicon of folk-etymology. In S. Sayres, A. Stephanson, S. Aronowitz, & F. Jameson (Eds.), *The 60s without apology* (pp. 360–377). Minneapolis: University of Minnesota Press.

Larsen, D. (1998). From the editor... *Cannabis Culture, 14,* 10.

Lart, R. (1998). Medical power/knowledge: The treatment and control of drugs and drug users. In R. Coomber (Ed.), *The control of drugs and drug users: Reason or reaction?* (pp. 49–68). Amsterdam: Harwood Academic Publishers.

Launders, D. (2000). Vancouver cops seize pot-kids. *Cannabis Culture, 26,* 22–23.

Launslager, D. (1994). From one to five: Multiple births and the family. In G. Basen, M. Eichler, & A. Lippman (Eds.), *Misconceptions: The social construction of choice and the new reproductive and genetic technologies* (Vol. 2, pp. 117–126). Maple Pond, ON: Voyageur Publishing.

Leal, P., Rozental, M., & Podur, J. (2001). *Barrancabermeja women's mobilization continues.* Retrieved November 26, 2001, from http://www.zmag.org/crisescurevts/colombia/mingacm2.htm

Lee, M., & Shlain, L. (1992). *Acid dreams: The complete social history of LSD: The CIA, the sixties, and beyond.* New York: Grove Press.

Leeders, F. (1992). Drug-addicted parents and their children. *International Journal of Drug Policy, 3*(4), 204–210.

Leonard, E. (2002). *Convicted survivors: The imprisonment of battered women who kill.* New York: State University of New York Press.

Levenson, J. (2001). Searching for a quick fix. *Prison Report Magazine, 55,* 12–13.

Levine, H.G. (1992). Temperance cultures: Concern about alcohol problems in Nordic and English-speaking cultures. In M. Lader, G. Edwards & C. Drummond, (Eds.), *The Nature of Alcohol and Drug Related Problems* (16–36). New York: Oxford University Press.

Lewis, S., Klee, H., & Jackson, M. (1995). Illicit drug users' experiences of pregnancy. An exploratory study. *Journal of Reproductive and Infant psychology, 13,* 219–227.

Lexchin, J. (1984). *The real pushers: A critical analysis of the Canadian drug industry.* Vancouver: New Star Books.

Lexchin, J. (2001). Globalization, trade deals and drugs: Heads the industry wins, tails Canada loses. *Canadian Centre for Policy Alternatives, 2*(8), 1–13.

Liazos, A. (1972). The poverty of the sociology of deviance: Nuts, sluts, and preverts. *Social Problems, 20*(1), 103–120.

Lief, N. (1976). Some measures of parenting behavior for addicted and non-addicted mothers. In *Symposium on comprehensive health care for addicted families and their children* (pp. 38–47). Rockville, MD: National Institute on Drug Abuse.

Lindesmith, A. (1965). *The addict and the law.* Bloomington: Indiana University Press.

Lindesmith Center-Drug Policy Foundation. (2001). *Over 100 top Latin American leaders call on President Bush to Halt "Plan Colombia" at Upcoming Summit of the Americas.* Retrieved April 20, 2001, from http://www.drugpolicy.org/lindesmith/news/pr-april6-01_letter.html

Little, M. (2003). The leaner meaner welfare machine: The Harris government's ideological attack on single mothers. In D. Brock

(Ed.), *Making Normal: Social regulation in Canada* (pp. 235–261). Scarborough, ON: Nelson Thomson.

Lloyd, R. (1998). Caught in the crossfire: Women are taking a stand in Colombia's struggle between corruption and justice. *The Drug Policy Letter, 35*, 19–20.

Logli, P. (1990). Drugs in the womb: The newest battlefield in the war on drugs. *Criminal Justice Ethics, 9*(1), 23–39.

Lowman, J., & Fraser, L. (1995). *Violence against persons who prostitute: The experience in British Columbia*. Ottawa: Department of Justice Canada.

Lyon, J. (2001). Family matters. *Prison Report Magazine, 55*, 3.

MacAndrew, C., & Edgerton, R. (1969). *Drunken comportment: A social explanation*. Chicago: Aldine Publishing.

Macdonald, P., Waldorf, D., Reinarman, C., & Murphy, S. (1988). Heavy cocaine use and sexual behavior. *The Journal of Drug Issues, 18*(3), 437–455.

Macdonald, S., Bois, C., Brands, B., Dempsey, D., Erickson, P., & Marsh, D. (2001). Drug testing and mandatory treatment for welfare recipients. *International Journal of Drug Policy, 12*, 249–257.

MacKinnon, M. (Ed.). (1991). *Each small step*. Charlottetown, PEI: gynergy.

Macrory, F. (1997). Drug use, pregnancy and care of the newborn: A guide for professionals. Paper presented at the Eight annual International Harm Reduction Conference, Paris, France.

Macrory, F. (2002). The drug liaison midwife: Developing a model of maternity services for drug-using women from conception to creation. In H. Klee, M. Jackson, & S. Lewis (Eds.), *Drug misuse and motherhood* (pp. 239–249). London: Routledge.

Macrory, F., & Crosby, S. (1995, March). Special care or segregation? The need for improvement in the provision of maternity services for drug-using women. Paper presented at the Sixth

International Conference on the Reduction of Drug Related Harm, Florence, Italy.

Maher, L. (1992). Punishment and Welfare: Crack Cocaine and the Regulation of Mothering. In C. Feinman (Ed.), *The criminalization of a woman's body* (pp. 157–192). New York: Haworth Press.

Maher, L. (1995). *Dope girls: Gender, race and class in the drug economy*. Unpublished doctoral dissertation, Rutgers, The State University of New Jersey.

Maher, L. (2002). Don't leave us this way: Ethnography and injecting drug use in the age of AIDS. *International Journal of Drug Policy*, *13*, 311–325.

Maher, L., & Dixon, D. (1999). Policing and public health: Law enforcement and harm minimization in a street-level drug market. *British Journal of Criminology*, *39*(4), 488–512.

Makkai, T. (1998). Drug courts: Issues and prospects. *Australian Institute of Criminology: Trends & Issues*, *95*, 1–8.

Malloch, M. (2000). *Women, drugs and custody: The experiences of women drug users in prison*. Winchester, UK: Waterside Press.

Maracle, B. (1993). *Crazywater: Native voices on addiction and recovery*. Toronto: Penguin.

Marlatt, A., & Baer, J. (1997). Harm reduction and alcohol abuse: A brief intervention for college-student binge drinking. In P. Erickson, D. Riley, Y. Cheung, & P. O'Hare (Eds.), *Harm Reduction: A new direction for drug policies and programs* (pp. 245–262). Toronto: University of Toronto Press.

Marshall, J. (1991). *Drug wars: Corruption, counterinsurgency and covert operations in the Third World*. Forestville, CA: Cohan & Cohen.

Martel, J. (2000). Women in the "hole": The unquestioned practice of segregation. In K. Hannah-Moffat & M. Shaw (Eds.), *An ideal prison? Critical essays on women's imprisonment in Canada* (pp. 128–135). Halifax: Fernwood Press.

Maruschak, L. (1999). *HIV in prisons 1997*. Rockville, MD: Bureau of Justice Statistics. United States Department of Justice.

Massey, J., Miller, S., and Wilhelmi, A. (1998). Civil forfeiture of property: The victimization of women as innocent owners of third parties. In Susan Miller (Ed.), *Crime control and women: Feminist implications of criminal justice policy* (pp. 15–31). Thousand Oaks, CA: Sage.

Matas, R. (2002, November 21). U.S drug chief wary of injection sites. *The Globe and Mail*, p. A16.

Matthews, L., Dawes, G., Nadeau, B., Wong, L., & Alexander, A. (1995). *The British Columbia Key Informant Study*. Unpublished manuscript, Simon Fraser University, Burnaby, BC.

Mauer, M., Potler, C., & Wolf, R. (1999a). Gender and justice: Women, drugs, and sentencing policy. *The Sentencing Project*. Retrieved June 21, 2000, from: http://www.lindesmith.org/library/sentenceproj2.html

Mauer, M., & The Sentencing Project. (1999b). *Race to incarcerate*. New York: The New Press.

Mawani, R. (2002). In between and out of place: Mixed-race identity, liquor, and the law in British Columbia, 1850–1913. In S. Razack (Ed.), *Race, space, and the law: Unmapping a white settler society* (pp. 47–69). Toronto: Between the Lines.

Mayes, L., Granger, R., Bornstein, M., & Zuckerman, B. (1992). The problem of prenatal cocaine exposure. *Journal of the American Medical Association, 267*(3), 406–408.

McCall, T. (2001). *This is not a rave: In the shadow of a subculture*. Toronto: Insomniac Press.

McCaughey, M., & King, N. (2001). *Reel knockouts: Violent women in the movies*. Austin: University of Texas Press.

McCoy, A. (1991). *The politics of heroin: CIA complicity in the global drug trade*. New York: Lawrence Hill Books.

McDonnell, K. (1986). Finding a common ground. In K. McDonnell (Ed.), *Adverse effects: Women and the pharmaceutical industry* (pp. 1–8). Toronto: Women's Educational Press.

McLaren, J., Menzies, R. , & Chunn, D. (2002). Introduction. In J. McLaren, R. Menzies, & D. Chunn (Eds.), *Regulating lives: Historical essays on the state, society, the individual and the law* (pp. 3–22). Vancouver: University of British Columbia Press.

Medrano, M. (1996). Does a discrete fetal solvent syndrome exist? *Alcoholism Treatment Quarterly, 14*(3), 59–76.

Mendez, J. (1990). *The "drug war" in Columbia: The neglected tragedy of political violence.* New York: Human Rights Watch.

Meza, R. (1998). The FARC, the war and the crisis of the state. *NACLA Report on the Americas 31*(5), 22–27.

Michals, D. (2002). From "consciousness expansion" to "consciousness raising." In P. Braunstein and Michael Doyle (Eds.), *Imagine nation: The American counterculture of the 1960s and '70s* (pp. 41–68). New York: Routledge.

Miethe, T., Lu, H., & Reese, E. (2000). Reintegrative shaming and recidivism risks in drug court: Explanations for some unexpected findings. *Crime and Delinquency, 46*(4), 522–541.

Mills, C. Wright. (1975). *The sociological imagination.* New York: Oxford Press.

Mintzes, B. (2000). *Protecting our health: New debates.* Montreal: DES Action Canada.

Mintzes, B., & Baraldi, R. (2001). *Protecting our health: New debates.* Montreal: DES Action Canada.

Misra, D. (Ed.). (2001). *Women's health data book: A profile of women's health in the United States* (3rd ed.). Washington, DC: Jacobs Institute of Women's Health and the Henry J. Kaiser Family Foundation.

Mitchinson, W. (2002). *Giving birth in Canada 1900–1950.* Toronto: University of Toronto Press.

Monbiot, G. (2001). Bush's dirty war in Colombia. *The Guardian.* Retrieved June 2, 2001, from http://www.corpwatch.org/issues/military/background/2001/gmonbiot.html

Monbiot, G. (2003, March 6–12). Out of the wreckage. *Guardian Weekly*, p. 11.

Mondragon, H. (2001). (J. Nielson & J. Podur, Trans.). Plan Colombia: Throwing gasoline on a fire. *Z Magazine.* Retrieved November 26, 2001, from http://www.zmag.org/crisescurevets/colombia/gas3.htm

Mondragon, H. (2001b). (Notes taken by J. Podur). Towards "humanitarian intervention" in Colombia? Based on a presentation given to a Witness for Peace delegation in July 2001. *Z Magazine.* Retrieved November 26, 2001, from http://www.zmag.org/crisescurevts/colombia/hemon.htm

Monture, P. (1989). A vicious circle: Child welfare and the First Nations. *Canadian Journal of Women & The Law, 3*, 1–17.

Monture-Angus, P. (1999). *Journeying forward: Dreaming First Nations independence.* Halifax: Fernwood.

Monture-Angus, P. (2000). Aboriginal women and correctional practice: Reflections on the Task Force on Federally Sentenced Women. In K. Hannah-Moffat and M. Shaw (Eds.), *An ideal prison? Critical essays on women's imprisonment in Canada* (pp. 52–60). Halifax: Fernwood Press.

Moore, D., & Valverde, M. (2003). Party girls and predators: "Date rape drugs" and chronotopes of gendered risk. In D. Brock (Ed.), *Making normal: Social regulation in Canada* (pp. 306–328). Scarborough, ON: Nelson Thomson.

Morales, E. (1996). The Andean cocaine dilemma. In B. Bagley & W. Walker III (Eds.), *Drug trafficking in the Americas* (pp.161–177). Miami: University of Miami, North-South Press.

Morgan, J., & Zimmer, L. (1997). The social pharmacology of smokeable cocaine: Not all it's cracked up to be. In C. Reinarman & H. Levine (Eds.), *Crack in America: Demon drugs and social justice* (pp. 131–170). Berkeley: University of California Press.

Morgan, O., & Vulliamy, E. (2003, April 10–16). Chasing riches in the ruins of Iraq. *Guardian Weekly*, p. 12.

Morgan, P., & Joe, K. (1997). Uncharted terrain: Contexts of experience among women in the illicit drug economy. *Women & Criminal Justice*, *8*(3), 85–109.

Morgen, S., & Weigt, J. (2001). Poor women, fair work, and welfare-to-work that works. In J. Goode & J. Maskovsky (Eds.), *The new poverty studies: The ethnography of power, politics, and impoverished people in the United States* (pp.152–178). New York: New York University Press.

Morgentaler, Smoling and Scott V. The Queen, 37 C.C.C. (3d) 449 (S.C.C.) (1989).

Morrison, D., & Siney, C. (1996). A survey of the management of neonatal opiate withdrawal in England and Wales. *European Journal of Pediatrics*, *155*(4), 323–326.

Mosher, C. J. (1998). *Discrimination and denial: Systemic racism in Ontario's legal and criminal justice systems, 1892–1961.* Toronto: University of Toronto Press

Mott, J., & Bean, P. (1998). The development of drug control in Britain. In Ross Coomber (Ed.), *The control of drugs and drug users* (pp. 31–48). Amsterdam: Harwood Academic Publishers.

Mulgrew, I. (2002, February 13). Innovative court helps addicts. *The Globe and Mail*, pp. A1, A16.

Mullings, L. (2001). Households headed by women: The politics of class, race, and gender. In J. Goode & J. Maskovsky (Eds.), *The new poverty studies: The ethnography of power, politics, and impoverished people in the United States* (pp. 37–56). New York: New York University Press.

Mumola, C. (1999). Substance abuse and treatment, State and Federal Prisoners, 1997. *Bureau of Justice Statistics Special Report.* Washington, DC: U.S. Department of Justice.

Murphy, E. (1973). *The black candle.* Toronto: Coles. (Originally published 1922)

Murphy, S., & Rosenbaum, M. (1999). *Pregnant women on drugs: Combating stereotypes and stigma.* New Brunswick, NJ: Rutgers University Press.

Musto, D. (1987). *The American disease: Origins of narcotic control* (expanded edition). New York: Oxford University Press.

Musto, D. (Ed.). (2002). *Drugs in America: A documentary history.* New York: Routledge.

Myers, B., Olson, H., & Kaltenbach, K. (1992). Cocaine-exposed infants. *Zero to Three, 13*(1), 1–5.

NACLA (2002). Profile Colombia. Drug Economies of the Americas. *NACLA: Report of the Americas, 36*(2), 13.

Nadelmann, E. (1993). *Cops across borders: The internationalization of U.S. criminal law enforcement.* University Park: Pennsylvania State University Press.

Naiman, A. (Ed.). (1996–1998). *The common good.* Monroe, ME: Odonian Press.

National Center for Policy Analysis (NCPA). (2002). *Idea House. Pharmaceutical Use.* Retrieved May 24, 2002, from http://www.ncpa.org/health/pdh/mar98.html

National Household Survey on Drug Abuse. (2000). *Alcohol use.* Retrieved July 2, 2002, from http://www.samhsa.gov/oas/NHSDA/2KNHSDA/chpter3.htm

National Institute for Health Care Management (NIHCM). (2002). *Prescription drug expenditures in 2001: Another year of escalating costs* (rev. ed.). Washington, DC: The National Institute for Health Care Management, Research and Educational Foundation.

Naylor, R. (1995). From cold war to crime war: The search for a new "national threat." *Transnational Organized Crime, 1*(4), 37–56.

Nelles, J., Hirsbrunner, H., Fuhrer, A., Dobler-Mikola, A., & Harding, T. (2000). Reduction of drug and HIV related harm in prison: Breaking taboos and applying public health principles. In D. Shewan & J. Davies (Eds.), *Drug use and prisons: An international perspective* (pp. 27–43). Amsterdam: Harwood Academic Publishers.

Nelson, J. (2002). "A strange revolution in the manners of the country": Aboriginal-settler intermarriage in nineteenth-century British Columbia. In J. McLaren, R. Menzies, & D. Chunn (Eds.), *Regulating lives: Historical essays on the state, society, the individual and the law* (pp. 23–62). Vancouver: University of British Columbia Press.

Ng, R. (1988). *The politics of community services: Immigrant women, class and state.* Toronto: Garamond.

NHTSA. (2000a). *Traffic safety facts 2000: Alcohol.* Washington, DC: U.S. Department of Transportation National Highway Traffic Safety Administration.

NHTSA. (2000b). *Traffic safety facts 2000: Children.* Washington, DC: U.S. Department of Transportation National Highway Traffic Safety Administration.

NHTSA. (2002). *Fatality analysis reporting system (FARS) web-based encyclopedia.* Washington, DC: U.S. Department of Transportation National Highway Traffic Safety Administration. Retrieved July 5, 2002, from http://www-fars.nhtsa.dot.gov/

NIDA. (2001). *Nationwide trends. INFOFAX.* Bethsesda, MD: National Institute on Drug Abuse, National Institute of Health.

Noble, A. (1997). Is prenatal drug use child abuse? Reporting practices and coerced treatment in California. In P. Erickson, D. Riley, Y. Cheung, & P. O'Hare (Eds.), *Harm reduction: A new direction for drug policies and programs* (pp. 174–191). Toronto: University of Toronto Press.

No Free Lunch (2003). *Pharmaceutical Facts.* Retrieved from http://www.nofreelunch.org/factsfallacies.htm

Nolan, J. (2002). Separated by an uncommon law: Drug courts in Great Britain and America. In J. Nolan (Ed.), *Drug courts in theory and in practice* (pp. 89–112). New York: Aldine de Gruyter.

Noonan, S. (2002). Of death, desire, and knowledge: Law and social control of witches in Renaissance Europe. In G. MacDonald (Ed.), *Social context and social location in the sociology of law* (pp. 91–129). Peterborough, ON: Broadview Press.

Norsigian, J. (2001, May 13). *The media and women's health: Sorting fact from fiction.* Public lecture, Gathering Forces Conference, Mount Saint Vincent University, Halifax, NS.

Nugent, J. (1994). Cross-cultural studies of child development: Implications for clinicians. *Zero to Three, 15*(2), 1–8.

Oakley, A. (1984). *The captured womb.* Oxford: Basil Blackwell Publisher.

Oakley, A. (1992). *Social support and motherhood.* Oxford: Blackwell.

Office of National Drug Control Strategy (ONDCS). (2003). *National Drug Control Strategy.* Retrieved October 8, 2003, from http://www.whitehousepolicy.gov/publications/policy/ndcs03/appa.html

O'Hanlon, M. (2003, October2). Gun deaths hit record low, Statistics Canada reports. *The Globe and Mail*, p. A5.

O'Hare, P. (1994). Starting harm reduction. *The International Journal of Drug Policy*, *5*(3), 199–200.

Omolade, B. (1994). *The rising song of African American women.* New York: Routledge.

Oscapella, E. (2001). Renne Boje—affidavit. Retrieved May 10, 2001, from http://www.cfdp.ca/eoaff.htm

Oziewicz, E. (2003, June 2). U.S. states, not Canada, led way in decriminalization, critics told. *The Globe and Mail*, p. A8.

Palmer, C., & Horowitz, M. (2000 edition). Images of women and drugs in myth and history. In C. Palmer and M. Horowitz (Eds.), *Sisters of the extreme: Women writing on the drug experience* (pp. 4–18). Rochester, VT: Park Street Press.

Paltrow, L. (1992). *Criminal prosecutions against pregnant women. Reproductive freedom project*. New York: American Civil Liberties Union Foundation.

Paltrow, L. (2001). The war on drugs and the war on abortion: Some initial thoughts on the connections, intersections and the effects. *Southern University Law Review, 28*(3), 201–253.

Paltrow, L., Cohen, D., & Carey, C. (2000a). *Governmental responses to pregnant women who use alcohol and other drugs: Year 2000 overview*. Retrieved March 12, 2003 from http://www.advocatesforpregnantwomen.org/articles/gov_response_review.pdf

Paltrow, L., Cohen, D., & Carey, C. (2000b). *Governmental responses to pregnant women who use alcohol or other drugs: Year 2000 Overview: An Analysis*. Retrieved March 12, 2003 from http://www.advocatesforpregnantwomen.org/articles/gov_response_review.pdf

Paltrow, L., Cohen, D., & Carey, C. (2000c). *Governmental responses to pregnant women who use alcohol and other drugs: Year 2000 overview: Federal and state by state statutes and regulations*. Retrieved March 12, 2003 from http://www.advocatesforpregnantwomen.org/articles/gov_response_review.pdf

Paul, D. (2000). *We were not the savages: A Mi'kmaq perspective on the collision between European and Native American civilizations*. Halifax: Fernwood.

Peele, S. (1989). *Diseasing of America: Addiction treatment out of control*. Toronto: Lexington Books.

Peele, S., & Brodsky, A., with Arnold, M. (1991). *The truth about addiction and recovery*. New York: Simon & Schuster.

Peele, S., & Bufe, C., with Brodsky, A. (2000). *Resisting 12-step coercion: How to fight forced participation in AA, NA, or 12-step treatment.* Tucson, AZ: See Sharp Press.

Penfold, S., & Walker, G. (1983). *Women and the psychiatric paradox.* Montreal: Eden Press.

Pepinsky, H., & Quinney, R. (1997). Thinking critically about peacemaking: Reflections from two proponents. In B. MacLean & D. Milovanovic (Eds.), *Thinking critically about crime* (pp. 109–114). Vancouver: Collective Press.

Petchesky, R. (1990). *Abortion and woman's choice: The state, sexuality, and reproductive freedom.* Boston: Northeastern University Press.

Peugh, J., & Belenko, S. (1999). Substace-involved women inmates: Challenges to providing effective treatment. *The Prison Journal, 79*(1), 23–44.

Pfohl, S. (1994). *Images of deviance and social control: A sociological history* (2nd ed.). New York: McGraw-Hill.

Piven, F. (2001). Welfare reform and the economic and cultural reconstruction of low wage labor markets. In J. Goode & J. Maskovsky (Eds.), *The new poverty studies: The ethnography of power, politics, and impoverished people in the United States* (pp. 135–151). New York: New York University Press.

Plant, M. (1985). *Women, drinking, and pregnancy.* London: Tavistock Publications.

Plant, M. (2000). Alcohol and its effects: Drinking during pregnancy. In M. Plant & D. Cameron (Eds.), *The Alcohol Report* (pp. 34–38). London: Free Association Press.

Plant, M., & Cameron, D. (Eds.). (2000). *The Alcohol Report.* London: Free Association Press.

Pollack, S. (2000). Dependency discourse as social control. In K. Hannah-Moffat & M. Shaw (Eds.), *An Ideal Prison? Critical essays on women's imprisonment in Canada* (pp. 72–81). Halifax, NS: Fernwood.

Prisoners with AIDS/HIV Support Network (PASAN). (1994). *HIV/AIDS in prison: Background materials.* Ottawa: Correctional Service of Canada.

Podur, J. (2001a). A way out for Colombia. *Z Magazine*, *14*(10), 45–48.

Podur, J. (2001b). Colombian women's organizations. *Z Magazine.* Retrieved from http://www.zmag.org/criesesurevts/colombia/womencol.htm

Quinney, R. (1997). Socialist humanism and critical/peacemaking criminology: The continuing project. In B. MacLean & D. Milovanovic (Eds.), *Thinking critically about crime* (pp. 114–117). Vancouver: Collective Press.

Rafter, N. (1990). *Partial justice: Women, prisons, and social control* (2nd ed.). New Brunswick, NJ: Transaction Publishers.

Ramsay, M., Baker, P., Goulden, C., Sharp, C., & Sondhi, A. (2001). *Drug misuse declared in 2000: Results from the British Crime survey.* London: Home Office Research, Development and Statistics Directorate.

Rapping, E. (1996). *The culture of recovery: Making sense of the self-help movement in women's lives.* Boston: Beacon Press.

Ratner, M. (1993). Sex, drugs, and public policy: Studying and understanding the sex-for-crack phenomenon. In M. Ratner (Ed.), *Crack pipe as pimp: An ethnographic investigation of sex-for-crack exchanges* (pp. 1–35). New York: Lexington Books.

Razack, S. (1998). *Looking white people in the eye: Gender, race, and culture in courtrooms and classrooms.* Toronto: University of Toronto Press.

Redden, J. (2000). *Snitch culture…how citizens are turned into the eyes of the state.* Venice, CA: Feral House.

Reinarman, C. (1979). Moral entrepreneurs and political economy: Historical and ethnographic notes on the construction of the cocaine menace. *Contemporary Crises, 3,* 225–254.

Reinarman, C. (1988). The social construction of an alcohol problem: The case of Mothers against Drunk Drivers and social control in the 1980s. *Theory and Society, 17*(1), 91–120.

Reinarman, C. (2000). The social impact of drugs & the war on drugs: The social construction of drug scares. In S. Tree (Ed.). *The war on drugs: Addicted to failure* (pp. 58–65). Washington, DC: Institute for Policy Studies.

Reinarman, C., & Duskin, C. (1999). Dominant ideology and drugs in the media. In J. Ferrell & N. Websdale (Eds.), *Making trouble: Cultural constructions of crime, deviance, and control* (pp. 73–87). New York: Aldine de Gruyter.

Reinarman, C., & Levine, H. (1997). The crack attack: Politics and media in the crack scare. In C. Reinarman & H. Levine (Eds.), *Crack in America: Demon drugs and social justice* (pp. 18–51). Berkeley: University of California Press.

Reinarman, C., & Levine, H. (2000). Crack in context: Politics and media in the making of a drug scare. In R. Cruthchfield, G. Bridgges, J. Weis, & C. Kubrin (Eds.), *Crime readings* (2nd ed. pp. 47–53). Thousand Oaks, CA: Pine Forge Press.

Reitsma-Street, M., & Prentice, A. (2002). *Women and housing: Past, present and future. Report Cards from the Present.* Victoria, BC: Women's Housing Action Team of Victoria Area.

Rennie, Y. (1978). *The search for criminal man.* Toronto: Lexington Books.

Report of the Aboriginal Committee. (1992). *Liberating our children, liberating our nations.* Victoria, B.C.: Ministry of Social Services.

Reynolds, E. (2001). *Hormonal pollution alert: Protecting our long-term health, protecting the environment.* Montreal: DES Action Canada.

Rhoads, D. (1983). A longitudinal study of life stress and social support among drug abusers. *International Journal of Addiction, 18*(2), 195–222.

Riley, D. (1995). Drug testing in prisons. *The International Journal of Drug Policy*, *6*(2), 106–110.

Riley, D., & Oscapella, E. (1996). Canada's new drug law: Some implications for HIV/AIDS prevention in Canada. *International Journal of Drug Policy*, *7*(3), 180–182.

Ritson, B., & Thorley, A. (2000). Alcohol and its effects: General effects. In M. Plant & D. Cameron (Eds.). *The alcohol report* (pp. 5–34). London: Free Association Press.

Roberts, D. (1997). *Killing the black body: Race, reproduction and the meaning of liberty*. New York: Pantheon Books.

Roberts, D. (2002). *Shattered bonds: The color of child welfare*. NY: Basic *Civitas* Books.

Roberts, A., Jackson, M., & Carlton-Laney, I. (2000). Revisiting the need for feminism and Afrocentric theory when treating African-American female substance abusers. *Journal of Drug Issues*, *30*(4), 901–918.

Robins, L., Helzer, J., & Davis, D. (1975). Narcotic use in southeast Asia and afterwards. *Archives of General Psychiatry*, *32*, 955–961.

Robins, L., & Mills, J. (Eds.). (1993). Effects of in utero exposure to street drugs. *American Journal of Public Health* (Supplement to Vol. 83), 1–32.

Robinson, J. (2001). *Prescription games: Money, ego, and power inside the global pharmaceutical industry*. Toronto: McClelland & Stewart.

Roe v. Wade, 410 U.S. 113 (1973).

Rose, K. (1996). *American women and the repeal of prohibition*. New York.: New York University Press.

Rosenbaum, M. (1997). Women: Research and policy. In J. Lowinson, P. Ruiz, R. Millman, & J. Langrod (Eds.), *Substance abuse, a comprehensive textbook* (pp. 654–665). Baltimore: Williams & Wilkins.

Rosenbaum, M. (1981). *Women on heroin.* New Brunswick, NJ: Rutgers University Press.

Rosenbaum, M., & Murphy, S. (1987). Not the picture of health: Women on methadone. *Journal of Psychoactive Drugs, 19*(2), 217–226.

Rosenbaum, M., Murphy, S., Irwin, J., & Watson, L. (1990). Women and crack: What's the real story? *The Drug Policy Letter, 11*(2), 2–6.

Roth, R. (2000). *Making women pay: The hidden costs of fetal rights.* Ithaca, NY: Cornell University Press.

Rothen, D. (1997–98). Methadone in provincial prisons in British Columbia. *Canadian HIV/AIDS Policy & Law Newsletter, 2*(4) & *4*(1), 27–29.

Ryes, A. (1996). Drug trafficking and the guerrilla movement in Colombia. In B. Bagley & W. Walker III (Eds.), *Drug trafficking in the Americas* (pp. 121–130). Miami: University of Miami, North-South Press.

Sales, P., & Murphy, S. (2000). Surviving violence: Pregnancy and drug use. *Journal of Drug Issues, 30*(4), 695–724.

Sanders-Phillips, K. (1998). Factors influencing health behaviors and drug abuse among low-income black and Latino women. In C. Wetherington and A. Roman (Eds.), *Drug addiction research and the health of women* (pp. 439–462). Rockville, MD: National Institute on Drug Abuse.

Saunders, D. (2000, April 1). Editors made deals on antidrug articles. *The Globe and Mail*, p. A2.

Saunders, D. (2002, October 5). What do you do with a problem like Noelle? *The Globe and Mail*, p. F2.

Savoie, J. (2002). Crime statistics in Canada, 2001. *Juristat, 22*(6), 1–22. Ottawa: Canadian Centre for Justice Statistics.

Saxakali Magazine (1997). Drugs, minority women and the U.S. prison economy. *Saxakali Magazine, 2*(2), 1–7. Retrieved June 29, 2001, from http://saxakali.com/saxakali-magazine/esxmag3s.htm

Sayres, S., Stephanson, A., Aronowitz, S., & Jameson, F. (Eds.) (1984). *The 60s without apology*. Minneapolis: University of Minnesota Press.

Schellenberg, C. (2002, June). Children, women, and families, and the medical diagnosis of fetal alcohol syndrom (FAS). Paper presented at the Sixth Annual Institutional Ethnography Network Conference, University of Victoria, B.C.

Schlosser, E. (2003). *Reefer madness: Sex, drugs, and cheap labor in the American black market*. Boston: Houghton Mifflin.

Schlosser, E. (1998). The prison-industrial complex. *The Atlantic Monthly*, *282*(6), 51–77.

Schumacher, M. (1992). *Dharma lion: A critical biography of Allen Ginsberg*. New York: St. Martin's Press.

Scott, P., & Marshall, J. (1998 edition). *Cocaine politics: Drugs, armies, and the CIA in Central America*. Berkeley: University of California Press.

Second Women. (2002) *The second women's march for peace*. Retrieved June 14, 2002, from http://tao.ca/~ccsc/June14_2002womensmarch.htm

SenGupta, S., & Peterson, J. (1999). *Mandatory injustice: Case histories of women convicted under New York's Rockefeller drug laws*. New York: Correctional Association of New York.

Sentencing Project & Human Rights Watch. (1998). *Losing the vote: The impact of felony disenfranchisement laws in the United States*. New York: Author.

Shapiro, H. (1992). *Drugs, pregnancy, and childcare: A guide for professionals*. London: Institute for the Study of Drug Dependence.

Shaw, M. (2000). Women, violence and disorder in prisons. In K. Hannah-Moffat & M. Shaw (Eds.), *An Ideal Prison? Critical essays on women's imprisonment in Canada* (pp. 61–70). Halifax: Fernwood.

Shearer, R., Myers, L., & Ogan, G. (2001). Treatment resistance and ethnicity among female offenders in substance abuse treatment programs. *The Prison Journal*, *81*(1), 55–72.

Shell, S. (2002). Drug treatment courts: A traditional perspective. In J. Nolan (Ed.). *Drug courts in theory and in practice* (pp. 173–187). New York: Aldine de Gruyter.

Shulman, A. (Ed.). (1972). *Red Emma speaks: Selected writings and speeches by Emma Goldman*. New York: Random House.

Siney, C. (1994). Team effort helps pregnant drug users. *Midirs Midwifery Digest, 4*(2), 229–231.

Siney, C. (1995). *The pregnant addict*. Cheshire, UK: Books for Midwives.

Siney, C. (Ed.). (1999). *Pregnancy and drug misuse*. Cheshire, UK: Books for Midwives.

Siney, C., Kidd, M., Walkinshaw, S., Morrision, C., & Manasse, P. (1995). Opiate dependency in pregnancy. *British Journal of Midwifery, 3*(2), 69–73.

Single, E., Van Truong, M., Adlaf, E., Ialomiteanu, A. (1999). *Canadian profile: Alcohol, tobacco & other drugs*. Toronto: Canadian Centre on Substance Abuse & Centre for Addiction and Mental Health.

Skelton, C., & Ovenden, N. (2000, December 1). B.C. hails Ottawa's plan for drug courts. *The Vancouver Sun*, p. A1.

Sleeth, P., & Barnsley, J. (1989). *Recollecting our lives: Women's experience of childhood sexual abuse*. Vancouver: Press Gang.

Smart, C. (1984). Social policy and drug addiction: A critical study of policy development. *British Journal of Addictions, 79*, 31–39.

Smart, C. (1989). *Feminism and the power of the law*. London: Routledge.

Smart, C., & Smart, B. (1978). Women and social control: An introduction. In C. Smart & B. Smart (Eds.), *Women, sexuality and social control* (pp. 1–7). London: Routledge & Kegan Paul.

Smith, N. (1996). *The new urban frontier: Gentrification and the revanchist city*. New York: Routledge.

Snyder-Joy, Z., & Carlo, T. (1998). Parenting through prison walls. In Susan Miller (Ed.), *Crime control and women: Feminist im-*

plications of criminal justice policy (pp. 130–150). Thousand Oaks, CA: Sage.

Solomon, R., & Green, M. (1988). The first century: The history of nonmedical opiate use and control policies in Canada, 1870–1970. In J. Blackwell & P. Erickson (Eds.), *Illicit drugs in Canada*. (pre-publication ed., pp. 88–116). Toronto: Methuen Publications.

Sowder, B., & Burt, M. (1980). Children of addicts and nonaddicts: A comparative investigation in five urban sites. In *Heroin-addicted parents and their children: Two reports* (National Institute on Drug Abuse Services Research Report, pp. 19–35). Washington, DC: U.S. Department of Health and Human Services; Public Health Service; Alcohol, Drug Abuse, and Mental Health Administration.

Spittal, P., Craib, K., Wood, E., Laliberte, N., Li, K., Tyndall, M., et al. (2002). Risk factors for elevated HIV incidence rates among female injection drug users in Vancouver. *Canadian Medical Association Journal*, *166*(7), 894–898.

Stanton, A. (1980). *When mothers go to jail*. Lexington: Lexington Books.

Starks v. State, No. 94104 (Okla. Ct App. 2001).

State of South Carolina v. Regina D. McKnight, No. 00–GS–26–0432, 00–GS–26–3330, S.C. Court of General Sessions (May 14–16, 2001).

Statistics Canada. (2000). *Women in Canada 2000: A gender-based statistical report*. Ottawa: Minister of Industry.

Sterk, C. (1999). *Fast lives: Women who use crack cocaine*. Philadelphia: Temple University Press.

Stevenson, G., Lingley, L., Trasov, G., & Stansfield, H. (1956). *Drug addiction in British Columbia: A research survey*. Unpublished manuscript, University of British Columbia, Vancouver.

Stewart, R. (1998). Dorothy Gaines: Guilt by association. *The Drug Policy Letter*, *35*, 17–18.

Stone, M., Salerno, L., Green, M., & Zelson, C. (1971). Narcotic addiction in pregnancy. *American Journal of Obstetrics and Gynaecology 109*(5), 716–723.

Strong, T. (2000). *Expecting trouble: What expectant parents should know about prenatal care in America.* New York: New York University Press.

Sullivan, D., & Tifft, L. (1980). *The mask of love: Corrections in America.* Port Washington, NY: Kennikat Press.

Sullivan, D., & Tifft, L. (2000). *Restorative justice as a transformative process.* Voorheesville, NY: Mutual Aid Press.

Sullivan, D., & Tifft, L. (2001). *Restorative justice: Healing the foundations of our everyday lives.* Monsey, NY: Willow Tree Press.

Sunny Hill Hospital For Children. (1992). *Potential long term NAS problems.* Vancouver: Author.

Swanson, J. (2001). *Poor-bashing: The politics of exclusion.* Toronto: Between the Lines.

Swift, K. (1995). *Manufacturing "bad mothers": A critical perspective on child neglect.* Toronto: University of Toronto Press.

Tamayo, J. (2001). U.S. civilians on frontlines of drug war in Colombia. *Knight Ridder.* Retrieved June 5, 2001, from http://www.corpwatch.org/issues/military/background/2001/jtamayo.html

Tart, C. (1969). Introduction. In C. Tart (Ed.), *Altered states of consciousness* (pp. 1–10). New York: Anchor Books.

Taylor, A. (1993). *Women drug users.* Oxford: Clarendon Press.

Terry, C., & Pellens, M. (1970). *The opium problem.* Montclair, NJ: Patterson Smith.

Theidon, K. (1995). Taking a hit: Pregnant drug users and violence. *Contemporary Drug Problems, 22,* 663–686.

Thomas, K. (1973). *Religion and the decline of magic.* New York: Penguin Books.

Toepell, A. (1997). Harm reduction efforts inside Canadian prisons: The example of education. In P. Erickson, D. Riley, Y. Cheung, & P. O'Hare (Eds.), *Harm reduction: A new direction for drug policies and programs* (pp. 453–472). Toronto: University of Toronto Press.

Tokatlian, J. (1996). Drug summary: A Colombian perspective. In B. Bagley & W. Walker III (Eds.), *Drug trafficking in the Americas* (pp.131–147). Miami: University of Miami, North-South Press.

Trebach, A. (1982). *The heroin solution.* New Haven: Yale University Press.

Tupper, K. (2002). Entheogens and existential intelligence: The use of plant teachers as cognitive tools. *Canadian Journal of Education*, 27(4), 499–516.

Turnbull, L. (2001). *Double jeopardy: Motherwork and the law.* Toronto: Sumach Press.

Urgent Action Network (UAN). (2001). *Urgent action appeal update.* Amnesty International USA. Retrieved November 20, 2001, from http://www.amnestyusa.org/urgent/newslett.html

United States Department of Health and Human Services. (2002a). Administration for Children and Families, Administration on Children, Youth and Families, Children's Bureau. "The AFCARS Report: Preliminary Estimates as of April 2001," 2. Retrieved July 8, 2002, from http://www.acf.dhhs.gov/programs

United States Department of Health and Human Services. (2002b). Administration for Children and Families, Administration on Children, Youth and Families, National Clearinghouse on Child Abuse and Neglect Information. "Foster care national statistics April 2001," 2. Retrieved July 8, 2002, from http://www.calib.com/nccanch/upbs/factsheets/foster.cfm

U.S. Department of Justice. (1999). *Prisoners in 1998.* Rockville, MD: Bureau of Justice Statistics.

U.S. Department of Justice. (2000a). *Compendium of federal justice statistics, 1998.* Rockville, MD: Bureau of Justice Statistics.

U.S. Department of Justice. (2000b). *Correctional populations and facilities. Drugs and Crime Facts.* Washington, DC: Bureau of Justice Statistics.

U.S. Department of Justice. (2000c). *Incarcerated parents and their children*. Rockville, MD: Bureau of Justice Statistics.

U.S. Department of Justice. (2002). *Crime in the United States, 2001*. Washington, DC: Federal Bureau of Investigation.

U.S. Federal Bureau of Prisons. (2002). *Statistical Data*. U.S. Department of Justice. Retrieved February 17, 2003, from http://www.bop.gov

U.S. Federal Bureau of Prisons. (2003) *Quick Facts*. Federal Bureau of Prisons. Retrieved January 17, 2003, from http://www.bop.gov/fact0598.html

Ussher, J. (1991). *Women's madness: Misogyny or mental illness?* Amherst, MA: The University of Massachusetts Press.

Utting, D. (2003). *Government urged to re-think penalties as more cannabis users "grow their own."* Retrieved May 7, 2003, from http://www.jrf.org.uk/pressroom/releases/140403.asp

Valbuena, A., with Chomsky, N., & Perez, R. (2001). Free Trade Area of the Americas (FTAA), Plan Columbia and the Resistance of the Indigenous U'wa People. A lecture presentation at the Indigenous Organization of Columbia, [Recorded by Roger Leisner] MIT, Cambridge, MA.

van de Wijngaart, G. (1991). *Competing perspectives on drug use: The Dutch experience*. Amsterdam: Sets & Zeitlinger.

Vega, W., Kolody, B., Hwang, J., & Noble, A. (1993). Prevalence and magnitude of perinatal substance exposures in California. *New England Journal of Medicine, 329*, 850–854.

Vernotica, E., Lisciotto, C., Rosenblatt, J., & Morrell, J. (1996). Cocaine transiently impairs maternal behavior in the rat. *Behavioral Neuroscience, 110*(2), 315–323.

Wagner, D. (1997). *The new temperance: The American obsession with sin and vice*. Boulder, CO: Westview Press.

Wagner, M. (1994). *Pursuing the birth machine*. Camperdown, Australia: ACE Graphics.

Waldorf, D., Murphy, S., Reinarman, C., & Joyce, B. (1977). *Doing coke: An ethnography of cocaine users and sellers.* Washington, DC: Drug Abuse Council.

Waldorf, D., Reinarman, C., & Murphy, S. (1991). *Cocaine changes.* Philadelphia: Temple University Press.

Walker III, W. (1996). The Bush administration's Andean drug strategy in historical perspective. In B. Bagley & W. Walker III (Eds.), *Drug trafficking in the Americas* (pp. 1–21). Miami: University of Miami, North-South Press.

Walkinshaw, S., Shaw, B., & Siney, C. (2002). Neonatal abstinence syndrome. In H. Klee, M. Jackson, & S. Lewis (Eds.), *Drug misuse and motherhood* (pp. 213–223). London: Routledge.

Warner, J. (2002). *Craze: Gin and debauchery in an age of reason.* New York: Four Walls Eight Windows.

Waterston, A. (1999). *Street addicts in the political economy.* Philadelphia: Temple University Press.

Weber, M. (1976). *The Protestant ethic and the spirit of capitalism.* London: George Allen & Unwin.

Websdale, N. (2001). *Policing the poor: From slave plantation to public housing.* Boston: Northeastern University Press.

Wedsdale, N., & Ferrell, J. (1999). Taking the trouble. In J. Ferrell and N. Websdale (Eds.), *Making trouble: Cultural constructions of crime* (pp. 349–364). New York: Aldine de Gruyter.

Wedderburn, D. (2000). *Justice for women: The need for reform.* London: Prison Reform Trust.

Weich, R., & Angula, C. (2000). *Justice on trial: Racial disparities in the American criminal justice system.* Washington, DC: Leadership Conference on Civil Rights & Leadership Conference on Education Fund.

Weil, A. (1972). *The natural mind.* Boston: Houghton Mifflin.

Weil, A., & Rosen, W. (1998 edition). *From chocolate to morphine: Everything you need to know about mind-altering drugs.* Boston: Houghton Mifflin.

Welch, M. (2002). *Detained: Immigration laws and the expanding I.N.S. jail complex.* Philadelphia: Temple University Press.

West, A. (2001). HIV/AIDS education for Latina inmates: The delimiting impact of culture on prevention efforts. *The Prison Journal, 81*(1), 20–41.

West, G. (2000). Critiquing the globalization of penality and imprisonment: Conceptualizing penal abolition globally. In W. Gordon & R. Morris (Eds.), *The case for penal abolition* (pp. 17–41). Toronto: Canadian Scholars' Press.

Whitner v. South Carolina, 492 S.E.2d 777 (S.C. 1997).

Williams-Peterson, M., Myers, B., Degen, H., Knisely, J., Elswichk, R., & Schnoll, S. (1994). Drug-using and nonusing women: Potential for child abuse, child-rearing attitudes, social support, and affection for expected baby. *International Journal of the Addictions, 29*(12), 1631–1643.

Willis, E. (1992). *No more nice girls: Countercultural essays.* Hanover, NH: University Press of New England.

Winick, C. (1962). Maturing out of narcotic addiction. *Bulletin on Narcotics, 14*(1), 1–7.

Winnipeg Child and Family Services (Northwest Area) v. G., (D.F.) [1997] 3 S.C.R. 925. Retrieved July 2, 2003, from http://www.lexum.umontreal.ca/csc-scc/en/pub/1997/vol3/html/1997scr3_0925.html

Withington, T. (2003, April 10–16). American forces patrol the world. *Guardian Weekly,* p. 5.

Wodak, A. (1992). Beyond the prohibition of heroin: The development of a controlled availability in Australia. In P. O'Hare, R. Newcombe, A. Matthews, E.C. Buning, & E. Drucker (Eds.), *The reduction of drug-related harm* (pp. 49–61). London: Routledge.

WOLA (2002). Taking stock: Plan Colombia's First Year. *Colombia Monitor, 1*, 1–12.

Wolfe, T. (1999). *Counting the cost: the social and financial consequences of women's imprisonment.* Report prepared for the Wedderburn Committee on Women's Imprisonment. London: Prison Reform Trust.

Wo/Men's Alliance for Medical Marijuana (WAMM). (2003). *Home Page.* Retrieved May 7, 2003, from http://www.wamm.org/

Women's Commission for Refugee Women and Children. (WCRWC). (1999). A charade of concern: The abandonment of Colombia's forcibly displaced. New York: Women's Commission for Refugee Women and Children.

Wood, E., Keer, T., Spittal, P., Li, K., Small, W., Tyndall, M., et al. (2003a). The potential public health and community impacts of safer injecting facilities: Evidence from a cohort of injection drug users. *Journal of Acquired Immune Deficiency Syndromes, 32*(1), 2–8.

Wood, E., Kerr, T., Spittal, P., Tyndall, M., O'Shaughnessy, M., & Schechter, M. (2003b). The health care and fiscal costs of the illicit drug use epidemic: The impact of conventional drug control strategies, and the potential of a comprehensive approach. *BC Medical Journal, 45*(3), 130–136.

Woodiwiss, M. (2001). *Organized crime and American power.* Toronto: University of Toronto Press.

Zarin-Ackerman, J. (1976). Developmental assessment of all infants born to the family care program. In *Symposium on comprehensive health care for addicted families and their children* (pp. 99–106). Rockville, MD: National Institute on Drug Abuse.

Zinberg, N. (1984). *Drugs, set, and setting: The basis for controlled intoxicant use.* New Haven, CT: Yale University Press.

Zion, J. (1998). The use of custom and legal tradition in the modern justice setting. *Contemporary Justice Review, 1* (1), 133–148.

Index